ADVOCATING OVERLORD

ADVOCATING OVERLORD

THE D-DAY STRATEGY AND THE ATOMIC BOMB

PHILIP PADGETT

Potomac Books

AN IMPRINT OF THE UNIVERSITY OF NEBRASKA PRESS

All rights reserved. Potomac Books is an imprint of the
University of Nebraska Press.
Manufactured in the United States of America.

Library of Congress Cataloging-in-Publication Data
Name: Padgett, Philip, author.
Title: Advocating Overlord: the D-Day strategy
and the atomic bomb / Philip Padgett.
Description: Lincoln: Potomac Books, an imprint of
the University of Nebraska Press, 2018.
Identifiers: LCCN 2017052569
ISBN 9781612349626 (cloth: alk. paper)
ISBN 9781640120488 (epub)
ISBN 9781640120495 (mobi)
ISBN 9781640120501 (web)
Subjects: LCSH: Operation Overlord. | World War,
1939–1945—Diplomatic history. | Atomic bomb.

Classification: LCC D756.5.N6 P33 2018
DDC 940.54/2142—dc23 LC record available at
https://lccn.loc.gov/2017052569

Set in Scala OT by E. Cuddy.

For Mary and Lauren
In memory of John and Mary Jane

CONTENTS

List of Illustrations   ix
List of Acronyms   xi
List of Code Names and Military Operations   xiii
Note on Time   xv

Prologue   I
1. Symbol, the Casablanca Conference   11
2. Campaigns of Attrition   41
3. cossac's Ninety Days to Deliver a Plan   57
4. The Trident Conference's Illusion of Agreement   70
5. Mission to Moscow   93
6. cossac's Plan Emerges   103
7. The Green Hornet   114
8. Hammer and Tongs   121
9. Revolt in London and Washington   147
10. The Fishing Trip   162
11. From One Attorney to Another   173
12. The Happy Time at Birch Island   184
13. Plain Speaking on the Potomac   190
14. A Presidential Directive   207
15. Blenheim on the Hudson   221
16. Overlord Reaffirmed in Quebec   235
17. Bolero Unleashed   251
18. Sealing the Quebec Decisions   274
Epilogue   299

Acknowledgments   315
Notes   319
Bibliography   359
Index   367

ILLUSTRATIONS

Photographs

Following page 194

1. Franklin Roosevelt, Winston Churchill, and the Combined Chiefs of Staff, Casablanca, January 1943
2. The Anfa Hotel in Casablanca, January 1943
3. Winston Churchill and the British Chiefs of Staff aboard RMS *Queen Mary*
4. RMS *Queen Mary*, converted for war
5. Churchill and Roosevelt at the Trident Conference
6. Joint Planning meeting in Algiers, June 1943
7. Lt. Gen. Sir Frederick E. Morgan, COSSAC
8. Morgan and Maj. Gen. Ray Barker, U.S. Army, deputy COSSAC
9. COSSAC's July 1943 plan for D-Day
10. The COSSAC teams who carried the plan to Churchill and the JCS
11. "The Whitefish Bay U.S. Navy Exploring Expedition 1943"
12. U.S. Army generals Dwight D. Eisenhower and George C. Marshall, June 1943
13. A section of Mainz, Germany, gutted by RAF firebombing, August 1942
14. Allied Combined Chiefs of Staff at the Quadrant Conference
15. The escort carrier USS *Bogue* (CVE-9), June 1943
16. One of *Bogue*'s U-boat kills, minutes from its destruction, June 1943
17. VLR B-24 Liberators of the RAF Coastal Command

18. Transport ship USS *Susan B. Anthony* (AP-72) in fast troop convoy UT-5
19. Germany's Enigma encryption machine
20. U.S. Sigaba encryption machine
21. U.S. Sigsaly voice encryption system
22. Douglas C-54 Skymaster transport plane
23. Stalin, Roosevelt, and Churchill during the Eureka Conference
24. A field of halftracks in England prior to D-Day
25. Battleship USS *Texas* (BB-35) in 1943
26. U.S. First or Twenty-ninth Division infantry wade toward Omaha Beach on D-Day
27. Omaha Beach on D+1, June 7, 1944
28. The first atomic bomb, Trinity, moments after detonation on July 16, 1945
29. Trinity fifteen seconds after detonation

Maps

1. Major Allied Conferences, 1943   38
2. Fast Troop Convoy UT-10, New York to United Kingdom, March 23–April 4, 1944   266
3. The COSSAC 1943 Overlord Plan and D-Day as Carried Out (Neptune)   300

ACRONYMS

A3	early radiotelephone voice encryption system
ASF	Army Service Force
ASW	antisubmarine warfare
AT	troop convoy designation, United States to UK
B-17	four-engine heavy bomber
B-24	four-engine heavy bomber (with transport and maritime patrol variants)
BA	British Army
C-54	four-engine transport aircraft
CBO	Combined Bomber Offensive
CCS	Combined Chiefs of Staff (Allied)
CIGS	Chief of Imperial General Staff (UK)
COS	Chiefs of Staff (UK)
COSSAC	Chief of Staff to Supreme Allied Commander, an organization and an officer's title
CVE	escort aircraft carrier
CU	convoy designation, Caribbean to Liverpool
ETOUSA	European Theater of Operations, U.S. Army
HF/DF	high frequency direction
HMS	His Majesty's Ship
HX	convoy designation, Halifax (later New York) to Liverpool
HXS	convoy designation, Halifax (later New York) to Liverpool, slow
JCS	Joint Chiefs of Staff (U.S.)
JIC	Joint Intelligence Committee
JPC	Joint Planning Committee (UK)
JSSC	Joint Strategy Survey Committee (U.S.)

JWPC	Joint War Planning Committee (U.S.)
KMF	convoy designation, Firth of Clyde to Mediterranean
MKF	convoy designation, Mediterranean to Firth of Clyde
OKW	Oberkommando der Wehrmacht, German Supreme Command of the Armed Forces
ON	convoy designation, outbound north, Liverpool to Halifax
ONS	convoy designation, outbound north slow, Liverpool to Halifax
OPD	Operations Division (U.S. Army)
OSRD	Office of Scientific Research and Development (U.S.)
RAF	Royal Air Force
RCMP	Royal Canadian Mounted Police
RMS	Royal Mail Ship
RN	Royal Navy
S-I	code name, atomic bomb development, U.S. term equivalent to Tube Alloy
SHAEF	Supreme Headquarters Allied Expeditionary Force
TA	Tube Alloy
TU	fast troop convoy designation, British Isles to United States
USA	U.S. Army
USAAF	U.S. Army Air Force
USAT	U.S. Army Transport
USN	U.S. Navy
USS	United States Ship
USSBS	U.S. Strategic Bombing Survey
UT	fast troop convoy designation, United States to British Isles
VHF	very high frequency
VLR	very long range
WSA	War Shipping Administration

CODE NAMES AND MILITARY OPERATIONS

Abraham	code name for Quebec City
Anakim	operation name, Allies' proposed invasion of Burma
Arcadia	code name, Allies' first conference, Washington
Avalanche	operation name, Allies' invasion at Salerno, near Naples, Italy
Bolero	operation name, U.S. buildup in UK
Cockade	operation name, series of 1943 Allied deceptions
D-Day	designated day for Normandy landings, the first phase of Overlord
Enigma	Germany's text encryption machine
Eureka	code name, Allies' sixth conference, Tehran
Gold	Normandy beach, British landing point
Gymnast	operation name, Allies' North Africa landings; became Torch
Husky	operation name, Allies' invasion of Sicily
Jubilee	operation name, raid on Dieppe, France
Juno	Normandy beach, Canadian landing point
Jupiter	operation name, Allies' invasion of Norway; not conducted
Manhattan Project	secret U.S. project to develop and produce atomic bomb
Neptune	operation name, Allies' amphibious and airborne landings, Normandy
Omaha	Normandy beach, U.S. landing point

Overlord	operation name, liberation of northwestern Europe
Pointblank	operation code name for the Allies' Combined Bomber Offensive
Quadrant	code name, Allies' fourth conference, Quebec City
Rankin	operation name, Allies' contingency for a German collapse
Roundhammer	plan name, cross-Channel attack
Roundup	plan name, U.S. cross-Channel attack
Rudge	early COSSAC planning exercise
Sextant	code name, Allies' fifth conference, Cairo
Sickle	code name, AAF buildup and supply in UK
Sigaba	U.S. text encryption machine
Sigsaly	U.S. voice encryption machine
Sledgehammer	operation name, Allies' contingency cross-Channel attack
Sword	Normandy beach, British landing point
Symbol	code name, Allies' second conference, Casablanca
Terminal	Allies' conference following VE-Day, Potsdam
Tindall	operation name, Allies' deception related to Norway
Torch	operation name, Allies' landing in North Africa
Trident	code name, Allies' third conference, Washington
Trinity	code name for first atomic bomb test
Tube Alloy	code name for British atomic bomb project
Utah	Normandy beach, U.S. landing point

NOTE ON TIME

All times given are local. London (Greenwich Mean Time) is five hours ahead of the time in Washington DC. Moscow is three hours ahead of London time. For military operations, time is stated according to the military twenty-four-hour clock.

ADVOCATING OVERLORD

Prologue

Good night, then sleep to gather strength for the morning. For the morning will come. Brightly will it shine on the brave and the true, kindly upon all who suffer for the cause, glorious upon the tombs of heroes. Thus will shine the dawn. Vive la France!

—Winston Churchill, BBC broadcast to the people of France, October 21, 1940

Belfast's waterfront pubs and streets were quiet, empty of Allied sailors, the night of June 3, 1944. In the fifth year of the war for which Belfast was a vital base for Allied warships defending the North Atlantic sea lanes, a night absent the sounds of sailors seemed impossible. But the night was quiet. Like ports throughout the United Kingdom, day and night for a year, Belfast also had witnessed the unloading of ships bearing the inflowing transatlantic flood of troops, equipment, and materiel for the growing Allied armies. But in recent weeks, the harbor's activities could be seen, instead, to be . . . loading. Did that outflow and this night's quiet hint at the start of D-Day?

Barely visible offshore in rain-swept Belfast Lough were the hulking outlines of the U.S. Navy's Battleship Division Five: *Texas*, *Arkansas*, and Pearl Harbor attack-survivor *Nevada*. Each had taken turns escorting twelve fast troop convoys east across the North Atlantic in an eight-month surge of U.S. forces to the United Kingdom. With the onset of spring, the old but still deadly sluggers of "BatDiv 5" had remained forward, one by one assembling in Belfast as part of the gathering invasion force.

Aboard the battleships' leader, uss *Texas*, as in each of the many ships gathered, the crew had been briefed for the mission to come. Now *Texas* was a sealed ship. Inside, the passageways were quiet except for the hum of ventilators. Tense anticipation had given way to fatigue from the exacting work to get the 27,000-ton ship ready for sea and for battle. In darkened berthing spaces, the crew slept.

At 0200, on June 4, *Texas* received the expected order flashed to a thousand recipients in the British Isles: "Carry out Operation Neptune." D-Day, the amphibious phase of the campaign to liberate Western Europe and defeat Nazism, Operation Overlord, was beginning.

The battleships slipped quietly from their moorings. Building speed to 15 knots, *Texas* steamed down the channel to open water in tactical command of her BatDiv 5 sisters, following in a column astern, and screened by five destroyers. Joining them from the darkness were the Free-French Navy cruisers *George Leygues* and *Montcalm,* the Royal Navy cruiser HMS *Glasgow*, and more destroyers. In the gray dawn, the bombardment group, designated Task Group 129.2, steamed into the Irish Sea and came to course 160 degrees, heading south by southeast. Through the day's heavy rain, the silhouettes of many more ships could be seen in all directions from the bridge of the *Texas*. Allied ships of all types were present—battleships and cruisers of other bombardment groups, transports, landing ships, destroyers—all on parallel south-southeasterly courses.

Notified in the night that D-Day had been postponed, the ships reversed course northward at dawn to mask their intentions from possible German reconnaissance through the daylight hours of June 4. Then in the dim northern twilight came a new message. D-Day was on for June 6.

In the Bristol Channel at 2204, like a mighty giant that had stepped back to flex before leaning once again into a colossal task, the rain-lashed armada reversed course once more. The "prospect of fair weather for the next 48 hours [was] reported very good." So all hoped. By the morning of June 5, "steaming as before following swept channels around Land's End," Task Group 129.2 sailed into the English Channel.[1]

For the crews aboard Free French *George Leygues* and *Montcalm,* anticipation was mixed with a particular anxiety. The terrible destruction soon to be inflicted on occupying German soldiers by shells from their ships' six-inch guns might also cause the death or wounding of many innocent French civilians. How many? Unknowable.

Known and bracing to every officer and *marin* aboard, however, was this. As Land's End grew distant in the west, so too receded for them four and a half years of wandering the Atlantic from Norway to West Africa. Since 1939 the French cruisers' crews had sailed for the Third Republic, then collaborationist Vichy, then gone into a lengthy refit in Philadelphia for the Allies. Wakes curved as helms were spun to bring the Task Group to new course 090 degrees, and the two cruisers entered La Manche. This day they were sailing for France.

Soon after the Task Group turned into the Channel, USS *Nevada* and its accompanying destroyers bore off to rendezvous with the ships of Force Utah. Off Portland Bill in the late afternoon of June 5, *Texas* logged, "Many convoys of LST's, LCT's, combat loaded transports, and squadrons of Fire Support Ships and escorts in sight in all directions heading towards rendezvous area."[2] That, just ahead, was a ten-mile diameter marshaling area, hectic with ships and nicknamed "Piccadilly Circus." From there, ten channels that had been swept through German and British minefields and marked covertly branched off toward five D-Day landing beaches on the Normandy coast: two British, one Canadian, and two American.[3] Led by HMS *Glasgow* and other Royal Navy escort vessels, all crews at general quarters, the ships of the *Texas* bombardment group advanced silently into their designated channel leading to Omaha Beach.

Theirs was only a portion of the largest amphibious armada the world had ever seen. Before D-Day ended, 358,000 Allied soldiers, airmen, sailors, coast guardsmen, and merchant mariners would thrust 156,000 of their number onto the landing grounds and beaches of Normandy against fierce opposition. By day's end, an estimated 9,000 Allied participants would become casualties, 3,000 of whom would be dead.[4]

Now blurred by the passage of three-quarters of a century, these events leading to the Allied defeat of Nazi Germany might casually be mistaken for a progression of logic and certainty. There would be a cross-Channel invasion of France. After all, Winston Churchill had told the French people in 1940 that the Allies would return. Breaking out on the offensive from their Normandy lodgment, the western Allies, together with the Red Army pressing forward from the east, would win complete victory in the European theater of operations, certainly by 1945. The path to D-Day's eve, however, had been neither straight nor certain.

To become a viable military campaign, Overlord, the strategy ultimately chosen in the west, needed a clear military objective, a plan, a Supreme Allied Commander, the forces for him to implement the plan, and, most important, leadership's endorsement. Eighteen months before D-Day, none of that had been defined. The process for doing so was stormy. As months passed, disagreement persisted. The very concept of what would become Operation Overlord was disputed hotly.

By the end of 1942, the pivotal Allied victories at El Alamein, Midway, and Stalingrad had tipped the war's balance in the Allies' favor. The threat of defeat by the Axis powers of Germany, Italy, and Japan had been eliminated. The Allies now could concentrate on offensive action to win World War II. Approaches to the European offensive had been discussed in 1942, some calling for quite unrealistic overreach given the resources then available. In 1943, the Allies could begin serious planning for military victory because of their improved strategic position and the fact that the great engine of North American industry was reaching full wartime production. The burning question for the Allies was how exactly they best could win. Answering that question with a plan to act upon the Allies' strategic advantages, hard won in 1942, was anything but resolved between Great Britain and the United States.

Certainly not agreed was that the liberation of Western Europe should begin, as the Americans advocated, with a cross-Channel assault at the time and place of the Allies' choosing. Instead, intense dispute raged at the highest levels of Allied leadership over the emergent competition of concepts for what should be the strategy for liberation. Should that be the American vision of an explosive offensive across northwestern Europe striking into the Nazi citadel? Or should it be the British preference for a series of thrusts from the Mediterranean into the "soft underbelly" of Europe while banking on the mounting pressure on Germany, from maritime blockade, all land fronts, and the sky above? The hoped for objective of the British strategy option was to force the political-economic collapse of Hitler's Reich much like Germany's unexpected collapse in 1918.

The issue was not simply a dispute confined to which was the best military strategy. Roots of the internal alliance conflict were to be found in differing conceptions for the desired result for the war in Europe, differing British and American perceptions of each other's capabilities and intentions, and each nation's evolving perception of its own—and the other's—role in the world. A constant factor influencing everything was the actual disparity in their national strength. The differences fed on each other throughout 1942 to create a near-toxic relationship between the British and American military chiefs. This carried into the new year despite its promise.

Inevitably in the swirling complexity of a world war, the military strategy dispute, even so broadly defined, did not proceed for long in isolation from other issues. Emergent, at least among a few select and critical decision makers, was an ever closer proximity of the unresolved strategy question to another great Anglo-American secret, their quest to develop an atomic bomb. That venture, anticipated to be joint, had instead ruptured.

Late in 1942, openly applying a rationale of practicality underlaid by their personal views of U.S. national security interests, and belief that their intent was endorsed by President Franklin D. Roosevelt, American scientists unilaterally cut Britain's scientists out of most of the Manhattan Project. That was the super-secret effort to develop an atomic bomb to which British research had made a strong early contribution. Prime Minister Winston Churchill was alarmed by the American turnabout. Foreseeing a postwar world that would be dominated by the United States and the Soviet Union, each to be atomic-armed, Churchill was convinced that a British atomic bomb would be essential to ensuring Britain's de facto independence. Yet, as Churchill was made acutely aware by his own atomic research leaders, wartime Britain lacked the resources and some of the knowledge to develop the bomb on its own.

Opposed though Churchill was to the U.S.-advocated cross-Channel invasion-based strategy, he wanted full British access to the Manhattan Project. He also wanted an Anglo-American security relationship that would endure beyond the war.

Nineteen forty-three opened with the first of what would be five major conferences that year involving Roosevelt, Churchill, and their military chiefs. The Allies picked up the discussion where 1942's wrangling over a winning offensive strategy had left off. Although mostly freed from the specter of the threat of defeat, relations between the British and American military chiefs remained mired in distrust and acrimony. Soon, separately but in parallel, Churchill was resisting the Americans' military strategy preference while pressing for restoration of British access to the Manhattan Project—and a broader Anglo-American atomic agreement. As British-American circular arguments on strategy raged, the growing intensity of Churchill's atomic sharing entreaties was met with American scientific leadership resistance and political leadership ambivalence.

The separate issues of European strategy and atomic bomb cooperation, now closed off by the Americans, came into ever more frequent and intimate proximity over the passing months, evident candidates for a quid pro quo. Yet only a very few of the actors had the "need to know" to be privy to the existence of both highly classified subjects and thus their potential to affect the political dynamics of the alliance, should they become linked. Churchill and Roosevelt knew.

Although planning cooperation blossomed between middle-ranking Allied military officers, among their own commanders

Anglo-American guidance for conduct of the war remained locked in differences and confrontation. Against these arguments at the top, the war's imperatives were becoming compelling. By mid-1943, the need to pick a single strategy and implement it was becoming so urgent as to lessen the importance of which strategy.

A letter written by an important British civilian advocate for the American position on strategy captured the exasperation felt on both sides of the Atlantic. In mid-June Churchill's close adviser and friend, Lord Max Beaverbrook, wrote to his American counterpart, Harry Hopkins with FDR. On the seeming Allied incapability to agree on one primary strategy, Beaverbrook declared, "If we are not prepared to accept the risks, face the difficulties, suffer the casualties, then let us concentrate at once exclusively on the production of heavy bombers and think in terms of 1950."[5] An end to the war in 1950? That was a prospect for a postwar world that in hindsight is too devastating and unstable to contemplate.

Advocating Overlord is the story of the British and American struggle to devise and commit to the liberation strategy that achieved victory in Europe in May 1945. The story is told from January 1943 when, heartened by the prospect of winning, the question of deciding on an Allied offensive strategy took on new urgency, leading to their decision in August and its sealing in December 1943.

This was a transformative year for how the United States came to see and act upon its role in the world. Isolationism's hemispheric defense-based strategies were left behind. Instead, the Roosevelt administration decided to engage globally, permanently accepting the full import of the rendezvous with destiny that FDR had foreseen in 1936. The United States became the guarantor of relationships from which would emerge the postwar cornerstone alliances of stable, free societies that provide both assurance and deterrence through collective security and cooperation. That new role, taken up by Roosevelt and his military leaders in 1943, depended on by allies and understood by adversaries, has endured to this day.

This is a tale of success that also carries a caution to be drawn from the obstacles to be overcome by national leaders who in 1942–43 found cooperation between their countries retarded by stereotyping and suspicion. Distrust and prejudicial oversimplification had filled the void when collaborative international endeavor dissipated in the shortness of two decades between the Armistice of 1918 and the outbreak of World War II. The resulting friction that held up agreement on a winning Allied strategy is a sharp reminder to us today. The corrosiveness of ill-informed stereotypes cannot be turned off and collaboration turned back on, like throwing a switch, even in the face of a shared existential threat. In our time of challenges to community from xenophobic nationalists who question the value and continuance of proven mechanisms for collective security, economic, and environmental well-being, that history confronts us with a lesson to be recalled again.

Advocating Overlord is also the counterbalancing story of a rising generation of young military leaders who moved past national biases and the animosity demonstrated among their own senior commanders, British and American. Instead, they joined in a genuinely connected endeavor as the only sure path to find a way to accomplish what they had been told was infeasible and, by inference, not universally desired among their chiefs to whom they reported, Operation Overlord. Their success at convincingly arguing the viability within achievable conditions of a cross-Channel assault-based liberation strategy advanced the emerging consensus. Their advocacy for their Overlord plan, even to the point of violating orders, quelled a nascent American crisis of confidence and helped to set the conditions to bring closure to the strategy debate. However, also necessary for closure were two more, sequential elements, one only achievable between Roosevelt and Churchill directly.

Circumstantially but strongly evident as the first element is this linkage. The American determination, with key British supporters, to base Allied strategy for Europe on a cross-Channel assault and Churchill's need to reestablish Anglo-American collaboration on atomic weapons, and do so in the context of a relationship extending beyond World War II, did become the two sides of a quid pro quo. That happened in the Quadrant Conference when, a few hours after the final strategy document had been agreed to and presented to them, Roosevelt and Churchill signed a second, secret atomic agreement on August 19, 1943. *Advocating Overlord* examines through primary documents the development of this much-overlooked story. These point to the increasingly intentional, step-by-step elevation of the question of resuming atomic cooperation with a concurrent awareness of the need to settle on strategy. The credibility of oral assurances at the top fell away. Imperative became the need for one leader to act followed by the other in response, each in writing. They did so.

The Quadrant Conference in Quebec effectively set the Allied strategy and reopened atomic cooperation. But it did not prevent revisits to the strategy question by Churchill. The strategy decision, and assignment of its command to an American, had to be sealed by creating as an irreversible new fact on the ground in Britain the concentration of forces to invade the Continent in 1944. This, which became the second element for closure, had been anticipated.

Even as the ink was drying on the two Quadrant agreements, fast troop convoys began to sail. In the eight months that followed the first Quebec Conference, more than one million troops were transported to the British Isles for Operation Overlord without losing a single soldier to enemy action, manifesting that the Battle of the Atlantic had been decided. Before the Quadrant Conference, before the apparent quid pro quo atomic agreement for strategy reaffirmation, the achievability of this massive transfer of troops, their equipment, and materiel in time for D-Day had been promised by the U.S. Army Chief of Staff, Gen. George C. Marshall. He did so to gain the commitment of the ultimate advocate for Overlord, Franklin D. Roosevelt.

This then is the story of how the advocates for Overlord, British and American, prevailed against operational and political adversity to win the Allied commitment to D-Day. Only a very few of the actors then knew that in so doing, a link was made between two events that would profoundly shape the twentieth century with effect to this day, the liberation of Europe from Hitler's tyranny and the advent of the atomic bomb. Just as we are indebted to the millions on all fronts who by their bravery and sacrifice in combat achieved the victory over Nazism in 1945, our debt to these advocates for Overlord endures.

1

Symbol, the Casablanca Conference

From a worm's eye viewpoint it was apparent that we were confronted by generations and generations of experience in committee work, in diplomacy, and in rationalizing points of view. They had us on the defensive practically all the time.

—Gen. Albert C. Wedemeyer, U.S. Army, February 1943

One cannot help suspecting that the U.S. Military Authorities who are now in complete control wish to gain an advance upon us, and feel that, having now benefitted from the fruits of our early endeavors, they will not suffer unduly by casting us aside.

—Message to Winston Churchill from Sir John Anderson, Tube Alloys director, January 20, 1943

In November 1942, the Moroccan sky had reverberated from the shock waves of the bombs and naval guns of an invading Allied force. Now the January stillness was broken by throbbing bass quartets of heavy aero engines. From north and south, the top political and military leadership of the United Kingdom and the United States were converging on Casablanca to parley. Their ally, the Soviet Union, would not be represented because Joseph Stalin, although invited, claimed he needed to remain in Moscow to direct military operations.

Arriving first from the south in two four-engine c-54 transports on January 11, 1943, were the Joint Chiefs of Staff (jcs) of the U.S. Navy, Army, and Army Air Force. They included Army Chief of Staff Gen. George C. Marshall, Adm. Ernest King, commander of the Navy, and Lt. Gen. Henry "Hap" Arnold, Army Air Force commander.[1] Traveling with the jcs to Casablanca was British Army Field Marshal Sir John Dill, head of the British military liaison in Washington. Dill's perceptiveness, tact, and his friendship with Marshall would be crucial to the Anglo-American alliance at Casablanca and in the year ahead.[2]

Marshall had won Roosevelt's respect when he alone openly disagreed with the president during a White House meeting five years earlier. Although he was told by others that his dissent had ended his career, Marshall was chosen by FDR in 1938 to be Army chief of staff. Admiral King had served throughout the Navy that he now led. During the First World War, King had spent time with the Royal Navy. Abrasive and authoritarian by nature, King came out of that experience as an Anglophobe as well. But because he was intelligent and insightful, King often would bring the British and American chiefs to the central point of their discussion. Arnold learned to fly from the Wright Brothers. He was an aviation pioneer and a firm advocate for air power. The American chiefs arrived fresh in crisp uniforms, but with limited staff and little preparation. This was a mistake.

Having arrived in Miami, Florida, secretly by train from Washington the previous night, Roosevelt took off aboard the Pan American Airlines flying boat *Dixie Clipper* for Casablanca on January 11 at 6:00 a.m. His party flew a three-day, mirror image J-shaped course via the Caribbean and Brazil to West Africa. At Bathurst on the Gambia River, January 13, they transferred to an Army Air Force c-54, nicknamed *The Sacred Cow*, for the onward flight to Casablanca.[3]

Franklin Delano Roosevelt was a wealthy, sixth-generation patrician from New York's Hudson River valley, unpretentious, and a Democrat. After serving as assistant secretary of the Navy he loved, he was stricken with polio. Roosevelt never gave in to this affliction. He was elected governor of New York in 1928 and president in 1932 in the depths of the Great Depression. In a time when there was concern for democracy's viability against the challenges of Fascism and Communism, and when populist domestic demagogues preached division, FDR governed through optimistic pragmatism and appeals for unity. His New Deal eventually brought the country through the Depression, only to face a new world war.

FDR came to Casablanca halfway into his unprecedented third term and with politics never far from his mind.

The flight to Casablanca made FDR the first U.S. president to fly and the first since Woodrow Wilson to depart the country while in office. In North Africa, he would become the first U.S. president to review troops in the field since Abraham Lincoln.[4] The president brought with him his close adviser, Harry Hopkins, and selected White House staff. FDR's chief of staff and chairman of the JCS, Adm. William Leahy, took sick en route and had to be left in Trinidad to recover.[5]

To Casablanca from the north on January 13 came four Royal Air Force B-24 bombers, converted into transports. Each flight had arced well out to the west over the Atlantic to avoid detection from German-occupied France or neutral but Axis-sympathizing Spain. Churchill's B-24, *Commando*, carried the British prime minister, his immediate staff, and FDR's emissary, Averill Harriman. Crowded onto the three following B-24s in "grim conditions" were the British military Chiefs of Staff (COS) and their support.[6] Led by the chief of the Imperial General Staff (CIGS), Gen. Sir Alan Brooke, were Admiral of the Fleet Sir Dudley Pound, Air Chief Marshal Sir Charles Portal, Combined Operations commander Vice Adm. Lord Louis Mountbatten, and others.

More than three years of war had tested the British chiefs, men already hardened by combat in the First World War. Until recently, they had fought this war desperately short of resources and come back from defeat after defeat. Each had a worldview shaped by the experience of empire. Gen. Sir Alan Brooke was an exemplar strategist who seemed perpetually critical of those around him and personally unhappy. Professional in his public demeanor, Brooke was scathing in his personal diary. Under unrelenting pressure from the Germans, Pound had kept Britain's maritime lifelines open. A fighter and bomber pilot in World War I, Portal had been a pioneer in the use of air power for imperial policing of tribal areas.[7] That became part of the base of experience from which developed the interwar notion that an adversary population could be bombed into political submission. Mountbatten, who had risen quickly, had a reputation for dash to the point of recklessness that had been deepened by the disastrous August 1942 Dieppe raid. But from his experience of combined operations, Mountbatten brought a readiness to innovate to the prospect of an eventual return to the Continent.

By January 1943, Churchill already had led a full and influential life, rich in adventure. Becoming Britain's prime minister at the country's most desperate hour in May 1940, he rallied the British people with his eloquent determination while secretly beating back domestic advocates for capitulation. Serving as his own minister of defense, Churchill had a direct involvement in leading Britain's war and day-to-day presence in its councils that could intimidate organized dissent, even when his chiefs disagreed with his ideas.[8] He could drive his ministers and military chiefs to distraction, particularly Brooke, with his fire hose of "action this day" memoranda and fits of temper. But Churchill kept his subordinates informed of his actions and thinking while Roosevelt kept his cabinet and military chiefs guessing.

Difficult and cold, the British flights also brought the prospect of a subtropical respite from winter and London's wartime privation. So, clad in a silk nightshirt, Churchill nearly froze on his flight.[9] The cos arrived tired and disheveled.[10] However, the British had been preceded by a large, well-prepared, and equipped support team that included an innovative floating headquarters ship, HMS *Bulolo*, which was a signal advantage.[11]

For the site of the conference, code-named Symbol, an Anglo-American team had selected Anfa, a Phoenician town five miles west of Casablanca with a view of the Atlantic Ocean. The airport, two miles away, could accommodate the heavy B-24s. Easily protected in the middle of a traffic circle with fourteen comfortable, even lavish villas nearby was the hilltop Anfa Hotel.[12] With four stories and wrap-around balconies, the hotel featured Le Restaurant Panoramique in the center of a rooftop terrace. Rounded and painted white with the occupying Americans' stars and stripes snapping in the breeze, the little art deco hotel resembled an excursion steamer putting out for a jaunt on the nearby ocean.

Or was it a flagship for the villas? Commandeered together, they became "Anfa Camp" for the Symbol Conference.

Britain and the United States were convening in Casablanca to address the open question of global strategy for the coming year, particularly how best to reenter the European continent and defeat the Axis in the west. Commanded by Lt. Gen. Dwight Eisenhower, the successful November 1942 landing of a 107,000-man Anglo-American army in Morocco and Algeria put the Allies at the beginning of a new phase of the war. They were on the offensive. Foreseeable at the start of 1943, in the fresh knowledge of the cost to win, was the challenge ahead. Although the 1942 victories of Midway, El Alamein, and Stalingrad in its final phase were having greatly positive consequences, they were but an opening. These hard-fought battles had delivered the Allies out of a defensive war to the geographic threshold of taking the offense onto the Continent and in the Pacific against still-formidable enemies.

Should the Allies misstep, Germany conceivably could force a favorable outcome for itself in the form of a stalemate, possibly yielding an armistice. Distraction from the war in the Pacific risked allowing Japan the opportunity to entrench its forward position to the point of impregnability. If the British and American teams arriving in Casablanca needed a cautionary metaphor to balance the flush of recent victories, they had only to look to their successfully landed North African army's current situation. Advance to the east was bogged down in Tunisia's winter cold and mud.[13]

Soon after U.S. entry into the war in December 1941, the Americans and the British faced imminent threats of defeat both in Europe and the Pacific. They responded by agreeing at the Arcadia Conference in Washington to establish a critically important, ultimately successful body to command their worldwide fight. The British Chiefs of Staff, navy, army, and air force, and their American counterparts stood up as a Combined Chiefs of Staff (ccs) to prosecute the war globally from Washington. Their permanent representatives met daily in Washington, and the chiefs themselves met at Anglo-American summits. In Casablanca, over just ten days, the ccs would hold their fifty-fifth through sixty-ninth meetings.[14]

Creation of the facility for defining and directing collective action, however, was far from a guarantee of Anglo-American agreement on what was needed and how to achieve it. Although Churchill and Roosevelt quickly developed an affinity for each other, whether or not Churchill saw this quality in the president, each man remained firm in pursuit of his nation's interests. Privately, Churchill was dismissive of FDR's intellect and thought him malleable. The prime minister was to learn otherwise. The British and American military chiefs and their staffs came to their alliance with very different views of the world, their nation's role in it, threats, and how to deal with them. The British and Americans were facing a harsh reality.

The bond of collective security forged in winning the First World War had been broken in intervening years by corrosive misperception, bias, and resentment. That could not now be reversed easily or quickly, even to meet shared existential threats. Perhaps this was inevitable between two cultures whose similarity could be as deceptive as their military traditions were different. Prevailing over the many Allied military disasters and near-disasters of 1942 had come at the cost of accelerated and intensified Anglo-American friction. Everyone gathering in Casablanca knew that the now urgent question drawing them together, offensive strategy had already been their frequent ground for conflict.

At the highest level, the United States and United Kingdom were in agreement that Germany was the most dangerous enemy. Japan could not win standing alone. But if the Allies were distracted to defeat Japan first, Germany—allowed time and latitude to stymy the Soviet Union and to consolidate the captured resources of occupied Europe—could become impregnable. Thus the Allied strategy of "Germany first" rested on a compelling but intellectual argument. For Americans, however, both among the public and tugging at the military leadership, particularly in the U.S. Navy, the emotional case favored strategic priority for retaliating against a Japan that had attacked first in the Pacific.

In the American public's divided opinion on war priorities, Roosevelt and his Democratic Party perceived a nascent political threat. Republicans were seeking to build in 1944 on gains they had won in the off-year November 1942 congressional elections. An open question in 1943 was whether Roosevelt would seek reelection to the presidency in 1944 for a fourth term. Public adulation of Gen. Douglas MacArthur, who had escaped the devastating defeat and capture of his American and Filipino troops, was seen as a potential Republican election opportunity. In 1942, through Michigan senator Arthur Vandenberg and Connecticut congresswoman Claire Booth Luce, Republicans had floated a "MacArthur for president in 1944" bubble in which MacArthur, commanding in the Southwest Pacific, was an innocent if somewhat interested party.[15] Anticipating attractiveness to voters in the 1944 presidential contest, which might flow from altered public opinion, especially if FDR declined to run for a fourth term, the "draft MacArthur" advocates were preparing in 1943 to appeal again to voter emotions with a "Pacific first" political campaign strategy.

Not coincidentally, Madame Chiang Kai-shek was embarking on a barnstorm tour of the United States to build on the public's demonstrated instinct to support China. Arriving in Casablanca with the sting of his party's off-year election drubbing still fresh, FDR knew that Madame Chiang was to address both houses of the U.S. Congress in February, a month away.[16]

Among Roosevelt's military chiefs, competition for resources often led the Army and Navy to divided positions on strategy. The European and Pacific theaters demanded generation of military forces and weapons in unprecedented quantities, even as response to the theaters' differing geographies fueled interservice competition. The U.S. Navy's leadership constantly pleaded for more resources for the Pacific where in fact the Army and Navy both struggled to fulfill bare minimal needs. The Navy tended to characterize allocations to the European theater as taking from the Pacific to the benefit of the Army in a zero-sum game. Given the shortage of steel and other materials, this often described the actual if not the intended result.

Although their motives might diverge, the U.S. Army and the Navy, nevertheless, could join in reaction to British initiatives that diverted the American buildup of forces in the British Isles away from the quick-thrust strategy of cross-Channel attack the JCS wanted. Pressed to their limit, the JCS's response was to play the Pacific card. In July 1942, they had recommended to Roosevelt that if cross-Channel attack was not to be the Allies' strategy, then the United States should shift attention and resources away from Europe and toward a "Pacific first" strategy, only to be rebuffed by FDR.[17] Nevertheless, in CCS meetings, the Americans would warn the British of this U.S. contingency option. They would do so again at Casablanca.

Roosevelt, his Republican Secretary of War Henry Stimson, and Harry Hopkins took in a larger picture and generally sought balance between the two opposing views. They tended to the more measured view that the British had not been wrong in 1942 to resist a cross-Channel attack as premature. Resolute in their determination that Hitler must be defeated first, they also were concerned about leaning too far in favor of further British proposals for operations in the Mediterranean and the Balkans. Doing so would risk a public perception of the prospect for a longer war for objectives peripheral to U.S. interests, specifically objectives of the British Empire. Secondary to Roosevelt and Hopkins's objective goals for the war, but not excluded from their considerations was that this could redound to the advantage of domestic political opponents who would not put Europe first.

The U.S. military chiefs went into World War II with a sequential strategy for fighting the global conflict, based on the goal of winning a short war. First, defeat Germany in Europe as the most dangerous threat,[18] shift to the Pacific to defeat Japan, and then come home. Before 1943 ended, the third objective, coming home, would be deferred indefinitely by a transformational change in perception of the role of the United States in the world.

The way to achieve the first objective and facilitate the second, in the view of the U.S. chiefs, was a violent, overwhelming thrust across the English Channel, through northwestern Europe, into the German citadel. Planners for this objective in early 1942, then overseen by recently promoted Brig. Gen. Dwight Eisenhower, conceived Operation Roundup to be a massive offensive by forty-eight divisions, thirty U.S. and eighteen British, supported by 5,800 aircraft. Roundup's U.S. planners optimistically foresaw such a force being assembled in the United Kingdom by April 1, 1943. With the Soviet Union then waging a desperate, as yet uncertain, defense against invading Axis armies, the United States also envisioned a much smaller emergency invasion to take pressure off the Soviets in the event of their imminent collapse. This contingency operation, named Sledgehammer, called for a cross-Channel assault with whatever forces were available in the UK. The objective was to draw some German divisions out of Russia with the threat of an Allied lodgment in the west. The U.S. planners anticipated shipping available to sustain just five divisions supported by 700 aircraft for Sledgehammer by September and October 1942.[19] Sustainment was not the same thing as an opposed landing of a force of this size on the Continent. For that, the needed amphibious lift did not then exist.

The U.S. plans and estimates were wildly optimistic from their inception. To advocate for them, U.S. Army chief of staff Marshall and Navy commander in chief Ernest King,[20] accompanied by Harry Hopkins representing FDR, had gone to London in April 1942. The JCS opposed the idea of an amphibious invasion of North Africa, Gymnast, as a diversion of resources. They were keeping on the table the U.S. option to switch their priority to the Pacific.

The British chiefs and Churchill initially expressed to Marshall and King assent, mild but disingenuous, for the cross-Channel attack strategy, even though the majority of forces for Sledgehammer would be British. They believed that neither the United States nor Britain would have the means to mount and complete either cross-Channel operation in 1942–43, unless Germany were suddenly to collapse from within as it had in 1918. That contingency, which the Americans acknowledged, the British were seeking to induce through aerial bombing and maritime blockade. The British chiefs' own strategy of peripheral attack, principally around the Mediterranean while attempting to weaken Germany, was then in gestation. Learning through Harry Hopkins that FDR's goal was to get U.S. troops into the fight in Europe before the end of 1942 "in the most useful place, and in the place where they could attain superiority,"[21] Churchill and the British chiefs saw their out. Hopkins's candor had determined for them that the president was less fixed on the point of initial engagement in Europe than his military chiefs were.

Marshall, King, and Hopkins returned to London in July 1942 with more specific instructions from their commander in chief. These FDR had developed in consultation with Hopkins. This time, Churchill learned from Hopkins that Roosevelt had taken first priority for the Pacific off the table and that getting U.S. forces into combat in the European theater in 1942 was the president's priority. So Churchill knew that he could resist Marshall's cross-Channel strategy for 1942–43 and advance his own Mediterranean strategy without risk. He did so.[22]

In London in July, Marshall, King, and the newly established American command staff with help from Lord Mountbatten's Combined Operations Command labored to produce a better plan for Sledgehammer as a precursor for Roundup. They offered their result in vain. FDR's directive and Churchill's informed resistance left no alternative to an invasion of North Africa as the next operation. Over the months that followed, the American chiefs fiercely argued for their preference. In the end, they had to accept resurrection of the renamed plan for an Anglo-American invasion of North Africa, Operation Torch, which was carried out in November 1942.

With their own European strategy kicked into the indeterminate future, the U.S. chiefs arrived in Casablanca in January 1943 with little confidence in Roosevelt's ability to resist Churchill and with hard feelings toward their British counterparts. They feared that the North African landings they had been forced to accept were but the first step along an endless path into the Mediterranean. There were plenty of doubts and suspicions about capabilities and motives on both sides.

Among the U.S. military staff still could be found adherents to the view of America's isolationists that the United States had been duped into World War I by the British. There was lingering suspicion, influencing staff papers signed off by U.S. service chiefs, that the British put priority on preserving their empire in context with a favorable postwar European balance of power. They could lapse into thinking that this goal drove the British position on strategy as much as their desire to defeat the Axis.[23] The JCS and their lieutenants' admiration for Britain's firm stand alone against Hitler's onslaught in 1940–41 was mixed with their sense that recurring defeats had eroded their British counterparts' aggressiveness.

Members of the British Chiefs of Staff perceived the United States to be lacking in military leadership capability to match its potential in manpower and materiel. That was not an unreasonable conclusion to draw from early U.S. overreach to advocate for a cross-Channel invasion that the British considered naïve and from initial stumbles by the U.S. military in the dark year of 1942. The British were acutely sensitive to the fact that General Marshall specifically had no experience leading armies in combat.[24]

Self-doubt and friction also dogged internal relations between each country's military and political leadership. Winston Churchill's micromanagement, flashes of ill temper, and stream of "action this day" directives exasperated the British COS and affected their personal opinions of his leadership ability.[25] For his part, having struggled to generate requested troops and resources only to endure British defeat after defeat in battle, Churchill apparently had come to suspect the capability of his military chiefs.[26]

The U.S. Joint Chiefs of Staff felt that FDR could not be relied on to stand up for U.S. goals and strategy against Churchill's persuasiveness. The chiefs had felt undercut by Roosevelt's shift from support for a cross-Channel invasion to instead redeploy forces for the invasion of North Africa that both FDR and Churchill desired. While outwardly supporting General Marshall's advocacy in London for a cross-Channel attack, Roosevelt's key aide, Harry Hopkins, had privately signaled more flexibility to Churchill.[27]

Marshall was astute enough to understand how the JCS had been maneuvered into accepting Operation Torch, the invasion of

North Africa. But the military's reliance and confidence in Harry Hopkins endured out of necessity. Beyond their unanimous appreciation for Hopkins's personal commitment to winning the war, the JCS knew this former social worker of frail constitution had an unequaled ability to draw decisions from the evasive Roosevelt. Marshall and Hopkins also had in common the bond between fathers whose sons were on active duty. Each would come to grieve the death of a son in combat.[28]

* * *

Winston Churchill brought with him to Casablanca from London a brand-new problem, one entirely different from military strategy and closely held. Britain's participation in the super secret Anglo-American work to develop an atomic bomb and access to information on its new discoveries in physics had been curtailed by the Americans. First together in the same theater at Casablanca, but standing well apart, the two issues, European war strategy and the ostensibly joint quest for an atomic bomb, would move onto the same stage and ever closer in proximity as 1943 progressed.

In October 1941, President Roosevelt had proposed that the two nations' efforts on weaponizing atomic energy should be "coordinated and even jointly conducted."[29] Believing they were ahead of the Americans on the science, the British at first had demurred. Then the British changed their minds after further considering the vast intellectual and financial resources required, access to natural resources, and the relative safety from military threat gained by basing the project in North America.

Since an informal oral agreement reached during a meeting between FDR and Churchill at the president's Hyde Park, New York, estate in July 1942, Britain and the United States had been moving toward a coordinated effort to speed research and produce an atomic bomb.[30] The Anglo-American scientific community's knowledge of discoveries by German scientists, combined with intelligence reports, persuaded them that they were in an all-out race to beat the Third Reich to the bomb. The British established an advance team of scientists in Montreal anticipating closer involvement with the Americans. But, only six months later, the U.S. side of the project put the British on notice that exchange of information on atomic weapons research would be sharply limited.[31]

On the day of departure for Casablanca, January 11, Churchill received a letter from Sir John Anderson, the lord president of the Privy Council, written with the concurrence of Lord Cherwell, the paymaster general and Churchill's scientific adviser. Anderson and Cherwell were the prime minister's principal advisers on atomic matters. The letter notified Churchill of the new restrictive U.S. policy on cooperative atomic bomb information interchange, the project that the British code named "Tube Alloys" and their American counterparts called "s-1."[32] For the British, the new U.S. restrictions plunged the project into crisis.

Writing for both men, Anderson said, "This development has come as a bombshell, and is quite intolerable." Anderson and Cherwell recommended "that an approach to President Roosevelt is urgently necessary." On the attached extract from the U.S. memorandum detailing the specifics of what was to be withheld, Churchill circled in red two references to "element forty-nine," code for plutonium by then identified as the most potent fissile material for a bomb. At the top of the first page, he wrote and circled a single word, *Symbol*, the code name for the conference with Roosevelt in Casablanca to which Churchill would fly that night.[33]

Weaponizing the energy of the atom, a possibility to which British science had contributed so much important early research, was foreseen by Churchill to become a fundamental determinant of political-military power in the postwar world. That world was likely to be dominated by the United States and the Soviet Union. In January 1943, awareness of the postwar importance to Britain of having its own bomb was dawning apace with unfolding realization that the decision to shift atomic research to North America for sound reasons had an unintended consequence. Achieving an independent British atomic weapon capability had become dependent on a nation that for its own reasons might not accommodate British interests.

Beyond an Anglo-American race to acquire an atomic bomb before Hitler, Churchill understood that this also was a unilaterally British issue for the future that demanded attention in the present. Could Anglo-American pursuit of an atomic bomb continue as a joint endeavor toward a result equally available to both countries?

The overt reason for the new U.S. policy, as explained to the British, was based on a security principle. The British suspected, however, that there was a deeper reason not stated to them.

Oversight for atomic research and its product on the U.S. side was through the Military Policy Committee, involving Vice President Henry Wallace, Secretary of War Henry Stimson, George Marshal, Office of Scientific Research and Development (OSRD) director Vannevar Bush, and Brig. Gen. Leslie Groves. Since September 1942, Groves had command of the Manhattan Project, created to produce an atomic bomb from the scientists' research. Leading implementation of the project for the United States was a civilian-military management team: Bush, his OSRD deputy director, James Conant, and Brig. Gen. Groves. Physicist Robert Oppenheimer led the scientific team.

Dr. Conant was a chemist and president of Harvard University. Dr. Bush had come from directorship of the Massachusetts Institute of Technology's Electrical Engineering Department to become president of the Carnegie Institution. Then, as the first presidential science adviser, he became director of OSRD. That organization had vast influence on science's contribution to the U.S. war effort.

By late 1942, strongly encouraged by Groves, Bush and Conant had concluded that the United States was making 90 percent of the effort and providing 90 percent of the investment to develop and build a bomb for this war, while Britain's level of effort could not yield a bomb in time for the current war. Bush and Conant would come to the position that sharing knowledge of how to produce such a weapon with a foreign nation was neither in the U.S. national security interest nor within the scope of FDR's war powers. In their later correspondence, they can be seen to be jointly concerned that sharing knowledge of the bomb could not be done without an alliance that would constrain U.S. latitude to act in its own national security interest. Churchill's end goal, not openly put to the Americans until September 1944, in fact was an alliance that would continue after the current war.[34]

The three men chose to employ a narrower rationale to meet their concern. They convinced the Military Policy Committee that in the context of FDR's legal authority to wage the current war, information shared with the British and the British-sponsored team in Canada should be based strictly on the principle of "need to know." The British should receive all the information that would help advance the areas of their participation contributing to the project for this war, but were not entitled to any other information. The three men expressed their decision as a straightforward extension of the principle of need to know that was in effect throughout the U.S. war effort. Bush and Conant believed that their action was consistent with what the president wanted: an impression that FDR fostered with his December 28, 1942, acceptance of all the Military Policy Committee recommendations and later did nothing to discourage.[35]

Dr. Conant informally described the imminent U.S. policy change to the British representative to the project in Washington, Wallace Akers, on December 11, 1942. Following the Military Policy Committee's decision, Conant outlined the new policy in a letter that he wrote with Bush's knowledge and sent to the British on January 2, 1943, via the Anglo-Canadian team working on the project in Montreal. Conant then wrote on January 7 a more extensive memorandum that detailed how the new policy would be applied to specific elements of the project, the details of which became known to Akers.[36]

Wallace Akers was a principal engineer at Imperial Chemical Industries, on loan to the government to help lead British atomic research. The Americans, Bush, Conant, and particularly Groves, were opposed to Akers as the British representative on the grounds that an ICI executive would gain for his company and country a postwar global competitive advantage in atomic power generation.[37] Possibly they actually saw more than their match in the cultured and thoughtful Akers's effectiveness in representing British interests through his hard work and perceptiveness.[38]

Even without the assumed conflict of interest and interpersonal tension, a rupture in cooperation would have been impossible to avoid. The new American policy's negative impact on British interests spawned an Anglo-American standoff in Washington that immediately became a crisis in London.

The British were quick to see that restricting their participation on a "need to know" basis would result in an essentially one-way flow of information to the benefit of the United States and to the detriment of essential aspects of their own atomic research. Although not expressed by them in these words, the British position was that the corollary to "need to know" was their U.S. ally's obligation to share. From an impression that the OSRD civilians, Bush and Conant, found General Groves intimidating, the British almost immediately began to suspect a deeper motive beyond the stated concern for security. They believed that the U.S. military desired to take exclusive control of atomic research.[39]

So it was that Winston Churchill arrived in Casablanca, where his military chiefs would engage in certain-to-be-fraught military strategy discussions, with the rupture of Anglo-American atomic information interchange very much on his mind. At the outset of 1943, the British COS themselves had little if any knowledge of the importance or even the existence of the Tube Alloys project. Neither were they aware of the newly contentious issue's presence at Casablanca.[40]

Within two hours of their 13 January arrival, tired though they were, the British COS met with Field Marshal Sir John Dill, who briefed them on the Americans' general military strategy position and relations among the American chiefs. This was time well spent. The British chiefs were forewarned by Dill that their American counterparts for multiple reasons strongly opposed following up the recent landings in North Africa, Operation Torch, with new initiatives in the Mediterranean. The Americans thought it would reduce the likelihood of a major cross-Channel assault into France. According to Dill, they also thought Mediterranean operations would draw resources away from the bombing of Germany and expend scarce naval craft and merchant shipping for less than optimal returns. A diversion to the Mediterranean would retard operations in Burma [Myanmar], which the Americans thought were significant to keeping China in the war, Dill said. The American chiefs, in Dill's assessment, questioned the strength of the British commitment to the war in East Asia. In pressing for a rapid defeat of Hitler, the Americans believed that if given time to dig in by a drawn-out European campaign, Japan would become impossible to defeat. Dill also told the British chiefs of friction between the U.S. Army under Marshall and the Navy under King.[41] The informative meeting with Dill concluded, British cos next met with Churchill at 6:00 p.m. and briefed him on their position going into the negotiation with the Americans. General Brooke then met with General Marshall for dinner followed by "a long talk."[42]

* * *

President Roosevelt arrived in Casablanca late on the afternoon of January 14. He was taken to the villa set aside for him in Anfa Camp, whereupon Harry Hopkins immediately fetched Churchill from his villa for drinks. The president then summoned the British and American chiefs to join the two leaders for a convivial dinner that lasted late into the night.[43] When the lights were extinguished for an air raid warning that turned out to be false, the evening ended with the faces of the assembled illuminated by candlelight.[44]

The following morning, Marshall, King, and Arnold met with FDR, Hopkins, and Harriman for the last time before the JCS sat down with the British. Marshall led the briefing of the president, speaking with the benefit of his talk with General Brooke the evening before.[45] Marshall quite accurately told FDR that the British chiefs' strategic concept for Europe called for first expanding bombing of the Axis and that they favored expanded Mediterranean operations as the best means to force Germany to disperse air resources. Marshall told FDR that the British favored Sicily over Sardinia for the next Allied operation. In Marshall's observation, the British were "extremely fearful of any direct action against the Continent until a decided crack in the German efficiency and morale has become apparent." Marshall told FDR that any operation in the Mediterranean "will definitely retard Bolero," the transatlantic buildup of U.S. forces in the British Isles for a cross-Channel attack into France. Marshall found the British and U.S. chiefs to be in agreement on giving priority to defeating the U-boats.[46]

That afternoon, curtains were drawn across the Anfa Hotel's broad windows. The Combined Chiefs of Staff sat down to their first substantive meeting. It started out well enough.

General agreement came quickly on the first topic, fulfilling antisubmarine warfare (ASW) requirements. For that the CCS had good reason. Everything the Allies were doing and hoped to do depended on shipping. Before the onset of winter storms in the North Atlantic brought partial relief to the convoys, November 1942 had seen the U-boat wolf pack predations at their worst. Sinking of Allied and neutral shipping set a new monthly record at 636,907 tons.[47] The U-boat threat had to be countered by spring, whatever the Allies' strategy choice for Europe.

Everywhere, the Allies always were short of surface escorts to protect the convoys. Only the introduction of operationally ready, new construction escort vessels could provide relief. Also agreed by the chiefs was that patrolling aircraft were highly effective in suppressing the U-boats. However, ASW patrolling required a lot of aircraft and flying time. The absolute "minimum requirement for Atlantic basin and UK home waters was 120 to 135 long-range bombers," according to Admiral Pound.[48] With this language, the note takers glossed over internal interservice contentions under way in both London and Washington on the allocation of bombers.

The most critical need was not for long-range but for *very* long-range (VLR) bombers to close a mid-Atlantic Ocean gap in air coverage where U-boats still enjoyed too much freedom to hunt. Competition was sharp between bombing advocates and ASW commanders for the still too few vlr candidate aircraft. Agreeing to the need, but kicking distribution into the future, the ccs directed the Combined Staff planners to assess and report the minimum requirements for escorts, aircraft carriers, and land-based aircraft to secure the United Nations' sea communications everywhere during 1943.[49]

Lt. Gen. Dwight Eisenhower, the supreme Allied commander in North Africa, entered the room after a rough, trouble-plagued flight from his headquarters in Algiers. He briefed the ccs on the current situation in North Africa and followed up with a briefing on his proposed attack with U.S. forces on the Axis-held Tunisian town of Sfax. Eisenhower's plan was sharply criticized by General Brooke for its lack of coordination with the British First and Eighth Armies, neither of which would be in a position to support the attack. As a result, Brooke said, the proposed U.S. attack risked being defeated in detail by Gen. Erwin Rommel's German forces.[50]

Criticism of Eisenhower's plan could not help but stir British perceptions of inexperience and inadequacy in U.S. generalship. That was an inauspicious lead into what followed. The Combined Chiefs of Staff next turned to strategy for the European theater, so beginning three days of deadlock.

Gen. Sir Alan Brooke led off. He first set up the options for a cross-Channel attack into northwestern Europe and then described in some detail the slim advantages such an attack offered. Not for the first time, the negatives associated with a cross-Channel attack were easily cited and difficult to counter in the absence of rigorous Allied planning for this strategy option. Brooke, with the benefit of planning for the British alternative, then described a Mediterranean strategy that offered many options with good potential and cascading advantages. A great benefit in Brooke's view was that focus on the Mediterranean, by limiting a buildup of tactical air units, would allow a greater heavy bomber force to be built up in the United Kingdom than if the Allies concentrated on invading France.[51] Thus, in a larger sense, the emerging Mediterranean strategy supported the British preference for defeating Germany through attrition and would diminish materiel resources for the American-preferred alternative.[52]

The British chiefs, deft in their serial coordination, countered successive, weak U.S. criticisms of the British position and an uncoordinated defense by the American chiefs of their own bid for greater priority and resources for the Pacific theater.[53] The British then moved the discussion on to the advantages of following up anticipated success in North Africa by next attacking Sicily not Sardinia.[54]

From this meeting, the ccs reconvened at 5:30 p.m. for the first of three plenary sessions with FDR and Churchill. There Roosevelt made statements that favored Mediterranean operations.[55] This indicated to the British that, once again, a division on strategy existed between the president and his jcs as it did among the ccs themselves. That was their opening to isolate General Marshall and his desire for a cross-Channel attack, as had been done in 1942 when the decision was made in favor of the North African landings.

In London, meanwhile, the anxiety of Britain's Tube Alloy scientific leadership ratcheted up. That evening they received from the British Scientific Mission in Washington Wallace Akers's transmission of the text of the Conant memorandum detailing seven specific areas in which information exchange would be withheld or limited.[56] As yet, Anderson and Lord Cherwell had received no response from Churchill in Casablanca.

On January 16 the ccs met twice more on the issues of strategy. Their discussion went along much the same lines as the day before. General Brooke wrote in his diary that this was a slow and tiring process. The slog was fueled by Brooke's growing disdain for the American chiefs, particularly what he saw as the absence of a sense of strategy among Marshall's "very high qualities."[57]

General Brooke possibly was reacting to Marshall's challenge to the British chiefs in this day's ccs meetings to articulate their best plan for defeating Germany. In so doing, Marshall, by his use of argument alone, clearly was trying to compensate for the absence from the conference of a prepared U.S. staff comparable to that of the British. Given that the British had cited aid to the Red Army as a key to victory, Marshall insisted that logic compelled them to invade the Continent. Thus in the meeting, Marshall attempted to set a strategy of direct action against the strategy of attrition. Still, he was ready to take an additional step with the British into the Mediterranean, to Sicily, if doing so would be the last step before committing the Allies to giving priority to the cross-Channel attack-based strategy. To Marshall, direct attack across the Channel and then on into Germany itself was "the main plot" of the war in Europe.[58]

At 5:00 p.m., the British and U.S. chiefs parted to report and consult separately with their leaders. General Marshall conveyed to FDR the importance to the British of obtaining a crack in German morale as a prerequisite for a return to the Continent.[59]

"A desperate day!" was how Brooke began his diary account of how, on the following day, Sunday, January 17, the ccs wrangled again over strategy. The chief of the Imperial General Staff concluded that in his opinion, the Combined Chiefs were "further from obtaining agreement than we ever were!" Admiral King and General Marshall had been emphatic on the need to maintain pressure on Japan. Warning that the immense cost in resources to engage the Japanese affected every other United Nations operation worldwide, Marshall ominously warned that "a situation might arise in the Pacific at any time that would necessitate the United States regretfully withdrawing from commitments in the European Theater." Hearing the Americans' advocacy for the Pacific, particularly Marshall's stark warning, the British chiefs concluded that the bedrock principle of defeating Germany first was back on the table. They directed their staff to prepare a new paper with which to confront this issue on the following day.[60]

The ccs resumed meetings on January 18. For the strategy debate at this conference, the day would be decisive. They began by discussing a contemplated amphibious landing, Operation Anakim, to retake Burma, then a Japanese-occupied British colony, as a step to keep China in the war. Around Anakim and the larger question of the allocation of effort to the Pacific again swirled the fundamental question. Was the Anglo-American commitment to the concept of defeating Germany first still firmly shared?[61]

The British attempted compromise by offering agreement with the U.S. Pacific strategy but, referring to the new British COS paper, "provided always that its application does not prejudice the earliest possible defeat of Germany." That drew a response from Admiral King that the British statement could be read to mean that "*anything* which was done in the Pacific interfered with the earliest possible defeat of Germany and that the Pacific theater should therefore remain totally inactive" (italics in the CCS meeting minutes). Air Marshal Sir Charles Portal attempted to counter King's objection by citing the immediate opportunity for engaging Germany in the Mediterranean and increasing bombing of Germany directly out of the United Kingdom, thereby assisting the Russians. But Portal helped nothing when he admitted that it was impossible to say exactly where the Allies should stop in the Mediterranean. The chiefs' argument went on at length, finally turning to other subjects with nothing resolved.[62]

Gen. Sir Alan Brooke left the morning meeting despairing to Field Marshal Sir John Dill, "It is no use, we shall never get agreement with them!" Dill, who in 1941 had been eased out and replaced as CIGS by Brooke, told the younger man that most points already were agreed between the two allies. After lunch, the two met in Brooke's hotel room where Dill ticked off the remaining points of disagreement and asked how far Brooke would go to get agreement. When Brooke replied that he would not move an inch, Dill replied, "Oh, yes, you will. You know that you must come to some agreement with the Americans and that you cannot bring the unsolved problem up to the Prime Minister and the President. You know as well as I do what a mess they will make of it."[63]

Air Marshall Portal came into the room with a similar proposed plan for agreement. The paper Portal carried had been written by his assistant chief of staff, Air Vice Marshal Sir John Slessor, over lunch at the hotel's rooftop restaurant. With consensus among the three British officers, Dill left to discuss their proposal with his friend Marshall.[64] When the CCS reconvened at 3:00 p.m.,

Brooke presented the compromise paper, which was accepted with few changes. The chiefs then briefed Churchill and Roosevelt, who gave the plan their approval, after which everyone was photographed together.[65] The smiles were tight.

Over the next three days, the ccs moved toward a concluding conference document with actionable objectives. They agreed that "the defeat of the U-boat must remain a first charge on the resources of the United Nations." Also agreed was that Soviet forces must be sustained by the greatest volume of supplies possible that could be transported to Russia without prohibitive cost in shipping. Operations in the European theater would seek to defeat Germany in 1943 with the maximum forces that can be brought to bear. In the Mediterranean, this would mean the occupation of Sicily and seeking to enlist Turkey in the war. From the United Kingdom, this would mean "the heaviest possible bomber offensive against the German war effort" (from Air Vice Marshal Slessor's paper), limited amphibious raids as may be practicable, and "assembly of the strongest possible force . . . in constant readiness to reenter the Continent as soon as German resistance is weakened to the required extent."[66]

The last objective was qualified to be limited by the needs of the Mediterranean and operations in the Pacific and East Asia to the narrow extent that those had been approved. The much discussed recapture of Burma (Anakim) was approved subject to all of the other calls on time and resources. Operations against the Marshall and Caroline Islands, after the recapture of Rabaul, were approved if not prejudicial to Anakim.[67]

Self-evident in the concluding ccs document of priorities for 1943 were many provisos subject to future interpretation. Between its lines was the British belief, a hope at this stage shared by Roosevelt, that Hitler's Reich could be induced to implode by forcing a collapse of German morale.

The contentious issue of European theater war strategy had been consigned to an uneasy agreement with the expectation of another major conference in the spring of 1943. The Combined Chiefs used their remaining days in Anfa Camp to address issues that, although of a lower order, would have a decisive effect on prosecution of the war in Europe.

The chiefs took up better coordination of the bombing of occupied Europe and Germany. At Casablanca, the U.S. Army Air Force and the Royal Air Force leadership were allies in the advocacy of air power, while disagreeing on how to use their respective long-range bombers. The RAF's campaign, ever increasing through 1942, was based on night area bombing of German cities. The still-small but soon to grow USAAF operations were founded on a belief in the effectiveness of daylight precision bombing of defined military-industrial point targets. Bombing results, or their lack to date, was a source of criticism for both operations. The RAF and USAAF banded together at Casablanca and won endorsement for integrating their different operations as a day-and-night Combined Bomber Offensive.

At their sixty-fifth meeting on January 21, the Combined Chiefs approved a governing "directive" to the RAF and USAAF operational commanders with the objective of "the progressive dislocation of the German military, industrial, and economic systems, and the undermining of the morale of the German people to a point where their capacity for armed resistance is fatally weakened."[68] How the Combined Bomber Offensive was implemented would become important to opposition to the cross-Channel attack-based strategy and also, through a collateral effect on the Luftwaffe still to unfold, the success of that very strategy.[69]

On January 22, the Combined Chiefs took a significant if less noticed decision to discern the viability and substance of cross-Channel attack. They agreed to establish in London an Allied team to plan for a return to the Continent. Previous separate and thinly resourced planning efforts would be replaced with an integrated, stand-alone organization of British and American composition. General Brooke said that a special staff for cross-Channel operations should be set up without delay. Among the structures recommended by General Marshall was that the head of the team should be designated the chief of staff to the still-to-be-named Supreme Allied Commander.[70]

In what must have been a bitter pill for the American delegation to Casablanca, the proposal to form the new unit took as a given that "there is no chance of our being able to stage a large scale invasion of the Continent against unbroken opposition during 1943." The proposal then described activities for which planning was needed including small-scale amphibious operations, such as reoccupation of the British Channel Islands, and readiness for a pick-up invasion to exploit "a sudden and unexpected collapse of German resistance." The example planning activities led lastly to planning for an invasion in force in 1944.[71] Beyond setting the year 1944, specifics as to timing and the means for implementing these plans were left to be determined.

The ccs did recognize the need and committed to providing the new planning unit with a "clear directive . . . setting out the objects of the plans and the resources likely to be available."[72] Although the details were uncertain, the mandate to begin genuinely allied planning to liberate the Continent now was a fact. Whether a cross-Channel attack-based strategy could succeed was an open question.

* * *

As the Combined Chiefs argued toward a military strategy compromise, essentially limited in scope to 1943.[73] Winston Churchill took up the separate crisis over a break in Anglo-American atomic information interchange. Acting on Sir John Anderson's January 11 letter of deep concern, Churchill made an approach to the Americans. Instead of appealing the new restrictive policy directly to Roosevelt, the prime minister elected to take the issue to FDR's close adviser, Harry Hopkins.[74] Churchill had developed a liking for Hopkins and placed deep trust in him. For that he had good reason. Hopkins was to Churchill a frequent source of intimate, often decisive insight into the thinking of the ever-smiling but often inscrutable Roosevelt.

The details of this exchange between the prime minister and Hopkins have not survived. However, Churchill found Hopkins's response on Tube Alloys information interchange satisfactory.

From Casablanca on January 18, Churchill's assistant secretary sent a message to Sir John Anderson in London. The message said that the prime minister "spoke to Mr. Harry Hopkins about this matter and was assured that the President, while he did not wish to telegraph about it, knew exactly how it should be handled, and it would be entirely in accordance with our wishes."[75]

By January 19, the crisis in London had reached the boiling point. That day, possibly unaware or not privy to the message about Churchill's initiative in Casablanca, British Tube Alloy scientists and program managers began to discuss responding to the new U.S. policy by withholding British information.[76] By the following day, Anderson and Lord Cherwell were discussing the scientists' restrictive response. In a "Note for the Record," William Gorell Barnes wrote that, on January 20, Anderson and Cherwell "decided that, for the time being, we should continue to give the impression of not withholding information from the Americans regarding our progress on Tube Alloys, but, at the same time, should be careful not to give away any important secrets until the position has clarified."[77]

That may have mollified the scientists, but the anxiety of the Tube Alloy leadership in London had not been stilled. Also on January 20, again writing on behalf of Lord Cherwell as well as himself, Anderson sent an immediate precedence, "Hush Most Secret" telegram to Churchill. Anderson conveyed nothing of the equivocal guidance he and Cherwell had given to the Tube Alloy scientists. Of the new U.S. policy, much as he already had said in his January 11 letter, Anderson told Churchill that "there is to be no further interchange of information in regard to many of the most important processes. . . . Pretext for this policy is need for secrecy, but one cannot help suspecting that the U.S. Military Authorities who are now in complete control wish to gain an advance upon us and feel that, having now benefitted from the fruits of our early endeavors, they will not suffer unduly by casting us aside. . . . We hope you will be able to prevail upon the President to put matters right. If not, we shall have to consider drastic changes in our programme and policy."[78]

On January 23, Churchill himself sent a "Hush Most Secret" message of reply directly back to Sir John Anderson stating, "I may be obtaining most satisfactory personal assurances but it is thought better not to send telegraphic instructions from here."[79] Churchill's personal message reassured the Tube Alloy community, if only for the present.[80]

* * *

The Casablanca Conference was extended three days in large part to allow for delicate maneuvering by Roosevelt and Churchill to bridge the estrangement between two competing French leaders. They were Free French Gen. Charles de Gaulle and the surviving leader of the former Vichy forces in North Africa, Gen. Henri Giraud.[81] Through a process of cajolery and threats with lots of help from Harry Hopkins and British Foreign Minister Sir Anthony Eden, the endeavor culminated in a much-photographed and wary public handshake by the two generals before Churchill and a delighted FDR.

This happened at a concluding garden press conference on January 24, forever to be remembered for Roosevelt's controversial declaration that the Allies would prosecute the war until the Axis surrendered unconditionally. FDR's preceding remark that the French generals' handshake reminded him of the ending of the American Civil War with a handshake between Robert E. Lee and Ulysses S. "Unconditional Surrender" Grant left an impression that the president's announcement of an Allied policy was impromptu. It was not.

On January 7, before any of them left for Casablanca, Roosevelt told the JCS that he would discuss with Churchill "the advisability of informing Mr. Stalin that the United Nations were to continue on until they reach Berlin, and that the only terms would be unconditional surrender." He did so, and in the days before the January 24 press conference, Churchill approved provided that Italy was left out of the declaration.[82] By the conclusion of the military talks in Casablanca, with everyone aware that the second front could not be opened in 1943, FDR and Churchill had still

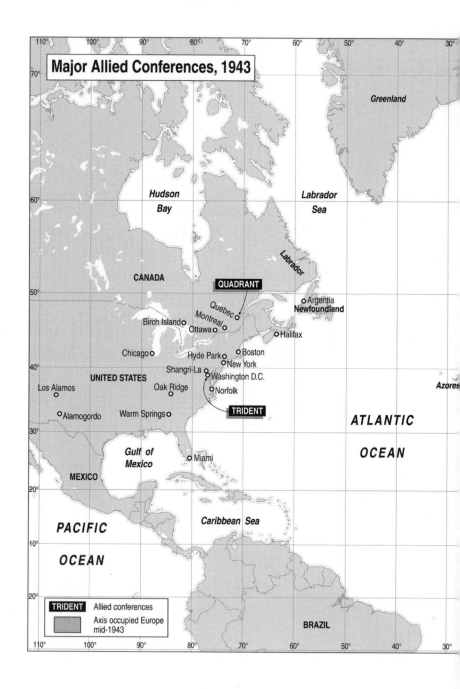

Major Allied Conferences, 1943

stronger reason to reassure Stalin that his western allies would not attempt to end the war short of Nazism's unconditional surrender. Speaking from a prepared text, that reassurance was Roosevelt's intent.[83] FDR's unconditional surrender statement remains controversial to this day.

Churchill and Roosevelt departed Casablanca by road for Marrakech. There they enjoyed an evening of peace in a villa with a sublime view from the villa's tower of the Atlas Mountains at twilight. On the morning of January 25, Roosevelt flew off to retrace his route back to Washington.[84] In two hours, Churchill made his only painting of the war as a future gift to FDR and left for Cairo and a meeting in Turkey with that country's president, Ismet Inönü.[85]

Except for Brooke, who went with Churchill, the British chiefs returned to London satisfied with the commitment to invade Sicily as the next Allied operation but also with the responsibility to set up the new Allied organization to plan for a return to the Continent. The American chiefs returned to Washington with an acute sense of having been bested roundly by superior British coordination and staff work. Knowing the ccs would meet again in the spring, they vowed not to come off second again.

2

Campaigns of Attrition

It might be true to say that the issue of the war depends on whether Hitler's U-boat attack on Allied tonnage, or the increase in application of Allied air power, reach their full fruition first.

—Winston Churchill, July 21, 1942

What would come of the Casablanca decisions on strategy, however tentative, would be shaped by the Allies' current engagement with their enemies at sea and in the air. Three and one-quarter years into the war, the Allies and the Axis were waging intense and sustained operations against each other with dissimilar weapons but similar primary objectives. In the Atlantic, unrestricted submarine warfare by German U-boats sought the collapse of Britain through economic strangulation. The British Royal Air Force night bombing offensive against Germany aimed to force the political-economic collapse of the Reich. Each campaign, U-boats and bombers, grew out of lessons drawn from World War I and would fail to achieve its primary objective. But in 1943 the outcome of each was still to be determined. Understanding how the commitment and concentration of Allied forces for Overlord emerged from deliberations in 1943 requires understanding the influence of the effects, real and perceptual, of these campaigns of attrition, starting with the bombers.

Under the RAF interpreter's stereo magnifier, the post-raid aerial photograph's clusters of hundreds of tiny rectangles with dark, concave centers resembled the microscopic cell structure of a leaf. But the gray veins enclosing the clusters were in fact the streets of Cologne, Germany's fourth largest city in 1943. Defined by still-standing walls, each rectangle contained the collapsed and blackened remains of fire-gutted housing. The photo revealed just a small fraction of Cologne, less than one-quarter of 1,785 acres that by 1943 the Royal Air Force claimed had been "completely devastated" by Allied bombing.[1] This photo and others like it would be published in a British Air Ministry progress report as evidence of bombing success. Housing was a target, an important one to the British.

Out of limited experience with long-range bombing late in World War I, interwar theorizing produced a strategic conception of victory through air power as an alternative to the grinding slog of positional warfare on the ground. Through aerial bombing, the theory held, the population of an industrialized society could be terrorized into forcing their government to change or abandon a policy of war.[2] Offering an alternative to politicians and to military staffs, averse to any repeat of the gore of the last war, and leverage for proponents of the new technology of air power, this untested theory was widely held and publicly acknowledged in industrialized Europe, the United States, and Japan. In the next war, governments, editorialists, and even fiction writers wrote that civilian populations would be a legitimate target for the purpose of breaking their morale.[3] In all countries in the interwar years, among the labels for the concept could be found "terror bombing." That term and the concept itself drew criticism but also found direct, facile application after war came.

Adolf Hitler put a premium on destroying, as he put it, his enemy's "will to resist." In September 1940, he told planners of Operation Sea Lion, the pending invasion of the UK, that "a systematic and long-drawn-out bombardment of London might produce an attitude in the enemy which will make Sea Lion unnecessary."[4] Roosevelt was assured by Churchill's frequently shared "evidence," and he believed in the coercive potential of aerial bombardment. They saw the air power strategy as an alternative path to early victory, short of the need to assault occupied Europe and risk a repeat of the land conflict of World War I. From early in their wartime conversations until well into 1943, the two leaders shared this view, their separate degrees of conviction fluctuating.

Looking ahead in August 1941 to a European war for which the

United States did not yet have an army to deploy, Roosevelt saw bombing as "the only means of gaining victory."[5] Roosevelt's view would evolve in a different direction as his army grew in size and combat experience. Although skeptical of Bomber Command's results early in the war, Churchill recognized bombing as the only way to hit back at Germany directly after Dunkirk in 1940. He maintained his commitment to bombing even when, at a low point, he deemed it "better than doing nothing."[6]

The problem lay in achieving air power's theoretical promise under actual wartime conditions with the technologically developing instruments at hand in the early 1940s. Theory ran into the reality of determined and increasingly skilled German defenses and weather in northern Europe. Forced by defenses to fly its missions at night, Bomber Command also suffered the consequences of having left celestial navigation out of its basic training syllabus prior to 1941.[7]

From 1942 through 1943 with the aid of the H2s bombing radar, only half of the bombs dropped on Germany by RAF Bomber Command fell within one and three-quarter miles of their intended target. That was an improvement over 1941 when only one-quarter of bombs fell within five miles of their aiming point.[8] For its night offensive, Bomber Command could not find, let alone hit, precision targets. Cities were what the bombers could hit.

The RAF bombing strategy adopted in London was channeled by the technological and operational limits of the bombing force available. Churchill's science adviser, Dr. Frederick Lindeman (later Lord Cherwell), produced a note to the prime minister purporting that, through area bombing of cities, 10,000 RAF bombers could "de-house" one-third of Germany's population by mid-1943. The loss of home, Lindeman argued, would be particularly damaging to German morale.[9] It was assumed that essential war production plants would be within the areas bombed when in fact industry tended to be on the periphery of old European city centers. However, at the time of Lindeman's study, the RAF had not even one-tenth of the heavy bombers assumed in his study. At its peak, the combined RAF and USAAF heavy bomber force would be only a fraction of the size of Lindeman's assumed force. The note was debated, criticized, and found persuasive by Churchill.

If anything, Lindeman's note gave evidence of a strategy already in adoption.[10] Although of questionable relevance in the 1940s, how World War I had ended encouraged belief in the proposition, perhaps as much as did loathing of a repeat of trench warfare. Shortly after its army mounted a large and dangerous offensive on the western front in 1918, Germany had surprised the Allies by collapsing internally and then seeking an armistice from within the resulting chaos.

The fact that Hitler had not profited from a similar bombing strategy directed against Britain that inflicted 40,000 deaths between August 1940 and June 1941 was rationalized away by the British.[11] The Luftwaffe's limited bombing capacity for the Blitz of Great Britain was contrasted with the already larger and growing Allied bombing capacity and dismissed.

Bombing to compel a nation to change its policy by shattering its people's morale had yet to be accomplished, proponents argued, because the bombing so far had been insufficient. What was the solution? Look to better accuracy from target location aids like "Gee" and airborne radars such as the H2S and then bomb more. In the assessment of bombing proponents, the experience of World War I was a teaser. Strategic bombing's potential was still being explored. Who could say that applying technological innovation and greater effort would not achieve this theory's promise?

The U.S. Army Air Force arrived in England for the war in Europe with a different doctrine and strategy, despite its attraction to and study of area bombing of complex industrial societies. USAAF Chief of Staff Lt. Gen. Hap Arnold and Maj. Gen. Carl "Tooey" Spaatz, who established the Eighth Air Force in England in 1942, were skeptical of RAF area bombing strategy. They had been made wary by what they had observed on the ground in London under Luftwaffe bombs during the Blitz, just as the RAF leadership was skeptical of the Americans' bombing doctrine alternative.

The UK-based Eighth Air Force would apply the USAAF doctrine of precision bombing in massed daylight raids, seeking the interrelated benefits of mutual protection and targeting accuracy. The heavy bombers would fight through to their targets relying on the defensive strength of large, tight bomber formations. Hits on targets would result from the Norden bombsight's "in the pickle barrel" accuracy, albeit accuracy that had been demonstrated in unopposed daylight flight through the clear, peaceful skies of the American Southwest. The American bombers would be directed against a list of military and military-industrial targets. Target sets would be prioritized by their strategic importance to the broader military effort. Implementing this targeting strategy, the initial American bombing force in England cut its teeth with limited effect in raids on facilities related to U-boat production. To follow would be sustained, larger efforts against functionally defined sets of facilities producing fighter aircraft, synthetic oil, and ball bearings, a component critical to all sorts of weapons.

Against determined defenses in the weather conditions of northern Europe, the strategy's theoretical promise of bomber self-defense and bombing accuracy, when put to practice, eluded the Americans. The fighters initially available to escort American daylight bombing raids lacked the range to stay with the bombers all the way for penetration to targets deep in Germany. After the escorting fighters withdrew, the unescorted bomber formations suffered heavy losses from Luftwaffe interceptors. Bombing through cloud cover or haze, frequent conditions in northern Europe, was far from precise. Bombing radar in the early 1940s could discern only large ground features, such as the bend of a river flowing through a city. Under these limitations, as 1943 progressed, more and more U.S. bombing targets were in fact area targets.[12]

The British and American bombing campaigns had been linked together in the Combined Bomber Offensive, Operation Pointblank, and subordinated to support the objectives of Allied forces as a whole at the January 1943 Casablanca Conference. Expecting that their differences on tactics would prove to be complementary in a day-night assault, not coincidentally promoting the cause of the victory through air power proponents, the chiefs of staff of the RAF and USAAF, Sir Charles Portal and Henry Arnold, had merged the objectives of both strategies in the directive establishing the Combined Bomber Offensive (CBO).

The CCS approved as the CBO primary objective: "The progressive destruction and dislocation of the German military, industrial, and economic system, and the undermining of the morale of the German people to a point where their capacity for armed resistance is fatally weakened."[13] The directive, CCS 166/1/D, continued with language on priorities and systems to be attacked that was too general to be of use in operational planning. But the air services' planners would work that out. The directive enfolded other British and U.S. services' expectations from strategic bombing, expressed at Casablanca, and bridged national air service differences over area vs. precision bombing.

Embedded in the primary objective was the belief that the German people, if subjected to enough suffering, could be induced to seek an end to the bombing by rebelling against their government. Almost a year later, in November 1943, a joint report by the British Ministry of Economic Warfare and Air Intelligence on the effects on Germany of the bombing stated that "the housing situation and the general morale are both so bad that either might cause a collapse before industry became unable to sustain the war effort."[14] They were wrong.

The basis of the German people's resilience had a deeper complexity, one that the Nazi leadership manipulated and Allied intelligence officers, economists, and analysts of the bombing campaign alike apparently missed. Two factors were at work. As a practical matter, Allied bombing caused German civilians to draw closer to the government on which they depended for emergency response, medical aid, and immediate socioeconomic relief, as well as defending them from air raids.[15] The second factor was a sense of fatalism at work within a population living under total dictatorship.

An unbridgeable disconnect between the Allies' expected bombing cause-and-effect and German civilian perception emerges from recent analysis by Nicholas Stargardt, firmly based in primary sources. The German people's perspective of the bombing was not that of a free, blameless society coming together to resist an external attack, as was that of the British public during the Blitz. Working against the Allies' notion was a perception, broadly held among German civilians, that the bombing was a terrible retribution for their own collective sin in the immediate past. That sin the German people felt powerless to undo.

General knowledge of what the Nazi regime had done to the Jews became well known among the public within Germany and in occupied territory, through widespread unofficial, interpersonal communication about anecdotal events. That was intentionally reinforced by leaks in official speeches and inferences in publications. Over time, Hitler's propaganda minister, Josef Goebbels, encouraged the public to develop a sense of complicity in these actions.[16] The public came to perceive the regime's acts as having been largely perpetrated in their name in the period from Kristallnacht in 1938 through 1941 and 1942, by which time most of the transports to concentration camps had occurred. Although the Holocaust was continuing on an industrial scale, ultimately murdering six million European Jews and millions of others, all innocent, the public's perception was that the city bombings were Allied retribution for horrific acts that, by then, were beyond being undone.[17] Goebbels told himself in his diary on March 2, 1943 that "a movement and a people, which has broken the bridges behind itself, fights much more unreservedly than those which still possess the possibility of retreating."[18]

The perceived impossibility of retreat, however, did not gain for Goebbels a reinvigorated popular resolve to fight on. The German public acknowledged in their private communication a burden of guilt, however they viewed the regime. Turning to patriotism and religion for consolation, instead of resolving to fight, they resigned themselves simply to endure.[19]

Tens of thousands of Allied airmen died carrying out the long and dangerous bombing raids. For the year 1943 alone, 25,175 RAF and USAAF airmen were killed or became prisoners of war in combat operations almost all of which were over Germany. That bomber crews endured the loss of comrades, fatigue, and moral injury to take to the air again and again testifies to their courage.

By the end of World War II, the blunt instrument of Allied bombing, dropping almost 2.7 million tons of explosives and incendiaries, had caused the deaths of an estimated 600,000 Europeans.[20]

Yet the internal collapse of Germany, similar to that which ended World War I, could not be induced in Nazi Germany. Measuring against Allied bombing target sets and the German war economy as a whole, the U.S. Strategic Bombing Survey would find that the U.S. bombing achieved only limited or negative results. The USSBS also found that, starting in 1942, Hitler's armament minister, Albert Speer, had rationalized an under-mobilized German economy to achieve "a threefold increase in armaments production."[21] The Combined Bomber Offensive did not spare the Allied armies from the need to end the Reich with a violent overland thrust.

The Allies' bombers, however, did produce a critical collateral benefit. Whatever their accuracy, the very destructiveness of the bombers effectively made them magnets for intercepting Luftwaffe fighters pulled back from the eastern front and Italy to defend the Reich. The Luftwaffe's second in command, Field Marshal Erhard Milch, stated that "Germany is the real front line. The bulk of our fighters must go for defense of the homeland."[22] Those fighters if redirected to other missions had serious potential to disrupt any Allied reentry into the Continent.

The arrival in England of a superb Allied fighter plane with the range to escort bombers all the way to any target in Germany, the American-designed and built, British-improved, single-engine P-51 Mustang, gave bombing a new dimension in full. General Arnold, chief of the USAAF, knew that a team of eminent historians were about to advise him that bombing by itself was a futile instrument to compel Germany's political-economic collapse. Arnold began to see in the P-51 greatly expanded benefit from the Eighth Air Force's role in the Combined Bomber Offensive.[23] That was to draw Luftwaffe fighters into the sky where escorting Allied fighters could shoot them down and kill pilots, as the bombers went on striking fighter production facilities on the ground. The Mustang pilots delivered on achievement of this objective. The accumulated loss of experienced, difficult to replace German fighter pilots, who went up to defend Germany from the bombers, even more critically than the fighter planes lost, would be a major contributor to why the Luftwaffe failed to counterattack the Allies in numbers from the air on D-Day.

* * *

However, at the conclusion of the Casablanca Conference, the Allies gave first priority not to the Combined Bomber Offensive but to countering the enemy's campaign of attrition, the U-boats preying on shipping. For 1943, with good reason, the Combined Chiefs agreed that "the defeat of the U-boat must remain a first charge on the resources of the United Nations."[24] On winning that long-running sea battle depended sustaining the British Isles, supplying the bomber offensive with fuel and ordnance, aiding Russia, and transferring the might of North America across the Atlantic to liberate the Continent from the west. From a convergence of factors, the Allies could predict a climax coming to the sea battle. However, in the race to gain dominance in that critical, multifaceted struggle, the Allies entered 1943 with a disadvantage of their own making.

The Battle of the Atlantic had begun within hours of the outbreak of war between Great Britain and Germany and would not end until VE-Day, five and a half years later, after the loss of 3,797 vessels (including 781 U-boats) and more than 72,000 lives, Allied and Axis. Hitler's intent was to crush Britain by strangling the flow of military and economic aid from her empire and from the United States. German and Italian submarines would sink 14,687,231 tons of merchant shipping.[25] The U-boats would not so much be driven from the sea as they would be frustrated at a critical point in the war by a vast network of Allied forces to detect and hunt the submarines. In early 1943, the Allies were approaching but had not yet reached that point.

From the outset of World War II, despite their experience with U-boats in the previous war, the Allied commitment to rigorous protection of merchant shipping and the means to do so developed in stages. In the beginning, the almost complacent attitude toward tonnage sunk by U-boats was that the British merchant marine, largest in the world, could absorb the losses that could be reduced by the convoy system. Supplanting that was a sense that North American shipbuilding could make up the losses. Then the war suddenly was expanded to global scope by the outbreak of hostilities with Japan. The expanded demand on resources and production capacity for all needs plus long sailing times in the vast Pacific threatened to overwhelm all assumptions. Embraced and acted on in London and Washington by 1943 was the calculation that one ship that survived in service one year was worth two new ships built.[26]

From 1939 through 1943, there were not enough escort vessels in the Allied navies to cover the convoy routes and also cover all the other major naval operations. Destroyers to escort and support a major amphibious landing, such as Operation Torch in North Africa in 1942, had to be withdrawn from convoy escort assignments well in advance of their new assignment and could not be returned to the convoys until long after its conclusion.[27] The punishing conditions of the Atlantic Ocean itself taxed the operational availability of the escorts that were designated for convoy duty.

Given their limited antisubmarine warfare (ASW) resources, the Allies' goal was less to sink U-boats than it was to move as much cargo as possible through the sea lanes safe from U-boat attack. Detecting U-boats and redirecting convoys to evade the submarines was essential.

The Allies' success in breaking the German Enigma message encryption machine lent invaluable insight into the content of radio messages to and from the U-boats—when decryption was possible. The naval Enigma always was particularly challenging to the codebreakers in Bletchley Park because the machine was more sophisticated and its operators were better trained and disciplined. After the Germans upgraded their naval Enigma machine with an additional electromechanical rotor, U-boat message internal content was dark to the Allies for ten months from March 1942 into January 1943. U-boat success in finding convoys and the number of ships they torpedoed soared.[28]

Aerial patrolling significantly helped to protect convoys in multiple ways. Upon detecting an aircraft, U-boats would submerge for their own safety, even though the aircraft may not have seen them. Slow as most convoys were, U-boats were slower underwater. A submerged U-boat, reduced to 8 knots from its surface speed of 18 knots, would lose contact with a convoy. By reducing the number of U-boats that got within attack distance of the convoys, aircraft enabled the surface escorts to defend more efficiently instead of becoming overwhelmed by threats. Into 1943, however, the acute shortage of escorts made the risk of overwhelming attack all too common.

The vastness of the North Atlantic left a huge area, through which convoys to the British Ilse had to pass, beyond the patrolling range of most land-based aircraft available to the Allies. The U-boats found particular success in attacking the convoys, while unhindered by long-range antisubmarine patrol aircraft, in this area beyond air patrolling range from bases in the UK, Iceland, and Newfoundland. The Allies called this void the Mid-Ocean Air Gap. There, with only intermittent help from intelligence, the convoy-escorting Allied destroyers, frigates, and corvettes faced the wolf packs on their own through harrowing days and nights.

A solution was at hand for the Allies in the form of B-24 Liberator heavy bombers converted to *very* long-range (VLR) maritime patrol capability. Just forty would do the job. But from 1941 through 1942 in London, the British Admiralty and RAF Coastal Command on one side and RAF Bomber Command on the other argued over the allocation of B-24s. In Washington, a similar dispute festered between the U.S. Navy and the Army Air Force with the added factor of competing Pacific requirements. Bombing, insisted its advocates, was offensive, and hunting U-boats was defensive. Of air patrolling to counter the U-boats, RAF Bomber Command's Arthur Harris, a ferocious advocate for bombing as the key to victory, insisted, "The purely defensive use of air power is grossly wasteful . . . looking for needles in a haystack. . . . Bomber Command provides our only offensive action yet pressed home directly against Germany."[29]

Harris's position was one that easily resonated with bomber aviators. The lot of those on antisubmarine air patrols was seemingly interminable hours of flight in noisy, vibrating, cold aircraft through often foul weather for few U-boat encounters. If forced to ditch, the frigid waters of the North Atlantic presented a virtual death sentence. According to Air Marshal Sir Charles Portal, the ratio of flying hours on patrol to U-boat detections was 250 to 1.[30]

The response from the Royal Navy with RAF Coastal Command's strong agreement was put succinctly by the Home Fleet commander in chief, Adm. Sir John Tovey, on June 7, 1942: "Whatever the results of the bombing of cities might be, it could not of itself win the war, whereas the failure of our sea communications would assuredly lose it."[31]

Well into 1942, as losses to U-boats mounted, Churchill vacillated. On October 24, 1942, despite his own doubts about bombing performance to date, Churchill directed that "we encroach as little as possible upon our bomber effort against Germany. . . . At present, in spite of U-boat losses, the Bomber Offensive should have first place in our air effort."[32] Weeks later, reacting to the sinking of ninety-four ships, primarily in the Mid-Ocean Air Gap, Churchill reversed himself. He took action through the reinstituted Cabinet Anti-U-Boat Warfare Committee, which could overrule any ministry or military headquarters. Forty Liberators would be allocated to Coastal Command for conversion to VLR standards and the closing of the Air Gap.[33] At the Casablanca Conference, as one prompt response to an appeal from the British, the Combined Chiefs of Staff increased the authorized number of VLR B-24s to eighty.[34]

An appeal from First Sea Lord Adm. Sir Dudley Pound had presented a stark choice: "The Naval Staff consider the situation so serious in the Atlantic that it is necessary to decide whether reinforcements for our escorts, air and surface, on the Atlantic trade route must be given priority over all other commitments, including offensive operations." Authorization was a long way from having VLR bombers operational over convoy routes. Conversion of the big B-24s was demanding.

Even with extreme priority for the program's needs, conversion encountered delays.[35]

The winter storms of December and January had brought not cessation but a lull in U-boat attacks. With better weather starting in February, losses to U-boats began to surge again toward new tonnage records.

The U-boat force reached peak strength in 1943 with the highest number of U-boats operational at sea and the highest rate of new boats and crews becoming operational. Promoted by Hitler to the commander in chief of the Kriegsmarine at the end of January 1943, Grand Adm. Karl Doenitz had 116 U-boats at sea by March out of 160 available for operations in the Atlantic, a very good ratio.[36] Such numbers allowed Doenitz to deploy U-boats in echelons of wolf packs in the mid-Atlantic where the threat from Allied aircraft was minimal. Lone U-boats were sent hundreds of miles farther west and east to detect and trail approaching convoys until the alerted packs could close in for the kill.[37] Doenitz was also intercepting Allied radio communications. Early in the war, the proficient German naval communication intelligence unit, Beobachtung-Dienst, had broken and subsequently overcome improvements to a number of British and American codes. This included an Anglo-American code used for convoy messages that the Germans called Frankfurt.[38]

In early 1943, the Allies were again able to read the internal content of the Germans' naval Enigma-encrypted messages to and from the U-boats after a ten-month blackout.[39] This time, however, the benefit accruing from the restored intelligence was limited by the increased pervasiveness of the threat. By early 1943, so many U-boats were operating in the North Atlantic as to make it nearly impossible to use the intelligence for evasive routing of convoys.

In February, losses to U-boats rose to 312,004 tons sunk.[40] An assessment by the Anti-U-Boat Warfare Committee in London on March 8 portrayed the situation fully in its grim scope. According to the committee, the Allies occasionally needed to protect up to six convoys simultaneously, three or four of which would be in the mid-ocean area where VLR aircraft were essential. The committee stipulated, "We must be ready to deal with up to three convoys each being attacked by a pack of U-boats." The supporting Annex gave sober detail to what was meant in February and March 1943 by "attacked by a pack," finding that "present U-boat density in the North Atlantic certainly allows 20 to 25 U-boats to be concentrated against each of two convoys simultaneously during their period in the danger zone [Mid-Ocean Air Gap], and it is probable that three convoys could be attacked at the same time. This certainly will be the case in the near future as the number of U-boats at sea is increasing."[41]

Recognizing that "the number of U-boats now at sea [has] reduced very considerably the chances of evasive routing," the option remaining was to enable every convoy "to fight its way through numbers of U-boats." From that came a determination to "make the U-boats pay for their successes a price which they cannot accept." This was seen to be a rate of exchange of one U-boat sunk for every two ships lost from convoys, a ratio that in fact had been achieved on occasion through coordinated action by a strong enough force of surface escorts and patrolling aircraft.[42]

From across the Atlantic, eight days later in an about-face, came the U.S. Joint Chiefs of Staff's unequivocal acknowledgment of the crisis at sea that only recently Admiral King had dismissed offhandedly. The difference was that Roosevelt had intervened.[43] In a memorandum to the Combined Chiefs recommending more VLR aircraft, the JCS recognized correctly that an improvement would come in July, but also that "the resources now at hand and to become available within the next few months are inadequate to cope with the submarine menace which is becoming more and more critical. . . . The only means for quickly increasing the effectiveness of our ASW measures is to divert heavy bombers from other assignments . . . , it seems that the only possibility is to divert these planes from the bombing of Germany."[44]

Writing in the third person, the U.S. chiefs, although "loth [sic] to recommend" reducing the Combined Bombing Offensive, concluded nevertheless that "they would be derelict in their duty were they to leave any stone unturned in the search for means to improve the submarine situation." The JCS recommended transferring 128 heavy bombers to antisubmarine operations.[45]

The Allies now were aligned in their appreciation for the severity of the immediate crisis and took steps to commit to meeting it. Previously, the allocation among the Allies of areas of responsibility for convoy protection and cooperative ASW command structure had developed piecemeal as much through changing political-military circumstances as through strategy.[46] That, now, was changed for the better. Allied convoy and antisubmarine warfare commands and committees would be able to make, and did make, more insightful decisions on organization and tactics.

At the Allies' March 1943 Convoy Conference in Washington, convoy protection responsibility in the North Atlantic was assigned to the British all the way west to the Grand Banks, where a new Canadian Northwest Atlantic area of responsibility under a Canadian commander would begin. The Central Atlantic was assigned to the U.S. Navy.[47] These were not exclusive areas. Coordination flexibility was improved between Allied navies to meet specific needs.

Decisions requiring construction of additional complex escort ships and patrol planes took time to show results. The number of VLR bombers operationally available at the end of March to confront the U-boats in the mid-ocean air gap had increased from fourteen to twenty out of a fleet of thirty-four such aircraft in RAF Coastal Command.[48] New escort ships, whose design benefited from hard-won experience, were coming off the shipbuilding ways and working up. Their time at sea confronting U-boats, however, remained several months away.

In March, the Allies' grim, near-term prediction for the sea battle became reality when losses to U-boats reached a monthly peak for 1943 at 567,401 tons.[49] The U-boats, however, were beginning to pay more for their successes. In epic running battles, often with support from the air precluded by distance and weather, Allied convoy escorts inflicted heavy losses on the wolf packs.[50] Fifteen

U-boats were sunk in February and fifteen more in March. The Battle of the Atlantic was turning.

Although the Battle of the Atlantic would continue to the last days of the war in Europe, requiring enormous devotion of Allied resources, the failure of the U-boats, becoming manifest in 1943, ultimately would be absolute. Britain would survive, not starve. In the advancing spring of 1943, advocates for direct attack across the Channel could be confident that timely transatlantic transfer to Europe of the might of North America was becoming assured.

3

COSSAC's Ninety Days to Deliver a Plan

Well there it is; it won't work, but you must bloody well make it.
—General Sir Alan Brooke, Chief of the Imperial General Staff

In April, as the battle at sea was beginning to turn in the Allies' favor, the joint organization established at the January 1943 Casablanca Conference to prepare for the Allies' return to northwestern Europe, finally took form in London. Although the directive to the new organization was still evolving through transatlantic drafting, British Lt. Gen. Sir Frederick Morgan was assigned to lead this team as the Chief of Staff to the Supreme Commander (Designate). Morgan would begin with an American deputy, but with the supreme Allied commander still to be chosen. To name the new organization, Morgan simply drew from his new job title to create an acronym. "COSSAC" would be to the point for those with the "need to know" and, in its élan, potentially misleading to outsiders and enemies.

Morgan's suitability to lead the task had been plumbed by the British Chiefs of Staff (COS) and Winston Churchill. Lt. Gen. Sir Hastings "Pug" Ismay, the prime minister's chief military assistant, gave Morgan a file of previous planning work on assaulting Germany through northwestern Europe. Ismay asked Morgan for a reply within twenty-four hours to "elaborate the means by which the expedition was to be organized and undertaken." Morgan responded with a memorandum on cross-Channel attack that he discussed with the COS on 24 March 1943.[1] Churchill then interviewed Morgan on April 4. In a note back to Ismay, in which the prime minister approved the layout and draft directive to COSSAC as proposed by the COS, Churchill also passed judgment that Morgan "seems a capable and sensible officer."[2] Perhaps as relevant, given the toxic environment into which Morgan was being thrust, the 1928 Staff College report that Ismay shared with Churchill had seen in Morgan "a keen but kindly sense of humor which should prove a great asset to him."[3]

Morgan queried Lt. Gen. Jacob Devers, recently arrived in London to take up command of the European Theater of Operations, U.S. Army (ETOUSA), for his recommendation for an American deputy for COSSAC. Among the Americans in London, Devers replied, "Well, the logical man is Ray Barker. He's been in this racket all along. He's more familiar with it and is more deeply immersed in it than anyone else."[4]

Pairing Morgan with Barker for Anglo-American leadership of COSSAC proved to be inspired. They shared similar military backgrounds as artillery officers. Each came to the task with a measure of understanding and affinity for the other's national culture. Barker had visited Britain and enjoyed studying its history. Morgan simply liked Americans. From time spent in contact with Canadian units in France in World War I and in 1940, Morgan had gained an appreciation for North American idioms and mannerisms that served him well with his allies.[5] The Americans in turn quickly came to accept Morgan. Their assessment was, "He's a straight shooter."[6]

The two were well aware that the friction between the senior British and American officers above them sometimes approached open hostility. However, neither allowed suspicion and questioning of his ally's motives or abilities to constrain candor or cooperation with each other. Morgan and Barker turned to advantage circumstances of security, urgency, shortage, and the unknown to build COSSAC into a community of purpose that would evolve to set a standard for integrated Allied effort.

At their first meeting as chief of staff and deputy in April 1943, Morgan set the tone with a small but telling act. He snipped a Royal Artillery brass button from his tunic and exchanged it for a brass button from Barker's U.S. Army uniform. From then until the Quadrant Conference in August, each general went around the COSSAC offices and to external meetings, British, American, and joint, wearing a token from his ally's army.[7] They each ignored jibes about "going "Yank" or "going native." Theirs was a clear statement of trust and joint endeavor to comrades and often fractious superiors.

COSSAC was allotted office space in Norfolk House in St. James Square, an easy walk from the Admiralty, War Office, Cabinet War Rooms, and other London centers of authority that were key to COSSAC's mission. Morgan, however, did not consider this an auspicious location. The building had been the site for an earlier series of planning efforts that, with the exception of the Torch invasion, came to nothing good. Morgan rued Norfolk House's "reputation as a home of lost causes." The first of the new team to arrive found little to begin with beyond a few desks, chairs, and a dropped pencil.[8] Yet the separate British and American planners of cross-Channel attack rallied on COSSAC from across London, and the organization made its start.[9] Their plan for a "full scale assault against the Continent" was due to be submitted through the British COS in ninety days.

Setting the purpose of COSSAC in the first meeting of his staff, April 17, Morgan broke from a general assumption in stating that "although the primary object of COSSAC is to make plans, I am certain that it is wrong to refer to it in any way as a 'planning staff.' The term 'Planning Staff' has come to have a most sinister meaning: it implies the production of nothing but paper. What we must contrive to do somehow is to produce not only paper but ACTION."[10] Acknowledging that neither he nor the COSSAC staff began their task with executive authority, Morgan concluded with an irresistible challenge to his young officers:

> My idea is that we shall regard ourselves in the first instance as pri-
> marily a coordinating body. We plan mainly by the co-ordination of
> effort already being exerted in a hundred and one directions. We dif-
> fer from the ordinary planning staff in that we are, as you perceive,
> in effect the embryo of the future Supreme Headquarters Staff. I do
> not think I can put the matter any better to you than by quoting to

you the last words of the CIGS, who said: "Well there it is: it won't work, but you must bloody well make it.[11]

The organizational form of COSSAC initially followed the British staff model on the assumption that the supreme Allied commander would be a British officer with an American deputy. Over time in the absence of precedent, except for the command staff established by French Marshal Ferdinand Foch in World War I, the merging of effort led COSSAC's organizational form to develop following function, not nationality. COSSAC came to be staffed accordingly, as Morgan had intended from the outset.

Barker later said of COSSAC, "Here was a team, and whether a man wore a U.S. or a Crown [uniform insignia] made not a bit of difference. . . . No one thought about whether a chap was British or American or Canadian [or] South African."[12] By the time General Eisenhower was appointed Supreme Allied Commander and the Supreme Headquarters, Allied Expeditionary Force (SHAEF) emerged, absorbing COSSAC, the initial, deliberate practice of assigning a British and an American deputy to each section had been replaced entirely. Throughout SHAEF's organization, a carryover from COSSAC, a single section leader was assigned on the basis of matching ability to need with little regard to nationality.

The activating directive from the Combined Chiefs of Staff to Morgan, defining the task at the initiation of COSSAC's work, was developed through March from alternative U.S. and British-recommended language and completed in April 1943. The directive blended both national views of the way ahead. At the first COSSAC meeting, Morgan read the COS version of the directive to his staff on the assumption that this draft would be approved by the Americans. Obvious between its lines was an expectation that further discussion at the highest Allied level, or events in Europe not under Allied control, would determine the strategy ultimately to be selected. The British draft of the task stated:

Our objective is to defeat the German fighting forces in North-West Europe. To this end the Combined Chiefs of Staff will endeavor to assemble the strongest possible forces (subject to prior commitments in other theatres) in constant readiness to reenter the Continent if German resistance is weakened to the required extent in 1943. In the meantime the Combined Chiefs of Staff must be prepared to order such limited operations as may be practicable with the forces and materiel available.[13]

The directive further ordered COSSAC to develop plans for three operations. First listed, and relevant to either the British or American preferred strategy for return to the Continent, was to prepare a series of operations over the summer of 1943. Termed Cockade, these operations were intended, through feints and deception, to test German strength in northwestern Europe and draw the Luftwaffe into air battles in which its capacity to oppose an Allied invasion, be that reactive or proactive, could be degraded by attrition. The task listed second was to plan "for a return to the Continent in the event of German disintegration at any time from now onwards with whatever forces may be available." This would become known as Operation Rankin. The third, and last, task was to plan "for a full scale assault against the Continent in 1944 as early as possible." Not yet named, this would become Operation Overlord.

Thus, from the outset, the competing British and U.S. views of strategy comingled in COSSAC's governing directive: Rankin's contingent reaction to opportunity, if offered by an internal collapse of the Reich, and Overlord's proactive assault against Germany's main force in the West as it stood at a time and place of attack unilaterally determined by the Allies. The U.S. Joint Chiefs of Staff–recommended draft differed from the British by setting the objective to "destroy" German forces in northwestern Europe and narrowed the date for full-scale assault to "the spring of 1944."[14] This became the agreed directive for cross-Channel assault when issued by the CCS on April 26.[15]

While actively engaged in planning and coordinating resources for deception operations under its first task, Cockade, COSSAC would also endeavor to develop plans required by its second and third tasks, Rankin and Overlord. In 1944, upon implementation of Overlord, plans to initiate Rankin continued to be maintained and updated regularly for many months beyond D-Day as a contingency response to a potential internal collapse of Germany.

The activating directive to COSSAC designated the British Chiefs of Staff to be the source for COSSAC's further guidance as required and as COSSAC's reporting channel to the Anglo-American CCS. The latter instruction would become challenging at a critical moment.

The directive also told Morgan to maintain close contact with the headquarters of ETOUSA. COSSAC was forbidden to interact with Allied military staffs other than British and American until told to do so by the COS, a stricture that was not easily relaxed. For example, early thinking had Canadian units at the center of the force to be landed. However, the "lukewarm" COS only "tacitly conceded" in April 1943 the benefit of appointing a Canadian liaison officer to COSSAC, Maj. Gen. G. R. Turner.[16]

To initiate the development of its tasks, COSSAC had access to the considerable body of work and the corporate memory of London groups—British, American, and joint—which had been assessing and planning for an Allied return to northwestern Europe, in some cases, since the Dunkirk evacuation in 1940. This included the lessons to be learned—many at a high cost in casualties—from raids on the Continent planned and conducted by the British Combined Operations Headquarters led by Vice Adm. Lord Louis Mountbatten. Inherited work also contained the output of a British committee, the Combined Commanders, with whom COSSAC's new American deputy, Maj. Gen. Ray Barker, had participated as the liaison officer from the U.S. Army in Europe. Among the Combined Commanders' products was a February 1943 outline plan that had not been formally approved. Called Operation Skyscraper, this plan laid out an assault on France's Cotentin Peninsula very similar in location and size to what Overlord eventually became.[17]

However, at COSSAC's initiation in April 1943, a viable plan to act on the generalized and debated intent to reenter the Continent through northwestern Europe was anything but clear. Many challenges and uncertainties revolved in kaleidoscopic combinations, each demanding consideration both separately and in relation to the others. Darkening all of COSSAC's planning was the shadow of interwar and current war professional skepticism: was a large-scale opposed amphibious assault viable at all?

Hitler's assertions about the strength of his defenses at the water's edge, the Atlantic Wall, were obvious. Equally obvious was the British aversion to incurring again anything like the casualties of World War I. To be added to this was extensive, objective analysis of the costly, unsuccessful Anglo-French landing at Gallipoli in 1915. Professional military opinion, developed in the interwar years and by no means limited to the British, tended to the view that amphibious success was very doubtful against an adversary who easily could concentrate and reinforce from the interior of a continent.[18] Freshly underscoring this conclusion in Europe was Operation Jubilee, the failed large-scale Anglo-Canadian raid on Dieppe in August 1942. Of Jubilee's principally Canadian raiding force of 6,000, more than 3,300 had been killed or captured. Sobering too was admission by the operational commanders and service chiefs that the much larger, better coordinated, and supported American landings in Morocco in November 1942 against weak, brief French resistance succeeded in large measure by luck.[19]

Almost alone in the interwar years, the U.S. Marine Corps had continued to develop amphibious doctrine and tactics in anticipation of their mission to assault Japanese-occupied islands in the Pacific. However, the Marines' island-centric task description did not address the assumption of a defending adversary's reinforcement from the interior of a continent. Even the Marines entered World War II with no purpose-designed and built amphibious assault equipment.[20]

The Allies were starting on parallel tasks near the bottom of a steep challenge. Against the experts' odds, they had to learn how to succeed in amphibious assault while creating the wherewithal to do so.

Potential landing beaches and the terrain behind them, from the Dutch coast to Brittany as far as Spanish border, had to be considered. However, from early days attention had tended to focus on two areas in France, the Pas de Calais and Normandy.[21] Would there be one landing or multiple landings? Concurrently or sequentially?

On the fundamental material questions, the Combined Chiefs of Staff directive to COSSAC was silent. How many Allied divisions of what type could COSSAC anticipate being available at which phases for a "spring of 1944" assault? Silence from the CCS. In direct, crucial relation to the number of divisions, what was the capacity of the shipping that would be available for the amphibious assault and follow-on buildup and sustainment? Silence.

Definition of shipping requirements was impossible absent knowledge of how many divisions would be in the assault. The most that Morgan could offer in May 1943 was to warn the British COS of the obvious: that the required number of landing craft would be "large enough . . . to present a very serious problem, which has no precedent."[22]

COSSAC knew with certainty only one thing. With its own champion, the Supreme Allied Commander, still to be designated, cross-Channel attack was last in line for assignment of scarce amphibious lift behind named commanders already leading scheduled operations around the world.

What would be the quality of the Allied troops the ships would land on the coast of northwestern Europe? On May 19, as the CCS were struggling with their compromise agreement at the Trident Conference, Lieutenant General Morgan, in London and unaware that the very issue was on the table in Washington, minuted his staff on this question. Combat-experienced troops, he told them, would be vital to success.[23] Where would these troops come from, and at the expense of which other operations?

There were crucial, operations-shaping, but unresolved geographic, geologic, hydrographic, meteorological, and technical questions and challenges. Which beaches and their inland terrain, in combination with which ports capable of supporting the landed forces, offered viable prospects for a successful military assault and follow-on offensive? On what axes of advance? Without intervening rivers and their estuaries impeding the just-landed national armies' capability to support each other in battle? Which combination of beaches and terrain also offered the best potential for rapidly establishing advanced, tactical airfields? Were the assault and follow-on forces really dependent on seizing French Channel ports for sustainment, or were nascent ideas for over-the-beach logistical support on an enormous scale a viable alternative to capturing ports? In that case, for which beaches specifically? For how long at what capacity? In spite of the Channel's fearsome weather?

Taking all of this into consideration, where lay the relative advantage for Allied fighter planes flying from England in support? For the Luftwaffe opposing them in the air and attacking the Allied landing force? How were the assault troops to receive sufficient fire support in the critical moments before they hit the beach? What constituted sufficient fire support, from the sea and from the air, against a strongly fortified and defended coast? That was a type of assault with which, by the spring of 1943, the Allies had had no experience with the disastrous exception of Dieppe and the luck-retrieved confusion of Torch. Would the answer for fire support promise conditions allowing a landing in daylight? Or would a need for compensating surprise drive the assault toward a predawn landing, which would be an offshore organizing nightmare for the navies?

Lacking guidance from the ccs on the critical factors, cossac could begin its work in April 1943 only by making initial assumptions about strategic objectives and the forces required to be available to achieve them. Specific to its third task, cross-Channel attack into Europe, Morgan directed his staff to apply a broad assumption about resources and the timing of their availability. Their task, he said, was to reconquer Europe with an Allied army that would grow to number 100 divisions, 15 of which would be British (or more precisely, Anglo-Canadian) and 85 American, complemented by powerful air forces and naval forces of similar proportion.

Most of this force was still in North America. As cossac started its work, Morgan told his staff that only the advanced guard of this huge force was in the United Kingdom and subsequent to securing ports on the Continent, the bulk of these forces would enter the theater directly from across the Atlantic. Therefore, COSSAC must address its tasks with "a map which starts at one end in San Francisco and the other end in Berlin."[24] Morgan lost no time in hanging precisely such a map in his office. Morgan, who had been left to define Overlord's military purpose himself, cast the operation's strategic objective with equally broad scope:

> Our ultimate object is to wage successful war on land in the heart of Europe against the main body of the German strategic reserve. It is true that we have to cross the enemy's beaches, but that to us must be merely an episode. True, it is a vital episode and, if it is not successful, the whole expedition will fail. We must plan for crossing the beaches, but let us make sure that we get that part of the plan in its right perspective as a passing phase.[25]

COSSAC was going for Berlin.

COSSAC measured the operation's ultimate objective against three factors. These were (1) the strength of enemy opposition to be encountered; (2) the enemy's disposition and the quality of Allied forces to be applied, plus (3) the requirement to focus assets then available in the United Kingdom (bombers, for example) on preparation of the battlefield. The approach enlightened planning as it broadened the scope of the task.

Morgan concluded that the cross-Channel attack into northwestern Europe must be considered to have begun already in April 1943. He pressed the COSSAC staff to embrace their work with this assumption as a given and recommended this view to the Chiefs of Staff.

Infused as COSSAC was from the outset with energy and purpose, doubts about the strength of higher command support for their enterprise also tugged at Morgan, Barker, and certainly their perceptive principal staff officers. From direct experience and participation, they knew of the "corrosive and potentially explosive mixture" of strategy discussions in London and Washington into which COSSAC was introduced. The new organization proceeded

with its work while Morgan pondered alternative, conflicting interpretations of cossac's purpose. As he later described the alternatives, "Was it to be a form of chemical agent to induce a sea,
land, and air change so that there might be brought about unity of
intent, unity of method, and so unity of action? Or was it perhaps
to be as a scapegoat upon which could be heaped responsibility
for what seemed in the eyes of each to be the sins of the other?"[26]

Morgan did not want to presume upon the still-to-be-named
Supreme Allied Commander's authority by developing for him
only a single option. Also, the driving question for initiation of
Overlord had to be resolved: which of the most favored potential
entry points to the Continent best met Allied needs?

To make a start, Morgan focused cossac's work on a competitive assessment of the two alternative entry points that consistently came out of previous groups' attention to the problem of
cross-Channel assault, the Pas de Calais and Normandy. The British Army contingent at cossac was assigned to develop the Pas
de Calais option, and the U.S. Army group was given the task of
developing an assault into Normandy. cossac's Air and Naval sections would help each team as needed. The possibility of multiple
assaults, one in each area, was left open, as was the possibility that
the odds against success would be compounded to such a degree as
to force a conclusion that any cross-Channel assault was unfeasible.

Acting as close but neutral observers to the competition would
be Morgan, Barker, and a very carefully selected few: Gen. Sir Bernard Paget, commander of the British Home Forces from which
many of the divisions to cross the Channel would be drawn, ETOUSA
commander Lt. Gen. Jacob Devers, and the chief of Combined
Operations, Vice Adm. Lord Louis Mountbatten.[27]

To start the two teams on common ground, on May 25 Morgan
issued to them his own outline plan for what he called Operation
Rudge. Into Rudge Morgan incorporated all of the operational and
logistical criteria common to an assault in either area, specifying
that cossac had determined that the landings should be on the
coast of France, but taking care in the wording of Rudge not to
suggest a preferred choice of where. On the teams' response to

these criteria, the options of landings in the Pas de Calais or Normandy would be assessed.

COSSAC's U.S. Army and British Army planners approached their task from different perspectives. In addition to knowing General Marshall's strong preference for direct action to conclude a short war in Europe and then turn to the Pacific, the American planners had an appreciation for the enormous surge of troops and materiel building in North America and soon to be projected across the Atlantic. The British planners, conditioned by almost four years of thin reserves and shortages, were influenced by the long game strategy of their military chiefs and their prime minister to wear down the enemy through attrition.

Morgan used his Rudge paper to eliminate that difference in perception at the outset, at least within COSSAC. He affirmed to his teams that only one of these strategies could motivate them by stating, "The decision to invade Europe in 1944 will imply at once the abandonment of long term policies of attrition in favor of the short term policy of direct assault." Just as unequivocal was Morgan's anchoring of the magnitude of the challenge in "the inescapable fact that while the armies of the assault must be for the most part inexperienced and untried in war, those of the defense may well contain strong cadres of battle-hardened soldiers. This inequality is further emphasized by the fact that the attack must consist of that most intricate of all military operations, the seaborne assault."[28]

The already complex interrelationship of beach and landing ground characteristics and enemy strength was further compounded to frustrate the teams' assessments by the resource questions left unanswered in the April 26 CCS directive to form COSSAC. Morgan's projection of the size of the ultimate force to liberate Europe was reasonable. But specific to the cross-Channel assault into France itself: how many Allied divisions, how many ships, how many planes? The teams' response was to begin by developing their assessment of how many resources of what type they thought would be required for the assault without any clear knowledge of how many resources they actually would have.

At that time, even the name of the cross-Channel operation had been rendered ambiguous by past conceptions of its size. The original plan for a forty-eight-division assault presented by the U.S. Army to the British in 1942, and so far in excess of what the Allies could field in 1942 as to be considered naïve, had been code-named Roundup. The subsequently proposed contingency plan for a cross-Channel attack with whatever divisions were at hand in the United Kingdom, either as an emergency response to an imminent collapse of the Soviet armies or in response to an internal collapse of the Third Reich, was code-named Sledgehammer.[29] Subsequent Anglo-American discussions of cross-Channel attack evolved toward an operation of a size somewhere between these two options that tentatively was called Roundhammer.

As COSSAC in London wrestled with the awesome, multifaceted challenge of an Allied return to Europe, at least some answers to their most basic questions were emerging from contentious Anglo-American discussions in Washington. Included would be the name for the operation that would stick, Overlord.

4

The Trident Conference's Illusion of Agreement

One of the constant sources of danger to us in this war is the temptation to regard as our first enemy the partner that must work with us in defeating the real enemy.

—Gen. Dwight D. Eisenhower, letter to Brig. Gen. Thomas Handy, early 1943

On Tuesday, May 11, 1943, the American and British Chiefs of Staff, Churchill, and FDR were convening again, this time in Washington. A British delegation arrived at 6:30 p.m. and met their counterparts directly at a hotel cocktail party.[1] Trident would be the follow-on conference for which the need had been so evident at the close of Symbol in Casablanca.

The Americans entered this conference with a determination not to be dominated, as they had been at Casablanca, by their British guests' better staffing and preparation.[2] The Americans were hopeful, though not confident, that this time Roosevelt would stand firm with them in his meetings with Churchill, particularly on strategy for Europe.

Certainly the Americans had prepared themselves as best they could, much better than they had for Casablanca. In advance of Trident, they produced and approved rigorous staff papers in six topical categories expected to be discussed. Better prepared, the American joint staffs were primed and standing by to make an agile response to any negotiating contingency as indeed they were called to do. By the time Trident concluded, the staff had produced thirty-seven formal studies in twenty days.[3]

Also stirring in the background in the spring of 1943 was a transformation in how American decision makers, political and military, viewed the security of the United States and its role in the world. Among shapers of U.S. policy could be heard rising calls for a newly internationalist and global outlook, particularly in the form of "Atlanticism."

In April the influential newspaper columnist Walter Lippmann had published in Boston his new book, *U.S. Foreign Policy: Shield of the Republic*. On the basis of his sweeping summation of the sources and the evolution of U.S. security and foreign policy interests since the American Revolution, Lippmann forecasted global interests and prescriptions for securing them in the context of the twentieth-century industrialized world. He sought to shake off as forever obsolete the isolationist "hemispheric" perspective of the United States living shielded behind the barrier of two great oceans.

It its place Lippmann found "the shield of the republic" to be engagement in the world. Looking to win the war and embrace interests shared with postwar Europe, Lippmann argued that the United States could not allow any potential foe to control Western Europe. The freedom and security of nations on both sides of the Atlantic, he wrote, rest on an enduring interdependency. Therefore, the Atlantic Ocean should be viewed neither as a frontier for the United States nor as a geographic division between the Old and New Worlds. It should be "the inland sea of a community of nations allied with one another by geography, history and vital necessity."[4] A corollary was Lippmann's projection of the essential U.S. security relationship to East Asia that pointed to a Pacific community.

As a manifestation of American nongovernmental, intellectual response to the global changes being thrust on the United States by war, Lippmann's book also provided a welcome framework for operational needs. In March, expanding on a pre-Casablanca request from Roosevelt, the JCS had set planners to studying the parameters of a global postwar system of air bases. That was to be defined in the context of "the broader subject of worldwide military problems which will confront the Joint Chiefs of Staff as soon as the Axis power surrenders—and which, therefore, must be studied now in order that we may be fully prepared."[5]

The military leadership of the United States found Lippmann's book, published after their embarrassment at Casablanca and one month before Trident, to be exceptionally timely. Historian Mark Stoler concludes that jcs planners "certainly did" read Lippmann's book, which would become a best seller, be popularized in national print media, and even be made available to U.S. troops in a 25-cent paperback edition.[6] Lippmann's book was read by Secretary of War Henry Stimson and Adm. Ernest King. Stimson recommended the book to Gen. John Hull, then a key U.S. Army planner, with his strong endorsement of the need for a new U.S. foreign policy.[7] King, who sent Lippmann a note of thanks, told an off-the-record press conference, "We are grown up now and we have got to evolve a foreign policy and stick to it."[8]

The British Chiefs of Staff arrived for Trident with their understanding of their country's role in the world already long confirmed by centuries of imperial rule. They had two concerns, one basic and one immediate.

Most basic to the cos and Churchill was that Great Britain's fighting capacity was fully engaged. In its fourth year of total war, having stood alone for a year and a half early in the struggle, Britain had nearly emptied its treasury. Britain was at the limit of the home islands' manpower pool. The number of operational British divisions had peaked at eighteen. The day was approaching when some divisions would have to be disbanded in order to maintain the rest at full strength and reorganized as mobile expeditionary formations.[9]

Beyond these immediate and quite tangible military force issues, centuries of experience encouraged the British to a long view. They knew from current Allied planning that well over one million American troops would be inserted into Europe for a direct assault strategy. Obvious to them was the postwar political influence that would accrue to the United States from an American force of such size in Europe. The opportunistic strategy of weakening Germany by attrition and only then pouncing was the only military option remaining through which Britain could continue in a continental war as an equal partner in the Alliance. From the same long experience, British leaders, particularly Churchill, were acutely aware that the western Allies should conclude the war in

72

Europe in a strong political-military position on the ground in Europe relative to that of Russia.

Flowing from their unvarnished understanding of the demands of the task still ahead and their finite means was the cos's immediate concern, the military capability of their ally on whose military and materiel capacity they were critically dependent. Gen. Dwight D. Eisenhower had made serious mistakes while leading the first major Anglo-American ground operation in North Africa. These mistakes were military in nature against the Germans and political in dealing with collaborationist Vichy and the Free French. Their effect on the British General Staff was to fuel a conclusion that Eisenhower would have to be, and could be, managed by the British as a figurehead Allied military leader with British commanders of superior experience and ability actually running operations.[10] Some went so far as to advocate putting well-equipped U.S. troops under British officers. In the ranks, seasoned British troops who had experienced the uncertain American efforts in North Africa could be heard in pubs singing a biting ditty that drew the title of a then-popular film into parody: "How Green Is My Ally."[11]

Yet within forty-eight hours of the Combined Chiefs commencing their new round of talks at Trident, and despite Allied operational and political mistakes in North Africa, Axis resistance ended there in Allied victory. Allied forces, which now included Free French ground combat units, bagged 275,000 German and Italian prisoners, which exceeded the number of Axis troops killed or taken prisoner at Stalingrad in 1942.[12]

A U.S. Army planner present at both conferences concluded that, before victory in North Africa, the collective attitude at Casablanca had produced decisions limited to the year 1943 and characterized by "wishful thinking relative to our [Allied] Atlantic strategy and a nebulous approach to Pacific strategy." When the ccs gathered for Trident, after the Tunisian victory, the thinking was "stronger, the decisions clearer, and the strategy more global and more realistic."[13] Logistics, critical to victory, got its due.

High on the agenda for the Trident Conference were the questions of which geographic axis the Allied armies should pursue for their reentry into Nazi-occupied Europe and when this reentry should take place. As at Casablanca, however, the strategy debate at Trident tapped deeper, divergent roots of national capabilities, priorities, and history on both sides. It was painfully evident in the tenor of discussion during its first week that the Trident Conference would be colored by personal suspicions of motives and bias deeply held on both sides.[14] These would be tough negotiations.

At the first formal meeting of Trident, a plenary in the White House Oval Office at 2:30 p.m. on May 12, the ccs received guidance from the president and the prime minister. Roosevelt, joined by Churchill, began by remarking on how far the Allies had come in one year since the prime minister and General Brooke were last in that very room. In 1942, they had received the shocking news of the fall of Tobruk followed by Roosevelt's immediate offer to divert Sherman tanks and armored artillery from then-scarce American stocks to the British in Egypt. There followed in this opening meeting of Trident Churchill's and Roosevelt's exposition of their respective views of the tasks before the ccs. Though put gracefully by the two leaders, clear to all was the conflict inherent in resumption of the strategy discussion.

The prime minister promptly set out the Mediterranean as "the first objective." Among the five objectives that followed, Churchill raised a cross-Channel attack and the buildup of forces for that strategy fourth. Defeat of Japan was last.[15]

Roosevelt's response to the heart of Churchill's position began indirectly. He started by saying that he always had been a firm believer in attrition. He expressed surprise and optimism about the cordial reception that Churchill got on his post-Casablanca "fishing trip" to Turkey, always a potential key component in Churchill's Mediterranean strategy. FDR stated that perhaps Turkey could be induced to adopt a favorable attitude toward the United Nations by diplomacy alone, implying a limit to his support for military operations as leverage. Then, referring to the scheduled Allied invasion of Sicily, the president asked rhetorically, "Where do we go from HUSKY?" By way of answer,

FDR continued that he had "always shrunk from the thought of putting large armies into Italy." Acknowledging the need to employ the surplus of Allied forces that would be in the Mediterranean following the conquest of Sicily, Roosevelt also warned of the humanitarian burden that would fall to the Allies if Italy were to be occupied. Roosevelt then made a firm statement in support of either a Sledgehammer or Roundup cross-Channel operation for 1944.

The meeting minutes summarize his remarks as being that "if one or the other were to be mounted in the spring of 1944, preparations should begin now. ROUNDUP and SLEDGEHAMMER have been talked about for two years, but as yet none of these operations had been accepted as a concrete plan to be carried out at a certain time. Therefore he wished to emphasize that SLEDGE-HAMMER or ROUNDUP should be decided upon definitely as an operation for the spring of 1944."[16]

Roosevelt's comments then shifted to the Pacific theater and support for keeping China in the war. Taken together, FDR's remarks summed up his Joint Chiefs of Staff's priorities in competition for resources with what they saw as Churchill's war-lengthening interest in the Mediterranean. Thus ended Trident's initial White House meeting with each nation's military chiefs having gotten their leader's backing for their opening position, positions that were in direct conflict.

The first short week of negotiation by the Combined Chiefs of Staff began on Wednesday morning, May 13, in the Board of Governors Room of the Federal Reserve Building on Constitution Avenue. Quickly, along a path that led through the reduction of the German Air Force and its implications, the CCS came to their fundamental difference on strategy for Europe.

Admiral King stated that if reduction of the Luftwaffe was an overwhelming success, the Allies then must be in position and ready to exploit that with a cross-Channel operation on the scale of Roundup. JCS chairman Admiral Leahy, supporting King, added that it "might be unwise to divert or maintain in the Mediterranean forces which could be used in a cross-

Channel assault." General Brooke replied for the British: unless operations in the Mediterranean continued, "no possibility of an attack into France would arise."[17]

There it was, as General Marshall then stated, "the heart of the problem . . . at the crossroads." The British were insistent that an attack into France would be possible only if the German Army in France had been significantly weakened by redeployment of divisions to fight the Allies in the Mediterranean. The Americans were convinced that further operations in the Mediterranean would continue to vacuum up Allied troops and resources and thereby deny building up the concentration of forces in the UK for a cross-Channel assault ever. While the JCS at Trident spoke of the Roundup concept in terms of twenty to twenty-five divisions, not its earlier forty-eight, both sides continued to argue their position in absolutes: the Mediterranean or cross-Channel attack, formulated as either Roundup or Sledgehammer. Brooke stated that halting Mediterranean operations after Husky to cross the Channel would lengthen the war. Marshall said that further Mediterranean operations would commit the Allies through most of 1944 with serious implications for the Pacific. The war in Europe, he argued, would be prolonged, causing "a delay in the ultimate defeat of Japan, which the people of the U.S. would not tolerate."[18]

General Brooke agreed that the war in Europe must be ended as quickly as possible. However, he said that "seizure of the Brest Peninsula, which was all we could now achieve, would merely lock up 20 divisions."[19] Arguing from the context of the size of the armies fighting in northwestern Europe in World War I, Brooke stated that no major operations would be possible until 1945 or 1946.

General Brooke's elaboration went to a significant difference between the United States and British forces. The United States benefited from the opportunity to conceptualize and build its forces from the start for the expeditionary offensive, whereas Britain now faced a transition from a defensively structured force to an offensive force structure. Brooke stated that the RAF was a largely static force then transitioning to mobility to support an expeditionary army. British manpower was at its limit. To create

the logistical services necessary to fight a continental war on the move, two of the twelve British divisions then in the UK probably would have to be cannibalized.[20]

Marshall's response to Brooke sought to go to the essence of the COS's thinking. To Marshall "it appeared that ROUNDUP was still regarded [by the British] as a vague conception." Did the British chiefs, he asked, "regard Mediterranean operations as the key to a successful termination of the European war?"[21] Apparently, yes.

The CCS took up other topics at length including China, Southeast Asia, and the Azores. On European strategy, however, they continued intransigently to argue variations of these opposing positions through the end of Trident's first week. Their afternoon progress meeting with Churchill and Roosevelt at the White House on Friday, May 14, was consumed by consideration of China, Burma, and India: no progress on Europe and no easing of raw feelings. The following day, the CCS did agree to direct the British and American planners to produce two new studies in consultation with each other: defeating Germany "by concentrating on the biggest possible invasion force in the UK as soon as possible" and, alternatively, a plan to defeat Germany that "accepts the elimination of Italy as a necessary preliminary."[22] The CCS ordered that both studies be ready for presentation to them on Monday, May 17.

On Saturday, after a short meeting, the Combined Chiefs flew south into Tidewater Virginia for a weekend at the living history museum, Colonial Williamsburg, which was then in restoration. This was a well-planned diversion that by mutual agreement included no discussion of the war. Briefly, the chiefs found collegial respite from their terrible responsibilities. However, on return to business in Washington, May 17, nothing had changed. General Brooke wrote in his diary, "Another very disappointing day. . . . Again discussing 'Global Strategy,' which led us nowhere." On Tuesday, the U.S. Joint Chiefs had to admit that their planners' paper on the European theater was not yet ready and that they still were considering the British paper. Brooke concluded that "the Americans are now taking up the attitude that we led them down the garden path," first to North African, then to Sicily, and now would do so again.[23]

Washington on Wednesday, May 19, was enduring the oppressive heat that can afflict the city as early as spring. In the Federal Reserve Board of Governors Room for a second week, the ccs discussion was hotter still. This decisive day for a very contentious conference began with sharp attacks by each country's military chiefs on the other's position. General Marshall, who held the conference's rotating chairmanship that day, cleared the room of all but the British and U.S. chiefs. With staff gone, the dialogue continued to be frank and tough. Now "off the record," however, the chiefs on both sides rediscovered their capability to be flexible.[24] By 6:00 p.m., the Combined Chiefs had reached an agreement.

Agreed was that the Allies would assemble and prepare twenty-nine divisions for the invasion of northwestern Europe through France. The initial assault would begin with the landing of nine divisions on the target date of May 1, 1944. In the Mediterranean theater, General Eisenhower would be directed to capitalize on the conquest of Sicily with continued Allied assaults, at times and places that Eisenhower would determine, as pressure intended to eliminate Italy from the war. The now definitive Anglo-American commitment to an assault into northwestern Europe on the specified date and the direction to Eisenhower to follow up on Sicily with further action were put to paper.[25] Not written down was an oral quid pro quo agreement that an Italian campaign would continue in exchange for this, the first of ultimately three British commitments to a cross-Channel assault in 1944.[26]

General Brooke considered the unwritten acceptance of continued operations against Italy to be a "triumph as Americans wanted to close down all operation in the Med after the capture of Sicily." Brooke found the compromise to be "not altogether a satisfactory one, but far better than a break up of the conference!"[27] From his perspective, General Marshall foresaw being dragged along by the British in a campaign up the Italian peninsula, at least as far as Rome, as a price he would have to pay for British concessions to the American preference for a cross-Channel assault strategy.

78

The JCS had succeeded at the Trident Conference in committing General Brooke, in writing, to more than just invading northwestern Europe via a cross-Channel assault on May 1, 1944, now designated Overlord. They had won British commitment to the transfer of seven combat-experienced Allied divisions, starting November 1, 1943, from the Mediterranean to the UK for Overlord, a commitment that would be tested again and again.[28] As this day of hard-won if fragile military agreement ended, Brooke noted in his diary, a thunderstorm broke the heat.[29]

Over the following three days the Combined Chiefs turned their attention to the Pacific and to global shipping. Only to a degree were the issues less contentious than those of the European theater. Thanks to accelerated shipbuilding and recent success against the U-boats, the forecast for shipping was adequate to the CCS's global plans.

On May 24, they turned to drafting the culminating Final Agreed Summary of Conclusions.[30] All the national and service-favored arguments then rose back to the surface. Fortunately, if with difficulty, the Chiefs held to the agreements of the preceding days, notably those on European strategy. These already had been briefed in draft to the president and prime minister and accepted by both leaders on May 19. At 4:45 p.m., the Combined Chiefs traveled the short distance to the White House for photographs and a final meeting with Roosevelt and Churchill.

There, the torturously negotiated agreement crashed against the suddenly contrary position of Winston Churchill. Brooke recorded in his diary for May 24 that "the PM entirely repudiated the paper we had passed, agreed to, and had been congratulated on at our last meeting!! . . . Now we are threatened by a redraft by him and more difficulties tomorrow!" Reflecting on this White House meeting in 1957, Brooke recalled: "Some of the alterations [Churchill] wished to make were on points we had been forced to concede to the Americans in order to secure more important ones. From the attitude he took up the American Chiefs might well have believed we had gone behind their backs in an attempt to obtain those points through Winston."[31]

Indeed, fairly or not, the U.S. Joint Chiefs arrived at the conclusion of the Trident Conference prepared to put little faith in the commitments of their British counterparts. However, viewing Trident through an aperture widened to include concurrent discussions at the White House, just six blocks from the chiefs' negotiation, suggests a reason for Churchill's sudden change of mind on May 24. As at Casablanca, there were two overarching issues under independent but parallel discussion during Trident. Less obvious than Allied military strategy, but vital to Churchill, was the issue of resuming Anglo-American atomic cooperation. This had become more urgent.

Churchill had left Casablanca in January believing that his raising of the atomic cooperation issue with Harry Hopkins had gained a promise of redress from FDR. He thought he had oral assurance, indirectly through Hopkins, that the matter would be handled "entirely in accordance with our wishes."[32] Instead, since January, the gap between the U.S. and British atomic programs had widened and acquired new substance.

Churchill went to Trident in May with the U.S. interruption of Anglo-American interchange of atomic information very much on his mind. The months since the conclusion of the Symbol Conference and the start of Trident had seen frequent high-level but fruitless communication between Washington and London on the issue of atomic information exchange. That impasse now combined with a sharpened British understanding of their own limited options to increase the level and urgency of Churchill's concern.

Churchill's confidence in the viability of an atomic bomb had been reinforced on April 7 by a Tube Alloys progress report from Lord Cherwell. Of the easier, more certain path to a bomb, using "light uranium" [U235], Cherwell described a bomb with 10 to 40 pounds of nuclear material "equivalent to 10,000 to 40,000 tons of T.N.T." Although he himself would not go quite so far, Cherwell wrote, "The experts are prepared to bet 100 to 1 on its success."[33]

At Churchill's request, on April 15, the Tube Alloys leaders had assessed anew their prospects for developing on their own a British atomic bomb.[34] Their conclusion was that the design and construction of a British bomb was unlikely to be completed in less than four years. The scientists believed that would be after the current war would end. They concluded that a postwar bomb would be possible with immediate construction of facilities in Britain and Canada. However, this could be done only at a staggeringly prohibitive cost in resources already critically needed by Britain for other uses to win the current war, a war that in May 1943 had only just tipped toward eventual Allied victory.

Beyond the financial expenditure, separate development of a British atomic bomb would require 20,000 laborers, a quarter possessing already scarce skills; 500,000 tons of steel already in heavy wartime demand; and an additional half million kilowatts of electricity. Parallel but separate British and American efforts to develop the bomb were foreseen by the British only to exacerbate the challenge of postwar atomic arms control already assessed to be difficult. The British scientists' recommendation to Churchill, which he took with him to Washington as a task, was to redouble efforts to restore full Anglo-American interchange of atomic research information.[35]

When on April 29 Sir John Anderson forwarded to Churchill the assessment made in response to the prime minister's request, he introduced a concern new to the dialogue, one certain to arouse Churchill. Anderson wrote: "We must always remember that the Russians, who are peculiarly well equipped scientifically for this kind of development, may well be working on the Tube Alloys project somewhere beyond the Urals and making great progress. It is incumbent upon us to make every possible effort to bring about an effective co-operation between the United States and ourselves." At the top of the first page of Anderson's cover note, Churchill wrote and then circled *Trident*.[36]

While at the Trident Conference, and well aware that his military chiefs and the Americans were in hot debate on strategy, Churchill received a cable on May 15 from Anderson. The encrypted cable made the task of quickly restoring information exchange and cooperation imperative. The United States had secured contracts that locked up the entire Canadian production of uranium and deuterium (heavy water). Anderson informed Churchill that, should the British opt for an independent program to develop an atomic bomb despite its already prohibitive requirements, they would have to do so without adequate sources for these essential ingredients.[37]

There was more to the information, received from Canada a day earlier, that had stimulated Anderson's cable to Churchill, but he held that back. The prime minister would have found it an enlightening background to his attempts so far to move the Americans off their position. Dean C. J. Mackenzie in Canada had noticed a sea change in the confidence level of the American scientific leaders of s-1. He observed that Vannevar Bush and James Conant, who up until January 1943 had seemed doubtful of an atomic bomb's practicability, had since March appeared "quite confident that Bombs will become available in reasonable quantities in time to be used in this war, and this has made all those concerned with the Policy direction of the American project absolutely firm on the question of Security."[38]

Trident had been preceded by a month and a half of intensified communication between London and Washington on the suspension of atomic information interchange. Following Churchill's lead, the British had gone through Harry Hopkins, Roosevelt's closest adviser. On March 20, Hopkins took to Roosevelt another cable from Churchill that reminded him that the prime minister was still awaiting word from Hopkins of a resolution. At FDR's direction, Hopkins sent the Churchill correspondence to Bush and requested a reply. Bush, who had become more confident of success in the quest for the bomb, according to C. J. Mackenzie, responded with a long defense of the U.S. "need to know" policy. Probably for the first time in his communication with Hopkins, Bush inserted a concern that he shared with his deputy, Dr. James Conant, and Manhattan Project director Brig. Gen. Leslie Groves. They suspected that the British were more interested in a postwar commercial advantage in nuclear power plants than they were in a bomb to help win the current war.[39]

As a result, no significant action on Churchill's request advanced in Washington. That prompted Churchill to renew his request through Hopkins with another cable on April 1 that alluded to higher stakes. Churchill wrote that should the United States and Britain take separate paths to develop an atomic bomb, that would be a "somber decision."[40]

Receiving no reply from Washington, there followed on April 13 a message to Hopkins from Foreign Secretary Anthony Eden. Eden's query repeated Churchill's hint at a possible parting of the ways: "Have you any news for me about the very secret matter we discussed? You will realize that we have various decisions to make if there has to be a separate development."[41]

Hopkins did not receive Eden's message until after he had met on April 13 with the British ambassador, Lord Halifax, at the embassy in Washington.[42] There, according to Halifax's account of the meeting in a letter to Eden, dated April 14, Hopkins "opened up on the secret scientific matter that [Eden] had spoken to him about." Hopkins expressed to Halifax "very little doubt" that both the U.S. and British sides had "a tendency to hold back information from one another, since this scientific research was necessarily largely in the hands of persons who had been and would be again in the employ of big business, and therefore had their eye on postwar interests on either side."

Hopkins's understanding of the substance of the issue would evolve in the month to come. However, his approach to its resolution endured. As he expressed that to Halifax April 13, the ambassador wrote, Hopkins thought the only path to resolution was for "the President and Prime Minister to agree that the pooling of knowledge system should not be confined to the war, but to carry over into post-war times." Halifax told Eden that Hopkins considered the issues involved too big to be decided at a level below Churchill and Roosevelt and that Hopkins "foresaw considerable possibility of trouble" if not resolved. Halifax recounted that Hopkins said he "had been having much talk with Vannevar Bush" and that "Winston was pressing him on the matter but that he had nothing definite to say at the present time."[43]

The following day, Hopkins replied to Eden, via a message sent for him by Halifax in British channels: "Your message regarding secret matter received. I am going to send you on Monday [April 19] a full telegram about the matter. On further enquiry I find it has many ramifications and I therefore am anxious to send you my views fully." Eden never received the later telegram from Hopkins, if ever one was sent.[44]

Harry Hopkins probably was not fully conversant in April 1943 on the specifics of the position of the British and that of the American scientists and General Groves. He knew enough, though. Hopkins's response to Eden, through Halifax, directly communicated the position that atomic information interchange could be restored only through an agreement at the Roosevelt-Churchill level, and in doing so Hopkins signaled to the British the possibility that the agreement could take into account postwar considerations of the parties.

That this discussion did not progress further through the channel to Anthony Eden, or at all before the British arrived in Washington for Trident, suggests that Hopkins was acting with instructions from Roosevelt. As important as resumption of access to atomic information was to Churchill, there remained an open issue at least as important to the U.S. side, Churchill's assent to a cross-Channel attack as the basis of the principal strategy for the victory campaign from the west in Europe.

As the Combined Chiefs worked at the Federal Reserve Building on Monday, May 24, to consolidate their many and varied conclusions into an agreed statement of Allied global military strategy, the open issue of atomic information sharing at last was under direct, high-level U.S.-British discussion at the White House. Churchill and his science adviser, Lord Cherwell, met for two and a half hours over lunch at the White House with Roosevelt, Vice President Henry Wallace (a member of the Military Policy Committee), and Harry Hopkins.[45]

Churchill was aware of the direction in which the CCS military strategy negotiations were proceeding, both from the Combined Chiefs' briefing to him and FDR on May 19, and from daily direct reports from his own COS Committee. The prime minister knew that the military conclusions from those difficult talks were to be presented that afternoon to the two leaders for their endorsement.

Churchill put to the Americans, over lunch, the still-open issue of U.S. constraints on atomic research cooperation with British scientists. According to Hopkins's summons to Vannevar Bush the next day, Churchill "formally raised the question of interchange on S-1."[46] Answers to Churchill's satisfaction remained pending.

Two hours after the May 24 lunch, the CCS arrived at the White House and presented the final results of their collaboration. At this point, Churchill stunned the chiefs, British and American, by repudiating in some detail the agreements on Allied strategy that he had accepted in draft on May 19, only five days earlier.

Most interpretations of Churchill's reversal of support for much of the chiefs' compromise outcome, then and since, have been that he was reacting to the absence in the document of an explicit, written commitment to invade Italy and advance British objectives in the Mediterranean.[47] That certainly was a central concern for the prime minister but not the only one in the moment.

A further explanation suggests itself for consideration, one not then apparent to the military chiefs, but given the separate White House discussion of joint atomic research at the lunch just concluded, likely very evident to Roosevelt and Hopkins. Was Churchill signaling resumption of full exchange of atomic information as the quid pro quo for his support of a cross-Channel attack in 1944?

The evidence for this is circumstantial, based on the ensuing meetings on May 24–26, 1943, and what the official histories have concluded from what is known about the context of these meetings. The meetings' sequence is enlightening, however, and merits attention.

Following his outright dissent from the agreed strategy findings that afternoon, Churchill worked through the night of May 24, attempting to reword the Trident agreement to include a definite written commitment to invade Italy, while the British Chiefs of Staff continued attempts to persuade him to drop his main objections.[48] During the evening, Harry Hopkins approached Churchill and said, "If you wish to carry your point you will have to stay here another week . . . even then there is no certainty."[49] General Brooke later credited Hopkins's intervention with getting Churchill to scale back his changes, which in the end did not alter the principles of the written strategy agreement.[50]

Surely there was more to the Churchill-Hopkins conversation. Building on a month and a half of long-distance entreaties, culminating in their lunch meeting with Roosevelt that day, did Churchill raise again with Hopkins the open issue of resumption of atomic information interchange? Perhaps in the context of his assent to a cross-Channel attack?

What is known is that the following day, on short notice to Vannevar Bush, Hopkins convened a meeting between Lord Cherwell, Bush, and himself to address the issues in atomic information interchange. At some time between their lunch on May 24 and this May 25 meeting, Hopkins would have told Churchill that he would do this.

On May 25, with the last-minute issues of the Trident strategy document temporarily settled, but with no one confident of their durability, the military principals of the Trident Conference prepared for their departure from Washington. That day at the White House, as Hopkins had promised to Churchill, Bush and Hopkins met with Cherwell to seek an agreement to end the impasse on Anglo-American atomic information interchange.[51]

The meeting was frank, at times blunt. Bush reviewed for Cherwell and Hopkins the history of the U.S. position and defended the "need to know" principle for access to classified information as being applied to U.S. government and U.S. private sector participants in the Manhattan Project as well as to British participants. That proved to be too narrow an explanation to accommodate the larger issue. All of the participants knew that the operative justification being applied by the U.S. side was "need to know" in order to win this war. Creation of a British atomic capability for after the current war was not an access criterion acceptable to U.S. leaders for the project, unless they were so directed by the president. Asked by Bush whether he disagreed with this principle or its application, Lord Cherwell replied that he "disagreed with the principle itself."[52] After extended discussion of interest in commercial applications of atomic energy, of which the United States suspected the British, Cherwell stated to Bush and Hopkins that the United Kingdom wanted the data from the current research not for commercial purposes but to be able to build its own atomic bomb after the war.

Recounting the meeting, Bush wrote that in stating his understanding of what Lord Cherwell had said, "Mr. Hopkins reiterated it and emphasized it, that the reason the British wish [for] the information was so that in the period immediately after this war they would be able to develop the weapon for themselves very promptly and not after a considerable interval."[53] Bush and Hopkins were in agreement that taking the purpose of Anglo-American cooperation beyond the needs of winning the current war to address a British political-military interest in the postwar world was a matter that would have to be settled at the highest level by Roosevelt and Churchill.

Ending the meeting, Hopkins cautioned Lord Cherwell on the constitutional limits of the U.S. president's war powers. Roosevelt could authorize sharing with the British through an executive agreement that, unless continued by whoever succeeded him as president, would be binding only on his own administration, Hopkins told Cherwell. Under the Constitution, Hopkins continued, FDR could not make international commitments binding on future presidents except by means of a treaty that would have to be ratified by the Senate.[54] The compelling need to preserve the secrecy of the Manhattan Project put a treaty as the vehicle for a solution out of the question.

The meeting clarified and sharpened Hopkins' understanding of the issue with the British on atomic research sharing. Asked by Bush if Hopkins wanted him to discuss the meeting with the other members of the Military Policy Committee that advised FDR on s-1, Hopkins told Bush, "No, nothing more to be done at this time." Expecting Hopkins would brief FDR, Bush told Hopkins that he would "sit tight and do nothing unless and until I heard from him further on the matter."[55]

Bush developed a belief, in which he probably was wrong, that Hopkins did not brief FDR on the meeting. Later communications to Hopkins from Cherwell and Churchill suggest that Hopkins briefed FDR within a day.[56] With the two countries' positions on atomic information sharing clarified but unreconciled, military strategy for Europe remained at issue at the highest level into the night.

Churchill's commitment to his view of the path to victory ran deep, a path along which FDR had been unwilling to follow him this time. Pacing in his White House bedroom on May 25, before proceeding to a night meeting with FDR, Churchill said in exasperation to his physician, Lord Moran, "The President is not willing to put pressure on Marshall. He is not in favor of landing in Italy. It is most discouraging. I only crossed the Atlantic for this purpose. I cannot let the matter rest where it is."[57] And he did not.

Alone in the White House in their meeting that ran into the early hours of May 26, Churchill and Roosevelt struggled to draft language for a cable to Stalin to tell him the results of the conference. As they did so, they discussed the main outcomes of Trident. Churchill received Roosevelt's oral agreement that Anglo-American full interchange of information on atomic bomb research should resume.[58] Although the absence of a written record of this specific meeting leaves no evidence either way, FDR's assurance possibly was understood to be in exchange for Churchill accepting the ccs compromise position at Trident, which included the commitment to Overlord for May 1, 1944.

In his May 26 message to Sir John Anderson, Churchill informed the Tube Alloys director of FDR's agreement to resume sharing atomic information without stating that FDR's assent was oral. Without referring to the limits of FDR's war powers, and with a hint of tentativeness, Churchill told Anderson that he "understood that his ruling would be based upon the fact that this weapon may well be developed in time for the present war and that it thus falls within the general agreement covering the inter-change of research and invention secrets."[59]

Churchill's interpretation of the basis for FDR's oral agreement in his cable to Anderson does not square with the assessment Hopkins gained from Lord Cherwell and reviewed with Cherwell at the time for clarity. This was that with restored access to information the British foresaw achieving their own atomic bomb "very promptly" after the war. That assessment is likely what Hopkins told FDR at some time in the interval between the conclusion of Hopkins's meeting with Cherwell and the president's late night session with Churchill, May 25–26, when FDR orally gave Churchill some assurance on atomic information interchange.[60] There was advantage for both leaders in a loose assumption about when a joint Anglo-American endeavor might produce an atomic bomb. In any case, Churchill's cable and Cherwell's earlier thank-you to Hopkins, written May 30 after Cherwell returned to London, credit Hopkins with the result of FDR's oral agreement.

* * *

Trident, the contentious third U.S.-British conference in Washington, officially had closed. But few if any on either side considered debate of its issues to have ended. Reluctantly, the British Chiefs of Staff had agreed at Trident to an Allied strategy that gave priority to an assault across the English Channel. Set for May 1, 1944, and now called Overlord, the goal of the strategy was to defeat Hitler by direct attack through northwestern Europe and into Germany. Overlord was to take priority over operations in the Mediterranean championed by Churchill, who, to the consternation of the British as well as U.S. Joint Chiefs of Staff, almost had upset the agreement in the last days of the conference. Few American participants in Trident believed that Churchill's new commitment to cross-Channel attack would hold. To the Americans, proof of that came quickly in a de facto addendum to Trident engineered by Churchill.

Washington's morning calm, May 26, 1943, shattered as the pilots of Winston Churchill's camouflage-painted Boeing 314 flying boat, *Bristol*, revved one after another of the plane's reciprocating engines. Then, all four engines at deep bass full throttle, the pilots set *Bristol* racing across the surface of the Potomac River. *Bristol* lifted through a steady rain and banked into the mist northeastward en route to Algiers via Newfoundland and Gibraltar.[61]

Along on the flight with the prime minister and Gen. Sir Alan Brooke were two last-minute, reluctant American passengers: Army Chief of Staff Gen. George C. Marshall, at Churchill's insistent request to President Roosevelt, and Marshall's aide, Lt. Col. Frank McCarthy. Marshall had been scheduled to take three days' leave after Trident and then depart on a long overdue trip to the Pacific with Navy commander in chief Adm. Ernest King. Only six hours before the morning flight, Marshall learned that instead he would accompany Churchill in the opposite direction. At the last minute, President Roosevelt had relented to Churchill's request to take Marshall along to continue Allied strategy discussions at General Eisenhower's headquarters in North Africa.[62]

Marshall, the principal proponent for direct attack, was certain as to Churchill's purpose in taking him along to North Africa. The prime minister intended to continue discussion to attempt realignment of Allied strategy for the European theater, supposedly already set at Trident, to restore precedence to Churchill's preferred Mediterranean strategy. Indeed, seeing Marshall as his strongest opponent in the Allied strategy debate, Churchill intended to do precisely that.

General Brooke, Chief of the Imperial General Staff, had a more nuanced interpretation of Marshall's presence. He was concerned that Churchill's last-minute attempt to reverse the ccs decisions at the Trident Conference would rekindle American suspicions. Brooke worried that Churchill's flight with Marshall would be interpreted "as an attempt to swing Eisenhower in our direction at the expense of decisions arrived at in Washington."[63] Marshall's presence on the trip, Brooke felt, would be offsetting.

The generals' misgivings were not the only ones likely to be found aboard *Bristol*. Flying away from Washington, as Marshall privately doubted the durability of Churchill's commitment at Trident to a cross-Channel invasion and as Brooke fretted, Churchill probably pondered whether FDR's spoken word would be confirmed by U.S. action to restore atomic information access.

Most immediate, however, was the task of framing the words to tell Joseph Stalin that the cross-Channel invasion, key to the second front promised to the Soviet premier for 1942 and then delayed until 1943, now had been reset at Trident for 1944. The night before, FDR and Churchill, each a master of language, had struggled together to find a way to convey this difficult message to Stalin. En route to Newfoundland, Churchill tried again to draw a cohesive message from the folder of cable drafts that he and Roosevelt had produced. Soon he gave up and turned the task over to Marshall.

Taking up a small, unlined pad and a pencil, the general started fresh. Two hours into the flight, Marshall returned to Churchill with his own draft, which survives and is remarkable for its few strike-outs and erasures.[64] So impressed was the prime minister that without changing a word he sent it to Roosevelt from Newfoundland with the recommendation that Marshall's version be their joint message to Stalin, and it was.[65]

Grasping at any possible diversion to continue delaying an inflight discussion of strategy for the European theater, Marshall drew Churchill into recounting the effects on Parliament of the late-eighteenth-century impeachment trial of the governor-general of India, Warren Hastings; then the 1941 landing in Scotland of Hitler's deputy führer, Rudolf Hess; and then Churchill's role in the crisis precipitated by the 1936 abdication of King Edward VIII. Each time, apparently unsuspecting of Marshall's tactic, Churchill responded with extended fascinating remarks. By the time the steward called them to dinner, Marshall had succeeded in deflecting for that day any discussion of Allied strategy.[66]

Arriving with Churchill at Eisenhower's headquarters in Algiers, Marshall sat down with the American Supreme Allied Commander for North Africa and his mostly British deputies, flush with the

Allies' fresh victory in Tunisia and its huge haul of POWs, for three days of conference with Churchill. In this reinforced company, Churchill pressed Marshall with his case for invading the Italian mainland.

Churchill's private physician, Lord Moran, three months later heard directly from Marshall and wrote down the general's account of how that went. To Moran's recollection, Marshall told him: "I did not think that the moment had come for a decision. It would be better, I said to the Prime Minister, to decide what to do when the attack on Sicily was well under way. I wanted to know whether Germany meant to put up a stiff resistance on southern Italy or whether she would decide to retire to the Po [River] as Winston suggested. I wanted more facts." To Churchill, Marshall seemed focused on details that the prime minister dismissed in favor of his own broader vision. Marshall told Moran, "I tried to argue that we must exercise great discretion in choosing what to do after the conquest of Sicily. I said to the Prime Minister that I would be content if Sardinia were taken before the invasion of France. He replied that the difference between taking southern Italy and Sardinia was the difference between a glorious campaign and a mere convenience."[67]

According to Lord Moran, Churchill returned to London happy in his belief that he had won his point.[68] That was an illusion. Marshall had decided not to continue the argument. On returning to Washington on June 7, Marshall reported that he believed he had protected the Trident decisions without damaging his good relationship with Churchill.[69]

In closer alignment among U.S. and British strategists was their contemplation of the Soviet Union. During their Trident meetings, their concern for keeping the Soviet Union in the war against Germany still was strong. Yet emerging was a parallel concern that would grow as the year progressed: the postwar political-military position of the Soviets on the ground in Europe relative to that of the western Allies.[70] As the Combined Chiefs of Staff met, unbeknownst to them or Churchill, Roosevelt had initiated his own mission to engage Stalin.

5

Mission to Moscow

He, himself, he said would tell Churchill and Churchill would understand.

—Ambassador Joseph E. Davies, May 5, 1943

All the while that Churchill, Roosevelt, and their senior civilian and military leadership were negotiating the way ahead for the western Allies at the Trident Conference, FDR's emissary was engaging to the east. His charge was FDR's initiative to foster a personal relationship with the other critical partner in the Alliance, Soviet premier Joseph Stalin. Roosevelt intended to act alone, leaving Churchill out and uninformed. The prime minister, FDR believed, had had his turn,

Churchill had flown to Moscow in August 1942 to meet with Stalin. The prime minister's difficult task had been to inform the Soviet premier that there would be no opening of a second front in France in 1942. As they met, Leningrad had been under German siege for more than 350 days, and advancing Germans were putting Stalingrad under heavy pressure. Churchill responded well to sharp Russian criticism of the Allies, according to Ambassador Averill Harriman, who accompanied him. However, the meetings with Stalin had gone poorly.[1]

To soften the message of no second front in 1942, Churchill had promised Stalin a huge Allied offensive in the west for 1943. Based on his projection of having eight to ten times more landing craft by then, Churchill told Stalin, the offensive would involve twenty-seven American and twenty-one British divisions, half of which would be armored.[2] It was clear from an early stage in the May 1943 Trident Conference that nothing like those numbers of divisions or landing craft would be available to the Allies for an invasion of France in 1943. When the Combined Chiefs of Staff began the conference, they already knew that, in fact, the second front could not be opened until 1944 at the earliest. Roosevelt interpreted that as his opportunity to make an overture of his own to Stalin.

On May 20, as the ccs sat down to lunch in Washington, by now proceeding in somewhat smoother waters, Roosevelt's emissary, Ambassador Joseph E. Davies, arrived at the Kremlin in Moscow for a 9:00 p.m. meeting. Davies was received by Stalin and Foreign Minister V. M. Molotov to present a personal letter that the president had written to Stalin on May 5. Davies had flown, via Brazil, Africa, and the Middle East, over 12,000 miles to hand-deliver FDR's communication. At the conclusion of their friendly meeting, Stalin asked Davies to return to the Kremlin in a few days for his reply.[3]

Joseph Davies had been sent to Moscow previously as the U.S. ambassador in 1936. Before returning to Washington in 1938, Davies's naiveté about the Soviet Union in his public statements and writings had made him a target for FDR's domestic critics. However, Davies and his second wife, Marjorie Merriweather Post, had developed rapport with the principal figures in the ever-shifting Soviet regime. Davies's connections made him the perfect messenger for Roosevelt's personal and very secret initiative to Stalin in 1943.

Roosevelt believed that the one-on-one, agenda-free meeting that he was seeking with Stalin would provide a start on building a personal relationship with the leader of the Soviet Union, one similar to the president's relationship with Churchill. He hoped that such a relationship would facilitate understanding and discussion among the Allies of the great issues to come. Before departing for Moscow, Davies wrote in his diary that FDR's last instruction to him at the White House on May 5 "was to impress upon Stalin that as between friends there were no differences that could not be solved and agreed upon, if there was common purpose to win the war and to organize the peace."[4] Certainly, as president, Roosevelt's perception was that, together with Britain, they constituted the Big Three, each with differing national interests and with the United States, FDR believed, in the favored position of influence at the apex of the triangle. In making this overture to Stalin, FDR decided, Churchill would only be in the way.

Roosevelt bluntly told Stalin in his letter that he would not meet on British territory, citing Khartoum as his example. Roosevelt rejected Iceland as a venue "because for both you and me it involves rather difficult flights and, in addition, would make it, quite frankly, difficult not to invite Prime Minister Churchill at the same time." Upon receiving FDR's instructions, a worried Davies had asked the president if he had a concern that Stalin might misinterpret the exclusion of Churchill. Davies recalled that Roosevelt replied that he personally would inform Churchill and that Churchill would understand.[5]

Roosevelt proposed to Stalin that the two of them meet without military staffs in the summer of 1943. FDR proposed that he would be accompanied by Harry Hopkins, an interpreter, and a stenographer. He wanted the meeting to be very informal and produce no official declarations or agreements.[6]

While Churchill—unaware—was meeting in Washington with Roosevelt, the president's letter was being read to the Soviet premier in translation in Moscow. According to Davies's diary entry, "Stalin didn't flicker an eyelash. He never looked up from the sheet of paper on which he was 'doodling.' He looked taciturn and grim." Habitually, Stalin doodled wolves. When Davies's reading of the letter came to excluding Churchill from the proposed meeting, Stalin asked, "Why?" Davies replied that "Roosevelt and Churchill respected and admired each other, and although they did not always see eye to eye, they were always loyal. They were 'big' men, and on matters in difference, each could be relied upon. In fact each would insist on finding common ground to win the war."[7]

After some discussion of differing views among the leaders about the postwar future, Davies again stated. "If you and Roosevelt meet, you will understand each other," to which Stalin responded, "I am not sure." Davies wrote that he said, "Knowing what you both are trying to do, I am sure." Stalin countered, "But understanding alone is not enough. There must be reciprocity and respect." Davies responded, "If you knew the President as I know him, you would know that this is exactly what you would get and, in fact, you are getting now."[8]

Their talk turned to the shared Russian and U.S. disappointment in the delay from 1942 to 1943 in opening the second front. Their conversation went on into the night, covering a broad range of political-military topics as Stalin "continued to look down and 'doodle' with his pencil." At some point during the conversation, Davies indicated to Stalin that the question of the postwar Polish-Soviet border might be settled to the Soviet premier's satisfaction along the post–World War I Curzon Line.[9] In making his remark, Davies had to know that it would be interpreted by Stalin to be an indication from the U.S. president's envoy of openness to considering a postwar border redrawn at Poland's expense. Near the end of their two and a half-hour meeting, Davies recalled, Stalin said, "I think your President is right. I think he represents America as I understand it. He is a great man. You may tell your President I will be glad to meet with him."[10]

Stalin gave Davies a letter of affirmative reply in principle to FDR's invitation to a private meeting of the two leaders. The letter was to be hand-delivered to the president. In the text, Stalin wrote that he could not provide a definite reply because of the present military situation. Stalin proposed that the meeting between him and Roosevelt be arranged to take place in July or August. If Roosevelt was agreeable, Stalin would communicate the date of the meeting two weeks in advance. Roosevelt and Stalin then would fly to the rendezvous from their respective capitals. Davies was to tell FDR orally the place Stalin proposed for the meeting, Fairbanks, Alaska.[11]

Of course, Roosevelt had been anxious to know as soon as possible Stalin's response as to whether and when they could meet. FDR did not trust the security of such sensitive information if stated directly in a cable encrypted and handled by subordinate embassy staff. In their May 5 Oval Office meeting, he provided a solution. To cloak Stalin's answer, FDR gave Davies a simple code of the president's own devising for use within a cable. Only the two of them would understand its meaning. Davies described the code in his diary: "The word 'Jonquils' would mean June. The word 'Jolly' would mean July. 'Auction Bridge' would mean August. If it were to be in the middle of the month, the words would be 'literally in the center of things.'"[12] In this manner, Davies told Stalin and Molotov, he would cable to FDR the range of tentative dates, from mid-July to mid-August. The two hardened revolutionaries, no strangers to cryptic messages, found Roosevelt's code simple and ingenious. Without once referring to a meeting, Davies then cabled FDR "tentative" in the context of military operations and that they had listened on the radio to Churchill's "jolly great speech" to Congress while they were "in the center of things, playing auction bridge."[13]

His private message sent, Ambassador Davies sent additional cables from Moscow to FDR and Secretary of State Cordell Hull. As Churchill's plane from Washington was landing in the harbor at Gibraltar on the morning of May 27 to refuel for the flight to Algiers and to unload its London-bound passengers, FDR and Hull were reading Davies's cables: "There is complete agreement in principle. Some supplementary matters he gave me to be orally transmitted to the President." Carrying Stalin's letter to FDR, Davies then took off for Washington by the fastest route possible, via Siberia and Alaska. His C-54 by now had been christened by the crew in yellow Russian paint on its nose, *Mission to Moscow*.

Ambassador Davies reported to FDR in the White House on June 3 his apparent progress toward a bilateral meeting with Stalin. In Moscow, however, Stalin had received new reason to doubt his allies' expressed intentions. After Davies's departure and while he was still en route to Washington, Soviet intelligence on May 29 had reported to Stalin, from a source who claimed to have attended a Roosevelt-Churchill meeting during the Trident Conference, that launching the second front had again been delayed, this time until 1944.[14]

Back from a visit with FDR at Shangri-La on June 7, Harry Hopkins drove to Tregaron, Joseph Davies's graceful estate atop a wooded hill in northwestern Washington's Cleveland Park section.[15] Hopkins's purpose was to brief Davies on what had happened during the ambassador's globe-circumnavigating journey. He gave Davies a grim but accurate account of the contentiousness of the Trident Conference and the follow-up meeting in Algiers to which Churchill had taken General Marshall.

During Trident, the absence of a plan for a cross-Channel assault accepted as viable by the cos made resistance to that strategy easy on many practical grounds. The British Chiefs had pressed these hard in favor of the Mediterranean strategy. Still, Hopkins told Davies, the U.S. jcs had held their own and salvaged the conference with a written British commitment to a cross-Channel assault, but delayed until May 1, 1944. This was gained in return for an oral commitment to continue Allied operations against Italy. The subsequent Algiers meeting had confirmed the Americans' suspicions that the new agreement in principle to implement Overlord already faced determined British resistance led by Churchill. Looking to inform Stalin that the second front had been put off again, Hopkins asked Davies, "How would he take it?" To which Davies replied, "He wouldn't take it. It would raise hob."[16]

Davies was surprised to learn from Hopkins that, despite what the president had said to him on May 5, at no time during the Trident Conference had Roosevelt told Churchill that the purpose of Davies's trip had been to arrange an exclusively bilateral meeting between Roosevelt and Stalin. Worse, Churchill still did not know.[17]

Hopkins told Davies that Lord Beaverbrook, a close adviser to Churchill, advocate for the cross-Channel strategy, and often a bridge between the U.S. and British governments, had just been informed by FDR of the purpose of Davies's trip. Beaverbrook, Hopkins said, "told the President that Churchill would bitterly resent [a bilateral Roosevelt-Stalin meeting] and 'never consent' to it." All were in agreement, however, that Churchill's "bitter session" with Stalin in August 1942 had left FDR with the better opportunity to resolve misunderstandings and gain agreements with Stalin.

Hopkins's proposed solution, for which he asked and received Davies's endorsement, was to have Averill Harriman, who had grown close to Churchill and his family, tell the prime minister about FDR's initiative to Stalin before Beaverbrook saw Churchill.[18] In the event, Harriman and Beaverbrook went together to see Churchill.

Resolution of this disconcerting surprise, sprung on Churchill by Roosevelt, would include initiation of a fourth major Anglo-American conference, Quadrant. There, reaffirmation of cross-Channel attack as the principal Allied strategy for victory in Europe would be the central issue, but not the only important one.

Flying into the United Kingdom from Washington with the charge from Roosevelt to tell the prime minister about the president's communication with Stalin, Harriman and Beaverbrook went directly to Churchill's country estate, Chequers. They had a late night dinner and discussion with Churchill on June 24–25. According to Harriman's July 5 written account to FDR, the two men were tired from two days of flying, and Beaverbrook was in an ill temper. Churchill and Beaverbrook, close but volatile friends, argued at dinner. After Beaverbrook left at midnight, Harriman stayed to convey to the now-upset Churchill several messages from FDR including the gist of the letter Stalin had sent FDR in May in reply to FDR's proposal for an FDR-Stalin meeting without the prime minister.[19]

Whether or not Churchill had indications earlier from British diplomatic or intelligence sources is not known. Harriman's revelation of FDR's unilateral, exclusionary initiative to set up an initial bilateral meeting with Stalin confronted Churchill with circumstances that eclipsed his own effort at a trilateral meeting. From an inauspicious beginning, a two-hour "direct and frank" talk ensued between Churchill and Harriman. Wide-ranging, their discussion always came back to "the talk to [the] Russian and the question of the meeting."

Harriman reported to FDR by letter, written July 5, eleven days later, that Churchill "firmly believes a three-cornered meeting is in the interests of the war but he admitted that his viewpoint is colored by considerations of the reaction in Great Britain." Harriman wrote that his response to Churchill was based on two points: first, "the value of the intimate understanding that in all probability would result from a tête-à-tête, impossible with three persons" and, second, Harriman's explanation of public perception and reaction in the United States. Harriman concluded that Churchill had a "sincere desire and determination to back [FDR] up in anything [FDR] finally decided to do and, although I must emphasize his disappointment if he is not present, I am satisfied he would accept it in good part and that it would in the long run improve rather than adversely affect your relations with him." Harriman believed Churchill recognized the logic of a bilateral meeting followed quickly by a trilateral meeting of Churchill, Stalin, and Roosevelt.

Harriman had told Churchill on the night of their meeting that there was no need to rush his reply to FDR. However, Churchill cabled FDR promptly. Friday morning, June 25, in consultation with Foreign Minister Anthony Eden, Churchill prepared a reply to FDR and called Harriman to the No. 10 Downing Street Annex to read it. Harriman told Churchill that although he did not agree with Churchill's position, the cable draft "fairly expressed his [Churchill's] views." On the way out of that meeting, Harriman spoke with Eden, who "was not unsympathetic with [FDR's] position and was quite satisfied to let the decision rest with [FDR]."[20] Using the abbreviation of their nickname for Stalin, "Uncle Joe," Churchill's June 25 cable conveyed his strong dissent from the idea of an FDR-Stalin bilateral meeting, stating:

> Averill told me last night of your wish for a meeting with U.J. in Alaska *a deux.*

> The whole world is expecting and all our side are desiring a meeting of the three great powers at which, not only the political chiefs, but the military staffs would be present in order to plan the future war moves and, of course, search for the foundation of post war settlement. It would seem a pity to draw U.J. 7,000 miles from Moscow for anything less than this. . . .

> I do not underrate the use that enemy propaganda would make of a meeting between the heads of Soviet Russia and the United States at this juncture with the British Commonwealth and Empire excluded. . . . Nevertheless, whatever you decide, I shall sustain to the best of my ability here.[21]

Roosevelt replied to Churchill on June 28. His message was disingenuous. The president wrote, "I did not suggest to UJ that we meet alone but he told Davies that he assumed (a) that we would meet alone and (b) that he agreed that we should not bring staffs to what would be a preliminary meeting."[22] In fact, FDR's May 5 letter to Stalin had sought a venue that would facilitate avoiding an invitation to Churchill and FDR proposed in his letter not bringing military staffs. Stalin's response had been to ask Davies why Churchill would be excluded.[23] Churchill had received, through Harriman, only a selective oral gist of FDR's May 5 letter to Stalin and not until fifty days after it was written.

In his June 28 explanation, FDR gave his five reasons why a preliminary bilateral with Stalin would be advantageous to the Allied cause adding, "I want to explore his thinking as fully as possible concerning Russia's post-war hopes and ambitions. I want to cover much the same field with him as did Eden for you a year ago."[24]

FDR then proposed a full-dress bilateral conference with Churchill: "What would you think of coming over *soon* afterwards and that you and I with staffs should meet in the Citadel in Quebec?" Sequentially, this would mean an FDR-Stalin bilateral followed quickly by an FDR-Churchill bilateral with FDR occupying the center. FDR then expounded on meeting dates in a way that reinforced his proposal for a pair of bilateral meetings in this sequence:

> While UJ gave no definite dates he suggested the end of July or early August. This was wholly tentative and I do not expect to hear anything further until about the fifteenth of July.

> If he confirms this, I would be back about August fifteenth. I would have to be in Washington for a week but could easily get to some place in eastern Canada by the twenty-fifth of August.[25]

FDR agreed with Churchill that "later in the autumn we should most definitely have a full dress meeting with the Russians." He claimed the Russians would not favor flying Stalin to Scapa Flow.

FDR concluded with a philosophical attempt at conciliation: "I have the idea that your conception is the right one from the short point of view, but mine is the right one from the long point of view. I wish there were not distances." The long view/short view echoes a description Harriman may have used in reporting by telephone to FDR immediately after his June 24–25 meeting with Churchill. Harriman certainly used the terms later in his July 5 letter.[26]

Unknown to COSSAC and its invitees, as they prepared and conducted their own breakthrough Rattle Conference on Overlord in Scotland, FDR's revelation to Churchill of his bid to meet alone with Stalin and Churchill's sharp reaction were unfolding to the south in England. Resolution would include initiation of a fourth major Anglo-American conference at which reaffirmation of cross-Channel attack as the principal Allied strategy for victory in Europe—and the COSSAC plan for Overlord—would be on the table in a showdown.

After reading FDR's June 28 cable, Churchill replied on June 29 with his acceptance of Roosevelt's proposed course of action. Citing his most recent message on Stalin as the reason, Churchill expressed his skepticism: "I send you first of all the very unpleasant reply I have received from U.J. and my rejoinder. This certainly has its bearing on your proposal to meet him alone and I shall not seek to deter you if you can get him to come."[27] Churchill wrote that "in view of his attitude I think it important that this contact [the FDR-Stalin meeting] should be established." Churchill agreed to ask Canada to host a bilateral meeting between Roosevelt and Churchill and their staffs in Quebec for the latter part of August, which would be consistent with accommodating FDR's prediction of the timing for his meeting with Stalin.[28]

Initiation had begun for an Anglo-American follow-up conference to Trident that the two men hoped also would follow closely on a meeting with Stalin by FDR. The Overlord planners and operational commanders gathered at COSSAC's conference in Scotland did not know so yet, but they were assured now that whatever plan they could craft for Overlord was on the calendar for review at the highest level.

6

COSSAC's Plan Emerges

Adopt the outlook that Operation Overlord is even now in progress.

—Lt. Gen. Sir Frederick Morgan, COSSAC, to the British Chiefs of Staff, July 15, 1943

The elements from which the plan for an Allied return to Europe could be assembled began to emerge on June 3 in London when Lieutenant General Morgan was allowed to read the report on the just-completed Trident Conference. Immediately Morgan communicated to his staff from memory, with documents en route by courier, both welcome new information on the resources to be provided and the new name for the operation, Overlord.[1] Four days later, Morgan followed up with another memorandum with confirming, amplifying details. The essence of the plan that COSSAC ultimately would produce started to take shape.[2]

For Overlord, the cross-Channel attack-based strategy, COSSAC was told to plan for an initial force of twenty-nine Allied divisions. There were to be landing craft sufficient for an initial assault on the French coast by five divisions, three Anglo-Canadian and two American. Of these, one British, one Canadian, and one American division would be in the initial landing with one British and one American division aboard ships for immediate follow-up. The objective of the twenty-nine divisions was to establish a lodgment in Europe. This amphibious endeavor, imbedded within Overlord, would be named Operation Neptune. With the lodgment established, the buildup on the Continent then would continue with three to five divisions arriving each month from the United States for the breakout and thrust across northwest Europe into Germany.

The apportionment of divisions to assault function by nationality had been a political decision that also influenced operational planning. Fulfilled was the political mandate that the national armies fight side by side, while avoiding an impractical crossing of lines of communication and logistical supply. This was done through a right flank/left flank assignment, looking from the sea south into France. Envisioned was "a Southwestward thrust by the American forces, covered to the East and Southeast by operation of the British Armies."[3] More precisely, composition of the latter would be Anglo-Canadian.

COSSAC planners learned from the Trident report that "a considerable body of troops, both American and British, battle hardened in the campaigns of North Africa, shall be transferred from that theatre to the United Kingdom in time to take part in Operation OVERLORD."[4] This crucial enhancement to the fighting qualities of the assault force combined with the limited number of divisions for which amphibious lift could be provided shaped COSSAC's planning in major ways.

Up to that time, the expected qualitative disparity between unproven Allied assault troops and defending German land forces had tended to favor selecting the closer Pas de Calais. By landing at that point nearer to England, the planners hoped, the numerically superior but short-ranged Allied fighter forces could achieve air supremacy, which in combination with shorter turnaround times for ships bringing reinforcements would compensate, they hoped, for the disparity between the Allied troops' combat experience and that of the enemy. This was perilously thin logic, recognized as such by the planners.[5]

The Germans could study maps equally well. COSSAC's estimate from Allied intelligence was that the Germans had transformed the Pas de Calais into "the most strongly defended area of the French coast and the pivot of the German coastal defense system."[6]

The anticipated leveling of the fighting qualities of opposing land forces, which would result from the Trident-authorized transfer of battle-tested Allied divisions, freed COSSAC to expand its options. Flying range constraints would limit time over the alternative beachheads and thus the impact of Allied fighter aircraft.

Now, however, the availability of more experienced ground troops allowed planners to accept the lesser criterion of air superiority, not supremacy, in order to expand their consideration of landing areas farther afield than the Pas de Calais.

At the same time, the amphibious lift available would constrain the initial assault to only three divisions. From that, Morgan deduced that "we must rule out of count immediately any question of dispersion of effort. The subdivision of so small an assault force as three divisions will inevitably lead to grave risk of defeat in detail."[7] Entertainment of multiple simultaneous landings was out.

Although there were alternative options specific to the Normandy coast, the basic choice for the supreme Allied commander was emerging as entry into northwestern Europe at one place, either through the Pas de Calais or Normandy. To develop that, Morgan directed that "the first task of our Air Sections is to appreciate the possibility of creating by [May 1, 1944] an acceptable air situation in an alternative area, which we know from prior examination to be that of the coastal strip lying between Cherbourg and Dieppe."[8]

Barely below the surface was the COSSAC team's initial qualified reaction to the new knowledge of the resources to be available. The margin for success with forces and tactics to a degree untested would be very thin. They worried that a five-division assault force, even one composed of combat-experienced troops, might not be sufficient to succeed, and they wished for more troops and the craft from which to land them.[9]

In COSSAC's view, the larger challenges to increasing the striking power for the cross-Channel attack were those within the Allies' span of control. These would be obtaining more ships, landing craft, fighters, and transport aircraft, plus achieving and sustaining supply and force buildup through damaged ports and over the beaches. Indirectly within Allied control, through the aerial striking potential of the Allied bomber force, well escorted over France, would be reducing the strength of the opposing German air force by D-Day and limiting the rate at which German reinforcements could reach the invasion area. Myriad other factors affected each perspective on the problem.

Concluding his new appreciation of resources available and their implications on June 7, 1943, Morgan reminded COSSAC planners of the time remaining. If the outline plan for Overlord was to reach the CCS in Washington on schedule, August 1, Morgan would need to submit the plan to the approval process with the British COS Committee in London thirty-three days hence.[10]

Still, agreement on an outline plan for Overlord refused to emerge from the complex mass of variables and conflicting opinions. To facilitate a solution, Vice Adm. Lord Louis Mountbatten, the chief of Combined Operations, proposed to Morgan a conference, dubbed Rattle, for COSSAC and the men who would be the operational commanders of the invasion forces. For the purpose, Mountbatten offered Combined Operations' training center in the requisitioned Hollywood Hotel in Largs, a seaside resort west of Glasgow.

Accepting Mountbatten's very welcome offer, Morgan nevertheless found that he was "in radical disagreement . . . in many respects" with the syllabus for Rattle that Mountbatten also proposed. A new syllabus was drafted by COSSAC in which time for engagement with senior officers was reduced and time was increased at the end for follow-up staff work.

Overlord would be addressed by the conference in the sequence of its component operational parts: mounting of the operation; assembly and embarkation of forces; cross-Channel voyage; the assault; follow-up and buildup phases; administrative [logistical] aspects of the buildup, including movement and maintenance [supply] problems during this phase; and combined signals organization. Lengthy discussion of the system of command and control or employment of air or airborne forces was to be deferred on grounds that the commanders would determine that for themselves.[11]

This would be followed by a visit to a nearby Combined Operations training station, HMS *Dun Donald*, which specialized in beach assault and organization and procedures for integrated communication. Provided would be further explanation of the combined signals organization; landing ships, craft, and amphibians; and mobile radio direction-finding equipment. At *Dun Donald* participants also would inspect the layout of a headquarters ship. Such ships had proven themselves off North Africa for Torch in 1942, and shortly would do so again in the invasion of Sicily. Headquarters ships would be critical assets for the ground force command staffs on D-Day.

Back at Largs, the conference would conclude with the scope of combined training for the assault phase, proposed combined training cycles, summary of decisions reached during the conference, and more periods as required.[12]

Difficult to conceal, the gathering for a multiday conference of so many Allied operational commanders, including forty-some general and flag officers, presented a security challenge.[13] That was turned to the advantage of COSSAC's first task of deception and feint, Cockcade. The fact of the Largs conference was used to reinforce a specific deception, Operation Tindall, which was intended to convey to the Germans the false suggestion of active planning for an Anglo-Russian invasion of northern Norway that in part would be mounted from Scotland.[14] Conference participation was set, as Morgan recalled, to "include all the principal contestants in our COSSAC scheming as well as the chief leaders of thought from outside our organization."[15] Put another way, they were key skeptics.

The risk of a lengthy discussion of the "strategical problem," shorthand for the Mediterranean versus cross-Channel debate and a sure touch point for Anglo-American disagreement, worried the planners. To deal with that in advance, Morgan wrote a read-ahead "strategical problem" background paper. There he defined the "strategical problem" exclusively in terms of COSSAC's mandate from the Combined Chiefs of Staff, elaborated by the Trident agreements.[16] For the assembled commanders, the larger strategy debate thus would be taken off the table.

Good plan. Conference Rattle, held from June 28 to July 1, 1943, began, as hoped, with the participants focused only on the challenges of a cross-Channel assault as their "strategical problem." These alone, however, were of sufficient difficulty to frustrate agreement.

Among many challenges in the proposed operation, greatest concern was expressed for fire support for the assault troops between suspension of air and naval bombardment and the troops' hitting the beaches and getting their own artillery into action. Arguing from the lessons of their exercises, army participants urged a landing "just before first light." Naval participants responded that the vast number and array of ships and craft would make organizing the landing in the dark of night "almost an impossible problem." Landing in daylight would be necessary. Work to resolve this basic issue would continue.[17]

With agreement on a plan still elusive, Morgan and Mountbatten persevered. Then a glimmer of approval came from one critic. Participants coalesced in support that grew to approach enthusiasm. They fixed on a cross-Channel assault in the vicinity of Caen near the base of the Cotentin Peninsula with some of the landed forces, American, swinging southwest to capture the port of Cherbourg by the fourteenth day after the landing (D+14). Rattle participants concluded from the then-relatively weak local defenses evident at the time that the Germans did not believe the Allies could make a successful assault through the Caen area. Success "would turn upon our surprising them by maintaining larger forces through these beaches than they expected, as a result of efficient beach maintenance [logistical] organization and development of artificial ports."[18]

In June 1943, cross-beach efficiency even remotely approaching the scale of Neptune in support of Overlord had not been demonstrated in combat by the Allies. Artificial ports were a new idea. However, exercises to show that required rates of over-the-beach resupply could be achieved had begun in the spring and would continue.[19] Field tests of components for artificial ports, which were under way in the harsh weather along the Scottish coast, were building confidence that the Allies indeed could take their ports with them.

One evening from the roof of the hotel, Rattle participants

watched the departure of a vast convoy outbound from the Clyde Estuary carrying the First Canadian Infantry Division to the Mediterranean for the invasion of Sicily. Through a talented Women's Royal Navy Service signaler, First Canadian Army commander Gen. Andrew McNaughton sent a flashing light message to the men in the ships to wish them well in their fight ahead.[20]

For Canadians, the convoy was a reminder that their country's five-division, two-brigade overseas army was being split into two widely separated corps by the existence of two competing Allied strategies.[21] For all the Rattle participants, the coincidence of the convoy's departure was sobering. They knew that Operation Husky, the imminent invasion of Sicily, would provide a limited test in combat not just of Allied troops but of many of the weapons, systems, and amphibious assault tactics that would be crucial to the success of a cross-Channel invasion. Before the eyes of these Overlord planners and commanders also sailed tangible evidence of the larger "strategical problem" the conference organizers had sought to set aside so as to focus on coming to grips with the needs of Overlord: the Mediterranean strategy's continuing competition with the cross-Channel attack for scarce combat resources.

Returning to London, Lord Mountbatten reported on Rattle to the Chiefs of Staff Committee on behalf of COSSAC and Lt. Gen. Jacob Devers, commander of the European Theater of Operations, U.S. Army. With twenty days remaining and new focus on the areas of concern and endorsement from the conference, the COSSAC planners turned with a will to completing the Overlord Outline Plan.[22]

The men and women of COSSAC always tackled the challenge of a return to the Continent with determination equally matched by spirit. At one point the Army Section made light of the seemingly intractable problems of over-the-beach buildup with a skit satirizing the Navy Section and titled "Operation Overboard." For security, all copies had to be withdrawn and destroyed quickly.[23] Had he met them, Shakespeare would have recognized COSSAC's "happy few."[24]

Their plan was completed in time to meet Morgan's dead-line. Printed on pale green paper and marked "U.S.—Secret British—Most Secret," the plan endeavored to make the most of the limited forces allotted. Envisioned and illustrated in mostly hand-drawn maps, the units' nationality were type-distinguished with colored pencil symbols. There were three main landing beaches between Ouistreham in the east and Isigny to the west, two British and one American. On D-Day, each beach would be assaulted by one division. Each assault division would be supported by a brigade-equivalent of tanks. The American division also would be reinforced by a regimental combat team. Covering the flanks and the stretch between the British and American beaches would be units of British Commandos and U.S. Army Rangers. A British airborne division would be dropped in the area surrounding the city of Caen. There would be three smaller insertions of American paratroopers behind the American beach. Hand-drawn was a detailed representation of one of the two artificial harbors to be created. There was an elaborate map of Normandy's terrain with soil composition color coded as to suitability for tactical airfields.[25]

The objective of the plan was to strike with forces from the UK on the then-target date of May 1, 1944, to "secure a lodgment on the Continent from which further offensive operations can be developed." The area of the lodgment was required to have port facilities sufficient to maintain an Allied ground force of twenty-six to thirty divisions and enable augmentation of the force at a rate of three to five divisions per month from the United States and elsewhere.[26]

The "Digest of Operations" for Overlord gave the reasons why Pas de Calais and Caen-Cotentin areas were most favored by COS-SAC's planners. These included access to beaches that were more sheltered from prevailing winds than those at other sites, a critical factor for getting ashore and expanding and sustaining the force over the beach. In the COSSAC planners' designation of operational areas, the Pas de Calais was defined to be the area between Gravelines and the River Somme. Caen was the area between the

River Orne and the base of Cotentin Peninsula. The Cotentin Peninsula included the port of Cherbourg.

To the planners, the advantages to landing in the Pas de Calais were offset by several concerns. One was the concentration of German fighter aircraft in that area. That was compounded by the assessment that still more of the Luftwaffe could be brought to bear in response to an Allied landing with minimal redeployment from its concentration of fighters to the north to defend against the long-range bombing of Germany.

The need to expand the Pas de Calais beachhead to gain the use of ports would present an unappealing choice: either a push west across many water obstacles to the French Channel ports of Le Harve and Rouen or northeast along the Belgian coast to reach Zeebrugge or even Antwerp, an area also replete with water obstacles.[27] These included polders that the Belgians had flooded to good defensive effect against the Germans in World War I.

From its outset, a landing in the Pas de Calais would confront the strongest German beach defenses on the French coast. These could be defeated through "very heavy and sustained bombardment from sea and air." However, the planners concluded that bombardment would introduce a further negative. The exits heading inland from the beaches would be damaged to an extent that would impede movement to build up Allied forces in the lodgment to exploit the landing.[28]

Terrain opportunities for expansion of a Pas de Calais lodgment were considered to be poor. They would require military maneuvers that would be unsound "unless the German forces are in a state not far short of final collapse."[29]

The COSSAC planners proposed instead a landing in the Caen-Cotentin area on the basis of comparative advantages that had emerged in their studies. They had determined that, like the Allies, the Luftwaffe also would be penalized by the flying distance from their bases to the Caen-Cotentin area. That improved the balance of advantages in favor of Allied versus German air power over the lodgment area. The terrain behind the landing beaches offered better potential for expansion of the lodgment, while avoiding intertwining the lines of supply for different national armies. For that reason Anglo-Canadian forces were assigned to the left flank to push toward Caen and the Americans to the right flank (again, looking from the sea) to push south and then swing west to capture the ports of Cherbourg and Brest.[30]

In selecting the Caen-Cotentin area over the Pas de Calais, the geography and disposition of Axis forces and beach defenses in France in mid-1943 had led the COSSAC planners to a stratagem that exploited the advent of a new technical capability, artificial ports. As discussed at the Rattle Conference, the stratagem was this:

> An attempt has been made to obtain tactical surprise by landing in a lightly defended area—presumably lightly defended as, due to its distance from a major port, the Germans consider a landing there unlikely to be successful. This action, of course, presupposes that we can offset the absence of a port in the initial stages by the provision of improvised sheltered waters. It is believed that this can be accomplished.[31]

Tactical surprise and concentration of force were the plan's foundation. Turning the Caen-Cotentin area's outward operational unattractiveness to Allied advantage enabled surprise. In the planners' view, "Concentration of the assault forces is considered essential if we are to ensure adequate air support and if our limited assault forces are to avoid defeat in detail."[32]

The "Overlord Outline Plan" was recommended as having a "reasonable prospect for success" by the COSSAC planners mindful of, and apprehensive about, the limited resources they had been allocated for the initial assault compared with the operation's importance and complexity. Their recommendation was made conditional on achievement of three goals: sustaining and expanding the Allied force over the French beaches until a port could be captured; reducing German fighter aircraft forces to the greatest possible extent; and not having more than twelve full-strength, first-rank German divisions in the area on D-Day. Stated in the Outline Plan, Lieutenant General Morgan also emphasized these conditions in his letter of transmission to the COS Committee.

Morgan wrote to the cos that, "in my opinion, it is possible to undertake the operation described, on or about the target date named, with the sea, land, and air forces specified, given a certain set of circumstances in existence at that time." Dividing these circumstances between those under the Allies' direct control and those under their indirect control, he first summarized the former. These were foremost the challenge, being addressed, of sustaining the invasion force over the beaches for two to three months until French port facilities could be restored and, second, the need to supply required shipping, naval landing craft, and transport aircraft. From this Morgan concluded that "in view of the limitations in resources imposed by my directive, we may be assured of a reasonable chance of success on 1 May 1944 only if we concentrate our efforts on an assault across the Norman beaches about Bayeux."[33]

Morgan's letter then turned to circumstances only indirectly under Allied control. Morgan cited the need to reduce "as far as it is humanly possible" on land and in the air over France "to the narrowest possible margin" the difference in strength between German forces defending from behind strong fortifications and Allied forces landing on the beaches after a cross-Channel voyage. Noting that considerable capability existed to affect this margin with forces available and growing in the United Kingdom, Morgan concluded that the Allies, nevertheless, were "largely dependent upon events that will take place on other war fronts, principally on the Russian front, between now and the date for the assault." As a basis for sustained coordination of every Allied effort to this end, Morgan suggested that the cos "adopt the outlook that Operation OVERLORD is even now in progress."[34]

In London on July 15, Morgan submitted cossac's draft outline plan for Overlord to the cos Committee in anticipation of the Quadrant Conference. Later that day, Generals Morgan and Barker also would host a visit to cossac and brief the "Overlord Outline Plan" to a key American participant, Secretary of War Henry L. Stimson. The timing of that meeting and the conclusions Stimson drew from it would prove critical.

7

The Green Hornet

We [were] astonished that especially Mr. Roosevelt was speaking so freely.

—Kurt Vetterlein, *Deutsche Reichspost*

Churchill's question written on a chit attached to a memorandum about the suspect security of the transatlantic radio-telephone brought his secretary up short: "What is the radio telephone, and when do we use it? Do I ever use it? W.S.C." Below, John Martin wrote in reply, "You have used the radio telephone in talking across the Atlantic and to Cairo. J.M.M. 4 September 1942."[1]

The British were right to be concerned. From the autumn of 1941 until the middle of July 1943, the Germans intercepted, decrypted, and listened to almost every word spoken via the radio-telephone's supposed protection, the A3 encryption system. The intelligence acquired included potentially every transatlantic telephone call between Churchill and Franklin D. Roosevelt during that nearly two-year period. The translated intelligence product was distributed to high-level German military and political leaders including Hitler.[2]

Rapid, secure communication by text and voice across the barrier of the Atlantic Ocean and between far-flung headquarters everywhere else was vital to Anglo-American coordination. Equally vital to the Axis was protected communication between Berlin and Germany's deployed forces, embassies, and Axis allies.

The story of Ultra, the Allies' decryption and exploitation of German text messages encrypted on Enigma machines and broadcast over the air, has been told often. Also known is the story of Magic, the breaking and reading of Japanese encrypted messages. Diplomatic reporting from Japan's ambassador in Berlin back to Tokyo was a rich source of information about Germany for the

Allies. The corresponding British and American electromechanical text encryption systems were superior to the Germans' Enigma machine for sending text messages and were not broken by German cryptanalysts.[3]

Penetration into encrypted voice communication was another matter. There the Germans had gained the advantage. By responding to better secure their voice communication, the Allies shut off a valuable source of intelligence to the Germans eleven months before D-Day, a time during which the ability to talk by telephone securely and frequently across the Atlantic to plan and prepare for the invasion was vital to the Allies.

From the start of the war until July 1943, there was only one secure voice option available for calls by radiotelephone between Washington and London or elsewhere by the Allies. That was the commercial A3 system, employing 1920s technology.[4] The A3 was maintained in New York by the American Telephone and Telegraph Company and in London by the British Post Office for all transatlantic calls. Observing the A3 with interest was a young *Deutsche Reichspost* radio engineer, Kurt Vetterlein. Vetterlein believed that he could surmount the technical challenges to break the A3 system.[5]

To encipher spoken words, A3 depended on synchronizing keys at the send and receive ends with a precise time signal. Vetterlein and his colleagues built an apparatus of equivalent synchronized timing accuracy that could beat the A3's pattern of enciphering, which shifted every twenty seconds on a thirty-six-step cycle. The Germans' cryptanalytic key had to be changed every few seconds, even in the absence of an actual voice transmission, in order to stay synchronized with the A3 signal.[6] The apparatus worked.

Vetterlein was placed in charge of a small radio intercept unit and established in a commandeered youth hostel on the North Sea coast of the Netherlands, near Nordwijk. From there, and later from inland Eindhoven after coastal commando raids elsewhere raised concern, Vetterlein's unit continuously monitored the only radio frequency for A3 between London and Washington. Vetterlein's unit intercepted, recorded, decoded, and translated as many as sixty calls per day, but never fewer than thirty calls, made on the A3 link, which Churchill and Roosevelt used frequently.[7]

Listening to oral communication brought added value to intelligence.[8] Although sound was distorted in this early voice encryption system, interception of the spoken word could yield intelligence inferences from reactions not evident in text messages. For example, was the speaker making certain points with emphasis or, conversely, by hesitating?[9] Roosevelt and Churchill used code names, but through the distortion, German interpreters still could recognize their distinctive voices.[10]

Field-translated intercepts were sent by land line and courier to the ss in Berlin, then distributed to the Oberkommando der Wehrmacht (High Command of the Armed Forces), the Foreign Ministry, and senior Nazi leaders including Hitler. After Vetterlein's unit made some mistakes in translation, all of the raw intercepts were sent to Berlin for translation.[11]

From at least as early as December 1941, the Allies knew that the security of information transmitted with the A3 system's encryption was questionable at best. They went to work to develop a genuinely secure replacement. Doing so at the cutting edge of the day's technology, however, would take time. In the interim, the Allies sought to instill security consciousness in A3 users. They established censors in Washington and London to monitor A3 calls with authority to interrupt if classified conversation discipline broke down.[12] At the start of an A3 call, a "minder" would caution users on each end that the enemy was listening.

To the German intercept operators, that precautionary warning in itself became a "tell." Among Allied censors, there was natural reluctance to wag a finger at very senior A3 users. Thus the absence of a warning statement at the beginning of a call alerted the Germans that someone important was about to come on the line. Interviewed by historian David Kahn in 1967, Vetterlein recalled, "We were smiling about this." The question on Winston Churchill's chit attached to a memorandum on communication security shows that as late as September 1942, the prime minister was insufficiently aware of the threat.[13] As for the senior Washington participant, Vetterlein recalled to Kahn, "We [were] astonished that especially Mr. Roosevelt was speaking so freely."[14]

Communication security officers despaired that the response from A3 users at lower levels was to attempt to "talk around" sensitive information by using initials and euphemisms such as "the Big Man." This never is a good practice when under attack by a skilled service that could place each call into the context of an intelligence mosaic. In a note to all British cabinet ministers, the reality was put bluntly: "As far, therefore, as the enemy are concerned all radiotelephony transmissions should be looked on as having no more secrecy than if they were in ordinary speech, and we can be tolerably certain that they are all overheard by the enemy, who, we know, watch our wireless traffic."[15]

The Americans had entered the war with a bloody lesson in cost of not having a form of telephonic communication that engendered security confidence. Holding in hand, on the morning of December 7, 1941, the warning from American codebreakers that a Japanese attack in the Pacific was imminent, General Marshall also was confronted by his personal doubts about the security of the A3 voice encryption system. How to warn Hawaii, five time zones behind Washington, without risking compromise of the precious secret of American access into Japanese encrypted messages? The A3 radiotelephone would be faster but not sufficiently secure, Marshall decided. He instead sent the threat warning to Pacific commanders by coded radiotelegraph. Pearl Harbor received Marshall's warning while already under Japanese attack.[16]

Stung by the failure to warn of the Japanese surprise attack, the U.S. Army immediately began to look for a better voice encryption system. Since 1936, the Bell Telephone Laboratories had been exploring conversion of analogue voice into digital data. The promise in Bell's results led to an Army contract in 1942.[17]

By the beginning of 1943, building on its own research and early work by the brilliant British computing pioneer Alan Turing, Bell had produced a new system involving forty racks of equipment and weighing fifty-five tons. Essential to its functionality, the new system that digitized human speech for encryption, transmission, and decryption incorporated multiple fundamentally new technological developments. The patents for these would be kept secret for thirty-four years.[18] At a secret Pentagon ceremony to inaugurate its use between Washington and London, the president of Bell Telephone Laboratories, Dr. O. E. Buckley, gave a summary description for laypeople of what had been accomplished:

> Speech has been converted into low frequency signals that are not speech but contain a specification or description of it. Those signals have been coded by a system that defies decoding by any but the intended recipient. The coded signals have been transmitted over a radio circuit in such a way that an interceptor cannot even distinguish the presence or absence of the signals. At the receiving end, the signals have been decoded and restored and then used to generate speech nearly enough like that which gave them birth that it may be clearly understood.[19]

The system's cryptographic key was wideband thermal noise converted to a frequency shift keyed (FSK) audio tone in multiple frequencies and recorded on vinyl phonograph discs. These were shipped to system operators and, when used, synchronized to a precise time signal. The turntables on which the discs were played were, themselves, exceptionally constant in their rotation.[20]

Highly secure, this forerunner of the voice encryption systems used today was given the nonsense cover name Sigsaly.[21] The impenetrable system's only external signal was a buzzing suggestive of the frenetically undulating musical theme of a then-popular radio mystery program. That prompted another informal name for Sigsaly among its operators, the Green Hornet.

The Americans were extremely protective of both Sigsaly's revolutionary technology and the secret of its existence. That contributed to Sigsaly arriving in London as though from Mars. On February 15, 1943, Lt. Gen. Sir Hastings Ismay informed Churchill:

> A United States officer has just arrived in London with instructions to install an apparatus of an entirely new kind for ensuring speech

secrecy over the radio-telephone. The apparatus is an American invention, of which three are in existence. . . . We know little or nothing about it, except that it requires three rooms to house it and six men to operate it. . . . The only Englishman who has so far been allowed to see it is Dr. Turing of the Government Code and Cypher School. The Chiefs of Staff are not sure that he is sufficiently qualified on all aspects to be able to give a final opinion. . . . The fact that the Americans desire to retain complete control of this apparatus, and to prevent our experts from becoming familiar with it, is perhaps strange. Nevertheless, the Chiefs of Staff do not recommend that any objection should be raised by us at this stage.[22]

Churchill, by 1943, was fully appreciative of the German voice communication interception threat and, at least on this topic, unmoved by staff wariness of Americans. Taking up his red ink pen, at the bottom of Ismay's February 15 memorandum, the prime minister simply wrote, "Good."

Installation of Sigsaly proved to be time-consuming. Not until July 15, five months later, was a Sigsaly system, operated by the U.S. Army Signal Corps, up and running in London and Washington. The London system was located in a U.S. communications complex in the basement annex to Selfridge's Department Store. A secure line ran to Churchill's War Cabinet Office a mile away. Another Sigsaly was set up in the Pentagon in Washington with secure landlines to the White House and the State Department.[23] The Germans soon noticed a significant drop in the number of A3 calls and deduced that another secure voice system must have been put into use, but they never identified the purpose of Sigsaly's signal, let alone decrypted its traffic.[24]

Sigsaly apparently did not bring a complete end to use of the insecure A3 system by Churchill and Roosevelt. The evening of July 28, 1943, Vetterlein's unit intercepted and decoded a Churchill-to-FDR scrambled telephone call on a line between War Cabinet rooms and the White House. Their connection was the compromised A3, not the new secure radiotelephone link.[25] Churchill and FDR discussed the coup that had ousted Mussolini and how to approach the new Italian government. Alerted by the intercept, the Oberkommando der Wehrmacht concluded prematurely that secret Allied negotiations with the Italians already were under way, but took steps to move German troops, which proved prudent.[26]

The relative advantage in protection of their high-level communication had tilted in favor of the Allies. Suspected but unconfirmed by the Germans was that their own enciphered and broadcasted text communication had been compromised and was being read by the Allies. While Enigma hemorrhaged German secrets, equivalent Allied enciphered text was not readable by the Germans. Now Allied radiotelephone calls had gone dark to Berlin. Sigsaly was a boon for secure voice communication between Allied military leaders physically separated by the Atlantic at a critical time, the eleven months remaining before D-Day and the drive from the West to liberate Europe that would follow.

Denied the most valuable intelligence to be drawn from decryption of intercepted radiotelephone transmissions, German situation awareness had become fatally compromised. In order to gain actionable knowledge of Allied intentions in the West, the Germans were even more dependent on tactical reconnaissance and their agents infiltrated into Britain. Reconnaissance could be and was being fooled. All of their agents had been captured and turned against the Germans in a vast, integrated deception that focused increasingly on preparing the battlefield for D-Day.

8

Hammer and Tongs

My principal objective had been to visit troops. But when I reached London the PM virtually took possession of my movements for the first week.... These unexpected subjects were so important that I devoted the bulk of my time to their consideration and altered my trip accordingly.

    —Secretary of War Henry L. Stimson, August 4, 1943

Henry Lewis Stimson, at seventy-five years of age in 1943, was serving his fourth president. For the second time Stimson was the U.S. secretary of war. Patrician in background and education, Stimson had been appointed U.S. attorney for the Southern District of New York by President Theodore Roosevelt. He had served as President Taft's secretary of war. Having risen to the rank of colonel as an artillery officer in France in World War I, Stimson subsequently was appointed governorgeneral of the Philippines and then secretary of state by President Hoover. An internationalist and proponent of aid to Britain and France, Republican Stimson again was appointed secretary of war by Franklin D. Roosevelt, a Democrat, in June 1940. He took up his post as Britain was in the last days of a scramble to rescue its army from the beaches of Dunkirk and France was collapsing under the German Blitzkrieg.

In the new War Department Building and later at the completed Pentagon across the Potomac, Stimson and Army Chief of Staff Gen. George Marshall worked in close partnership from adjoining wood-paneled offices between which the door never was closed.[1] Stimson became a strong advocate for Marshall's strategy for taking the war in Europe to Germany through a cross-Channel attack into northwestern Europe. Both Stimson and Marshall served on the Military Policy Committee formed by FDR to advise him on the project to develop an atomic bomb.

Thursday morning, July 8, 1943, Secretary Stimson, his special assistant, Harvey Bundy, and his aides gathered at Washington National Airport in the Inter-Continental Hangar of Trans World Airlines. They were to begin the secretary's long-delayed trip to Britain to meet with U.S. forces and commanders in the European Theater.[2]

Their plane was a four-engine Douglas C-54 crewed and operated by TWA on contract to the Army Air Force. The plane had been modified to provide "every imaginable convenience aboard," and for Stimson's trip it carried extensive survival gear for a variety of climates from tropical to subarctic.[3] At 9:20, Stimson's plane took off into an overcast sky on the first leg. Theirs would become a 12,000-mile trip after Winston Churchill took over Stimson's schedule in Britain and, as a result, General Marshall urged Stimson to fly on to North Africa to get another opinion from Gen. Dwight D. Eisenhower.

Separately making their way by air from Washington to London, via New York, Lisbon, and Ireland, were FDR's science adviser, Dr. Vannevar Bush, and two antisubmarine warfare technology experts. Bush had been invited by Sir Stafford Cripps to attend a meeting of the War Cabinet Anti-U-boat Committee on July 15. The three Americans expected to use their time in Britain to work with their British colleagues in the Allied Anti-Submarine Working Group.[4] However, the coincidence of Bush and Stimson's presence in London would lead to a meeting with Churchill on July 22 critical to both Anglo-American cooperation on atomic bomb research and Allied strategy for the European theater. Bush, who had lunched with FDR on June 24, believed that he was prepared for an atomic research sharing discussion, but only if need be.[5]

Delayed by weather, Stimson's party finally took to the air again from Gander, Newfoundland, headed for Iceland on the evening of July 9. As their C-54 flew northeastward through the dusk of the subarctic summer night, 4,000 miles to the southeast, ten Allied divisions of Operation Husky began assaulting beaches and parachuting onto landing grounds in the invasion of Sicily.[6] The Allies were stepping onto a doorstep into the Continent from the south while, far to the east on the steppes of Russia, the titanic Battle of Kursk raged between 2.7 million German and Soviet soldiers.

After twenty-four hours inspecting troops and meeting with U.S., Danish, and Icelandic officials, Stimson flew on to Prestwick, Scotland. Arriving in Windsor by overnight train from Prestwick early on July 12, they took up residence at Stanwell, a sixteenth-century shooting lodge built for Henry VIII.[7]

Upon completing a day of initial meetings with British and American officials, Stimson went to No. 10 Downing Street to dine with the Churchill's, Ambassador and Mrs. John Gilbert Winant, and Foreign Secretary Sir Anthony Eden. Discussion quickly turned to Operation Overlord, which Stimson referred to in all his reports on this trip as "Round Hammer."[8] Churchill again expressed his apprehension about direct attack, and Eden "painted a rosy picture of the possibilities of stimulating trouble in the Balkans and Greece against the Nazis."

Stimson responded in the context of the approaching presidential election. He described to Churchill and Eden "the political danger of a delay, pointing out the tenseness of the situation in the U.S. and the danger of the people not understanding or approving further penetration of the Eastern Mediterranean; the consequent possible loss of prestige to the President, with the immense consequent damage to the Common Cause."[9] Stimson explained that "only by an intellectual effort had [the American people] been convinced that Germany was their most dangerous enemy and should be disposed of before Japan." Their anger at Japan's aggression, he said, competed with their acceptance of the "Europe first" strategy.[10] In his report on the trip, Stimson reflected that he did not think Churchill had had the situation in the United States explained to him that way before.[11]

After departing from the dinner, Stimson and Ambassador Winant told each other that they had been encouraged by Churchill's support for Bolero and Overlord, "with conditions . . . less destructful than before." Over conversations in the week that followed, but from this dinner particularly, Stimson formed an assessment of Churchill that he would express to General Marshall in a secure telephone call on July 19. The prime minister, Stimson observed, was prepared to keep his commitment to cross-Channel assault but that his impulsive attraction to tangential commitments could make preparations for the cross-Channel assault impossible. Churchill's commitment to advancing in Italy was strong.[12]

The next day, Stimson met with Brig. Gen. Ira Eaker, the commander of the U.S. Eighth Air Force. Stimson found Eaker "intensely interested in a thorough softening-up of the opposition on the Continent, and gave every evidence of desiring to go on according to the directive," meaning the Combined Bomber Offensive agreed upon at Casablanca in January.

Stimson sat next to Churchill again at a dinner in the secretary of war's honor given by Winant at Claridge's Hotel on July 14. The dinner was attended by most of the senior British and American officials whom the secretary would be seeing in the days ahead. Stimson observed that he and Churchill further discussed the matters they had gone over two nights earlier; the substance of their remarks to each other is not in the record.[13]

* * *

Now emerged the issue of sharing Anglo-American atomic information that soon would draw in Stimson. About to attend a July 15 meeting of the War Cabinet Anti-U-boat Committee, Dr. Vannevar Bush called on Churchill at No. 10 Downing Street. Escorted by Minister for Air Sir Stafford Cripps, Bush had expected the visit to take thirty seconds "to pay his respects." Churchill, however, confronted the American on the breakdown in atomic sharing and then floated his approach to a solution.

The essence of their exchange can be reconstructed from fragmentary accounts in British and American records. Bush wrote in 1970 that Churchill upbraided him for "ten to fifteen minutes" on the atomic information interchange issue describing the U.S. position as unfair, unreasonable, and nonsensical.[14] To support his position, Churchill produced a copy of the

January 1943 Conant memorandum. According to the British official history, Bush replied that he was "shocked at the document and doubted whether it had even existed," adding that he himself had never seen it.[15]

Bush, however, had communicated with James Conant about the drafting of his memorandum. He was involved in drafting the Military Policy Committee's December 15 recommendation to FDR, which was identical in substance if more constructively worded. Bush knew the committee's recommendation had been conveyed to the British and certainly knew of James Conant's communication with the British.[16]

According to Bush's own meeting notes, handwritten on No. 10 Downing Street stationery, the prime minister had more fundamental points. Churchill told Bush that he "had the Pres[ident's] word of honor to share equally." Churchill then alluded to "the threat from the East," underlined by Bush. Concluding his notes, Bush recorded Churchill's statement that the "Pres[ident] agreed that interchange should be resumed." According to Bush's notes, Churchill believed FDR's oral commitment had been made in an undated telephone call between the two leaders in response to a July 9, 1943, cable from Churchill.[17] According to U.S. records, FDR's response to Churchill's cable was to consult Harry Hopkins, who reminded the president of his oral commitment to Churchill, May 25–26, at the close of the Trident Conference.[18] FDR did not issue instructions to Bush to "renew" the information exchange until July 20, 1943. The textual meaning of that message from the president to Bush apparently was intentionally altered before it left Washington.

Conversing with Bush, Churchill introduced most of the elements of an Anglo-American agreement to resolve the matter. Churchill's points would evolve and expand. In this first airing, they included interchange of all information, commitment never to use an atomic weapon without the consent of the other party, and deferral to a decision by the U.S. president on British commercial use of atomic energy. Churchill avowed "no interest" in commercial aspects.[19]

When the prime minister had finished, Bush replied, "The American atomic energy development is now under the Army. The Secretary of War of the United States is in London, and I certainly do not propose to discuss this subject in his absence." Having asked for a follow-up talk early in their exchange, Churchill replied that he would defer the matter to "a full-dress discussion" later.[20] That afternoon, Bush apprised Harvey Bundy, Stimson's aide, of the meeting and the gist of Churchill's case. Bush used the next several days to prepare his own response.[21]

On the day he upbraided Bush, July 15, Churchill was generally combative and assertive. He approved Operation Gomorrah, a series of four night bombing raids by the RAF that would devastate the German city of Hamburg with fire storms now estimated to have caused between 37,000 and 40,000 deaths.[22] On July 15, Churchill also wrote to South African field marshal Jan Smuts, a close adviser, with regard to Allied strategy: "I will in no circumstances allow the powerful British and British-controlled armies in the Mediterranean to stand idle. . . . Not only must we take Rome and much as far north as possible in Italy, but our right hand must give succor to the Balkan patriots. . . . I shall go to all lengths to procure the agreement of our Allies. If not, we have ample forces to act by ourselves."[23] Although Churchill's conditions for Bolero and Overlord, stated to Stimson and Winant three nights earlier, may have been "less destructful than before," in his letter to Smuts, the prime minister was resolute in pursuit of his Mediterranean goals.

* * *

A short distance from No. 10 Downing Street, Stimson was visiting COSSAC, the Overlord planning office at Norfolk House, for what Stimson later described as "the most important meeting I had had." Stimson received a briefing by the U.S. deputy for COSSAC, Maj. Gen. Ray Barker, on the just-completed "Overlord Outline Plan" followed by a frank discussion with Lieutenant General Morgan and Barker. Both men impressed Stimson not only with their confidence in the plan but also with their deep concern about distractions that could dissipate the forces intended to be available when the time came for the cross-Channel attack. According to Stimson, Morgan candidly was "very fearful of delays caused by getting too deep into commitments in the Mediterranean." In particular, he felt that it was imperative that the divisions being released from the Mediterranean for Overlord on the first of November actually should be free to move back to the UK starting on that date and not merely to plan to come back."[24] Though probably known to the British COS Committee informally, these concerns had not been in Morgan's cover letter when he submitted the plan to them earlier that day.[25]

The fact that Morgan and Barker had presented the "Overlord Outline Plan" to the U.S. secretary of war soon would influence the two generals to send the plan to Washington before they had approval to do so from the British COS Committee. What Stimson heard from Morgan and Barker in London would also add critical weight to his report to Roosevelt.

Subsequent to meeting with Morgan and Barker, Stimson also talked with Lt. Gen. Jacob Devers, commander of ETOUSA, who was concerned about the delay of a large contingent from the United States that included one division. Stimson found Devers's fears to be similar to Morgan's.[26] A week later, on July 22, Stimson had lunch with Lt. Gen. John C. H. Lee, commander of the U.S. Army Service Forces. A concerned Lee wanted no curtailment of the flow of the logistical buildup of weapons and materiel into the United Kingdom, a position that complemented exactly the concern for the troop buildup expressed by Devers and the COSSAC planners.

* * *

That day from Washington, President Roosevelt continued his quest for a private meeting with Joseph Stalin. In a cable to Stalin, apologizing for a friendly fire incident in the North Pacific, FDR wrote, "I hope to hear from you very soon about the other matter which I still feel to be of great importance to you and me." Handwritten notation on the surviving copy of this cable reads,

"In President's letter to Stalin via Amb. Davies," who delivered it in Moscow on May 5, 1943.[27]

The following day Roosevelt cabled Churchill again. FDR had "still heard nothing from U.J." When he did hear from Stalin, he would let Churchill "know at once about ABRAHAM [the Quebec Conference]." He liked Churchill's suggested date.[28] In a breezy way, the president had reminded Churchill that the upcoming Anglo-American strategy conference, precise dates still to be determined, could be influenced by an exclusively bilateral meeting between the U.S. president and the leader of the Soviet Union.

* * *

Blocks away from the White House, the Combined Chiefs of Staff permanent representatives were meeting at the old Public Health Building. The American representatives had a new initiative. With Admiral King's support, General Marshall proposed to the CCS that Eisenhower be sounded out about a landing in Italy south of Rome as a flanking attack. Marshall's intent was to knock Italy out of the war. The Allies then could go on the defensive in Italy and concentrate on the buildup in the United Kingdom for the cross-Channel invasion. The British representatives at the CCS staff meeting enthusiastically endorsed Marshall's proposal and suggested landing south of Rome in late August.[29] The report from the July 16 meeting in Washington would not take long to reach Churchill in London.

Since Roosevelt's June 28 proposal to Churchill for a full-dress conference at the Citadel in Quebec City,[30] the U.S. military leadership and Harry Hopkins had been anxious to learn precisely when and where Churchill would land in North America for the gathering. Their concern was that Churchill would come early to meet privately with Roosevelt and—once again—influence him in favor of the British position on Allied strategy in advance of the Joint Chiefs' battle to control the outcome of the formal conference. Should that happen, the timing could be bad for the U.S. side. Marshall and King knew that internal support for the U.S. strategy for the conference was not yet solid. Some staff organizations in the Pentagon were experiencing doubts of their own about their commitment to cross-Channel attack.

For both countries' leadership, the regular CCS staff meetings in Washington were not just a forum for formal exchanges but also a fertile source of informal information. The Americans were alert for hints as to Churchill's next move in the contest for FDR's support for either of the strategy alternatives. At this CCS meeting, side conversations with the British about Churchill's intentions may have stimulated concern among American officers for an early visit to FDR by Churchill and triggered action to forestall that.

What is known from Harry Hopkins's telephone records is that late on Friday afternoon, after the close of the CCS meeting, the president's closest adviser spoke with the head of FDR's Secret Service detail, Michael Reilly, and the JCS chairman, Adm. William Leahy. Late the next morning, Hopkins spoke again by telephone with Reilly.[31] Reilly and Dewey Long of the White House Travel Office planned and organized the president's travels away from Washington.

Taken off the shelf at the White House was a proposal for a fishing trip to McGregor Bay in Ontario, Canada, 760 miles to the northwest, first put forward in April 1942 by Zenith Radio Corporation founder E. F. McDonald.[32] Coincidental or not, presidential travel began to be arranged with dates that would narrow Churchill's opportunities to meet with Roosevelt by hanging a "gone fishing" sign on the White House. Although FDR eventually would share advanced knowledge of the trip with Churchill, the out-of-country excursion deep into Ontario's north country would be kept unusually secret.

* * *

Saturday morning in England, July 17, the prime minister took the U.S. secretary of war on a daytrip to inspect coastal defenses. Churchill's special train steamed out of Victoria Station and, clear of London, picked up speed eastward through the countryside of Kent as its passengers sat down in wing chairs to breakfast.

They were bound for Dover and the Channel coast.[33] The train was equipped with a dining car, a generator, and communications that could be connected to London from anywhere on Britain's railways. At the heart of the train were two splendid early twentieth-century coaches that had been intended for royalty. Elegantly paneled, carpeted, and upholstered, the cars offered Churchill and his guests open saloons, bedrooms, a conference room, and an office for the prime minister.[34]

Detraining at Dover, the party inspected coastal artillery batteries that sometimes dueled with German long-range guns across the Channel, shelters for Royal Navy motor torpedo boats that went out to stalk and skirmish with German E-boats, and subterranean command bunkers "newly enlarged for major trans-Channel operations."[35] Churchill's agenda for Stimson, however, was anything but favorable to cross-Channel attack.

Back aboard the train, over lunch, Churchill pressed Stimson hard on alternatives to Overlord, producing a British cable that he had received based on the previous day's CCS staff meeting in Washington. Stating that Marshall wanted a study of Avalanche, an amphibious assault onto the Italian mainland at Salerno near Naples, Churchill argued to Stimson that the cable meant Marshall had come over to support Churchill's Mediterranean strategy. Stimson responded that Marshall only wanted to get the drive to Rome out of the way so as to focus on Overlord.[36]

Churchill then took Stimson into his onboard office for an earnest conversation alone and "at length" about the issue of atomic information sharing. Stimson recorded that Churchill was "most anxious that I should help him by intervening in that matter and he would hold himself open at any date to meet me, Dr. Bush, and Mr. Bundy during this coming week. He was to have present with him a few members of his staff, and the Lord President of the Council [Sir John Anderson, director of Britain's atomic program]."[37] Very likely, the prime minister used this conversation to sketch to Stimson the elements of the Anglo-American agreement forming in his mind which he had tried out on Vannevar Bush on July 15. Now expanded by Churchill beyond resuming information interchange, the agreement he proposed entered into aspects of a postwar atomic relationship between the two countries. In its scope, the proposed agreement could test the legal limits of FDR's war powers.

Already apprised by Harvey Bundy of Churchill's confrontation with Bush two days earlier, Stimson probably anticipated Churchill's approach on the train. Now, direct from the source, Stimson had a fuller understanding. As a member of the Military Policy Committee advising FDR, Stimson was well informed on this highly secret and complex topic. Stimson also was attuned to the tension between Churchill's enduring resistance to the U.S. strategy of direct attack and his intense desire for Britain to be restored to access to atomic weapons research.

* * *

In the afternoon on July 19, Stimson went to the U.S. Army's headquarters for European theater operations where, after generally reviewing his meetings in London and the state of CCS decisions on strategy with Lt. Gen. Jacob Devers and Maj. Gen. Alexander Surles, Stimson conducted a secure radiotelephone call over the new Sigsaly system with General Marshall in Washington. Stimson told Marshall of his impression of Churchill, that "he was honestly ready to keep his pledge as to 'Round Hammer,' but was impulsively likely to branch out into commitments which would make it impossible, and further that he was very set on a march to Rome." To Stimson's description of his Saturday response to Churchill, that Marshall's intentions for Italy were limited to facilitating renewed concentration on Overlord, Marshall replied, "That was exactly right, you were quite right, that was what I meant." Marshall then urged Stimson to travel to North Africa to get Eisenhower's view.[38]

* * *

The parallel, but separate, Anglo-American negotiation on resuming atomic cooperation, which came ever closer to the strategy negotiations, now advanced in London. That, however, began with a curious turn in Washington.

Prodded by Churchill again, and on the advice of Harry Hopkins,[39] President Roosevelt took action on Tuesday, July 20, to move forward the issue of atomic information interchange. FDR dictated an instruction to Vannevar Bush that would cause consternation among the leadership of the Manhattan Project. Knowing Bush was in London, the note to his science adviser was sent by courier to the Office of Scientific Research and Development, located at the Carnegie Institute at 1530 P Street, N.W., in Washington, for forward transmission:

Dear Van:

While the Prime Minister was here we discussed the whole question of exchange of information regarding tube alloys, including the building project.

While I am mindful of the vital necessity for security in regard to this I feel that our understanding with the British encompasses the complete exchange of all information.

I wish, therefore, that you would renew, in an inclusive manner, the full exchange of information with the British Government regarding tube alloys.

Sincerely yours,
Franklin D. Roosevelt[40]

The note was received at OSRD by Bush's executive assistant, Dr. Carroll L. Wilson. OSRD's communication procedure required paraphrasing the substance of a classified message, as a common additional security measure, before submitting it for encryption and radio transmission, in this case to the OSRD Liaison Office's London Mission.[41] Wilson was responsible for paraphrasing FDR's message, and he anticipated trouble.

As Bush's executive assistant, Wilson was involved closely with discussions and deliberations between Bush and James Conant. Wilson had drafted the original uranium development agreement with the British. On receiving FDR's note to Bush on July 20, Wilson immediately recognized the significance of Roosevelt's instruction as a major step beyond the "need to know" policy toward the British. Wilson knew that Conant, Bush, and Groves were opposed to sharing further atomic information with the British.

Wilson's personal position on the matter is not evident in archived OSRD papers, but his actions are. Wilson consulted at least with Conant before forwarding FDR's instruction. He paraphrased the president's text for transmission in a manner sympathetic to the position of its opponents. On July 27, OSRD had the Navy encrypt and transmit the president's July 20 instruction to Bush in the following paraphrase:

> To Bush.
>
> Letter to you from your Chief requests you review in an inclusive manner full exchange with the U.K. on Essone. Conant taking no action and will not discuss with anyone awaiting your instructions on return.
>
> From Carroll L. Wilson[42]

In paraphrasing Roosevelt's text, Dr. Wilson replaced the critical verb, *renew*, with *review*, thus altering the instruction's intent. Wilson added for Bush information about how Conant would handle the matter until Bush returned. In a note to the president sent July 28 confirming that he had paraphrased and sent FDR's message, but not saying how it was paraphrased, Wilson wrote, "Tomorrow [July 29] I shall bring your letter to the attention of Dr. James B. Conant upon his return to Washington."[43] Apparent from the paraphrase sent to Bush, however, is that Wilson already had communicated with Conant about Roosevelt's instruction to Bush. That Conant knew the content of FDR's letter is evident in Conant's cable to Bush on July 29, received in London after Dr. Bush had left for Washington. Conant asked Bush if he wanted him to convene a meeting on the issue with the Military Policy Committee and General Groves in Bush's absence.[44]

Onward transmission of the president's instruction to Bush to "renew" full exchange with the British was held in suspense by Wilson for seven days, a week in which Vannevar Bush and Secretary of War Stimson would have a critical meeting with Churchill unaware of the president's new instruction. When the message did reach Bush, he still would be misinformed by its altered language. Not until Bush returned to Washington and saw FDR's original note was his misperception clarified.

* * *

Unaware that two days earlier Roosevelt had stepped into the issue but that his instruction was sitting in a safe in Washington, Bush sat down in London with Churchill, Stimson, and Lord Cherwell for their meeting on atomic information sharing to which, not by chance, Stimson added a separate meeting with Churchill on strategy for Europe.

The morning of July 22, Stimson, Harvey Bundy, and Bush met at Claridge's Hotel to prepare for their meeting that afternoon with Churchill and his key scientific advisers on the highly secret atomic sharing issue. On grounds of law and policy, particularly the limits of Roosevelt's war powers, Bush and Bundy advised caution. Neither wanted to see resolution of postwar issues with a foreign power, such as an atomic military capability or atomic power commercial advantage for Britain, determined by presidential executive action that might challenge congressionally authorized war powers constrained to steps necessary to win this war.[45] The essence of the information sharing policy in the 1942 Military Policy Committee recommendation to the president, then being implemented across the Manhattan Project, was access to information on the basis of "need to know" in order to win the current war. Without referring to other rumblings within the U.S. atomic leadership, if he knew about them, Bundy advised Stimson to frame his responses to Churchill within the limits of FDR's war powers.

Bush was taken through his position on interchange of information rigorously by Stimson. The secretary of war used the adversarial format of a mock trial to test FDR's scientific adviser's argument. Later in the afternoon, as they walked to No. 10 Downing Street, a satisfied Stimson told Bush to take the lead in the discussion of the s-1 matter according to Bush's approach to how atomic information sharing should be handled.[46]

Bush, who opposed sharing with the British, was surprised by Stimson's delegation to him of the discussion on S-1. The secretary of war earlier had made clear to Bush that he wanted a postwar Anglo-American partnership and considered Churchill's position on atomic sharing to be correct.[47] Bush asked Stimson directly if his intent was for Bush to speak for the American side from his own oppositional perspective of the issue. This Stimson affirmed. From that Bush concluded that the purpose of the exercise at Claridge's had been to confirm that "I had my arguments in order."[48]

True enough. However, with much of the summation that he himself planned to offer to Churchill already formed in his mind, and tasked by Roosevelt to press Churchill on cross-Channel assault, Stimson probably saw Bush's tactical role in the larger context of a strategy of quid pro quo.[49] There is irony in the fact that the boundaries of the OSRD director's extensive wartime responsibilities left Bush outside European strategy discussions. For those, Bush lacked the "need to know."

Stimson, Bush, and Bundy were received at No. 10 Downing Street by Winston Churchill, Sir John Anderson, and Churchill's science adviser, Lord Cherwell. Anderson and Lord Cherwell were the top leadership of Tube Alloys. Absent from accounts of the discussion that followed are allusions to Britain launching an independent atomic bomb development program. These certainly were in each participant's mind from previous discussions, as recently as one week earlier.

Beginning the meeting, Churchill recounted FDR's oral assurances to him on three occasions that atomic bomb research would be a joint enterprise. None of the president's assurances had been committed to paper and, obvious to the British, none had been acted on by U.S. Manhattan Project leaders. Churchill said the British were deeply concerned when they received James Conant's January 1943 memorandum "rigidly limiting the exchange of information" through a unilateral U.S. application of the concept of need to know.[50] Churchill, Cherwell, and Anderson all feared for Britain's position in a postwar world between the United States and Soviet Union, each atomic-armed, in the absence of a British atomic deterrent.[51] According to Harvey Bundy:

> The Prime Minister took the position that this particular matter was so important that it might affect seriously British-American relationships; that it would not be satisfactory for the United States to claim the right of sole knowledge in this matter. The Prime Minister further said that Britain was not interested in the commercial aspects but was vitally interested in the possession of all information because this will be necessary for Britain's independence in the future as well as for success during the war; that it would never do to have Germany or Russia win the race for something which might be used for international blackmail; and that Russia might be in a position to accomplish this result unless we worked together.[52]

Taking the lead in responding for the U.S. side, per Stimson's instruction, Bush emphasized that the U.S. position was based on cooperation to facilitate winning the current war, "that post war problems were separate, and that the difficulties of complete exchange lay in respect to post war matters, both political and commercial."[53] Churchill, supported by Cherwell and Anderson, replied that commercial interests were not a factor in the British position and that the United Kingdom would be willing to enter any agreement FDR thought fair, taking into account the relative contributions to the Manhattan Project of the two countries.[54]

Secretary of War Stimson then offered his own summation of the situation. With the advantage of five days to have considered what Churchill had said to him on the train trip to Dover, and having used Bush to present the U.S. case, Stimson now read from his prepared notes:

> 1. Two Governments in possession of an unfinished scientific hypothetical formula on which they are working.

> 2. Both Governments continue working on the development of that formula and are ready to interchange reports of their respective developments.

3. U.S. at large expenditure of public monies sets on foot construction out of which these formulae may be transformed into practical products; on the understanding that the U.K. may share these products for the joint object of winning the war.

4. U.K. now asks U.S. for running reports on its constructive designs and other manufacturing experience, in order that UK after the war is ended and its present strain of other construction is over, may be in a position to prepare itself to promptly produce against the danger of a new threat or a new war.

5. Should the U.S. grant this request unequivocally? Should it seek safeguards against any use of product except under political restrictions? Should it refuse the request as entirely uncalled for, under the original agreement between the President and the Prime Minister?[55]

Responding that Stimson's "was a trenchant analysis of the situation," Churchill offered to accept an agreement between himself and Roosevelt that the prime minister then outlined with five points:

1. A Free interchange to the end that the matter be a completely joint enterprise.

2. That each Government should agree not to use this invention against the other.

3. That each Government should agree not to give information to any other parties without the consent of both.

4. That they should agree not to use it against any other party without the consent of both.

5. That the commercial or industrial uses of Great Britain should be limited in such a manner as the President might consider fair and equitable in view of the large additional expense incurred by the U.S.[56]

The essence of a resolution of the atomic information sharing impasse had been put into play—in draft—but with political and military elements that could be agreed to only at the presidential–prime ministerial level. Stimson offered to convey Churchill's proposed agreement to Roosevelt. Churchill agreed to put the proposal in writing.

* * *

With the discussion of atomic weapons cooperation concluded, Stimson sent the others out of the room so that he could meet alone with the prime minister on the issue of equal importance and urgency to the United States, which was clearly still open, despite the Trident Conference. That was reaffirmation of cross-Channel assault as the primary Allied liberation strategy.

The two men began with by then familiar lines of opposition and "had it hammer and tongs," according to Stimson. Churchill, citing strong German resistance in Sicily, told him that "if he had 50,000 men ashore on the French Channel Coast, he would not have an easy moment, because he felt that the Germans could rush up in sufficient force to drive them back." His anger rising, Stimson accused Churchill in strong terms of reneging on the commitment to Overlord decided at the Trident Conference two months earlier, telling Churchill that his statements were "like hitting us in the eye." Questioned by Stimson, Churchill responded that he would not have Overlord if the decision were his, but would "loyally" implement the agreed strategy. However, Churchill remained eager to advance to Rome. Stimson replied that, while he did not question the sincerity of Churchill's promise, he also worried that Churchill did not allow for the long-term planning and preparation essential to an operation like cross-Channel attack. He told Churchill of his meeting a week earlier with COSSAC at which Generals Morgan and Barker expressed confidence in their Overlord Outline Plan but also concern for diversion of resources. Stimson closed the meeting by telling Churchill he would be "taking every step to try to prevent any further encroachment into the plans made for Round Hammer [Overlord]."[57]

Churchill's expression of intent to "loyally" follow the cross-Channel assault strategy well might have been a backhanded allusion to American disloyalty in not putting into effect FDR's oral—not written—promises in October 1941 and May 1943 of full exchange of atomic information.[58] As a former U.S. Attorney for the Southern District of New York, Stimson could neither miss nor ignore the lawyerly quality of Churchill's response on Overlord.[59] From his perspective, despite the light that seemed to be breaking early in his meeting with Stimson, Churchill almost certainly held a no less critical opinion of the "need to know" rationale for U.S. suspension of atomic information sharing with the British. From Stimson's last substantive meeting with Churchill on this trip, the secretary of war left for North Africa.

The meeting had produced a path that could resolve the issue of atomic research sharing with further negotiation. However, Stimson drew two conclusions with respect to Overlord that altered the impression of Churchill that he had expressed to General Marshall three days earlier and that would shape Stimson's recommendations to Roosevelt. Stimson was convinced that the British would continue every effort to find an alternative to Overlord, and knowing their prime minister's reticence, he moved toward the conclusion that the cross-Channel invasion could not succeed with any British commander.[60]

* * *

From No. 10 Downing Street, Vannevar Bush returned to the U.S. embassy. There he prepared a cryptic memorandum, to be sent by diplomatic pouch on July 23, to alert his deputy, James Conant, that an Anglo-American agreement on atomic information interchange was in preparation and probably would be delivered to FDR by the secretary of war. Citing pressure he encountered from the British, but believing that "the outcome is not going to be bad at all," Bush lamented, "I have had to go alone for there was no way whatever of stopping the progress nor would it indeed have been advisable to do so, and I merely hope that I have not made a lot of mistakes in advising the secretary."[61] Bush wrote to Conant while still ignorant of FDR's new instruction and then turned to the antisubmarine and other research business that had caused his trip to Britain.

As Stimson and Bush negotiated in London with Churchill on a way forward on atomic information interchange, FDR's new instruction to Bush of July 20 remained with Carroll Wilson at OSRD headquarters in Washington. Events, however, moved on.

Bush learned from Sir John Anderson on July 27 that another message to Churchill had arrived directly from FDR. Apparently assuming that his July 20 instruction had been received by Bush as he had written it and had been acted on, Roosevelt cabled Churchill that he had "arranged satisfactorily for the TUBE ALLOYS" and recommended that Churchill send over his "top man in this enterprise" to get "full understanding from our people."[62] Mystified as to the genesis of FDR's cable to Churchill, and concerned that the agreement outlined in the July 22 meeting with Churchill not be undercut, Bush sent an anxious radio message to Harvey Bundy, who was with Stimson in North Africa. On July 28, six days after meeting Churchill, Bush received in London the transmission of FDR's new instruction, but paraphrased in a way that altered the president's intent. Reading the misleading cable after the meeting, Bush recalled in his memoir that he concluded at the time, "Well this simply tells me to do what I am doing now."[63]

Scheduled to leave for Washington early the next morning, Bush still wanted instructions. He sent another radio message, now marked "urgent," to Bundy in North Africa. "Cable now informs me that my chief by letter requests me to review in inclusive manner full exchange with [UK]."[64] Secretary Stimson replied in an urgent message that evening, sent under Eisenhower's signature. He recommended that Bush "advise Hopkins for the President that the Prime Minister opened the matter with the Secretary and subsequent discussions went well, but emphasize that of course no commitments were made." The message closed with Stimson's assumption that he would be carrying back to FDR immediately Churchill's suggested settlement.[65] FDR's cabled invitation in hand, however, Churchill would not wait for that.

* * *

Concurrent with the meetings in London, preparations began for the fourth full-dress Anglo-American conference, Quadrant. On July 20, Churchill sent a cable to Roosevelt in Hyde Park that Canadian prime minister William Mackenzie King welcomed the proposal to hold the Quadrant meeting in Quebec City.[66] The following day, Churchill cabled FDR, "Planning arrive ABRAHAM 11,"[67] meaning the Plains of Abraham (Quebec City) August 11. Quadrant would commence in approximately three weeks, but of concern to the JCS, Henry Stimson, and Harry Hopkins, substantive talks at the top of the Alliance might occur earlier. Stimson's recollection was that Churchill told him on July 22 or 23 of his intention to travel to North America early in August in advance of the Quadrant Conference, not information that Stimson kept to himself.[68] Churchill's early arrival could only mean that the prime minister intended to meet with Roosevelt before the conference.

Actions initiated the previous week at the White House already had accelerated, ostensibly to give "the Boss" some rest in a remote venue before Quadrant. Thomas Beck at Crowell-Collier Publishing in New York had been the intermediary for the idea of an FDR fishing trip to the Great Lakes. On July 20, at 10:20 a.m., Harry Hopkins telephoned Beck to get the number for the originator of the proposal for the trip, E. F. McDonald in Chicago. Five minutes later, Hopkins called McDonald.[69] The next day, as Mike Reilly of the Secret Service was consulting with Hopkins about the trip, McDonald mailed a special delivery letter describing updated arrangements for fishing by the president in McGregor Bay, Ontario, "when and if the trip materializes."[70] The morning of July 22, Brig. Gen. John Deane of the JCS Secretariat met Hopkins at the White House without an appointment, and at 2:30 p.m. Hopkins met General Marshall at the Pentagon.[71] Probably on Friday morning, July 23, when McDonald's updating letter was received, the decision was made at the White House. Before the Quadrant Conference, FDR would be going fishing.

* * *

Secretary of War Stimson, on General Marshall's strong recommendation, had reached Scotland to embark on the long flight to North Africa to consult with Eisenhower. Taking off from Prestwick for Marrakesh on the evening of July 24, the Stimson party's c-54 flew west across Northern Ireland in the near-daylight of northern summer and west over the Atlantic before turning south. The navigator had planned to fly south along 14 degree longitude, but Stimson moved the southward leg further west to the 18th degree "for safety." This change put their course well beyond German radar range from the French coast and that of Luftwaffe JU-88 fighter bombers hunting for patrolling Allied antisubmarine aircraft, but still within the outer edge of normal operating area of Luftwaffe four-engine FW-200 maritime reconnaissance bombers flying out of Bordeaux.

There were reasons for prudence. With some frequency, Allied antisubmarine patrol aircraft were intercepted and shot down by the JU-88s in the Bay of Biscay, as had been a KLM airliner, en route from Lisbon to London with actor Leslie Howard on board only three weeks earlier. Less frequently, farther west, Allied very long-range, four-engine Liberators on antisubmarine patrols and the Luftwaffe FW-200s, hunting targets for the same U-boats, sometimes encountered each other and fought aerial duels. Stimson also knew from U.S. actions that, given foreknowledge of their movements, senior leaders were wartime targets for assassination. Only three months earlier in the South Pacific on April 18, in an intelligence-based planned ambush, American fighter planes had shot down two Japanese bombers, killing Combined Fleet commander and Pearl Harbor attack planner Adm. Isoroku Yamamoto and most of his senior staff.[72]

Stimson's aide, Colonel Wright, recounted, "The weather was most favorable for our purpose, since we passed the most dangerous area west of the Bay of Biscay with good cloud cover above and below," cruising at six thousand feet.[73] Drawing closer to the North African coast in the morning, Stimson's plane came within range of a protective response from Allied fighters if needed.

* * *

Events indeed were moving forward in Washington, stimulated by Stimson's report from London on Churchill's anticipated travel. On Sunday, July 25, from Shangri-La, FDR responded to Churchill's cable that Lady Churchill and daughter Mary would be coming with him to Quebec by inviting Churchill and family to Hyde Park for a visit to be concluded by August 15. On that day, Eleanor Roosevelt would leave Hyde Park on an inspection trip to the Pacific. Roosevelt also told Churchill, "I hope to go on a short trip to fish and sleep next Saturday [July 31]."[74] Based on subsequent British communication of new dates for Churchill to be at Hyde Park, FDR's message must have communicated something of the duration of the fishing trip.

A fishing trip? As Marshall in Washington viewed with increased foreboding the weeks ahead, across the Atlantic, the president's almost nonchalant mention of a fishing trip must have stimulated Churchill to wonder if he was the recipient of a political euphemism.

For two months, while their military chiefs grappled over strategy, the two western leaders had engaged in earnest communication about Roosevelt's desire to meet Stalin alone with almost no staff and without Churchill. FDR believed that such intimate informality would allow him to build trust with Stalin and, unburdened by an agenda, make progress on East-West issues in advance of the Big Three leaders meeting to address the critical war years ahead. After a strong protest in June, Churchill had accepted, grudgingly, the potential value in FDR meeting alone with Stalin in the context of a Churchill-FDR bilateral and Big Three meeting quickly following. Churchill never relaxed his concern for the effect on Britain's standing as an ally or its postwar position, subsequent to any wartime meeting with the Soviet leader that did not include Britain at the table.

The expectation, outlined by the Soviet premier in May, was that he would give FDR two weeks' notice of when he could be at a meeting place, probably in August. On that basis the president would organize the venue, suggested by Stalin to be Fairbanks, Alaska.[75] Roosevelt had told Churchill that he did not expect to hear from Stalin before July 15.[76] Then came word to Churchill from the president, setting back the date after which Churchill would be welcome at Hyde Park, that he would begin travel into a remote area of Canada a little more than two weeks beyond the date on which FDR had anticipated a response from Stalin. FDR had used a "fishing trip" in the vicinity of Cape Cod as a ruse to cover his meeting with Churchill at Argentia, Newfoundland, in 1941.[77] At Trident in May, FDR had called Churchill's post-Casablanca trip to entreat Turkey's president to enter the war on the Allies' side a "fishing trip."[78] FDR had demonstrated by his use of it a liking for this Americanism for an exploratory meeting. Given Churchill's heightened appreciation of the importance of Quadrant, a pre-Quebec meeting between FDR and Stalin was a source of anxiety for him.

Whatever concern he might have had, Churchill remained resolute in his position on strategy. The next day, building on Mussolini's demise, Churchill sent an effusive letter to FDR describing prospects for a Mediterranean strategy.[79] The British Chiefs of Staff held to their July 24 "stand fast" order to British forces in Mediterranean, pending a reappraisal of strategy at Quadrant.

Uncertainty about just when Churchill and the British delegation for Quadrant would arrive in North America was resolved in the United States by a message to the Joint Staff Mission from British cos for delivery to General Marshall. Received in Washington the afternoon of July 26, the message stated that "'Colonel Warden' [Churchill] will arrive at Halifax evening of the 9th by the same method as last time [aboard the *Queen Mary*]. Colonel Warden and his lady will then go to Hyde Park until 15th, since P.Q. [Roosevelt] does not come to Abraham until 17th." The British delegation would go directly from Halifax to Quebec, arriving there early on August 10 and "hoped all their opposite numbers from Washington will be able to arrive that day."[80] Sent Most Secret and Most Immediate, the message was hand-delivered to Col. Frank McCarthy, Marshall's aide.

The U.S. Joint Chiefs of Staff had their own conception of when the U.S. delegation should arrive in Quebec City and would not allow themselves to be rushed by the British. A new complication for the JCS, emerging from subordinate staff, was dissent from their goal for the fast-approaching conference. The JCS also remained uncertain about their commander in chief's commitment to that goal, reassertion of Overlord's primacy, and FDR was about to go fishing.

Mike Reilly and two Secret Service agents departed the White House on July 26 for Chicago, on the first leg of a reconnaissance to arrange for FDR's trip to Ontario. Uncertain about the dates for Churchill's trip to North America—and the possibility of travel by Stalin—Reilly and Dewey Long had stood by in suspense on the dates for FDR's trip until then.[81] During this interval, by some means, Churchill was informed that FDR could not receive him at Hyde Park before August 12 because he would be "fishing" or in Washington and that he would depart Washington on July 30. For thirteen days before Quadrant, the president would not be available to the prime minister except via cables.

Back at the White House from Shangri-La, Monday, July 26, FDR cabled Churchill that he had "arranged satisfactorily for the TUBE ALLOYS" and recommended that Churchill send over his "top man in this enterprise" to get "full understanding from our people."[82]

* * *

Working with Maj. Gen. Alexander Surles on Tuesday, July 27, in Algiers, Secretary Stimson compiled his notes on three days of meetings in North Africa with Generals Dwight Eisenhower, Carl Spaatz, and Jimmy Doolittle.[83] Stimson agreed with the generals he consulted in Algiers that, following the conquest of Sicily, an operation on the Italian mainland "seems not only advisable, but essential to cover the interim before mounting a powerful [cross-Channel] invasion offensive for a knockout." If the operation Eisenhower was developing for an amphibious landing at

Salerno (Operation Avalanche) was feasible, this would be preferable to a long, costly slog up the boot of Italy.

However, Stimson concluded that the operation was being advocated for two other reasons that were in conflict. He interpreted the British concept to be "the use of the favorable conclusion of such an operation as the basis for a ground operation in the direction of the Balkans or of the Mediterranean avenues of invasion." As to the goal of the operation for the American commanders in North Africa, Stimson interpreted that to be shaped instead by the needs and contribution of air power.[84]

Highly desired by Eisenhower and Spaatz (a desire shared in Washington by Marshall) were air bases on the Italian mainland as far north as Rome from which heavy bombers could attack southern Germany. Flying from Britain, its operations limited by weather, the Eighth Air Force's losses to steadily improving German air defenses were "approaching the margin of safety" at 10 percent, whereas flying in the south incurred losses of less than 1 percent and benefited from better weather. The airmen did not believe German air defense in the south could be developed to the extent it was in northwestern Europe. If this second axis of air attack could be established concurrent with the mounting of Overlord, Stimson and Major General Surles believed the Allies in the west "would have the maximum advantage in effect upon Germany both psychologically and militarily."

"However," they concluded, "the Southern effort must be strictly confined to this objective of the air attack. There must be no further diversions of forces or material which will interfere with the coincident mounting of the Round Hammer [Overlord] Project."[85] In Stimson's interpretation of what he had heard in Algiers, the American goal for assault on the Italian mainland left scant room for the British conception.

Stimson returned to Washington on Saturday, July 31, and went to his office in the Pentagon on Sunday.[86] He had missed President Roosevelt, who was by then 760 miles to the north in the Canadian bush.

9

Revolt in London and Washington

If we are not prepared to accept the risks, face the difficulties, suffer the casualties, then let us concentrate at once exclusively on the production of heavy
bombers and think in terms of 1950.

— Lord Beaverbrook to Harry Hopkins, June 1943

n London, on July 22, the day Stimson and Churchill conversed
at No. 10 Downing Street on atomic bomb cooperation and war
strategy, two blocks away in the bunkered Cabinet War Rooms
in Great George Street, Lieutenant General Morgan, COSSAC, met
with the British chiefs. Still awaiting the chiefs' endorsement of
his team's plan, which had such critical relevance to the imminent conference in Quebec, COSSAC now got further instruction
from Churchill's military leaders.

Having received, on July 15, COSSAC's final draft for the Overlord
Outline Plan, the British Chiefs of Staff, four days later, directed
Morgan to assign a small COSSAC team to accompany and support
the British Quebec Conference delegation. Morgan responded later
that day by asking permission to send a similar team to Washington to enlighten the U.S. Joint Chiefs of Staff as well.[1] Now,
attending the July 22 meeting of the war cabinet COS Committee, Morgan and his deputy, Barker, received their answer. Permission withheld.

Chief of the Imperial General Staff, Gen. Sir Alan Brooke told
Morgan that the COS had not yet examined the Overlord report. In
the presence of U.S. Army theater commander General Devers,
General Brooke told Morgan that "no discussion should take place
in Washington on plans for OPERATION OVERLORD and no [COS-
SAC] Staff Mission should proceed to America until the plan had
been examined by the Committee."[2]

During this meeting, in addition to the constraint on sharing its Overlord plan with Washington, cossac also received a telling query. The cos wanted to be told more about cossac's planning for its other task, Operation Rankin, the contingency for responding to an internal collapse of the German Reich.[3] Rankin was preferred by Churchill and his chiefs as an alternative to Overlord's direct assault at the time and place determined by Allies. However, Rankin could be implemented only in reaction to developments that might be influenced but not controlled by the Allies.

From their representatives in Washington, but not recorded as being discussed in the London meeting, the British chiefs knew about the dissent percolating among the American planners. Should that dissent prevail in Washington, the chiefs surmised, priority in Allied strategy would shift to the British-preferred Mediterranean strategy and cross-Channel assault would be subordinated and recast into a Rankin-like operation.

Denial of permission to send a briefing team to Washington thrust the London community of planners for Overlord into turmoil. By cossac's charter, the planning group reported to the Combined Chiefs of Staff in Washington through the cos Committee in London and received their orders through the British chiefs. If the Combined Chiefs "were in fact combined," Morgan later reasoned, denying cossac permission to brief the U.S. Joint Chiefs of Staff on the Overlord Outline Plan in advance of the Quadrant Conference was within the authority of the British chiefs.[4] Reaction against the cos order immediately began to build among the American officers in London and within cossac's primarily Anglo-American staff.

* * *

Stimson was flying his long, dog-leg course to meet with General Eisenhower in Algiers when Allied sparring over strategy sharpened at transatlantic distance between London and Washington. On Saturday, July 24, two days after withholding for the moment permission for cossac to share its draft Overlord plan with Washington, the British Chiefs of Staff leapt to take advantage of Marshall's expressed, though constrained, interest in an invasion of the Italian mainland. The COS responded to the Combined Chiefs of Staff with a message of strong support for invading Italy. Without waiting for Washington's reaction, they acted to give their position substance. British senior commanders in the Mediterranean were sent an order to "stop own movement of forces." From London the COS suggested that the United States do the same. This triggered a sharp reaction from the U.S. Joint Chiefs of Staff.[5] Even if meant as support for a new move into Italy, the order also could be interpreted as an act in opposition to Overlord. So it was seen in Washington.

In acting unilaterally to stop redeployment of their forces from the Mediterranean to Britain for Overlord, the British Chiefs of Staff had laid bare again the deepest anxieties of the U.S. Joint Chiefs. The JCS put no confidence in Churchill's acceptance, at the Trident Conference only two months earlier, of an Allied cross-Channel invasion of northwestern Europe in 1944. The JCS saw at best very fragile support among the COS for Overlord's direct assault, *versus* waiting for the opportunistic conditions for Rankin. Nagging at the JCS was their counterparts' demonstrated willingness to go along with strategy proposals from Churchill in which, they believed, the British chiefs themselves sometimes put no faith.

From experience, the JCS and, as Marshall knew, Stimson and Hopkins were deeply worried about Churchill's ability to turn their president's position away from what they saw as the best strategic interests of the United States. Now they knew for certain that the prime minister intended to come early to meet with Roosevelt before Quadrant. Perhaps his greatest concern, Marshall also knew that with Quadrant less than a month away, the U.S. strategy for Europe and for the conference was not firm; U.S. military planners, themselves, were sliding into a crisis of doubt about cross-Channel attack.

Events in the Mediterranean advanced independently from the Allies' control. On Sunday, July 25, the Italian dictator Benito Mussolini was ousted. On orders from King Victor Emmanuel III, Mussolini was arrested and replaced by Field Marshal Pietro Badoglio.[6]

As news broke in Washington and London of Mussolini's arrest and formation of the new Italian government, General Marshall traveled by car seventy-five miles to Shangri-La, the president's retreat in Maryland's Catoctin Mountains. Anticipating the imminent conference in Quebec, Marshall intended to impress on FDR the Joint Chiefs' objections to the British strategy. In his notes for the meeting, Marshall's objective was unequivocal and emphatic. Typed with underlining, that was: "To prevent, prior to the Quadrant conference, the making of commitments, verbal or written, affecting operations now under way or future operations."[7]

Basing his case directly on the cos "stop own movement" order and their message to the jcs of the previous day, Marshall argued that the British were spring-loaded to exploit for their own objectives any statement by the president or U.S. military leaders. He told FDR of the jcs's continuing "great difficulties" in determining "whether the proposals [the British chiefs] advance are those of the prime minister or are those of his military advisors. Are the ideas based on sound operational and logistics considerations from a military viewpoint or are they accepted by the cos (in some cases possibly against their better judgment) only because the Prime Minister wants them?" Marshall warned FDR, "Proposals contained in conversations or communications between the President and the Prime Minister prior to the conference will, if accepted by the latter, definitely tie the cos and thus interfere with what should be a calm and reasoned consideration of the issues involved."[8]

Fixed on the goal that out of Quadrant "must come a really *firm* decision as to whether or not we will cross the Channel against determined resistance" (emphasis in the original), Marshall appealed to FDR. If Roosevelt found it necessary to reply to any proposal from Churchill before the conference, Marshall implored, the president first should absolutely obtain the advice of his Joint Chiefs of Staff.[9]

Marshall's meeting with Roosevelt had been held at Shangri-La and away from White House bustle, but amid distractions from the news of Mussolini's overthrow. Marshall left not confident that his message had registered with the president. Context compounded his disappointment. In addition to the British "stop own movement" gambit, Marshall knew that, among his own planners, support of Overlord was wavering. Within the Pentagon, eight days earlier while Stimson and Churchill toured the Dover Cliffs area, the initial foray had begun into what the official U.S. Army history later would title the U.S. staff "Revolt Against Overlord."[10]

Allied troops deployed in the European theater, as of the summer of 1943, were split and neither the concentration of forces in the United Kingdom nor in the Mediterranean was sufficient in itself to implement a strategy for total defeat of the Axis in Europe.[11] Some U.S. strategy planners had become hesitant about reaffirming cross-Channel attack as the principal Allied strategy and were becoming persuaded that the successful landing in Sicily pointed to the Mediterranean-focused strategy as the bird in hand. The advocates for the cross-Channel attack-based Overlord strategy opposed the British Mediterranean strategy as too lengthy, too susceptible to still more diversions to the east, and too reliant on the hope of inducing defeat of Germany by political-economic collapse.[12]

The dissenters from Overlord, however, had a respected champion. Brig. Gen. John E. Hull was the chief of the Army's Operations Division (OPD) theater group and one of the early authors of the cross-Channel strategy. On July 17, Hull had stated his new view that "we should now reverse our decision and pour our resources into exploitation of our Mediterranean operations."[13] General Hull's was an opinion that could not be ignored.

As the Army chief of staff made his apparently fruitless round-trip to Shangri-La that Sunday, July 25, the seed of a dissent from Marshall's strategy that Hull had planted on July 17 was taking root. The senior Army and Army Air Force members of the Joint War Plans Committee (JWPC), Cols. William W. Bessell and Richard C. Lindsay, issued a paper attacking the Trident priority for the cross-Channel strategy. Bessell and Lindsay contrasted Bolero's goals to its limited accomplishment in building a U.S. force in the United Kingdom and compared that to the size of the Allied force in being then in the Mediterranean. They recommended that the U.S. acknowledge that the Soviet Union had been, and likely would continue to be, the main source of ground pressure against Germany and, given that, continue with Britain to bomb Germany from the air.[14]

The full JWPC acted to formally question the cross-Channel strategy in a report to the Joint Planning Staff. Building on Bessell and Lindsay's argument, the committee recommended that future Allied operations emphasize the Mediterranean and landings in southern France. They proposed that the cross-Channel strategy become the "final" action, not "the opening wedge for decisive defeat of the German armies." The JWPC alternative recommended leaving in place the seven combat-experienced divisions slated for transfer from the Mediterranean to the UK. Instead, they recommended that the shipping thus released should be used to bring seven fresh divisions from the United States to Europe.[15]

Monday morning, July 26, Bessell and Lindsay gained support for their position from the senior Navy member of the Joint Planning Staff, Rear Adm. Charles M. "Savvy" Cooke Jr. Cooke believed that Overlord, burdened by many operational and logistical challenges, should be subordinated to more certain operations in the Mediterranean and particularly in the Pacific.[16] In its sum, the Joint Planning Staff position advocated reversing the Trident decisions and accepting the British position, championed by Churchill and supported by his senior commanders, along with strengthened advocacy for U.S. Pacific operations.

As the U.S. Joint Planning Staff made its recommendations, challenging the position preferred by General Marshall and the other Joint Chiefs, Anglo-American skirmishing began for the control of the agenda for the Quadrant Conference. Typical of all international conferences is that this minuet of process-setting can steer the substantive outcome. While moving to check the staff crisis of confidence, the U.S. Joint Chiefs also began to reveal their hard-learned better footwork to those masters of the dance in London.

The British Chiefs of Staff submitted to the U.S. Joint Chiefs their "Proposed Agenda for Quadrant." Paragraph One inferred

that the purpose of Quadrant would be to examine the Trident decisions "in light of the situation existing in [July–August 1943]." Paragraph Two was "Strategy in the Mediterranean." Paragraph Three
was "Defeat of Japan." Overlord and Bolero-Sickle only appeared
as subheadings in Paragraph Four, "Operations from the UK"[17]

Within a day, the U.S. Joint Chiefs of Staff responded by submitting to the CCS the U.S. Proposed Agenda for Quadrant (CCS
288/1). The JCS intended to come to grips first with the Allies'
strategic goals that in turn would define objectives for operations.
Their intent was to not allow the COS an opening to employ their
tactic of flooding the discussion with comparative details so as
to avoid commitment to larger strategy decisions. In order by
its roman numerals, the U.S. proposal was: I Conference procedure; II Consideration of Overall Objective, Overall Strategic
Concept, and Basic Undertakings in support of Overall Strategic
Concept; III Consideration of specific operations for 1943–44 in
the European-Mediterranean area with (1) Bolero-Overlord and
(2) Sickle-Pointblank leading the list. Antisubmarine warfare, critical to success of transporting across the Atlantic of the massive
force required for Overlord, was listed third.[18]

The British chiefs' rejoinder to the JCS came from London to
the CCS in Washington on July 29, as their Proposed Agenda
for Quadrant (CCS 288/2). The COS expressed their hope "that
it may be possible to confine the Agenda as far as possible to
those specific issues on which decisions are required to govern
operations in the comparatively near future." They asked that
the U.S. Chiefs of Staff "dispense with lengthy discussions on
over-all strategic concepts or global strategy." They requested that
instead of exchanging more cables, the agenda be settled at the
first meeting of the conference, and again they asked that the
U.S. chiefs join the conference by August 10 or as soon thereafter as possible.[19]

Confident that their preferred agenda was firmly lodged, assigning priority to Overlord, the U.S. Chiefs had no intention of sitting down with the British in Quebec before the U.S. positions
were embraced in their full development by a unified U.S. team

that included the president. Marshall, with the full support of the JCS, was determined that this would be a team intent on winning.

Unfortunately, as the British chiefs knew, the U.S. team was not unified. The U.S. planners below the level of the Joint Chiefs were debating the relative merit of the Mediterranean strategy and cross-Channel attack, FDR's position remained ambiguous and, however delayed and curtailed in duration, a pre-Quadrant meeting between Roosevelt and Churchill could not be prevented by the U.S. chiefs.

In Washington, the absence of a viable Overlord plan—COSSAC's plan held in suspense in London—made both the British chiefs' and now the internal American challenges to the case for Overlord difficult to refute. London had gained knowledge from side conversations among CCS representative that, at staff-level in Washington, the internal cracks in U.S. support for giving priority to cross-Channel assault appeared to be expanding.

* * *

At Norfolk House, disturbed though COSSAC was by the chiefs' stricture against sharing with Washington their draft Overlord plan, COSSAC's mandatory, immediate task was clear: move ahead urgently on planning for Rankin in order to answer the COS question. Their Rankin planning had fallen well behind Overlord for a combination of reasons. Overlord was tangible, a defined opening phase starting point just across the Channel. The COSSAC staff had become united and stimulated by: the very challenges of Overlord; anticipation of the enormity of the still-pent-up but inevitable surge of forces to concentrate for a defined date for action, May 1, 1944; and their own shared desire to take the fight back to the enemy on the Continent.

In contrast, Rankin was a fog of "what if's." Practical operational responses to Rankin's three contingency cases were difficult to conceptualize. Each case was intended to react to a situation of "disintegration" determined not by the Allies but by the circumstances of unpredictable dissolution within enemy forces and leadership. Earlier, on the third of May, Lieutenant General Morgan had pointed out to the Joint Planning Staff in London that there was no official definition of "disintegration." He appealed to the Chiefs of Staff Committee to "lay down objectives . . . to enable him to decide what would constitute disintegration."[20] Set against the context of RAF bombing of Germany since 1941 with the intent of causing political-economic collapse, the absence in 1943 of a definition for disintegration, at a minimum, suggested a strategy unmoored. Compounding this was awareness that the Allied resources to respond to any Rankin option were assumed to come not from a planned buildup against a specified date, but from what forces would be at hand in the United Kingdom for action who knew when?

Accepting COSSAC's "Overlord Outline Plan" for their review in the July 22 meeting, the British chiefs had asked COSSAC for a Rankin plan that could be made operational on August 1, nine days hence,[21] and that "if undertaken in 1943, should be planned on the basis that there would be no opposition to our landing."[22] The COS wanted a Rankin plan, operational and ready to be initiated, in their quiver when they arrived at Quadrant as an opportunistic alternative to Overlord.

Despite the British chiefs' urgent deadline, Rankin planning advanced only haltingly. The COSSAC staff was fighting the ambiguity inherent to their Rankin task and an undercurrent of consternation that sharing of their jointly developed Overlord plan with Washington was being held up.

General Morgan saw the immediate impediment to planning for Operation Rankin to be in the wording of COSSAC's implementing directive. In a July 27 memorandum, intended to accelerate action to craft a Rankin plan, by then due to the chiefs in five days, Morgan told his staff: "The operation that was described to me as 'A return to the Continent in the event of German Disintegration' [was] not in fact an operation of war."[23] He directed COSSAC's principal staff officers to identify in the abstract military operations by type that would be required to varying degrees but in common by all the circumstances reasonable to a drawing inward by the Reich. Although abstract, identification of needed operations would provide a basis for assessing the resources necessary. Acting on the intelligence assessments he was given,[24] Morgan impressed on his officers the need for urgency in developing solutions to the amorphous demands of Rankin. Acknowledging the differences in Germany's situation in 1943 from those which brought on that country's chaotic implosion in the previous war, Morgan concluded that "nevertheless the sum total of all the various factors operating cannot be far from that of the factors which caused the German collapse in 1918. Once again, therefore, emphasis must be on speed in the evolution of a plan."[25]

Three abstract operational requirements were apparent immediately. To have a hope of averting chaos, the Allies needed to avoid being surprised by a German collapse or partial collapse, as they had been in 1918. That pointed to a need for sustained reconnaissance in strength. Allied aerial assets, signals intelligence, and the growing array of British Commandos and expected U.S. Army Rangers could meet that need. A collapse would trigger a need for rapid deployment to the Continent to fill the vacuum left by withdrawing German forces, particularly to capture strategic airfields from which a weakened Germany could be "overawed" into complete surrender. Allied airborne forces, to be transferred or returned to the UK for Overlord, could take that mission. Ports and transportation systems would need to be restored to operation rapidly to handle the surge of ground troops to complete the occupation. That would require prompt, accurate damage assessment and action by specialized engineering and salvage units. Across every circumstance would be the need for a robust Allied civil affairs capability attuned and responsive to the situation of the populous in each liberated country.[26]

In response, the planners developed three cases for Rankin. Case A considered a return to the Continent before the date for Overlord in the event of a substantial weakening of German capacity for resistance in France and the Low Countries. Case A was not considered feasible before the end of 1943, unless Germany was very near collapse and an adequate naval assault force was available. Case B assumed a return to the Continent if Germany withdrew from the extremities of the areas it occupied to make a defense at the Siegfried Line located east of the Rhine River. Case C responded to an unconditional surrender by the Germans mandating the need to occupy the Reich itself and other areas as rapidly as possible to enforce the surrender.[27]

Development of civil affairs planning and capabilities, which later would become a major effort within COSSAC, lagged across the three cases for Rankin. Civil affairs depended on the policies of the United Kingdom and the United States toward specific occupied countries. These policies, however, were still developing. COSSAC's own history of Rankin planning, written in May 1944 in the midst of war and near the eve of the D-Day invasion, provides a glimpse into both the quandary of civil affairs and wartime emotion, not without cynicism:

> That some delay should elapse before the main [Rankin] forces should follow those advance guards was inevitable but it might not be a disadvantage. There was bound to be a certain amount of "blood-letting" among the liberated peoples eager for revenge upon their quislings, and the delay in completing full occupation would both save the Anglo-American authorities from contamination and yet avoid the necessity of interfering and being compelled morally to save their enemies from very well-merited fates.[28]

In the event, civil affairs planning by COSSAC, SHAEF, and the Allied governments was overwhelmed at liberation by the enormous scope of Nazi barbarity, general destruction, loss, and the revenge, and sometimes-violent pursuit of pent-up political agenda that followed in Europe.[29]

* * *

As the month of July drew to its close, General Morgan recounted, "The British Chiefs of Staff had had ample opportunity, of which good use had been made, to familiarize themselves with our project in all its weak points as well as its strong particulars. In discussion the weak points naturally had bulked largest."[30] On July

27, cossac submitted to the cos the final draft of the Overlord plan and its appendices.

Knowledge of the nascent American staff hesitancy was spreading in London. When on July 27 Morgan asked Lt. Gen. Jacob Devers about the rumor of appointment of a U.S. Supreme Allied Commander, his friend demurred. Devers had been with Morgan in the July 22 meeting in which Gen. Sir Alan Brooke withheld permission to share the draft Overlord plan with Washington. Now Devers replied that he felt unable to answer Morgan's question in part because he was not sure of the attitude in Washington toward cossac. Washington's attention seemed to be shifting to the Mediterranean and the Pacific. Devers told Morgan he was very conscious of being at the end of a "3,000-mile-long limb."[31]

Among U.S. officers in London knowledgeable of Overlord, both within and outside the planning group, vigorous protests mounted against General Brooke's July 22 order constraining cossac, which they considered to be inequitable. Plainly evident to these officers was the cossac crash effort in response to the cos to develop a Rankin alternative to Overlord. Morgan's American deputy, Maj. Gen. Ray Barker, knew that General Marshall and the U.S. Joint Chiefs did not want to arrive at the Quebec Conference uninformed about the substance of the Overlord Outline Plan already presented to the cos.[32]

Less than a fortnight earlier, Morgan and Barker had given Stimson a full, candid briefing on the essentials of the plan that the British chiefs were now holding close. The two generals had revealed their own concerns about assembling the concentration of forces required for Overlord's success. They were acutely aware that withholding full details of the plan now would invite trouble with Stimson, who, while impressed by cossac's ability and commitment, was known to hold suspect the British commitment to Overlord. Through General Devers's remarks to Morgan on July 27, they also knew of the questioning of priority for the cross-Channel attack strategy then stirring within Washington, in part stimulated by advocates for the Pacific theater who saw their own opportunity in reacting to the British.

Certain that time was of the essence, Morgan and Barker also knew that direct appeal in London or Washington of the British chiefs' decision only would inflame the situation. The two generals found in the details of COSSAC's work grounds for taking action. They concluded that many key elements of the draft plan, now submitted to the COS, would have received, and should have had, closer examination and authorization from the U.S. planners in Washington had more time been available to do so. These elements affected critical U.S. long lead-time decisions on troops, logistics, and civil affairs that would have to be addressed and, they reasoned, "did not lend themselves to treatment over the trans-Atlantic telephone."[33]

Morgan had been given a legitimate order that thrust upon the career soldier an exquisite dilemma. Under the Combined Chiefs of Staff chain of command, COSSAC was responsible to and reported through the COS. Before COSSAC, Morgan had commanded a corps and had expectations that his next British Army assignment would be to take up a combat command. After consultation with the other British and American advocates for Overlord in London, Morgan acted on this inequitable treatment of his country's ally. Mindful of the bureaucratic reasons not to act, and potential consequences to his British Army career, on July 28, Morgan dispatched a team to Washington anyway, headed by Barker, with copies of COSSAC's plan to brief to the Americans.[34]

Military flights from Henley, outside London, direct to Prestwick, Scotland, to catch a transatlantic flight westward were an option for the team, provided they applied for and received an air priority order.[35] The Washington-bound COSSAC team, instead, chose a lower profile option for leaving London. They bought train tickets to Glasgow.

At 8:00 p.m., Wednesday, 28 July, the London Midland & Scottish Railway's Night Mail eased out of London's Euston Station on its express, limited-stop, overnight run north to Glasgow. Not listed on passenger timetables, the Night Mail was known informally as "the Ghost Train," because limited passenger accommodations indeed were available. In addition to mail cars, the train included a single rider coach with three to four passenger compartments. One was used by the guard (conductor). The other compartments often were used by the king's messengers who favored anonymous travel with speed and security.[36]

These attributes made "the Ghost Train" the perfect accommodation for Major General Ray Barker and three U.S officers from COSSAC who boarded that night to slip out of London on the first leg of their trip to Washington. Copies of the secret draft Overlord Outline Plan were locked in their government-issue briefcases of thick brown leather.[37] Barker and his team arrived in Glasgow at 5:00 a.m., July 29. Intent on making their flight west across the North Atlantic to Washington, the team took a staff car to the air terminal at Prestwick where their progress halted abruptly. Westbound planes had stopped flying.

The weather that had barely favored Secretary of War Stimson's homeward flight only hours earlier had closed in. A major tropical depression was advancing eastward over the North Atlantic inflicting chaos on flight operations. Flying out of southern Newfoundland already had been suspended and flying south of Iceland would be affected by July 31. Pilots in Prestwick were advised that they would have to wait two to three days for favorable flying weather westward.[38]

* * *

On another route, undeterred by weather or anything else, Anglo-American atomic negotiations also were transferring west across the Atlantic. As July moved toward its end, the next stage of talks on atomic research sharing was about to open, now in Washington. Friday, July 30, the White House received Churchill's reply to FDR's invitation to send "your top man" to Washington "to get full understanding from our people."[39] The cable informed FDR that Sir John Anderson would arrive in Washington by air on the coming Monday or Tuesday. Anderson would make contact with Wallace Akers, the senior British representative for Tube Alloys/s-1 in the United States, and then be ready to talk with anyone FDR wished.[40]

The Pentagon already had received a July 29 letter from Churchill to Henry Stimson to tell the secretary of war of FDR's invitation and travel by Anderson in response. Churchill informed the secretary that Anderson would get in touch with Stimson in Washington on the second or third of August and enclosed for Stimson his "Draft Heads of Agreement" setting out the four points Churchill proposed in their July 22 meeting in London.[41] Stimson still was en route home from North Africa and would not see Churchill's letter until he went into the Pentagon on Sunday, August 1, the day before Anderson would arrive in Washington.

Anticipating Anderson's arrival, opposition to an Anglo-American sharing agreement also went on paper that Friday, July 30. Dr. James Conant, Vannevar Bush's deputy at the Office of Scientific Research and Development, sent Bush a memorandum as deputy chairman of the Military Policy Committee. Noting FDR's directive to Bush to exchange information with the British on an "inclusive basis," the memorandum put on record Conant's "conviction . . . that a complete interchange with the British on the s-1 project is a mistake." Conant authorized Bush to quote him to "higher authority if you see fit" meaning the president.[42] The president, however, had plans.

10

The Fishing Trip

Well, Pa, I guess we gave them the slip good this time.

—Franklin D. Roosevelt to Maj. Gen. Edwin Watson, August 1943

On Friday, July 30, 1943, Winston Churchill was preparing to sail for North America. The prime minister was intent on arriving early to win over Roosevelt to the British position on Allied strategy for victory in the war in Europe even before the start of the Anglo-American Quadrant Conference in Quebec. Sir John Anderson, Churchill's head of atomic research, was flying to Washington from London to negotiate for British participation in the Manhattan Project. Research findings had been withheld from British scientists since the end of 1942. Churchill felt it was crucial to postwar independence that the United States share this research with his scientists. The new government in Rome that replaced Mussolini was dispatching emissaries to find a way out of the conflict with the Allies. Joseph Stalin was pondering whether he could leave Moscow in the near term to meet secretly with Roosevelt. U.S. Secretary of War Henry Stimson was flying back to Washington from his meetings in London and North Africa determined to persuade FDR to insist that Churchill accept the U.S. military's position on strategy to win in Europe—based on a cross-Channel assault through Normandy—and further insist that an American serve as the Supreme Allied Commander. And Roosevelt, focus of the hopes of each, was quietly leaving town to go fishing.

At 10:30 p.m. Friday, while Stimson's homebound plane was still over the Atlantic, skirting north of bad weather, Roosevelt's fishing party left Washington by train for McGregor Bay in Ontario, on the north shore of Lake Huron, 760 miles to the northwest.

From a railroad siding under the U.S. Bureau of Engraving on Fourteenth Street, a switch engine eased forward a string of five Pullman sleeping cars. The last "Pullman" in the train, displaying neither name nor number, was Roosevelt's armor-plated car, the 142-ton *Ferdinand Magellan*. Aboard the train with the president were Joint Chiefs of Staff chairman Adm. William Leahy; Office of War Mobilization director James Byrnes; naval aide de camp Rear Adm. Wilson Brown; Maj. Gen. Edwin "Pa" Watson; Rear Adm. Ross McIntire, the president's doctor; presidential valet Arthur Prettyman; and FDR's dog, Falla.[1] Also on the train was William D. Hassett, an assistant press secretary who would leave from Hyde Park, New York, in the morning to begin his own Vermont vacation.[2] Aboard too was a Secret Service detail that would increase to thirty when the advance team already at McGregor Bay was added.

Unusual secrecy cloaked this trip. Taking side streets from the White House to the Bureau of Engraving to avoid attention, and deferring any press release until a trip was completed were normal security measures. Breaking from precedent, however, no trusted news reporters were told in confidence about the president's departure from Washington or the nature of this trip.[3] No official photographs would be made.

For an off-the-record fishing trip, the Roosevelt party took along a lot of administrative support. Aboard, and surprised to have been invited, were presidential secretaries Grace Tully and Dorothy Brady.[4] Also on the train was Navy chief ship's clerk William Rigdon, on assignment to the White House.[5]

White House transportation officer Dewey Long, who with Mike Reilly of the Secret Service prepared the site in Ontario, had flown back to be on the train. Baltimore & Ohio Railroad general passenger agent Daniel Moorman, who worked with Long to organize this and many of FDR's other trips, was aboard. Per standard practice, the railroad from which the White House requested a trip was in charge from beginning to end, even if a trip involved as many as twenty-five other railroads and, as in this case, crossed an international border.[6] Moorman would stay with the train until its return to Washington.

Arriving at Virginia Avenue, still in downtown Washington, the Pullmans were consolidated with the Army Signal Corps communication car dedicated to FDR's travel. Also added was a sleeper for the communicators, a B&O dining car, and a baggage car. Joining the passengers aboard were ten Army radio operators with their commander, Major Greer, and the railroad and Pullman staff to maintain the train and serve the passengers for their ten-day trip into a remote area.

Now complete, the nine-car train was forwarded by the Pennsylvania Railroad under Capitol Hill and through the complex trackage of Washington Union Station to Anacostia Junction in Maryland. There with a change of engines, the train was handed over to the Baltimore & Ohio Railroad. By 11:05 p.m. the president's train was picking up speed on its run north to Hyde Park.[7]

Just eight days had passed since the White House received word that Churchill intended to arrive early in North America for Quadrant. With the U.S. position for Quadrant still undergoing internal debate, an early arrival by Churchill was an alarming prospect for the Overlord strategy's American advocates. The White House had taken action. The vacation, first recommended fifteen months earlier,[8] had been activated at the initiative of Harry Hopkins. With the president's calendar now filled with fishing, the possibility of another personal meeting between him and Churchill deftly had been put off until August 12.

The only overtly stated reason to be found today for the trip was to "get the Boss away for a week of rest and fishing."[9] This was unassailable on its face. Foreseeable was that the Allied agenda for 1943 would be packed with grueling conferences and international travel for Roosevelt. Unknowable by the participants, this fishing trip would be the last time that as a still reasonably well man FDR would escape the White House for a vacation, to the extent that he could escape.

Notable beyond rest and recreation was the juxtaposition of the timing of the trip with then imminent developments for core U.S. interests. Although not to be found openly discussed in the surviving trip planning records, these critical and complex issues, to the outcome of which Roosevelt was central, were very much part of the sudden decision to activate and, one week later, implement unannounced this presidential leisure trip so far from the U.S. seat of power.

Hopkins, Stimson, George Marshall, and the rest of the U.S. Joint Chiefs feared a meeting with Churchill before the Quadrant Conference. Such a meeting carried the risk of ad hoc agreements by Roosevelt with Churchill that could preempt the U.S. position for this conference, as had happened before, a position still in development and to which FDR had not yet expressed firm commitment. Hopkins, Stimson, and Marshall had become concerned in late July, the moment Churchill made known his intended early arrival in North America. The new vulnerability compounding General Marshall's concern was the emerging challenge from within American staff ranks to the central U.S. strategy objective for Quadrant, reaffirmation of Overlord. This stirring of opposition within the Pentagon was known to the British Chiefs of Staff and Churchill in London.

Soon to arrive in Washington would be Sir John Anderson to negotiate a resumption of virtually suspended U.S.-British atomic information sharing. Although Roosevelt had invited Churchill to send Anderson to Washington,[10] there would be no protocol need for him to meet Anderson if he was not in town. Anderson would have to meet, instead, with Roosevelt's science adviser, Vannevar Bush. Bush opposed sharing with the British and had shown firmness in dealing with Churchill three weeks earlier in London. By physically distancing himself, Roosevelt—ready to share but on his terms—thus was assured of spirited protection of the U.S. interest without having to draw down his own stock of goodwill with Churchill. So continued the apparent "bad cop/good cop" negotiating strategy FDR had applied to Anglo-American atomic cooperation for months. The part that Bush took in the gambit was never made plain to him by the president. Thus unaware, Bush always played his character with unfeigned rigor.

There were other issues in play, and Roosevelt was not beyond putting Churchill off balance. As FDR's train steamed north that

July night, an open question for FDR and Churchill was whether Stalin would act on the meeting FDR had offered and to which the Soviet leader had agreed in principle. The meeting was projected tentatively for Fairbanks, Alaska. FDR's destination in Ontario was on a reasonable vector from Washington to Fairbanks. Churchill, bound for Scotland to board the *Queen Mary*, had reason to wonder where FDR, enamored of the "fishing trip" euphemism, really was going. Close to departure, there did remain an intriguing degree of tentativeness to the fishing trip. Roosevelt's cousin, Margaret "Daisy" Suckley, recorded in her diary for July 28 that FDR had called her to say that he would be at Hyde Park on July 31, and "If he can spare the time he will leave that night for a fishing trip in Lake Huron . . . at a place without a name, on siding which used to serve a lumber camp. . . . Otherwise, he will simply stay here until Sunday night & return to Wash."[11]

Roosevelt left Washington without further communication from Stalin on the Soviet premier's promise of a bilateral meeting. So far as the Americans and the British knew, the window remained open for a meeting before the middle of August. Churchill, invited or not, departed for North America prepared to "remain . . . for as long as may be necessary" for the possibility of a meeting of the Big Three.[12] Perhaps by coincidence, the makeup of the fishing party, to be joined by Harry Hopkins, was a close approximation of the White House team (but not its military complement) that FDR later would take to the meeting of Churchill, Stalin, and himself in Teheran.

The timing and duration provided by the "fishing trip" into northern Ontario would have sufficed as cover for a Stalin-FDR meeting.[13] Suckley's diary entry, alluding to equivocation, and the separate Secret Service query about airfields in Canada hint that FDR was holding open the option to fly to Fairbanks to meet Stalin.[14] Had Stalin proposed a date, could Roosevelt have done anything other than go?

At the end of July 1943, the cohesion of the Big Three relationship was under strain for multiple reasons. No one in the West could be confident of knowing the relationship's strength

in Moscow. Since the Anglo-American Trident Conference decision in May to postpone again the opening of the second front
(Overlord) from 1943 to 1944, a decision from which the Soviets had been excluded, Roosevelt's desire to meet with Stalin
if anything had intensified. The Soviet leader's reaction to the
postponement had been profoundly negative and accusatory.
Then unknown to his allies, Stalin's disappointment in their
direct communication of the second front delay was compounded
by Soviet intelligence that inferred insincerity in earlier Allied
statements of commitment to the second front.[15] Stalin's communication to Churchill and Roosevelt implied loss of faith
in the Allies and that, if the Soviet Union was to face the Axis
alone, other options might arise.[16] Soviet ambassadors in London and Washington were recalled to Moscow. The ensuing
back-and-forth messaging between the western leaders and Stalin had coincided with rumors reaching the West from neutral Sweden, once again, about overtures between the Soviets
and the Nazis. These suggested in 1943 the possibility of some
form of armistice in the East and Soviet withdrawal from the
war against the Axis.[17]

FDR set the presidential record for train travel, logging 243,827
miles in 399 trips during his twelve years in office.[18] Train travel
gave back to Roosevelt a measure of the mobility that polio took
from him. He often told B&O's Moorman, "I love this country of
ours, every inch of it, and I want to take the time to really see it."[19]
To accommodate the president's desire, his train usually traveled
at 25–50 miles per hour during daylight with authority to make
up time at night.[20] Roosevelt himself often made the sleeping car
assignments for his traveling party.[21] He knew well the railroad
network in the United States and railroad procedures.

To his love for political campaigning, Roosevelt applied his
knowledge of the rails with the skill of a ballet master. During
campaign trips, the president liked the train to pull away just
as he ended his speech from the rear platform with the assembled crowd cheering. To accomplish this without leaving behind
Secret Service agents or reporters, who knew the routine, Roos-

evelt became adept at timing the end of his speeches precisely to completion of servicing of his train.[22]

The stated purpose of this trip was to get away from speeches, politics, and the pressure of wartime government. Roosevelt's invitation to the director of war production, James Byrnes, was so cast. Roosevelt told Byrnes, as the avid fisherman later recalled, "he knew I had been having a hard time settling feuds and 'holding the line' and he wanted me to try a fishing line."[23] Rolling north through Baltimore and Wilmington, William Hassett recounted, the fishing party gathered with FDR in the parlor of the *Ferdinand Magellan* where orangeade and lemonade were passed around with the shades lowered, a Hyde Park custom when drinks were served.[24] They chatted about the hectic wartime capital they were leaving for the peace of Canadian Shield country.

Two evenings earlier in a fireside chat by radio to the American people, Roosevelt had described his views for postwar demobilization. These included the essence of legislation that, when expanded by Congress, became the GI Bill of Rights.[25] Asked by his traveling companions about Republican criticism that the address had been "a bold bid" for the military service vote in 1944, Roosevelt joked that were he to limit his speeches to "how beautiful is the moon," he would be "accused of politics because young people like to sit under the moon."[26] Yet, beneath the conviviality, weighing on the president was fresh knowledge of the brutality of the war and the urgent need to decide how to end the fight in Europe victoriously and quickly.

Roosevelt left Washington with compelling evidence of the war's human cost and the horror of Nazi genocide that underlined the need for a prompt end to the war. That week, the first reports on the Royal Air Force's firebombing of Hamburg had reached FDR recounting the dropping of 2,000 tons of ordnance on the night of July 24–25, then 2,300 tons more the night of July 27–28.[27] The result was a firestorm that swept the city imperiling tens of thousands of civilians. Then, during the morning of July 28, two days before his departure, FDR received at the White House the Polish ambassador, Jan Ciechanowski, and a young Polish resistance officer, Jan Karski.[28] Extending to a full hour their meeting, scheduled for thirty minutes, and foregoing his penchant for taking over conversations, Roosevelt gave unwavering attention to Karski's eyewitness account of the German occupation of Poland. Karski's assessment was that, harshly though the Polish people were being treated, the Nazis were bent on exterminating Poland's Jews.[29] When Secretary of State Cordell Hull lunched with the president the following day, he later told the ambassador, Roosevelt could speak of nothing but his conversation with Karski.[30] FDR's responses to appeals like Karksi's on behalf of those oppressed by the Nazis distilled into "We will win the war."

The hotly debated issue, approaching a showdown in Quebec, was how to win. That was at the root of the Allies' way forward in Europe. Rolling north toward a week of fishing, that issue FDR could not leave behind.

Now in high gear, America's mobilization was organizing, training, and equipping overwhelming military forces that in the summer of 1943 still were largely in the United States. The intellectually based priority on defeating the Nazis first still held, but was in tension with the emotional desire for victory in the Pacific. For compelling military and political reasons, the massive power growing in the United States had to be projected against the enemy on the European continent soon. But where? Through the Mediterranean in the long game espoused by Churchill, or in direct assault across the English Channel as FDR's Joint Chiefs advocated?

Arriving Saturday morning at Highland, New York, Roosevelt and some of the party detrained to spend the day at Hyde Park where Eleanor Roosevelt was staying.[31] That evening, the party reassembled on the train for the run northwest on the New York Central Railroad to Buffalo and across the bridge into Canada.[32] At Hamilton, Ontario, at 3 a.m., a security contingent of Royal Canadian Mounted Police (RCMP) boarded the train. Now handled by the Canadian Pacific Railway, the train was designated "O.D. #1" Pacific-type passenger locomotive no. 2337, its elegant gray, maroon, and black livery gleaming, coupled to the train and accelerated north in predawn light.[33] The farm country of southern

Ontario soon was left behind. North beyond the high bridge above Parry Sound, the president's party awoke to the lakes and trees of the Canadian Shield. They sped past miles of near-wilderness. For Roosevelt, always up for an expedition, this was tonic.

At Sudbury, 2337 transferred the train to Locomotive 5183, a freight engine polished from buffer to buffer for this special duty. The sure-footed Mikado's traction was needed to pull the train with the heavy *Ferdinand Magellan* on the trip's last leg. Passing through the La Cloche Mountains on a twisting, single-track branch line, they reached the fishing site at the waterside hamlet of Birch Island, a whistle-stop station where the land narrows between McGregor Bay and the Bay of Islands. Roosevelt later said that he found the area reminiscent of "the Maine Coast— rocky, wooded, 100's of islands, cool on the whole, very nice."[34]

Like Maine, but younger. The more recent retreat of Ice Age glaciers left a land less evolved. The living rock of earth's crust, Precambrian granite and gneiss in warm pinks and terra cotta, was set in the vivid, fiery churn of its creation. Now flooded by meltwater that became the Great Lakes, the rocks had been ground smooth under the pressure of glacial ice. Barely eroded fissures yielded thin purchase for wind-sculpted pines and, inland, birch and maple. The artists who became known to the world as the Group of Seven in the early twentieth century found their distinctly Canadian vision in the convergence of these primal forces.[35]

The land has long been the domain of the Ojibwe. In the seventeenth century, through a modest narrow just a few miles from Birch Island and bridged by the railway centuries later, went French explorers in search of the Northwest Passage, Jesuit missionaries, and voyageurs who paddled west and returned east, laden with furs and knowledge of a vast new continent. Into this already historic, primitive beauty for relaxation and its fish came the president at 4:00 p.m. Sunday, August 1, still tethered to a world war, distant but for radio, telegraph wires, and dispatch planes.

Tiny Birch Island Station was ready for FDR after seven days' urgent effort by Canadians and Americans. Steps from the train, over a wheelchair ramp built by local carpenters, waited launches for FDR and his fishing partners. Wanting something "a little classier" for the president, the Navy had requisitioned a thirty-eight-foot Williams cabin cruiser.[36] Unknown to the Navy, there was serendipity in the craft's name, *Anna H.* Franklin and Eleanor had a special fondness for their only daughter, Anna.[37] FDR dubbed the boat his "fishing smack."[38] Anchored a few miles offshore was the Navy training ship USS *Wilmette* brought from Chicago for support. *Wilmette* officers and sailors in civilian clothes crewed the launches and the *Anna H* and provided an armed shore party to supplement the RCMP and Secret Service security detail. Royal Canadian Air Force planes patrolled the contemplated fishing area.[39] An Army Air Force float plane arrived each day with dispatches and newspapers forwarded overnight from Washington.

The Signal Corps communication car was connected quickly to special circuits established by Bell Telephone Company of Canada and the railway.[40] Through the network of copper wires of that day, the president was linked directly to the White House Map Room and from there to any place in the world. On arrival that Sunday afternoon, hoping the world could forebear, FDR and his friends went fishing.

The war did not stand still. The trip had been delayed to await assurance of success for the Allied forces landing on Sicily. There bitter street fighting raged, but Allied troops steadily advanced.[41] As FDR's train was crossing into Canada, 178 Army Air Force B-24 Liberators, each with a crew of ten, were taking off from Benghazi, Libya, en route to Ploiesti,[42] Romania, 1,850 miles away. Their mission was to bomb Ploiesti's vast and heavily defended oil refineries by attacking at near-treetop height to maximize their accuracy despite greater vulnerability. Before dusk at Birch Island, the devastating Ploiesti raid was completed, and fifty-four of the heavy bombers including fifty-one crews of ten men each had been lost, killed or captured.[43] On the eastern front, the Red Army pressed its offensive around Orel in hard fighting.[44] In the Solomon Islands, swimming for their lives hours after a nighttime collision with a Japanese destroyer, were the surviving crew of Navy Patrol Torpedo Boat 109 and their captain, Lt. JG John F. Kennedy.[45]

Within two days, knowledge that FDR had left Washington had spread among officials, diplomats, and reporters. Despite mounting pressure on White House press secretary Steve Early, no explanation of the president's absence, official or otherwise, was forthcoming. Ever more inventive rumors circulated about where Roosevelt had gone and why. Some of the rumors extended to Churchill, who shortly would depart by sea for Canada and the Quadrant Conference, a transatlantic passage necessarily cloaked in secrecy.[46]

Increasingly beleaguered, Early appealed for authorization to issue a news release. FDR declined the request, enjoying the journalists' pandemonium. Whenever he brought new signals to the president from the communications car, William Rigdon remembered, FDR would ask, "What's the latest? Where am I supposed to be now?" Rigdon overheard FDR say to Maj. Gen. Edwin Watson, "Well, Pa, I guess we gave them the slip good this time."[47]

At Birch Island, per FDR's practice on vacation each morning, two or three hours' attention was given to necessary decisions. Among these were the situation in Italy, how to deal with the French Committee of Liberation, and pressuring Portugal for antisubmarine air basing rights in the Azores.[48] On this trip, post dinner discussion between FDR, Brown, Hopkins, and Leahy on war issues, including items on the agenda for Quebec, extended late into the night.[49] Hopkins and Leahy both were advocates for Overlord. On that topic, from Washington by intention and from Churchill in London, who saw his opportunity in distant developments, the two competing strategy visions would come before Roosevelt again in this remote place.

11

From One Attorney to Another

When I parted with him, I felt that, if pressed by us, he would sincerely go ahead with the Roundhammer commitment but that he was looking so constantly and vigorously for an easy way of ending the war without a trans-Channel assault that if we expected to be ready for a Roundhammer which would be early enough in 1944 to avoid the dangers of bad weather, we must be constantly on the lookout against Mediterranean diversions.

—Secretary of War Henry Stimson to FDR, on Churchill's position, August 4, 1943

As FDR began his second day of fishing, Overlord advocates were stirring in Washington. Returning to work on Monday, August 2, Henry Stimson badly wanted to press Roosevelt to take a firm decision to champion the cross-Channel invasion-based strategy, Overlord, and to convey to him in person Churchill's proposed terms of agreement for resuming atomic information interchange. Stimson found General Marshall at his desk, but the president was away from the city.

Churchill's July 29 letter on the atomic cooperation impasse awaited Stimson. From it, the secretary of war became aware that, since he had left London for Algiers, there had been further communication between FDR and Churchill directly on the atomic bomb project. At FDR's invitation, the secretary learned, Churchill had sent Sir John Anderson, who also arrived in Washington that day to negotiate resumption of British participation in the Manhattan Project. The written memorandum for the president that Stimson hand-carried from Churchill was being overtaken by events.

That morning, and again in the afternoon, Stimson met with Marshall in the secretary's office that adjoined the general's.[1] Stimson gave him an accounting of his trip observations and conclusions as well as his firmly held opinion that Roosevelt should assert U.S. leadership on the future direction of Allied strategy. Agreeing with Stimson's views, Marshall replied by telling him about "some of the difficulties that were encountered here with the President."[2] Stimson proposed holding a War Council meeting, a serious step especially with the president absent. This the general rejected. With Assistant Secretary of War for Air Robert Lovett, Stimson reviewed the antisubmarine warfare situation with the benefit of his meetings in Britain.[3] Stimson was reconnecting with the War Department's urgent business after his absence of more than three weeks. Foremost in his mind, however, was communicating to Roosevelt on Overlord.

On August 3, Stimson succeeded in telephoning Harry Hopkins, then vacationing with his wife at a friend's home on Mount Desert Island, Maine, but scheduled to join FDR in Canada the following day. In his journal, Stimson wrote that he "begged [Hopkins's] help in getting at the President whom I apparently am not allowed to communicate with myself. He was very sympathetic and thought I ought to see him at once and said he would take it up." To prepare himself, Stimson recorded, "I spent a large part of today dictating out an attempted appraisal of the result of my conferences abroad so that I will have something on paper to use in case, as usually happens, the conversation with the President is broken and haphazard."[4]

Stimson, a seasoned attorney, wrote as if preparing a trial brief. Into his writing he poured his knowledge of the man who would read it, Roosevelt. The memorandum, although solid enough to stand alone, would present his evidence and argument. Stimson held back for now from stating overtly his strongly held conclusions and recommendations—in effect, his closing argument. Expecting to deliver the memorandum to FDR in person, Stimson planned to make his diplomatically sensitive summation orally.[5]

Stimson began by describing the forthright tenor of his conversations with Churchill. While at times their talks had been blunt, they were anchored in friendship, and he had gained a clearer understanding of Churchill's views than ever before.[6]

Stimson then summoned FDR's political instinct by telling of his first dinner conversation with Churchill and setting his account in a U.S. domestic political context. Churchill had criticized the fixed U.S. electoral calendar as a distracting influence on war strategy deliberations. Churchill saw a danger that the 1944 general election could lead to a change in U.S. leadership at a critical point in the war. Stimson wrote that, seeing an opportunity, he had replied by describing American voters' attitudes toward the war. He told the prime minister that becoming too involved in the eastern Mediterranean and further delaying the cross-Channel invasion indeed could increase the electoral danger. It could make voters susceptible to opposition "campaign arguments" about "being made to fight for interests which were really those of the British Empire. In other words, that the [Roosevelt administration's] war leadership in that respect was not good." Stimson wrote to FDR that he told Churchill such a development "would be a serious blow to the prestige of the President's war policy and therefore the interests of the United States."[7]

Stimson had made clear to Churchill in London, and now to Roosevelt by his retelling, the potential for emergence of a revitalized domestic political challenge to U.S. adherence to the basic U.S.-British policy of defeating Germany first. He closed this section by stating to FDR Churchill's preference for "a march on Rome with its prestige and the possibility of knocking Italy out of the war." But, Stimson noted, the prime minister eventually reaffirmed his May 1943 Trident Conference pledge to support the cross-Channel assault, "unless his military advisers could present him with some better opportunity not yet disclosed."[8]

Stimson's trip report to FDR then advanced three days to his July 15 visit with Generals Sir Frederick Morgan and Ray Barker, the former British and the other his American deputy, to be briefed on COSSAC's "Overlord Outline Plan."

Stimson, when in his fifties, had experienced combat as a colonel of artillery in World War I, leading batteries in support of the front line and at forward headquarters.[9] In the crisis-fraught year that had followed the attack on Pearl Harbor by Japan, Stimson had been a source of disagreement and aggravation for Roosevelt. Nevertheless, with Roosevelt, who played up his own modest adventures near the front in World War I, Stimson's assessment of military plans still carried the weight of authority born of experience.

He told FDR that the Allied cossac team believed that the cross-Channel assault could succeed on the Trident-specified date of May 1, 1944, with the forces allocated provided that reasonable conditions were met.[10] However limited in detail, that put before the president for the first time, via an experienced observer, a soundly based, qualified *Allied* projection of success for Overlord. The prospect of a successful cross-Channel assault had been heard previously by FDR only as an assurance from the U.S. Joint Chiefs, but without a foundation in analytical rigor, and never heard by him from the British.

Stimson then described at length the fears of the Allied cossac leadership and other U.S. generals in London that this favorable prospect could be undone by further diversions in the Mediterranean, including delay in transfer of seven, combat-experienced divisions to the UK for Overlord as promised in the Trident agreements. Elaborating on the risk to invasion buildup in the UK, Stimson told the president of General Morgan's specific concern that "the chief danger was of commitments made in perfectly good faith and in the belief that the delay proposed might be made up for by subsequent speed when as a matter of fact the effect of the delay would be the loss of the favorable summer and autumn season and throw the work of preparation into the winter season when such accentuated speed could not be attained."[11]

Without saying so directly, Stimson, a Republican, was reminding Roosevelt of his Democratic Party's losses in the 1942 midterm elections. Earlier that year, as signs of the American public impatience grew and mindful of preserving their support for the "Germany first" strategy, Roosevelt had set a goal of getting the U.S. Army into action against the Germans as quickly as possible. That October, with a grin and an imploring gesture, the president said to General Marshall, regarding the forthcoming landing in North Africa, "Please make it before Election Day."[12]

But the schedule for Torch could not be advanced, which FDR accepted stoically.[13] Whatever other issues influenced them, U.S. voters went to the polls in 1942 unaware of the imminent landing of U.S. troops to face the Germans in combat. FDR's Democrats lost forty-five seats in the House of Representatives and eight seats in the Senate.

By introducing the specter that even the *preparation* for Overlord might be delayed past the winter of 1943–44, Stimson implicitly raised the dire consequence. That was the risk of missing altogether the May–September window of favorable weather for a 1944 thrust across the English Channel. Thus Stimson put before FDR a choice now compelling in its political as well as strategic impact: override Churchill and keep Overlord on schedule for the spring of 1944, or face another election in November that year with U.S. goals for winning the war in Europe still distant and, this time, with the presidency at stake.

[handwritten margin note: domestic political implications]

Stimson returned to his conversations with Churchill. After briefly mentioning the important July 22 discussion of s-1, the Americans' shorthand term for the project to develop an atomic bomb, Stimson described in detail his confrontation with the prime minister on European strategy that immediately followed when they sent others from their No. 10 Downing Street room and closed the door. Withholding few of the atmospherics, Stimson told FDR that Churchill

> repeated assertions he had made to me in previous conversations as to the disastrous effect of having the Channel full of corpses of defeated allies. This stirred me up and for a few minutes we had it hammer and tongs. I directly charged him that he was not in favor of the Roundhammer operation and that such statements as he made were "like hitting us in the eye" in respect to a project which we had all deliberately adopted and in which we were comrades. I told him we could never win any battle by talking about corpses.[14]

Stimson, ever the former attorney, concluded his account by relaying an admission by Churchill that FDR could not fail to perceive as lawyerly. The cross-Channel assault would not be Churchill's choice but "having made his pledge he would go through with it loyally." Telling Roosevelt his last impression of Churchill's position before leaving London on July 24, Stimson returned to the issue of timing for Overlord:

> If pressed by us [Churchill] would sincerely go ahead with the Round-hammer commitment but that he was always looking so constantly and vigorously for an easy way of ending the war without a trans-Channel assault that, if we expected to be ready for a Roundham-mer which would be early enough in 1944 to avoid the dangers of bad weather, we must be constantly on the lookout against Mediter-ranean diversions.[15]

Stimson concluded his report to FDR with his visit to Eisenhower's headquarters in North Africa. He recounted the options opening in Italy after completion of the conquest of Sicily. In Tunis, Stimson had heard from the air power advocates on Eisenhower's staff, Generals Carl Spaatz and Jimmy Doolittle. They confirmed the opinion among air power leaders and COSSAC in London that Allied air forces could hold off German reinforcements sent to counterattack the Overlord landings. Stimson endorsed the view in Tunis that advances into Italy were justified at least to establish a position from which bombing of Germany from the south could begin. But on the prospect of an offensive up the Italian mainland, Stimson reported that Eisenhower, who impressed the secretary favorably, "said that if we were to be obliged to 'merely crawl up the leg,' it would be so slow that he thought we had better jump at once to Roundhammer."[16]

Henry Stimson completed his trip report on August 4. In the memorandum, Stimson had established for FDR the criticality—political as well as military—of implementing Overlord (which he called "Roundhammer") on schedule in the spring of 1944. He detailed the strength of Churchill's continuing resistance to Overlord in unequivocal terms and the danger to timing of the invasion inherent to Churchill's alternative options. He noted the opinion of Allied planners in London that Overlord was feasible and that the Allied commander in the Mediterranean, Eisenhower, recommended the cross-Channel thrust over an offensive up the Italian peninsula.

However, Stimson demurred from putting into his August 4 report his most profound and diplomatically sensitive conclusions from the trip. Of these there were principally three. Stimson had become convinced that the Allied assault into northwestern Europe could not succeed under a British supreme Allied commander. Therefore, he believed that FDR should assume openly the leadership of the Alliance that Churchill had offered to him in 1942. Roosevelt should insist on reaffirming the primacy of Overlord as the Allied strategy for Europe and insist that it be led by an American general as Supreme Allied Commander. A fourth point that Stimson did not put into this paper, because he would not put the general in an awkward position, was his recommendation of George C. Marshall for Supreme Allied Commander. Anticipating that he would present his report to FDR in person, Stimson intended to make these points in direct conversation. Nevertheless, even without these conclusions, Stimson's message to the highly perceptive Roosevelt was a powerful one.

Secretary Stimson showed his memorandum to Marshall. As he read it, the general knew that down the corridor senior staffers were arguing over whether to stick with the U.S. insistence on Overlord as scheduled or accept options in the Mediterranean. He knew also that Major General Barker, sent by British Lieutenant General Morgan in contravention of his superiors' instructions, finally had arrived in Washington with the COSSAC plan. With a persuasive case for Overlord, Barker was about to be thrust into the Pentagon debate. Marshall suggested no changes to Stimson's memorandum to the president, which contained no hint that Stimson would propose Marshall to command Overlord. Of that, the general had no knowledge.[17]

Stimson was prepared to fly up to Canada to present his findings in person, but Marshall, who controlled the Army's airplanes, would not allow him to do so. Instead Marshall advised sending the report by air courier to FDR's fishing camp in Canada. Marshall insisted that Roosevelt would be more likely to absorb the message if received in writing and presented to him by Harry Hopkins.[18] Stimson acquiesced, knowing that Hopkins, then flying to Birch Island by Navy PBY Catalina amphibious patrol bomber, agreed with the essence of the findings and, being deeply committed to the cross-Channel assault strategy, would champion his report.

Marshall's approach to dealing with FDR when the chips were down was based on what the general had learned over five years about what worked, or did not, to obtain a critical and firm decision from a president whose pragmatism often led others to perceive him to be irresolute. Seeing critical need and circumstance aligned again, the general applied his learning.

Marshall's most recent experience, a negative but confirming one, had been his drive to meet with Roosevelt at Shangri-La on July 25, just nine days earlier, where he attempted personally to persuade FDR to take a firm stand on Overlord and reject British alternatives. Having coincided with the distracting news of Mussolini's overthrow, Marshall considered his meeting with FDR a failure. This failure reinforced Marshall's lessons from two earlier critical successes.

The first positive lesson came from successful resolution of the "1938 Airplane Conference." As a response to Hitler's bellicosity, Roosevelt wanted Congress to include in the federal budget an appropriation for the purchase, massive in its prewar context, of 6,000 new combat aircraft. When his generals responded to the White House with a request that was balanced to fund fewer planes while adding aircrew training, air bases, and their protection instead of a simple mass acquisition of aircraft, the president blew up. All knew that, whatever form the request took, the massive funding required would be a very heavy political lift for FDR and his allies, one sure to draw fierce attacks from isolationists in and out of Congress. In the swirl of meetings that followed, Marshall enlisted the highly respected retired Gen. John J. Pershing, who commanded the American Expeditionary Force in World War I, for another White House discussion. Pershing and Marshall left that meeting convinced that FDR had not listened.[19]

On Pershing's stationery, Marshall then ghost-wrote a letter restating the case for a balanced appropriation, which Pershing signed. The letter was sent to the president at the Little White House in Warm Springs, Georgia. There, relaxing with Harry Hopkins, FDR considered the letter at length. More meetings and horse-trading followed, but in the end, the substantial appropriation passed by Congress was for a balanced expansion and enhancement of the Army Air Force. Marshall was convinced that Pershing's letter to FDR, received while absent from Washington, contributed significantly to this outcome.[20]

Marshall's second lesson in influencing FDR's decisions came in early December 1940. Much of the world already had been swept up in war. Great Britain, aided by its dominions and empire, stood alone in Europe against the Axis. Roosevelt was sailing the Caribbean aboard the Navy cruiser *Tuscaloosa* with a few of his closest friends. None, save Hopkins, were versed in the dangers manifest in Europe. Although he had announced that he would inspect the bases received under lease from Britain in exchange for fifty old destroyers, FDR had actually escaped Washington to go fishing.

On December 9, a Navy seaplane delivered to the *Tuscaloosa* a 4,000-word letter to Roosevelt from Churchill.[21] In a masterful *tour d'horizon*, Churchill gave FDR his assessment of Britain's situation and projection for the year to come. He ended his message with the ominous statement that Britain was nearing the exhaustion of its ability to pay for vital military supplies from U.S. sources. At that time, under U.S. law, this assistance was available only on the basis of "cash and carry": money up front and transportation in British ships. Churchill expressed his belief that FDR would see the moral imperative to continue support and that "ways and means will be found which future generations on both sides of the Atlantic will approve and admire."[22]

Marshall understood Britain's dire situation and the importance to the still far from war-ready United States of continued British resistance of the Axis. If orders from Britain for American-made armaments ceased, so too would end the expansion of defense production plants vital to winning the war into which the United

States itself was certain to be drawn soon. Marshall followed Churchill's letter and FDR's response to it closely.

In a quiet, sheltered place on the cruiser's deck, Roosevelt read and reread Churchill's letter. He discussed it with Hopkins and went back to read it some more. Hopkins later said that for several days he had no idea what FDR would do.[23] The only evident certainty was that Churchill had captured the president's attention. Toward the end of the fishing trip, possibly not until they returned to Washington, Roosevelt revealed to Hopkins his response as a near fully formed plan.[24] Aid to Britain would continue as "lend-lease" to be returned or paid for after the war. By this approach, vital expansion of U.S. means of defense production would continue as well. Months of debate would follow, but White House aide Robert Sherwood believed that FDR had won his case from the outset with his mundane metaphor of loaning a neighbor a garden hose to put out a fire.[25] Churchill would call the Lend-Lease Act "the most unsordid act in the whole of recorded history."[26]

Marshall had learned from these two experiences that if presented with a well-argued decision paper when relaxed and physically removed from the distractions of the White House, FDR would focus, make a decision, and embrace it as his own. Marshall had concluded in 1939 that, quickly losing interest in long White House discussions, FDR often took over the conversation. Informal meetings with FDR invited digression and trouble. Marshall later said that for this reason he never visited FDR at Warm Spring, Georgia, and only visited Hyde Park for FDR's funeral.[27] The way to reach FDR, Marshall believed, was instead to make a well-stated case on paper. "You have to intrigue his interest, and then it knows no limit," Marshall said.[28] Observing Churchill's success with FDR as their relationship progressed, Marshall amended his early commitment to just a single page to entertain more expansive memoranda. This was fortunate for Stimson, whose Brief Report ran to fourteen pages.

The best prospect for the success of such written communication was when FDR was away from Washington and relaxed, preferably with Harry Hopkins present. Stimson's report, combined with the occasion of Roosevelt's fishing trip that Hopkins shortly would join, offered just such an opportunity.

Stimson's report was packaged and addressed to Harry Hopkins at Birch Island. Stimson inserted a cover letter to FDR stating that he was sending this through Hopkins and not giving up entirely on a personal meeting, adding, "If you care to talk them over with me before [Churchill] arrives, I shall be very glad to fly up to you at such time as you may suggest."[29] Atop this, Stimson placed a "Dear Harry" note asking him to present the report to the president and hinting again, stated that Churchill had given him two other messages for FDR "as to one of which he has given me a memorandum for the President which I can bring up."[30] The package left the Pentagon at 5:00 p.m., August 4, for delivery by air courier to the president's party at Birch Island. Their hopes for getting a decision from Roosevelt rested on Stimson's written argument, Marshall's strategy, and Hopkins's ability to influence FDR. In Washington, the secretary of war and the Army chief of staff could only await developments.

12

The Happy Time at Birch Island

Events took place that will perhaps go down in history as the most momentous occasion of this World War II. This, of course, I cannot discuss for some
time to come.

    —Lt. John Manley to Lt. Ernest Loeb, September 9, 1943

In Canada, the business at hand for the president was fishing.
Roosevelt took fishing "so seriously that it was like working,"
in the opinion of James Byrnes, director of the Office of War
Mobilization. Nevertheless, Byrnes, a South Carolina country boy,
complained about waiting until afternoon to get onto the water.[1]

Admiral Leahy wrote in his journal that, by FDR's established
tradition, the party "had a daily pool into which each of the seven
or eight participants contributed one dollar to provide a prize to
the individuals who brought in the largest, the longest, and the
greatest number of fish. . . . In the final settlement of our pool at
the weekend only the President and I were winners. . . . Mr. Harry
Hopkins joined our party on August 4th and thereafter contributed his daily share to the winnings of those of us who were the
most successful fishermen."[2] There were plenty of fish—bass,
pike, pickerel, and lake trout—in the clear, deep water that in
the still of late afternoon could reflect the rocks so perfectly as to
leave boaters feeling suspended in space and time.

U.S. Navy Reserve Lt. John Manley knew the *Anna H* and the
waters well from prewar visits aboard her. The young officer cap-
tained the craft for FDR's trip. He wrote about the trip to his prewar fishing buddy serving in the Pacific, Ernest Loeb, whose family
owned the *Anna H*. Both men were of the generation of Americans
who came of age knowing only Franklin D. Roosevelt as their president. The dreamlike experience of being in the cockpit of the little

Anna H with his commander-in-chief and personalities he knew only from newsreels permeates Manley's letter. He wrote of eating from the same lunchbox, FDR sharing half his sandwich with the boatswain, and the president making sure the enlisted sailors got proper rest. He wrote to Loeb, "It is almost unbelievable how good the fishing was. We fished in the Current Bay and waters of McGregor Bay, across the peninsula and in the uncharted waters of White Fish Bay. . . . Saw F.D.R. pulling in a good sized small mouth, General Watson (Military Aid to F.D.R.) betting a dollar it isn't as big as the one he caught and Justice Byrnes picking up the bet of General Watson's and Harry Hopkins, the stake holder."[3]

The fishing party split itself between two boats usually with FDR, Leahy, Watson, Hopkins, Brown, and McIntire in the *Anna H*, and the rest with James Byrnes in the other boat. Of course rivalry and a daily pool immediately developed between the two craft. As they returned to the dock at the end of the day, FDR would pull alongside to show his catch with his observations on each fish.[4]

Mystified though most of the world was as to FDR's whereabouts, McGregor Bay residents knew. Their experience of the president's visit was of security, circling planes, machine gun–armed guard boats, and personal encounters with an affable FDR. E. D. Wilkins recalled to the *Sudbury Daily Star* that, while on the water and ruminating about the vagaries of Ontario politics, he looked up from his fishing pole to recognize immediately the smiling U.S. president. From across the water, FDR hailed Wilkins in a booming voice from the *Anna H* and asking, "What luck are you having?" When Wilkins raised a stringer with two bass, FDR called out to Wilkins, "We're going after some like that right away. We had good luck yesterday."[5]

Dusk each day brought cocktails aboard the *Ferdinand Magellan*. On their supposed and actual location there was "merry talk about the latest rumors and competitive talk about fishing exploits."[6] The end-of-day fresh fish dinners concluded well. Drawing from limitless wild blueberries and their finite sugar rations, local cottagers gifted the fishing party with homemade pies.[7]

The fateful issue of strategy for Europe's liberation, however, would not be put off. On the morning of Thursday, August 5, a graceful, float-equipped USAAF Beech C-43 air courier from Alpena, Michigan, set down on the water near Birch Island with the day's dispatches from Washington. In the pouch was Secretary of War Stimson's package addressed to Harry Hopkins and meant for the president. This was the first of three communications that would reach FDR before the sun set that day in a completely unanticipated collision of the competing strategies for Europe.

Even as Hopkins and Roosevelt were out on the water fishing and discussing Stimson's just-received memorandum, radiomen in the Signal Corps communication car, ashore, were decrypting a new, three-part message to FDR from Winston Churchill, relayed to them by the White House Map Room. The prime minister's message was a fresh appeal for the competing alternative to cross-Channel assault, action on Churchill's Mediterranean strategy. Soon there arrived the third communication from an unexpected source in London, another encrypted radio message, one that challenged Churchill's facts.

As the president's party had traveled north, the new government of Marshal Pietro Badoglio in Rome, deciding to contact the Allies about exiting the war, had sent out emissaries on July 30. One of these, the Marquis Blasco Lanza d'Ajeta, had arrived in Lisbon, Portugal, where he met with British ambassador Ronald Campbell.[8] Once relayed to London, Lanza d'Ajeta's oral message stimulated Churchill to press upon FDR again, strongly, his Mediterranean strategy preference. Late on the evening of August 4, Churchill passed to U.S. ambassador John Gilbert Winant his message no. 405, an assessment and recommended response to the Italian diplomatic initiative. Winant then transmitted it to FDR over the U.S. embassy circuit as requested by Churchill.

Seeing opportunity in the Italian overture, Churchill wanted urgent action in the Mediterranean. In his account to FDR, embellishing on what the ambassador had reported that Lanza d'Ajeta had said in Lisbon, Churchill gingered up his scene-setting with a dire picture of Italy following Mussolini's arrest. Although Ambassador Campbell's report on the meeting included no report by the Italian diplomat of internal unrest in Italy, Churchill inferred otherwise.[9] Citing no source other than Lanza d'Ajeta, Churchill wrote in his account to FDR:

> Every vestige [of fascism in Italy] has been swept away. Italy turned Red overnight. In Turin and Milan there were Communist demonstrations which had to be put down by armed force. 20 years of Fascism has obliterated the middle class. There is nothing [standing] between the King and the patriots who have rallied round him and rampant Bolshevism.[10]

Churchill continued with a summary of German forces within Italy generally reflecting the raw intelligence Campbell reported that Lanza d'Ajeta provided. On the basis of his description of internal unrest, German troop dispositions in Italy, and Churchill's acknowledgment that the option of an Allied thrust into the Balkans was not on the table, the prime minister again argued that "the sooner we land in Italy the better" and that by doing so the Allies "shall find little opposition and perhaps even active cooperation on the part of the Italians."[11]

The day's third message, arriving at Birch Island from London via the White House Map Room on the heels of Churchill's message, was from Ambassador Winant himself. Uneasy about the message he had sent for Churchill, Winant had spent the day checking further with British foreign secretary Anthony Eden, who also questioned the reliability of Churchill's information as sent to Roosevelt. Winant sent to FDR Eden's statement to him in full. Drawing from other intelligence, analyzed by professionals, Eden considered the military information from Lanza d'Ajeta exaggerated and possibly founded on a German deception. Eden's statement concluded, "My own strong feeling is that there is nothing in this approach that should deflect us from our present policy including resumption of the bombing of Rome." Courtesy of Eden, Winant added the full text of the British message from Lisbon on which Churchill had based his cable to FDR.[12] If the two messages from London were compared side by side, as Roosevelt could do, the basis for the prime minister's fresh entreaty to land in Italy looked thin.

The equation for success in getting an important decision from Roosevelt, which General Marshall had developed from experience, had rested on presenting for FDR's consideration a single idea. But now a directly competing idea had presented itself as well in Churchill's message 405. Each argument had a champion known and respected by Roosevelt, first Stimson and now Churchill. The duality was a new factor potentially altering Marshall's equation in unknown ways.

Marshall and Stimson in Washington had not foreseen the secretary of war's memorandum advocating a firm decision endorsing Overlord being considered simultaneously by FDR alongside its directly competing strategy concept. So, too, Churchill, now aboard the *Queen Mary* sailing toward Canada and a pre-conference meeting with Roosevelt at Hyde Park, did not know the timing or content of Stimson's report to FDR on his London and North Africa trip. Unknowingly, Churchill had risked overreaching with exactly the kind of "Mediterranean diversion" Stimson's memorandum warned FDR against.

Which course would the president choose if either? Famous for keeping his own counsel, Roosevelt did so now. Like the situation almost three years earlier, when FDR pondered Churchill's 1940 letter that spawned Lend-Lease, Harry Hopkins could not determine whether or not Roosevelt had come to a decision about the conflicting cases for Allied strategy.

Outwardly in the days that followed, something about Roosevelt had changed, at least in the opinion of his Canadian fishing guide, Donald McKenzie. "He talked more freely, whereas the first part of the week he seemed quite preoccupied." Asked, "Would you suggest that he had solved a problem that had been bothering him?" McKenzie answered, "Well he was very cheerful today [Saturday] when we were out fishing, and if he came here with a problem to solve I would say that he made some headway on it."[13]

Lieutenant Manley was in close quarters with Roosevelt throughout the week aboard the *Anna H*. He also attended at least one of two dinners FDR hosted aboard the *Ferdinand Magellan* for officers of the *Wilmette*. In his letter to his friend about the experience,

Manley wrote cryptically, "Events took place that will perhaps go down in history as the most momentous occasion of this World War II. This, of course, I cannot discuss for some time to come."[14]

Marshall and Stimson, by August 5, had learned about Churchill's long message to FDR from either the White House Map Room or Field Marshall Sir John Dill, Marshall's trusted source on British intentions.[15] From Birch Island, however, they received only the briefest message from Roosevelt to Stimson on August 5, stating that he had read Stimson's memorandum.[16]

The fishing party departed Birch Island by train at 10 p.m., August 7. Reilly and Long's original plan had been to make a circle to return along the beautiful Ottawa River and through Canada's capital.[17] However, there had been a security alert. An escaped German prisoner of war, Peter Krug, had been recaptured early August 5 near the railway in North Bay, Ontario, through which Roosevelt's returning train would have passed.[18] FDR's train instead retraced its route through Ontario, then directly back to Washington.[19]

As the train traveled south, a reply from Stalin to Roosevelt's invitation to meet informally arrived at the White House via the Soviet embassy. Because the German offensive on the eastern front had been delayed one month, from June to July, Stalin wrote, it would be impossible to "keep my promise" for a bilateral meeting with FDR during the summer or autumn of 1943. However, Stalin requested a meeting between the two countries when the situation allowed and suggested either Astrakhan or Archangel, each a city in the Soviet Union. Then he went beyond FDR's desire for informality. The meeting, Stalin noted, would require preparatory consultation on agenda and drafts of proposals. He concluded by saying, "I do not have any objections to the presence of Mr. Churchil[l] at this meeting, in order that the meeting of the representatives of the two countries would become the meeting of the representatives of the three countries."[20]

Late on the night of August 8, probably from Buffalo, New York, FDR sent Secretary of War Stimson a telegram that said only, "I hope you will lunch with me on Tuesday. Glad to have your memoranda."[21] Stimson and Marshall continued to wait in suspense.

13

Plain Speaking on the Potomac

The United States and Great Britain have now reached the crossroads in the war where perseverance in the practice of dispersing the limited resources and reversing or amending decisions involves a grave danger that the war will become stalemated or that decisive action leading to complete victory will be indefinitely postponed.

—Maj. Gen. Thomas Handy, U.S. Army, August 8, 1943

As Roosevelt fished in Canada, the converted Cunard liner RMS *Queen Mary* steamed westward in the Atlantic bearing Winston Churchill, the 230-member British delegation to Quadrant, and well secured below decks, thousands of Axis prisoners of war.[1] Brig. Gen. Kenneth McLean, Air Cdre. Victor Groom, and Royal Navy Capt. M. J. Mansergh, the COSSAC team sent along in support, attended the third aboard-ship meeting of the British Chiefs of Staff Committee and briefed them on the "Overlord Outline Plan."[2] The chiefs then wrote a covering note recommending that the Combined Chiefs of Staff approve the outline plan with the plan's three conditions. These were that the German Luftwaffe fighter force would be reduced in strength; German Wehrmacht reserve offensive forces in France on the target date would not exceed twelve full-strength division equivalents; and the artificial harbors would provide sheltered water for over-the-beach expansion and resupply of the landed Allied assault force.[3] The chiefs' note recommended authorizing COSSAC to proceed with detailed planning.[4] This was important, if qualified, progress.

Two days later, the COSSAC team members were relaxing in their cabin when McLean and Groom were summoned on short notice to explain the plan to Winston Churchill. The prime minister lay in the bed of his stateroom while the two officers set up their large-scale map and, as recounted by Churchill, "explained in a tense and cogent tale the plan which had been prepared for the cross-Channel descent upon France."[5] In the moment, the prime minister's preference for the Mediterranean strategy and his opposition to the cross-Channel assault were set aside. Churchill, who liked the COSSAC plan, was moved to show McLean and Groom his own plan, which involved ten armored brigades and "relied on 'violence and simultaneity.'" Churchill wanted the ground forces in COSSAC's plan increased by 25 percent. If approved, this would bring the assault force up close to the number of troops that COSSAC himself, British Lt. Gen. Sir Frederick Morgan, would have preferred from the outset. Told by the COSSAC men that making the troop increase would come down to a matter of landing craft, Churchill declared that more landing craft must be produced.[6]

The COSSAC men had emphasized to Churchill the importance of "Mulberry," the two artificial harbors for over-the-beach buildup and sustainment of the invasion force. That prompted a demonstration. Members of the British COS Committee crowded into the bathroom of Churchill's suite. According to Gen. Sir Hastings Ismay, the prime minister in his colorful dressing gown sat on the commode to observe while an admiral splashed his hands in the water at one end of the bathtub to make waves and a brigadier stretched a sponge across the other end to show the mitigating effect of the "Mulberry" block ships.[7]

The *Queen Mary* steamed on toward Halifax. Meanwhile Britons and Americans were talking in Washington. They would draw together closer still the separate issues of European war strategy and the atomic bomb.

* * *

After tumbling over Great Falls, the Potomac River, separating the District of Columbia from Virginia, flows south and broadens to become tidal and up to a half mile wide. In the routine of government in Washington, the phrase "across the river" is said frequently. "Across the river" might be spoken as a reminder of powerful third party interests in a pending decision or an announcement of travel a short distance to elevate a discussion.

During the first week of August 1943 with FDR away, intense discussion and negotiation of the critical issues separating Britain and the United States took place on each bank of the Potomac. In Virginia, talk at the Pentagon was of strategy for Europe and in Washington, across the river, sharing atomic information. Each would shape the impending meeting between Roosevelt and Churchill and, through their linkage, the outcome of the conference in Quebec.

At FDR's invitation to Churchill to "send over your top man in this enterprise," Sir John Anderson arrived at the British embassy in Washington, Monday, August 2.[8] Head of the British atomic bomb program, Anderson had flown over to negotiate resumption of atomic information sharing. Waiting for him was a telegram message of encouragement from the prime minister. Its source, back in London, was a chit on which in the upper right had been handwritten and underlined, "Explosives," and in the entirety of its body, "Best of luck—Winston."[9]

Anderson checked in with William Akers, Britain's resident liaison for the atomic bomb project and suspect to the Americans because of his long association with Imperial Chemical Industries. The American scientists saw in ICI a potentially powerful competitor for postwar commercial applications of atomic energy.[10]

Negotiation between Vannevar Bush and Sir John Anderson began almost quaintly via cross-town secure mail messengers. The afternoon of August 3, a letter to Anderson from his American opposite arrived by courier at Britain's shaded, red-brick Georgian-style embassy on Massachusetts Avenue. Bush had sent an extract from the December 15, 1942, "Conant memorandum" as written then. Bush had added his "Present interpretations" to the enclosed points as a baseline to which the British were invited to recommend modifications as a vehicle for an atomic information interchange agreement.[11]

Following some discussion between them of the Conant memorandum, the British scientist sent on August 4 a letter by courier to Vannevar Bush at the Office of Scientific Research and Development (OSRD) a mile away. Bush received Anderson's refinement of the wording of Churchill's July "Heads of Agreement" draft and a proposal for a second, more detailed agreement on implementation with Anderson's draft text of both.[12]

While negotiating with Anderson, and under pressure from colleagues, Bush continued to try to make sense of the confusion of instructions from the president that he encountered while in London. His anxiety was heightened by the July 30 memorandum from his deputy, James Conant, that awaited him in Washington. Conant reacted to FDR's July 20 instruction to Bush by reaffirming his own opposition, writing that "a complete interchange with the British on S-I is a mistake." Conant authorized Bush to quote him to "higher authority if you see fit." Roosevelt, absent from the city, was Bush's only higher authority.

Charged to negotiate on their behalf and acutely sensitive to divided opinion among his stakeholders, Bush completed a "Memorandum for the File Made as Original Only" with his account of the "Sequence of Events Concerning Interchange with the British on the Subject of S-I." To the memorandum Bush added two handwritten notes. First, "the President was out of town when Sir John & I both came to the U.S., so that I could not make immediate contact with him to clarify the somewhat general instructions in his letter to me [of July 20]. Aug 4 V.B." That was followed by "Letter from Sir John received Aug 4. Arranged to discuss with Mr. Stimson."[13] Bush encapsulated his view of the effect of the disparity between the critical verb in FDR's message as sent from the White House, via OSRD, and the message he received in London (*renew* replaced with *review*) as "a very strange bit of confusion."[14] Over the days of their negotiation, Anderson developed a sense that Bush lacked "the strength to control Dr. Conant."[15]

Bush spent August 5 consulting with the Military Policy Committee to develop a response to Anderson's letter and refining the draft agreement received the day before. Bush was able to review the material and hold discussions with Secretary Stimson, General Marshall, and Dr. Conant. Vice President Wallace was out of town, but at the conclusion of his consultations, Bush was confident that Wallace would support the committee's response.[16]

While Bush was consulting, Anderson crossed the Potomac to lunch with Stimson and Marshall. The lunch in Stimson's Pentagon office also included Stimson's aide, Harvey Bundy, who had participated in the key meeting with Churchill on Tube Alloys–s-1 in London on July 22. During lunch, according to Bundy, Stimson and Marshall, both members of the Military Policy Committee, "discussed s-1" with Anderson.[17] Stimson and Marshall, according to Anderson, stated to him their wish to fully restore Anglo-American collaboration.[18] If correct, this went farther than Bush, Conant, and Groves were prepared to go.

To Anderson's surprise, he found Stimson and Marshall minimally informed about the atomic bomb project. Anderson recorded that Stimson said that he had reached a new understanding of the issues.[19] From the scientist's perspective, Stimson may have shown only cursory awareness of physics-driven issues of the project, but he certainly understood the policy issues. His insightful summation of the Anglo-American atomic impasse in the July 22 London meeting that he and Bush had with Churchill had influenced the prime minister's draft agreement now in negotiation between Anderson and Bush. This second meeting with Anderson at the Pentagon reinforced Stimson's personal position that the atomic bomb should be a joint possession of the two countries.

Brought to Washington in its evolved form by Anderson, Churchill's proposed atomic agreement included five points. The four substantive points, unchanged from the July 22 London discussion, clearly went beyond reopening to the British of the current wartime research to develop an atomic bomb. They would establish a policy framework for a U.S.-British political-military atomic relationship with no stated limit to its duration. The four substantive points were as follows:

1. President Franklin D. Roosevelt and Prime Minister Winston Churchill together with the Anglo-American Combined Chiefs of Staff in Casablanca for the Symbol Conference, January 1943. *Left to right*: Lt. Gen. Henry "Hap" Arnold, USAAF, Adm. Ernest King, USN, Gen. George Marshall, USA, Adm. Sir Dudley Pound, RN, Air Chief Marshal Sir Charles Portal, RAF, Gen. Sir Alan Brooke, BA, Field Marshal Sir John Dill, BA, and Vice Adm. Lord Louis Mountbatten. © Imperial War Museums (NY 6074).

2. The Anfa Hotel, on a hill overlooking the Atlantic Ocean outside Casablanca, was the venue for Symbol Conference meetings in January 1943. U.S. Army Air Force photo, NARA (1031 AC).

3. Winston Churchill and the British Chiefs of Staff strategize in a stateroom aboard RMS *Queen Mary* en route to Washington for the Trident Conference, May 1943. © Imperial War Museums (A16709).

4. The Cunard liner RMS *Queen Mary*, converted for war, could transport 15,000 troops and took Churchill to North America for two conferences. © Imperial War Museums (A25913).

5. At the start of the May 1943 Trident Conference, Churchill and Roosevelt pose for photographs outside the White House in Washington DC. U.S. Army Signal Corps photo, NARA (208-PU-175C-4).

6. (*opposite top*) The Joint Planning meeting in Algiers, June 4, 1943. Flush with victory in Tunisia and gathered around Churchill, *left to right*, are Foreign Minister Anthony Eden, Gen. Sir Alan Brooke, Air Chief Marshal Sir Arthur Tedder, Adm. Sir Andrew Cunningham, Gen. Sir Harold Alexander, U.S. Gens. Marshall and Eisenhower, and Gen. Bernard Montgomery. Second from the left in the background is Maj. Gen. Thomas Handy, who flew to Algiers on short notice to support Marshall. © Imperial War Museums (NA 3286).

7. (*opposite bottom*) Lt. Gen. Sir Frederick E. Morgan, BA, was the Chief of Staff, Supreme Allied Commander (Designate), "COSSAC." His uniform bears the SHAEF insignia. © Imperial War Museums (EA 33078).

8. (*above*) Lt. Gen. Sir Frederick Morgan (*left*) congratulates his COSSAC deputy, Maj. Gen. Ray Barker, USA, on receiving the Order of the British Empire. U.S. Army Signal Corps photo, NARA (11583).

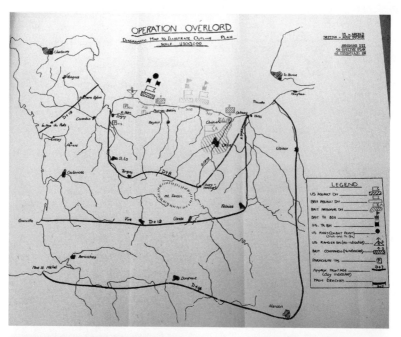

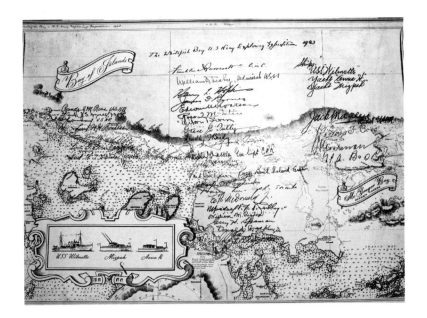

9. (*opposite top*) The COSSAC "Overlord Outline Plan's" hand-drawn depiction of a three-division assault on D-Day won the Combined Chiefs of Staff's approval at the Quadrant Conference. NARA (NM-84, 390/30/18/1, box 13, annex 3).

10. (*opposite bottom*) The COSSAC three-member teams who carried the "Overlord Outline Plan" to Churchill and to Washington reassembled at the Quadrant Conference in Quebec. *Left to right*: Captain Mansergh, RN, Captain Hutchins, USN, Brigadier McLean, BA, Major General Barker, USA; Air Commodore Groom, RAF, and Colonel Albrecht, USA. U.S. Army Signal Corps photo, NARA (178138).

11. (*above*) "The Whitefish Bay U.S. Navy Exploring Expedition 1943," a navigation chart of the waters around Birch Island, Ontario, signed by FDR and all the participants in his August 1943 secret fishing trip. FDR Library (Map #29-6-3.5).

12. (*opposite top*) Gen. Dwight Eisenhower, U.S. Army, the commander of Allied Forces in North Africa, together in Algiers, June 3, 1943, with his mentor, Army Chief of Staff Gen. George Marshall. FDR would choose Eisenhower to be Supreme Allied Commander in Europe. Courtesy of the George C. Marshall Foundation, Lexington, Virginia (GCM#973A).

13. (*opposite bottom*) A Royal Air Force reconnaissance photo of a small portion of fire-gutted dwellings, commercial, and public buildings following night bombing raids on Mainz, Germany, in August 1942. Housing was a target in an attempt to break morale. © Imperial War Museums (C 3378).

14. (*above*) At the Quadrant Conference, August 23, 1943, the Combined Chiefs of Staff and deputies gather in the Chateau Frontenac. These were tight quarters for discussing issues that were hotly debated.
Left to right: Vice Admiral Mountbatten, Admiral Pound, General Brooke, Air Marshal Breadner, Lieutenant General Ismay, Field Marshal Dill, Admiral King, General Arnold, Admiral Leahy, Lieutenant General Stuart, Vice Admiral Wells, and General Marshall. U.S. Army Signal Corps photo, NARA (178136).

15. The escort carrier USS *Bogue* (CVE-9) photographed off Hampton Roads, Virginia, June 20, 1943. *Bogue*'s hunter-killer group sank two U-boats on this cruise. U.S. Navy photo, NARA (71314).

16. (*opposite top*) Last minutes of U-118, caught on the surface and sunk by aircraft from USS *Bogue*, June 12, 1943. A depth charge, dropped from a TBM Avenger, has splashed into the water and will explode within seconds. Seventeen survivors were rescued. U.S. Navy photo, NARA (68694).

17. (*opposite bottom*) Anti-U-boat patrolling by very long range (VLR) B-24 Liberator bombers, such as these five in Northern Ireland, closed the Mid-Ocean Air Gap, thus helping to turn the Battle of the Atlantic in the Allies' favor. The antennae on the wing and nose are part of an early surface search radar. © Imperial War Museums (CH 18035).

18. (*opposite top*) The transport uss *Susan B. Anthony* (ap-72), decks packed with soldiers on a calm, sunny day, December 6, 1943. The "Susie B" is south of Nova Scotia, out of Boston, and bound for Britain in twenty-six-ship, fast troop convoy ut-5. U.S. Navy photo, nara (269623).

19. (*opposite bottom*) With great effort, the Allies broke the German Enigma machine's encryption of text messages. National Cryptologic Museum (Enigma File).

20. (*above*) Designed with an additional stepping function, the American Sigaba encryption machine was never broken and remained in service well beyond World War II. National Cryptologic Museum (Sigaba File).

21. The Sigsaly voice encryption system brought security to Allied transatlantic radiotelephone calls that, after July 1943, never again were decrypted or identified by the Germans. Sigsaly's fifty tons of equipment required six operators. Turntables for the phonographic crypto keys can be seen on the right. National Cryptologic Museum (Sigsaly Collection).

22. Travel to far-flung points around the world by Roosevelt and senior U.S. military officers and diplomats was facilitated by the Douglas c-54 Skymaster's significant passenger and cargo capacity, range, and comfort. Air Transport Command photo, NARA (28039AC).

23. Joseph Stalin, Franklin D. Roosevelt, and Winston Churchill pose atop the front steps to the Soviet Legation in Tehran, Iran, during the Eureka Conference, November 1943. Office of War Information, NARA (OWI 208-N-19478).

24. A sentry stands guard over a field of U.S. Army halftracks "somewhere in England" as the buildup for Operation Overlord mounts. Office of War Information photo, NARA (208AA42AA-3).

25. (*opposite top*) The battleship uss *Texas* (BB-35) as configured when escorting fast troop convoys across the Atlantic and for D-Day. U.S. Navy photo, NARA (208067).

26. (*opposite bottom*) Seen through the open ramp of an LCVP, infantry of the U.S. First or Twenty-Ninth Division wade toward Omaha Beach through surf and hostile fire from the heights on D-Day morning. U.S. Coast Guard photo by Chief Photographers Mate Robert E. Sargent, NARA (1041).

27. (*above*) One day after D-Day, despite continued sniping and mines offshore, Omaha Beach has been transformed as scores of ships unload U.S. troops, weapons, and supplies for the fighting inland. Twelve Landing Ship Tanks (LSTs) disgorge tanks, halftracks, guns, and trucks shuttled from England. Tethered barrage balloons float overhead to deter low-level air attack. U.S. Coast Guard photo, NARA (71287AC).

28. Dawn of a new anxious age. The first atomic bomb, Trinity, 1.5 seconds after detonation at 5:30 a.m. in the desert outside Alamogordo, New Mexico, on July 16, 1943. Los Alamos Scientific Laboratory photo, NARA (434-SF-2-13).

29. Fifteen seconds after detonating with the force of 18.6 kilotons of TNT, all that was swept up in Trinity's fireball roils into a mushroom-shaped cloud, still a specter today that challenges society to control the violence of war. Los Alamos Scientific Laboratory photo, NARA (434-SF-2-29).

1. A free interchange to the end that the matter be a completely joint enterprise.

2. That each government should agree not to use this invention against the other.

3. That each government should agree not to give information to any other parties without the consent of both.

4. That they should agree not to use it against any other party without the consent of both.[20]

The draft's fifth point established a process of governance for implementing the exchange of atomic information by creating a U.S.-British commission. Bush opposed sharing with the British except on the basis of "need to know" to win the current war. As a scientist, wary to step into foreign policy matters, Bush found his negotiating opportunity in the fifth point.[21] He agreed to the process while withholding the substance.

On Friday, August 6, Bush brought to a conclusion the negotiation with Anderson on the draft for an Anglo-American atomic research and policy agreement. The scope of agreement was narrow and specific. In a formal letter to Anderson, Bush reserved the first four out of five negotiating points as "matters of international understanding . . . [f]or the consideration of the President and the Prime Minister."[22] Bush told Anderson in his letter that he had reviewed the fifth point, on the process and governance of information interchange, with all of the members of the U.S. Military Policy Committee except Vice President Wallace who was away. The U.S. committee, he told Anderson, could accept the draft formulation for the governance body and process. They considered early selection of the Anglo-American Combined Policy Committee that would govern the information exchange process to be very important.

Bush wanted Anderson's statement of his intention to present the draft agreement as it stood to Churchill so that he, Bush, could "simultaneously transmit" this to the president.[23] The underlying message meant to be carried to both leaders was clear.

Although a process for cooperation was attainable, this would remain an abstraction with U.S. atomic bomb research closed to the British, unless Churchill came to terms directly with Roosevelt in an agreement on the substantive issues, all of which remained open. Only settling these would establish the atomic relationship that the prime minister considered so vital to Britain's postwar future. When next Churchill and Roosevelt met, one week hence at Hyde Park, the two leaders would do so knowing that each came to the table with a critical, open issue: the atomic bomb and Overlord.

These separate issues had come into intimate proximity in the White House during the Trident Conference the previous May and again in London in July. If resolution of Anglo-American differences might be found through their linkage, how much latitude did the president have under Congress's 1941 Declaration of War and the U.S. Constitution? At the War Department, following the previous day's lunch with Sir John Anderson, the large, long-term implications of the proposed atomic research and policy agreement with the British in fact was a source of concern.

Somewhere ahead, on the path to winning the current war, there was a threshold beyond which a treaty might be required for Anglo-American collaboration on creation of an atomic bomb, its control, and policy on its use. That especially would be so if the collaboration was intended to extend beyond this war. At the request of General Marshall, Harvey Bundy wrote a memorandum to Stimson to urge that these implications, pressed by Conant and Bush with support from Groves, be made clear to FDR.[24] Acknowledging his understanding of Stimson's view that the product of s-1 should be "the joint possession of the UK and the U.S.A.," Bundy advised Stimson:

> If you take the matter up with the President, I think it vital that he should understand that what Dr. Bush and Dr. Conant are really trying to do is to work out the agreement for interchange of information so that nobody, including the political opponents of the President, will be in a position to say that he acted otherwise than

under the war powers and for the sole purpose of winning the war. Therefore, they are strenuously of the opinion that the agreement should stand on a reasonable basis of *quid pro quo* and exchanges should be limited to the exchanges of information which will help expedite the s-1 development. They are trying to avoid at all costs the President being accused of dealing with hundreds of millions of taxpayers' money improvidently or acting for purposes beyond the winning of the war by turning over great power in the post war world to the U.K. without adequate consideration or without submitting such a vital question for consideration and action by both Executive and Legislative authority.[25]

Bundy submitted the memorandum to Marshall that day to check that it accomplished the general's intended purpose. Marshall replied, "I think it is o.k." At some later date, Brig. Gen. Leslie Groves, the military lead for the Manhattan Project (s-1), added a note to his copy: "Their views were in complete accordance with the opinions of the Military Policy Committee" of which Groves was a member. What would constitute "a reasonable basis of quid pro quo" to win the war might be seen differently, however, from the perspective of President Roosevelt and from that of his science adviser.[26]

Anderson and Bush now had closure if only so far as Bush would allow their negotiation to go. Writing to Bush from the British embassy on August 6, Anderson proposed that he submit their amended draft to Churchill and that Bush do the same with FDR.[27] This would take some time, as the president was out of the city fishing and Churchill was at sea headed for Canada.

The following day, Saturday, Bush prepared a package for transmittal to FDR on his negotiation with Anderson on atomic information exchange. In his cover letter Bush noted for the president that he had withheld comment from Anderson on the first four points of policy, deferring these to FDR and Churchill. Bush wrote, "I have encountered some strong opinions concerning them, but you will undoubtedly wish to consult on this broad aspect of the matter directly rather than through me."[28] Those "strong opinions" certainly included the clear statement by Churchill's science adviser, Lord Cherwell, to Bush in Harry Hopkins's presence on the last day of the Trident Conference, May 25, that Britain wanted to produce and possess an atomic bomb after the present war.[29] They also included Conant's equally clear intent—shared by Bush and Groves—that the enormous U.S. effort in the Manhattan Project should serve the U.S. objective to win the current war, not British postwar interests.[30]

* * *

All the while Bush and Anderson were negotiating on atomic research sharing in Washington, across the river at the Pentagon, General Marshal and his allies were restoring cohesion to the U.S. military position for the Quadrant Conference. Of immense help to them was the timely hand-delivery from London of cossac's Overlord Outline Plan.

As Stimson completed his trip report to FDR on August 4, Maj. Gen. Ray Barker, cossac's American deputy freshly arrived from London, was meeting with the U.S. Joint Planning Staff to brief and defend cossac's Overlord Outline Plan. This was the first of several meetings at the Pentagon in which the substance of the Allied plan would be revealed to U.S. military leaders and their staff. In the second meeting of the jps that day, Maj. Gen. Albert Wedemeyer and Brig. Gen. Laurence Kuter attacked the original and revised Joint War Plans Committee (jwpc) plans that favored the Mediterranean strategy. These two proponents of cross-Channel assault wanted to return to "sound strategic plans which envisage decisive military operations at times and places of our choosing, not the enemy's." In their view, Overlord must be the primary Allied strategy in fact as well as name.[31] But the challenge to primacy for Overlord in the U.S. position on strategy was not yet resolved.

On Thursday, August 5, the day when FDR in Canada was reading Stimson's report advocating Overlord with Marshall's endorsement, the debate within the Pentagon on sticking with that very strategy continued. In partial response to the criticism from Wedemeyer and Kuter, the Joint War Plans Committee shifted its view to favor a pincers assault on the peninsula of Europe with the cross-Channel and southern France invasions in mutual support.[32] From the perspective of Overlord's advocates, that was movement in the right direction. However, another staff group, Joint Strategic Survey Committee (JSSC), sent a memorandum to the Joint Chiefs of Staff calling attention to the "inviting promise of [the] new situation in Mediterranean" and expressing the Committee's willingness to "envisage encroachments" on the cross-Channel operation that might reduce it to a purely opportunistic effort to exploit "a marked deterioration" in Germany's Atlantic defenses."[33] In all but name, the JSSC had advocated the British strategy.

By a coincident action on this day, helpful to U.S. Army advocates for Overlord, Deputy Chief of Staff Lt. Gen. Joseph McNarny issued a directive reaffirming the Operations Division's authority as "the element within the General Staff having primary interest in overseas operations."[34] Within the Pentagon, OPD was the fountainhead of advocacy for Overlord.

While debate continued in the Pentagon, the start of Quadrant moved ever closer. That day, the U.S. Advance Team for the Conference flew from Washington to Quebec City.[35]

Viewing this American crisis of confidence from afar were the British Chiefs of Staff and, with interest second to no one, Morgan and his COSSAC team in London. From the Pentagon, August 5, Barker reported back to Morgan in London via the new, secure radiotelephone, Sigsaly. On the line with Morgan was Jacob Devers, U.S. Army commander of the European theater of operations.

Barker apprised the two generals of his meeting with the Joint Planning Staff. Summarizing their conversation in a report to his staff, Morgan wrote that Barker detected a "slight weakening of the American attitude [oppositional to Overlord] induced, as previously, by U.S. Navy authorities (NIWP Admiral Cooke). He is confident that he got there in the nick of time and reinforced a successful counter-attack by the War Department."[36] Barker reported that the Joint Planning Staff gave the Outline Plan a "good reception." On the movement of U.S. divisions to the United Kingdom, Barker had learned that two from the United States would be switched out.

More unsettling was Barker's news that the "War Department have asked if we should be broken-hearted if we did not receive the promised four divisions from Africa, but were given instead an equal number of divisions from the United States." Lt. Gen. Devers responded emphatically in the negative. The combat experience of the four U.S. divisions to be transferred to the UK from Africa was a quality vital to the success of D-Day. Devers ordered Barker to "stand out for the move from Africa as now arranged." In his assessment, Morgan warned his staff about the "danger of relying too much on promised reinforcement from Africa" and that it was "evident to me that both British and U.S. authorities are chiseling as hard as they can go."[37]

At its 100th meeting at noon on August 6, the Joint Chiefs of Staff discussed the COSSAC "Overlord Outline Plan" with Barker participating. Barker emphasized that the plan was from a U.S.-British point of view, that the existence of more than twelve full-strength German divisions in France would not mean that the plan would be impossible, but that in that event "special consideration as regards planning for the operation will be mandatory." Barker clarified for the Joint Chiefs the issues and conclusions on over-the-beach maintenance of logistics and told them that tests in Scotland showed the prototype piers for the artificial ports to be "rugged and serviceable." Marshall told the JCS that Maj. Gen. Thomas Handy, director of the Operations Division, was correct in stating the strategy choice to be between the Mediterranean with political results as its goal and, on the other hand, Overlord as an aggressive offensive action to achieve military results.[38]

Marshall asks Barker for his "frank opinion" of British attitude toward Overlord. In reply, "Barker said that every soldier of all ranks [in COSSAC] up to and including General Morgan and General Paget were 100 percent favorable toward Overlord. He said that when the Chief of the Imperial General Staff and others come under the 'sunlamp' of the Prime Minister, it is obvious that the latter's attitude is reflected and that everyone knows that the Prime Minister is always looking into the Mediterranean and especially into the Aegean." Absorbing this rich discussion of the "Overlord Outline Plan," and looking ahead to the Quadrant Conference, the JCS directed Barker to prepare a paper that would expand and clarify the ideas expressed in COSSAC's plan (accepted into the U.S. system as Report JCS 442).[39]

On Friday, August 6, the Joint Chiefs of Staff took to the offensive against the dissenters by sharply questioning the JSSC paper, a meeting in which General Marshall backed Overlord strongly. Chastised, the JSSC relented and produced a new, revised "Joint Chiefs of Staff QUADRANT and European Strategy" memorandum (JCS 443-Revised) now based on priority for Operations Overlord and Pointblank-Sickle, the Combined Bomber Offensive, and its transatlantic buildup and logistical support operation. Reflecting the position the JCS intended to take with the British chiefs, the paper stated that if the Quadrant Conference decision was made in favor of the Mediterranean, "OVERLORD should be affirmatively abandoned." Further, "If the British insist on a strategy for Europe which cannot be reconciled with the overall objective of ending the war as soon as possible, the U.S. Chiefs of Staff will have to consider transferring to the Pacific some of the U.S. resources now committed to Europe."[40]

Friday concluded with the staff again aligned in acceptance of the U.S. strategy concept approved by JCS. By Saturday morning the revised papers for JCS no longer bore any traces of support for making the "main effort in Mediterranean."[41]

Saturday, August 7, U.S. Joint Staff Planners submitted to the Combined Chiefs of Staff the U.S. intelligence case meant to support the JCS position at Quadrant, "Estimate of the Enemy Situation, 1943–1944, European-Mediterranean Area" (CCS 300/1). The intelligence estimate noted a favorable turn in the Battle of the Atlantic. It described Germany's basic task to be "gaining an advantageous negotiated peace by dividing her enemies politically . . . beating off their attacks, or by making her defeat so costly as to dissuade them from the task."[42]

This was a reasonable assessment of Germany from the Allied perspective in 1943 if a rational adversary was assumed and probably close to how the German General Staff saw their situation. Unaccounted for in the assessment was the perspective of Hitler and the Nazi leadership. Abundantly clear to most of them was that, short of now unattainable victory for Germany, an end to fighting also would bring their personal end.

As internal Pentagon discussions and the Bush-Anderson negotiations across the river moved to their separate resolution, Quadrant Conference preparations advanced further. Late that Saturday afternoon, the first of four special trains carrying the U.S. delegation departed for Quebec City.[43]

Already two days at sea were Winston Churchill and the full British delegation, having departed Faslane, Scotland, aboard RMS *Queen Mary* on August 5.[44] Averill Harriman and his daughter Kathleen were aboard. Harriman dined with Churchill every evening and then played Bezique, a nineteenth-century French card game from which Pinochle evolved. Harriman recounted, "Churchill still worried that the Americans, in their preoccupation with the climactic assault on the French Coast, would insist upon withdrawing troops [the seven divisions agreed at Trident] and landing craft from Mediterranean, effectively vetoing operations he had in mind for Italy."[45]

* * *

Sunday morning, August 8, with the U.S. staff revolt against Overlord ended, Maj. Gen. Thomas Handy was writing at his desk in the Pentagon. Handy had succeeded Eisenhower as the director of the War Department Operations Division. The Joint Chiefs, including Handy's boss, General Marshall, would meet with Roosevelt in two days with a further Churchill-Roosevelt meeting to follow imminently. The principals in Washington had received no information about how Secretary Stimson's report, guided in its presentation by Marshall's experience and Hopkins's presence, had been received by FDR. Thus for them, and for Handy as he wrote, the strength of the president's support for the now-unified U.S. military advocacy of Overlord was something still to be determined.

Handy spent the Sabbath writing a ten-page secret memorandum that, from the U.S. perspective, succinctly defined and prioritized the strategy decisions that must be taken by the United States and Great Britain at the Quadrant Conference.[46] Handy addressed his task with three developments in mind: Friday's jcs rejection of the Joint Strategic Survey Committee's bid to give near-term priority to the Mediterranean; Saturday's U.S. intelligence estimate that described Germany's basic task as attempting to gain an advantageous negotiated peace by dividing her enemies politically; and the already-begun deployment of the U.S. team to Quebec for Quadrant. Within twenty-four hours, Handy's memorandum would become the basis for the proposed Allied strategy paper that the U.S. chiefs would press upon the British, ccs 303.

Although setting a date for the cross-Channel invasion and the size of the force, twenty-nine divisions, Trident's expedient outcome, ten weeks earlier, had permitted continued parallel development of both the cross-Channel and Mediterranean strategies. After hesitating to consider again, the U.S. side was convinced that the United Nations had neither the time nor the resources to ride two horses. The U.S. military had come to agreement on its preferred mount, the cross-Channel assault.

Writing with a confidence reinforced by Marshall's endorsement of his strategic assessment the preceding Friday, Handy put to paper the essence of the concerns that the Joint Chiefs of Staff and their supporting planners had been voicing since the Trident Conference in May.

He set out the two choices. One was an opportunistic strategy of expanding operations in the Mediterranean, while relying on the bloodletting of the eastern front and internal weakening to bring Germany to the point of collapse. Or the Allies could affirm that only direct, explosive assault from the west across the Channel and into northwestern Europe, striking directly into Germany and joining with the Russian assault from the east, could defeat the Third Reich. Handy argued the case for cross-Channel assault as the superior choice. But above all, he concluded, Allied strategic indecision had to end at Quadrant. He wrote with emphasis that "even more vital to the achievement of victory than the particular course of action chosen is the pressing necessity of deciding what that course of action shall be and then sticking vigorously and whole-heartedly to that decision."[47]

Titled "Conduct of the War in Europe," the paper began by setting forth in unvarnished terms the consequences of the United Nations having "failed during the past year and a half to concentrate their forces and hold to decisions" in Europe. Handy concluded that the original objective of the Bolero plan for moving a U.S. force to the United Kingdom for a direct assault on Germany through northwestern Europe had been frustrated. Using then-available figures for the end of April 1943, the memorandum stated that the goal had been to have 1,047,000 U.S. troops in the UK for cross-Channel attack by that date. However, per the memo, at the end of April, only 452,000 U.S. troops were in Europe facing the Axis. Moreover, these were divided approximately equally between the UK and Mediterranean theater with 260,000 in UK.[48] At the time Major General Handy wrote his memo in early August, the number of U.S. troops in UK actually was 278,742, a mere 19,000 troop increase in four months.[49]

This end-of-July total fell 76 percent short of the U.S. Army's original Bolero goal of 1 million troops deployed to Britain by the spring of 1943,[50] on the way to 1.4 million U.S. troops fully ready for the cross-Channel invasion of Europe. The competition continued between force requirements in the Mediterranean and buildup for the cross-Channel invasion through Operation Bolero. In mid-July, three weeks before Handy's memo, the Combined Chiefs of Staff, at General Eisenhower's request, approved diversion to the Mediterranean of a convoy destined for the United Kingdom incurring a net subtraction of 66,000 troops from the buildup for Overlord.[51]

Handy could have added details of the composition of the U.S. forces in the United Kingdom. These illuminate the qualitative magnitude of the shortfall. Nine months after the transfer of forces from the UK for the November 1942 invasion of North Africa, the flow of U.S. ground combat troops to the British Isles had slowed to a trickle. Only one U.S. ground combat division, the Twenty-Ninth Infantry, remained deployed in Britain. Yet there had been no offsetting increases in troops deployed for other vital needs. Despite expanding and intensifying air operations, in significant part to implement Operation Pointblank, the reduction of Luftwaffe capability in advance of the cross-Channel invasion, the U.S. Eighth Air Force did not have enough crews in the UK to man all of its combat aircraft. Surviving aircrews, reduced in number by combat losses, were approaching exhaustion.[52] There were shortages among logistical support and engineering troops critical to preparing facilities in the United Kingdom that would provide the foundation for expansion of the U.S. force.

Compounding the quantitative shortfall in deployed forces, Handy wrote, was wasted logistical effort and operational planning in the United States and the UK. Handy explained that the effects were magnified in North America because of much greater geographic distances between factories, depots, camps, and embarkation ports. Although stating unequivocally that the North African landings, Operation Torch, had proved their value, Handy lamented that cargo capacity was squandered because hundreds of thousands of tons of supplies were transshipped through the UK to North Africa rather than being shipped directly from the United States. In the United States, preparation for operations that were kept in suspense by strategic indecision was causing units to be trained and equipped on a priority basis "for an agreed operation [cross-Channel assault] which is continually postponed, while a series of secondary operations [North Africa, Sicily] are undertaken for which they are either not required or unsuitable." The waste, Handy wrote, "if continued will certainly postpone victory, and may result in only a partial defeat of the Axis."[53] The COSSAC staff was in agreement with the last point, and Barker may have said as much in his Pentagon meetings, which Handy attended.

Handy found that as of August 1943, "the United States and Great Britain have two forces of limited size located in widely separated areas facing the European Axis. Neither of these forces nor their bases are at present adequate to launch an offensive which will bring victory quick and complete. Furthermore, it is doubtful that they are now sufficient to take full advantage of an opportunity presented by a major weakening of Axis power."[54]

By ensnaring themselves in a cycle of strategic indecision, maldeployment, and waste, Handy concluded, "The United States and Great Britain have now reached the crossroads in the war where perseverance in the practice of dispersing the limited resources and reversing or amending decisions involves a grave danger that the war will become stalemated or that decisive action leading to complete victory will be indefinitely postponed."[55]

Writing on Sunday, Handy knew that in two days the Joint Chiefs of Staff would meet with Roosevelt in the White House to discuss strategy for Quadrant and that two days later, the president would meet Churchill at Hyde Park, he and the JCS believed, basically alone. No one in Washington yet could gauge Roosevelt's commitment to the cross-Channel strategy (so clearly the choice of Marshall and the JCS) or the durability of FDR's commitment under Churchill's "sunlamp." More fuel for their anxiety as to whether and where the president would take a stand was about to come from Roosevelt himself.

General knowledge of the Americans' renewed resolve reached the British Quadrant delegation at sea aboard *Queen Mary* in an August 8 encrypted radio message from the British military mission in Washington. General Sir Alan Brooke, a passionate amateur ornithologist, concluded from the news that "we are to have a very difficult time of it at this Conference. Americans determined to carry on with preparations for re-entry into France and for Burma campaign at expense of Italy. They do not seem to realize the truth of the motto that 'A bird in the hand is worth two in the bush'!"[56]

14

A Presidential Directive

The President went the whole hog on the subject of ROUNDHAMMER. He was more clear and definite than I have ever seen him since we have been in this war and he took the policy that the American staff have been fighting for fully.... I could see that the military and naval conferees were astonished and delighted.

—Secretary of War Henry L. Stimson

President Roosevelt's train arrived back in Washington at 7:40 a.m. Monday, August 9, coming to a halt on the track underneath the Bureau of Engraving.[1] The members of the fishing party dispersed to their offices for the start of what would be an intense and decisive week. As they set the U.S. position for the Quadrant Conference, their activities quickly merged into the rhythm of consultations by the military chiefs and other principals who had not left Washington,

Vannevar Bush called Harry Hopkins at the White House an hour and a half into the business day. Bush requested and received an appointment to report orally and deliver the papers from his negotiation with Sir John Anderson on the drafted secret agreement on atomic weapons research and policy.[2]

Across the Potomac at the Pentagon, Secretary of War Stimson had returned to his office in the Pentagon from a weekend at his family home on Long Island, New York, at 9:35 a.m. Monday. Anticipating the separate meetings each would have with the president, Stimson and General Marshall met for almost an hour.[3] As Stimson took a telephone call from Harry Hopkins, who was reporting back on his discussion with FDR in Canada, Marshall joined a meeting of the Joint Chiefs of Staff.[4]

The Joint Chiefs of Staff were meeting that day for the 102nd time, with Leahy, Marshall, King, and Arnold attending along with thirty-nine other officers. The JCS agreed on the position that they would present to the Combined Chiefs of Staff for "consideration," Admiral King's choice of wording with Marshall's agreement, for adoption by the Combined Chiefs of Staff at the Quadrant Conference.[5] Titled "Strategic Concept for the Defeat of the Axis in Europe" and built on the conclusions in General Handy's August 8 paper, the JCS-recommended European strategy was forwarded to the CCS as "CCS 303."[6] Handy's paper itself was made required reading for all of the U.S. delegates to the Quebec Conference and, prior to Quadrant, was used by Marshall to communicate to Roosevelt the opportunity cost should the Allies fail to concentrate their forces promptly for a cross-Channel attack.[7]

In a continuation of tactics to control the meeting with the British, CCS 303 was organized to adhere to the agenda for Quadrant submitted by the JCS on July 27. This called for discussing first the overall strategic concept and undertakings in its support. This was a discussion that the British Chiefs of Staff preferred not to have at the start of the conference.

CCS 303 began with an overview of the enemy's strategic situation and United Nations strategy. The authors concluded that the Axis leadership probably was shifting its actual priority to ending the war on satisfactory terms and that they still possessed "strong defensive power" with which to achieve that. If the Allies' choice of strategy permitted their enemy the option, "A defensive strategy on the part of the Axis might develop into a protracted struggle and result in a stalemate on the Continent." In the circumstances before the Allies, CCS 303 concluded, "It is imperative, therefore, that the Allied Powers penetrate to the heart of the fortress of Europe, come to grips with the enemy, and thus bring about the early and decisive defeat of the Axis."

Complementing this argument for how to confound the enemy's likely intention, CCS 303 addressed the Allies' strategy options as an evolutionary choice. One option was the strategy of attrition that maritime power Britain historically favored and which the JCS considered to be rooted in the Napoleonic Wars. The other option was founded on the surging potential of land and air forces that reinforcement from North America could bring to bear. CCS 303 called for moving beyond hopes to effect a political-economic collapse of the Reich through attrition to choose, instead, direct assault for victory by a military result.

CCS 303 observed that comparative weakness early in the war was what had compelled the United Nations, then, to follow an opportunistic strategy of attrition. Now, argued the paper, the rapidly improving strength and position of the Allies relative to the Axis "demand an abrogation of opportunistic strategy and require adoption of and adherence to sound strategic plans which envisage decisive military operations conducted at times and places of our choosing—not the enemy's."

Turning from general to specific strategy options, affirmation of cross-Channel attack or expanded operations in the Mediterranean, the paper called for the CCS to choose at the Quebec Conference one of these as the dominant military strategy for the European theater. The JCS did not shrink from stating the choice to the British bluntly. On one hand, if the decision was that conditions in the Mediterranean justified putting the primary effort there, CCS 303 argued, then the Allies should concentrate strength in the Mediterranean and "concurrently . . . provide only sufficient forces in the British Isles to secure this important base and make available opportunistic forces to cross the channel if a German collapse should occur." Left unstated, but obvious for the British COS to conclude, was that this choice would mean no more than a reinforced U.S. corps (three divisions plus support) would be left in the United Kingdom with the number of USAAF long-range bombers perhaps, or perhaps not, equivalent to the force then conducting with the RAF the Combined Bomber Offensive. Also left as an unstated expectation was that the United States then would promptly direct increased attention and resources to the Pacific.[8]

CCS 303 called for reaffirmation, on the other hand, of the Trident decision in favor of the cross-Channel invasion as the primary strategy. CCS 303 declared that "Operation OVERLORD, carefully synchronized with the Combined Bomber Offensive, if given *whole-hearted* and *immediate support,* would result in an early and decisive victory in Europe" (underlined in the original). The balance of the sixteen-page paper set out prioritized operational elements of this cross-Channel invasion-based strategy. The paper specifically supported the Trident-agreed transfer of seven battle-experienced divisions from the Mediterranean to Britain for Overlord. After describing the options, the paper also recommended the invasion of southern France, in support of Overlord, with forces already in the Mediterranean.[9]

To prepare Stimson for his meeting with Roosevelt on Tuesday, Harry Hopkins crossed the Potomac for lunch and a discussion in the secretary's office that stretched into two hours. Their purpose, at Stimson's invitation, was to go over Stimson's August 4 "Brief Trip Report" and Hopkins's account of Roosevelt's reaction and receptivity when he discussed it with the president in Canada.[10] Despite having had ample time in Canada for discussion of Churchill's coincident and colorful appeal for prompt action to invade Italy, Ambassador Winant's cable calling into question Churchill's facts, and Stimson's memorandum, Hopkins had found that the president's reaction at the time had been inscrutable.

At Stimson's request, General Handy joined the luncheon meeting for thirty-five minutes near its end.[11] Having attended the JCS meeting and being intimately familiar with its output as the author of the source paper, Handy was well prepared to outline to the secretary of war and Hopkins the JCS's adoption of the strategy recommendation for Quadrant earlier in the day.

The Joint Chiefs' strategy paper, CCS 303, and the strong summation that Stimson withheld from his evidentiary August 4 memorandum, but which he intended to make to FDR the next day, bore the hierarchical and substantive differences in content to be expected between a military staff to military staff position and a cabinet member's political-military recommendations to the president. What they shared in common was a two-part thrust: decide firmly on one dominant strategy for the European theater at the Quadrant Conference and reaffirm the cross-Channel invasion. Remaining to be seen was whether the convergence of these recommendations from the military chiefs and the cabinet member could win Roosevelt's unequivocal commitment before the president met again with Churchill in four days' time.

At the White House, the many tasks awaiting Roosevelt that Monday included lunch with Secretary of State Cordell Hull to discuss a very full foreign policy agenda. After Hull left, and as Stimson, Hopkins, and Handy were meeting, Roosevelt met with his Army chief of staff, General Marshall.[12] Their discussion would stimulate Marshall's concern about the strength of the president's commitment to Overlord.

Roosevelt spoke to Marshall on the allocation of divisions to Overlord and to operations in the Mediterranean. The president stated his support for transferring seven combat-experienced divisions to Overlord from the Mediterranean but inquired about replacing them with a transfer to the Mediterranean of seven more divisions from the United States.[13] Roosevelt's query tested the limit of what could be done logistically to establish the required concentration of forces on one decisive axis of attack into Europe by May 1, 1944, then the date for the cross-Channel attack from the United Kingdom.

This raised in Marshall's mind an immediate concern. The Quadrant Conference was just over the horizon and FDR's preliminary meeting with Churchill was four days away. On one hand, the question implied that the president might not yet be persuaded that the time was at hand to affirm, once and for all, a dominant Allied strategy for the European theater. The strategy selected would govern the allocation of forces. Therefore, on the other hand, the president, by his question to Marshall, might also have been putting a test of resolve to his military chiefs before he confronted Churchill.

From that morning's meeting of the JCS, Marshall knew that the U.S. chiefs were firm in their position that future operations in the Mediterranean should be conducted within the capacity of forces already deployed there—less the seven divisions to be transferred to Overlord and not to be replaced in the Mediterranean. Immediately, upon returning from the White House to his office in the Pentagon, Marshall directed Major General Handy in precise, written detail to prepare no later than 11:00 a.m., August 10, a written answer to FDR's questions about troop lift possible for Priceless (the Mediterranean) and Overlord.[14] Marshall's direction to Handy anticipated the JCS meeting at noon on August 10 to prepare for their meeting with FDR later that afternoon and to set tactics the U.S. chiefs would employ in discussion with their British counterparts at Quadrant.[15]

By close of business, ahead of schedule, Marshall had his answer from Handy, based on options worked up by the Army chief of transportation. In essence, the answer was that movement of an additional seven divisions from the continental United States to the Mediterranean could be done under the most optimistic assumptions (no loss or further diversion of troop ships) if based on the May Trident commitment of 1.3 million U.S. troops in the UK, but not responsive to the new requirement for 1.4 million troops for Overlord and Pointblank. Handy recommended that full sealift be allocated to achieve a force of 1.4 million U.S. troops in Britain by May 1, 1944, for Overlord and Pointblank as the most effective contribution to the strategy for Europe. Handy noted that the representative of General Eisenhower, then commanding in the Mediterranean, had said that seven additional divisions would be nice to have but were not needed there. Handy's memorandum showed that transfer of an additional seven divisions from the United States to the Mediterranean would result in more divisions there than in Britain for Overlord, figures that are underlined by hand on Marshall's copy of the document.[16]

As Handy developed the response to FDR's query about divisions for the Mediterranean, Marshall and Stimson met twice more that afternoon to review Marshall's meeting with the president that day and "re: W. House conf" for the next day.[17]

Stimson wrote in his observations of these days that he was becoming even more convinced that an Allied strategy dependent on Overlord meant that "we must insist on getting an American commander and the only American commander we can probably get to be accepted by the President is George Marshall. I was very much interested to find as I went over with Harry Hopkins the suggestions in my mind that he agreed with every step and with my final conclusion."[18]

In parallel with preparation of FDR for the next round of military strategy debate, the atomic sharing issue moved into its next stage: updating the president. Shortly after 5:00 p.m., Dr. Vannevar Bush had his meeting with Harry Hopkins at the White House.[19] Bush briefed Hopkins on the outcome of his talks with Sir John Anderson on the proposed secret U.S.-UK atomic sharing agreement. Bush left with Hopkins the then-current draft of the information sharing agreement with its implementing process arrangements and the cover letter Bush wrote to Roosevelt on August 7. Bush's cover letter drew particular attention to the four political-military policy points that, at Bush's insistence, he and Anderson had left to the president and Churchill to negotiate directly.[20] Bush's meeting with Hopkins fulfilled his task in the "simultaneous" transmission of results of their negotiation to FDR, as would Anderson with Churchill as soon as they met in Quebec.

Meetings about Quadrant among the U.S. principals churned on in Washington through Monday when the *Queen Mary*, carrying Churchill and the huge British delegation to Quadrant, docked at Halifax, Nova Scotia. That afternoon the British boarded special trains to Quebec City.[21] Averill Harriman left Churchill at Halifax to travel to New York City. There Harriman would visit with family and consult with Hopkins before joining FDR and Churchill at Hyde Park for the "preliminary talks."[22]

Monday evening, Hopkins dined with the president at the White House.[23] From the day's meetings, Hopkins could relate the latest information on both U.S. preparations for Quadrant and the state of negotiation on an Anglo-American atomic agreement. Hopkins's meeting with Stimson had shown the president's adviser the consensus of agreement among Roosevelt's military advisers and commanders on strategy for Europe and their negotiating strategy for the conference. From Vannevar Bush, Hopkins had received an oral report and papers on the proposed secret agreement on British participation in atomic weapons research and subsequent policy. Significantly, the account of the Bush-Anderson negotiation conveyed to FDR its limited scope and what had been left to be settled directly between FDR and Churchill. Thus the president concluded his day knowing that his secretary of war and military chiefs were aligned on a strategy for Europe and objectives for Quadrant and that the central points of the atomic agreement, so desired by Churchill, were Roosevelt's to negotiate.

A mile and a half to the northwest at hilltop Woodley, his historic estate overlooking Rock Creek Park and the city, Henry Stimson was dining with his aide, confidant, and companion on his recent trip to Britain and North Africa, Harvey Bundy.[24] The day's events must have been prominent in their dinner discussion. From his meeting with Harry Hopkins that day to go over the president's reception of the August 4 trip report and, undoubtedly, Marshall's report on his meeting with FDR that afternoon, Stimson was pessimistic. He doubted the strength of FDR's commitment to Overlord with the Quadrant Conference beginning soon and FDR's next meeting with Churchill sooner still. Roosevelt went to bed at the White House with good reason to be confident about the chiefs' resolve and his own negotiating position. On the heights of Woodley Park, however, Stimson went to bed troubled.

Tuesday morning, August 10, Henry Stimson arrived at his office in the Pentagon. Having slept little through a hot night, he faced a challenging day. Stimson worked through his fatigue to dictate a new letter to the president again stating the heart of his August 4 report. Stimson had decided that his best course was to present his views on these critical matters to FDR in writing at their White House lunch.[25]

Compressed to a quarter of the length of his earlier report, Stimson's August 10 letter to the president concentrated on his essential conclusions from his trip to Britain and North Africa. From his meetings with Hopkins and Marshall the previous day, Stimson worried that FDR still had not fully appreciated the critical need for decisive and timely leadership in the meeting with Churchill and the conference that drew ever closer.

First among Stimson's points was that the Allies "cannot now rationally hope to be able to cross the Channel and come to grips with our German enemy under a British Commander." As his reasons, Stimson cited the years of defeats suffered by the British since 1939, the memory of British Empire combat casualties in World War I (almost one million killed), and the knowledge he saw as pervasive among senior British operational commanders that their prime minister and their chiefs could not put their heart into a cross-Channel assault. In an interesting choice of phrasing between two men deeply involved in their churches, Stimson then stated his second point: the strategy difference between the United States and the United Kingdom "is a vital difference of faith." The United States believed in massed U.S. and British Empire forces striking across northwestern Europe into the heart of Germany. The United Kingdom believed in eventual German political and economic collapse brought on by a strategy of attrition and aerial bombing. Third, in the circumstances, Stimson urged that it was time for FDR to "assume the responsibility of leadership." Stimson wrote that the Allies "cannot afford to begin the most dangerous operation of the war under halfhearted leadership." Two years ago, he said, Churchill had offered the United States leadership of the Alliance. The time had come, Stimson declared, that the British offer to the United States of leadership "should be accepted—if necessary insisted on." Fourth, Stimson concluded that "the time has come when we must put our most commanding soldier in charge of this critical operation at this critical time." That soldier, Stimson said, was George Marshall.[26]

After the letter was typed, Stimson read it again and signed it. Particularly because of Stimson's recommendation of Marshall for supreme command of the Allied forces, but also honoring the distinction between advice to the president from a cabinet member and that from a chief of staff of the Army, only then did he call General Marshall into his office to read the letter. Marshall raised no major objection to the letter, but he did not want an appearance of Stimson having consulted with him before writing it. Stimson told the chief of staff that this was why he had signed the letter first.[27]

On this morning, in contrast to one week earlier, Marshall could view the balance of Stimson's renewed call for the president to press the American strategy for Europe confident that the Joint Chiefs and U.S. military staffs were in agreement. The American planners were united with the Joint Chiefs in support of one primary strategy. Preparations for the military's afternoon meeting with FDR and for Quadrant continued. The memorandum concerning Allied Forces available in the Mediterranean, prepared by General Handy at Marshall's direction to answer the president, was forwarded by Marshall to Admiral Leahy at the White House.[28] The secretary of war took counsel from his aide, Harvey Bundy, in Stimson's office "re: White House appointment."[29]

At noon, the second special train taking members of the U.S. delegation to Quebec City departed Washington Union Station.[30] Also at noon, the Joint Chiefs of Staff sat down to prepare for their meeting with Roosevelt at the White House meeting at 2:00 p.m.

This 103rd meeting of the JSC had a certain anxiety about it, stimulated by FDR's question to General Marshall about sending seven more divisions from the continental United States to the Mediterranean to replace the divisions being sent to the UK for Overlord. Marshall told the JCS of his concern that neither FDR nor Churchill understood the near-term disruption to the war effort caused by switching resources back and forth between regions or the "far reaching effect on the shipping and production resources of the United States." Admiral King added that sending seven more divisions from the United States to the Mediterranean would "curtail planned Pacific operations" where shipping already had been withdrawn in support of Bolero-Sickle. Marshall thought the divisions, which would not arrive in the Mediterranean before June 1944, "would constitute in reality an expeditionary force available for use in the Balkans." Having reestablished unity within their own staff only days earlier, and with a meeting with FDR less than two hours away, the Joint Chiefs were uncertain about their commander in chief's intent.[31]

At 1 p.m., Stimson joined Roosevelt for lunch in the Oval Office. Stimson began by reminding Roosevelt of the substance of his

August 4 trip report, which he found the president "had very thoroughly in his mind."[32] Stimson then handed FDR his new letter. FDR, Stimson recorded, "read it through with very apparent interest, approving each step after step and saying finally that I had announced the conclusions which he had just come to himself."[33] Apparent was that Stimson's earlier trip report, conveyed to FDR and discussed by Hopkins at Birch Island, had indeed achieved the decisions Stimson sought. Confirming Marshall's strategy for presenting them, Roosevelt had made the recommendations his own.

Roosevelt and Stimson's meeting then turned to other matters including "current negotiations [with the British] about the atomic bomb." Stimson recalled that FDR "at once said that that was all settled." Settled they were only in the sense that Bush and Anderson had clearly defined terms of the agreement that could be reached only between Roosevelt and Churchill themselves and that, as the president knew, remained an open issue. Then, acting on the advice that Harvey Bundy had given him, at the strong urging of Vannevar Bush, Stimson raised concern about the second of four points in Churchill's proposal: that each government should agree not to use atomic bombs against each other. Roosevelt "did not think there was enough danger in that to make it worthwhile to amend it," according to Stimson, not venturing into the implied need for a treaty instead of an executive agreement. This suggests that FDR was ready to accept Churchill's points in an agreement to resume atomic information sharing and was holding his assent for the time and terms FDR found favorable.[34]

FDR had more fulsome and current information on the atomic negotiation than Stimson at this point, having the benefit of Hopkins's account to him the night before of Bush's status report. FDR also had been told by Hopkins that Churchill would receive a similar report from Anderson of what still remained to be agreed upon between the two of them. The negotiation was developing along the outline charted by Churchill and Stimson in their July 22 London meeting with the points of substance (versus process) left, at Bush's insistence, for Roosevelt and Churchill to negotiate directly. Within the span of three weeks, Stimson had participated in a meeting with first one of the leaders and then the other in which unsettled issues of the cross-Channel attack strategy and Anglo-American cooperation on atomic bomb research and postwar policy had arisen in intense and immediate, if unremarked, proximity.[35]

The time for the start of Roosevelt's 2:00 p.m. meeting with his JCS brought their lunch to an end. President Roosevelt invited civilian Secretary of War Stimson to stay for the FDR's meeting with the JCS as their commander in chief. Leahy, King, Marshall, Arnold, and the JCS secretary, Brig. Gen. John Deane, entered the Oval Office together.[36]

To the delight of the JCS and growing satisfaction of Stimson, Roosevelt affirmed to the chiefs in detail, point by point, the substance that they had been advocating. FDR endorsed reaffirmation of a cross-Channel attack in 1944 as the primary Allied strategy for victory in Europe. Not discussed, however, was the secretary of war's recommendation to the president of George Marshall for Supreme Allied Commander. FDR did say unequivocally that he wanted an American commanding the Allied forces. To support the basis for that, he directed the JCS to have the full complement of U.S. troops, then set at 18.5 divisions and their support, in the United Kingdom and operationally ready by D-Day.

By August 10, the "troop basis" (goal) for U.S. forces in the UK by D-Day, then May 1, 1944, had increased to 1.4 million.[37] To fulfill Roosevelt's directive, given Bolero's existing shortfall, the armed forces would move well over one million troops, plus millions of tons of weapons, equipment, and materiel, across the Atlantic in less than eight months.

Roosevelt, known for his inscrutability, had given his lieutenants direction with clarity and definition on the issue of strategy for Europe that had been mired in uncertainty and contention for more than a year. No one in the Oval Office that afternoon could doubt that embedded in their commander in chief's direction was an assertion of U.S. leadership of the alliance against the Axis. The chiefs and Stimson were elated. Briefed on the meeting by Stimson on his return to the office, Bundy concluded that

FDR had at last embraced the cross-Channel assault-based strategy for victory, Overlord.[38]

Beyond the strategy, its commander, and forces to implement it, Roosevelt also had signaled good reason for confidence in the strength of his direction to his chiefs. His message was one that Stimson and Marshall quickly could grasp. This was not necessarily so for others.

Writing for his memoir from what he was told by participants after the meeting, Gen. Albert Wedemeyer, an early planner and advocate for the cross-Channel assault strategy, quoted FDR as saying in the meeting with the JCS and Stimson that it was "unwise to plan military strategy based on a gamble as to political results." In Wedemeyer's opinion, "the remark made very little sense."[39]

Actually, the remark gave good evidence that FDR grasped the heart of the matter, Stimson's "vital difference of faith." In his briefing to FDR at Shangri-La on July 25, Marshall had argued for an Allied strategy based on direct action for a military result over one based, as Churchill advocated, on indirect action seeking to cause internal German political-economic collapse. Stimson had set out the evidentiary basis for this difference in his August 4 trip report, which FDR had discussed with Harry Hopkins at Birch Island, and stated the distinction directly in his lunch with the president just concluded. By his remark, FDR showed that he embraced not just the strategy of direct military attack but also the reason at its foundation.

Yet there remained for the chiefs and the secretary the anxious hope for FDR's new certainty to endure. As expressed in Stimson's diary, "If he can only hold it through in the conferences which he is going to have with the Prime Minister."[40] The first test of that would be FDR's meeting with Churchill at Hyde Park in less than two days.

As the JCS and Stimson returned across the river to their Pentagon offices, the third of the U.S. Quadrant delegation's four trains departed for Quebec City.[41] At 6 p.m., the British Quadrant Delegation arrived in Quebec City.[42]

The following day, Marshall took action on the president's

directive. He responded to FDR's instruction to have a preponderance of U.S. divisions in the UK on the target date for Overlord by committing to deploy not 18.5 but a full 19 divisions to
the UK by that date. He compared this force to the 14 (including
4–5 Canadian) divisions to be under British command on D-Day.
Marshall noted to FDR that in the Overlord buildup in France
to 60 Allied divisions, there would be 42 U.S., 13 British, and 5
Canadian divisions.[43] To Marshall, his memorandum was a critical step to reassure Roosevelt, who would be seeing Churchill
at Hyde Park the next evening, August 12, for two days of meetings before the president and prime minister went to Quadrant.

Through the Army General Staff's Operations Division, General
Marshall then sent an encrypted message to Allied Headquarters
in Algiers. Noting the participation of General Eisenhower's representative, Brig. Gen. Lowell Rooks, who had said an additional division from the United States would be nice to have for garrison duty
but not necessary, Operations Division summarized the opinion of
JCS and the Joint Planning Staff: forces then committed to the Mediterranean, minus the seven divisions to be transferred to Britain
for Overlord, would be adequate to attain the Allies' three desired
goals. These were to occupy Italy up to a line north of Rome, seize
Sardinia and Corsica, and make a diversionary effort into southern
France from the Mediterranean in May or June 1944. In the message, Marshall told Eisenhower that the JCS and the planners "estimated that 10 divisions will be sufficient to contain any remaining
German forces in Italy, unless Germany sends large reinforcements
to the peninsula, and that there will be available 14 offensive divisions and adequate combat aircraft to launch a combined amphibious and overland assault on Southern France in coordination with
the main effort of the initial 29 divisions across the channel."[44]

In a section marked for his personal attention, Marshall asked
for Eisenhower's views. Nevertheless, by this message, Marshall
sealed the transfer of 7 divisions out of Eisenhower's command
in the Mediterranean and back to the British Isles for Overlord.
Later in the year, the German Wehrmacht would test in Italy the
wisdom of the OPD planners and the JCS.

15

Blenheim on the Hudson

I can do more with the President by not pressing too hard at once. He is a fine fellow. Very strong in his views, but he comes around.

    —Winston Churchill, August 10, 1943

Delivered by a Canadian National Railway special train to Charny Station on the south bank of the Saint Lawrence River on August 10, Churchill was greeted by Canadian prime minister William Mackenzie King. They motored across the river to the Citadel, the historic eighteenth-century fortress above Quebec City. Their conversation during the drive and dinner that followed encompassed much of Churchill's goals, concerns, strategy, assessment of Roosevelt, and unfolding awareness of the immediate situation before him going into the Quadrant Conference. Mackenzie King recounted their conversation in detail in a memorandum for the record the following day.[1]

In the car, Churchill requested that he be billeted at the Citadel so that "he could readily keep in touch with the President." Mackenzie King agreed and noted that Churchill told him, "You and I would carry on the war from this side." Quietly, referring to the Axis, Churchill then said, "We have got them beaten, but it may take some time." In reply to Mackenzie King's question as to how long, Churchill replied, "One, possibly two years. On the other hand, no one knows what might happen in Germany. It might be six months, but there is also Japan."[2]

In explaining his intention not to rush back to Britain from North America after Quadrant, Churchill said, "Much more can be done by giving time for things to develop. I can do more with the President by not pressing too hard at once. He is a fine fellow. Very strong in his views, but he comes around." Mackenzie King had been briefed on British war strategy by his military leaders and Canada's External Affairs Ministry. He told Churchill that he "understood his difficulty would be to persuade the President not to be too quick about fighting from the North instead of from the South." To this Churchill replied, "Yes . . . there would have to be much careful work done there. That the trouble was the Americans did not realize how long it took to accomplish some things." Mackenzie King observed that Churchill believed getting into Germany by military assault would be very difficult and that Churchill "was entirely for going on with the war in Italy."[3]

During their drive, Mackenzie King told Churchill that the day before he had telephoned Roosevelt and spoken with him about the president's just completed fishing trip in Canada. In reply Churchill asked what success Roosevelt had had. Later in a sunroom in the Citadel, waiting to go into dinner, Churchill asked again about Roosevelt's fishing trip. Mackenzie King chose that point in his memorandum of the conversation to observe of Churchill, "He looked to me very much older."[4] Perhaps never to be known is whether a still-unresolved concern that Roosevelt would act to meet Stalin without including or telling Churchill prompted the prime minister to seek confirmation from Mackenzie King that the fishing trip indeed had been spent fishing in Canada.

In the context of steps taken to limit publicity, media access, and pomp at the Quadrant Conference, "Two or three times, [Churchill] referred to great events pertaining to the war being settled here in Canada. That this was a crucial time, and great decisions had to be made here. He felt it better not to have too much in the way of pressure."[5]

$* * *$

At the Citadel, Sir John Anderson, head of the British Tube Alloy project, was waiting when Churchill and Mackenzie King arrived. Mackenzie King invited Anderson to join the dinner party and then left Anderson and Churchill to talk, one critical conversation that evening to which Mackenzie King was not party directly.[6] Anderson had arrived in Canada on August 7, coming from Washington, where he negotiated the draft secret U.S.-UK agreement on atomic weapons research and postwar policy with Vannevar Bush. The purpose of this conversation with Churchill was to fulfill Anderson's part of the agreement with Bush for almost "simultaneous transmission" to Churchill and Roosevelt of the results of their negotiation. Whatever Anderson may have told the prime minister that evening, his written report left out the important information that only one of the five points had been agreed upon.

In their just-finished negotiation in Washington, at the insistence of Bush, the four points on political-military policy that Churchill considered so critical had been left on the table to be settled directly between Roosevelt and Churchill. In his written reply to Bush's concluding letter that set limits to the scope of their agreement, Anderson had found that "entirely satisfactory to me."[7]

As Roosevelt's negotiator, Bush had insisted on truncating his and Anderson's progress on the draft agreement, yielding only an administrative process with political-military substance withheld. Beyond Bush's personal reticence about his authority and the Military Policy Committee's concerns, the limitation should have signaled to Churchill that full attainment of his goal could be achieved only through his direct negotiation with Roosevelt. Anderson's August 10 written report to Churchill, conveying the full text of the agreement in draft, gave the prime minister no indication that the two scientists' progress had been circumscribed by the American. As to the result attained by Bush and himself, Anderson wrote simply that "the draft articles of agreement . . . should be jointly recommended to the President and yourself."[8]

Whether or not Churchill got a more circumscribed and enlightening oral report from Anderson, the prime minister's message to Lord Cherwell in London the following day was rosy. Churchill's telegram stated that "T.A. was settled as proposed subject to confirmation with President."[9]

With respect to his host, Churchill knew that Canada's participation in the Tube Alloy–Manhattan Project endeavor had revealed an independence of view and allowance for U.S. action perhaps supportive of Canadian interests but less so that of a team player for Empire.

Canadians in the project had expressed the view that the U.S. restriction on information interchange was reasonable in the context of who was doing what share of the work. More concrete and a serious barrier to British options for achieving an independent atomic weapon, Canada had allowed the United States to acquire Canada's entire near-term production of uranium oxide and heavy water.[10] Churchill's conversation with Mackenzie King suggests an attempt by him to rebalance Canada's position more to favor British interests.

Rejoining Mackenzie King, Churchill asked him if Anderson was pleased with the arrangements Churchill had made in regard to the atomic weapon development project including the British team working in Montreal. Mackenzie King replied that he thought Anderson was satisfied. His memorandum of conversation then recounted that Churchill said he, too, was satisfied and that "Churchill said it was too important a matter to let others get ahead of the rest of us on it. There had been some effort he thought on the part of the Americans to get ahead of the British."[11]

Later that evening, Churchill asked Mackenzie King to read the draft language agreed upon by Anderson and Bush on point five of the secret agreement, establishment of the process and committee to manage atomic weapons research information interchange. Mackenzie King recounted, "It suggested a Canadian member of the Combined Policy Committee, and [Churchill] asked me if I would be agreeable to his suggesting to the President that Mr. [C. D.] Howe [Canada's minister of munitions and supply] should become a member of the Committee. I agreed to this and to our seeing Sir John Anderson in the morning."[12]

* * *

At 8:00 p.m., Churchill received a communication from Stalin that contained congratulations upon the Allies' successful invasion of Sicily. It also stated that Stalin was sorry not to have been able to answer previous communications from Churchill for some time as he had been at the front with his armies. Stalin concluded his message by saying that he hoped to meet with Roosevelt and Churchill in the near future.

Although still expressing his pique with Stalin, Churchill acknowledged that the Soviet leader's readiness to meet with the two western leaders was welcome news. Just before the party left the dinner table, Gen. Sir Hastings Ismay entered the room to report to Churchill on discussion within the British Chiefs of Staff. Churchill showed him the message. Ismay's reaction was to say that they should start making arrangements for the meeting location right away, a process of three-way coordination that would prove difficult.[13]

Mackenzie King and Churchill spoke at length during dinner about Italy, the fighting in Sicily, and the confusion over timing and who would make the announcement about the participation of Canadian troops in the invasion of Sicily.[14] That provided an opportunity for Mackenzie King to press upon Churchill issues more fundamental to Canada's participation in the war. Although of a view that Churchill "cowed his colleagues" and "stifled discussion when it was critical and did not agree with his views," the Canadian prime minister pressed his points nevertheless.[15] Mackenzie King recounted:

I got a good chance both at dinner and after to speak of my problem which is Canada's problem—namely the need of our having the Canadian people feel that we were really having a voice in all matters pertaining to the war.

I explained that I fully understood the necessity of safeguarding the position of other United Nations and other Dominions, but pointed out that there were two lines of pressure which were very great. One [from] the opposition in Parliament [was] whether I was letting Canada's position go by default so that when it came to the time for the peace, we would have no real voice. The other pressure was from my colleagues in the Cabinet and from members of the Permanent Staff, E.A. [External Affairs], etc. who were always at me to be asserting more strongly Canada's position, not allowing anything to pass without taking it up immediately. . . . Churchill is very understanding in matters of this kind.[16]

At dinner, Churchill spoke of the recent surge in the number of U-boats sunk by the Allies in the North and mid-Atlantic and said that a statement on this was to be made for the Allies by Roosevelt. Mackenzie King took the opportunity to reply by calling Churchill's attention to the substance of Canada's participation in the war. He recalled, "I mentioned that the RAF was made up of a large number of Canadians. Also that 40 percent of the patrolling of the North Atlantic had been by our Navy, and that we were doing much of it before the Americans had entered at all. Churchill said he had not realized that the proportion was so large. I think the same figure was mentioned with regard to Australians, New Zealanders, etc., in the Royal Air Force."[17]

As their meeting ended, Churchill reiterated to Mackenzie King the importance to him of the Canadian prime minister's help to facilitate Churchill's close communication with Roosevelt during the Quadrant Conference and, by extension, at other times. Churchill's appeal was directed to a man with considerable potential to aid his cause. Roosevelt and Mackenzie King had attended Harvard University together when the Canadian was an upperclassman. A close, lifelong friendship developed between them in which the younger Roosevelt considered Mackenzie King a mentor. Mackenzie King described the conclusion of his meeting with Churchill thus:

> When I left, he insisted in walking out into the hall with me to say good-bye. . . . He said to me that the war was in a fluid state. Conditions were changing from day to day very rapidly. It would mean very much to him to be able to talk with the President, to be nearby where he could speak with the President, or run down to see him at a moment's notice. That more important than anything else was keeping the President's good-will and complete understanding between the two.
>
> He said he really is the one friend that we have, and we must keep in as close touch as we can with him.[18]

* * *

Wednesday evening, August 11, a Canadian Pacific train carrying Churchill, his daughter, Mary, personal staff, and his Canadian and British security detail departed Quebec City. The wine-red, four-car train of a sleeper and three beautifully appointed private cars, including the railway president's own car, *Mount Royal*, took the Churchill's to Niagara Falls for a morning visit on August 12. Crossing into the United States, they continued on to Springwood, Roosevelt's home at Hyde Park, New York, arriving at 6:30 p.m. Churchill took with him his private secretary and valet, leaving in Quebec City his senior civilian and military advisers. For Churchill, this was an unusually small entourage, particularly given his appreciation for the significance of the conversations he anticipated having with Roosevelt. A daily courier flight by the Royal Canadian Air Force would be his connection to the British delegation at Abraham. [19]

For Churchill's visit, Roosevelt had rearranged the décor of his home as a contextual reminder to Churchill of how far they had come together. Churchill would receive a firm message from the president on the U.S. position on Allied strategy to be taken at Quadrant. Roosevelt instructed his cousin Daisy Suckley to "Have the Churchill pictures hung together in the center section: F.D.R. & W.S.C. painting in the middle with the Atlantic Charter, etc., the drawing of W.S.C. by his teacher on the left panel, the painting [by] W.S.C. on the [right] panel."[20] The last was the sunset in Marrakesh that Churchill had painted and presented to FDR after the January 1943 Casablanca Conference.[21]

In anticipation of Churchill's weekend visit, Hyde Park teamed with assorted Roosevelt family members, friends, and White House staff. Although Churchill came with only his daughter and personal staff, Roosevelt had at hand for substantive discussions the support of his naval aide, Rear Adm. Wilson Brown, and the counsel of Harry Hopkins and Averill Harriman. Harriman had come up to Hyde Park from New York City after sailing to Halifax on the *Queen Mary* with Churchill. The Joint Chiefs of Staff need not have been concerned about Roosevelt being alone under the Churchill "sun lamp."

Eleanor Roosevelt was at Hyde Park for the Churchills' arrival. About to leave on an inspection trip in the South Pacific for the Red Cross, she had decided that going about her normal business was the best security cover for her impending departure.

On August 13, FDR and Eleanor, Churchill, Mary, and the gathered Roosevelt family, friends, and staff, Hopkins and Brown among them, motored from Springwood for swimming and a picnic lunch at nearby Val-Kill, the idyllic retreat Eleanor had built with FDR's encouragement.[22] Roosevelt drove the Churchills in his hand-controlled blue Ford convertible, the prime minister in a ten-gallon hat and a white tropical suit, but a suit, nonetheless, on a day when the temperature would climb to 93 degrees Fahrenheit.

After the picnic lunch, Roosevelt and Churchill moved off under a tree for a personal discussion. There Churchill found in FDR none of the propensity toward flexibility on strategy alternatives upon which Churchill had come to rely. Roosevelt instead asserted point by point the position of the ascendant United States that the British long had anticipated as inevitable. He expressed his solid commitment to confirming the cross-Channel invasion, Overlord, for May 1944 as the principal Allied strategy in Europe under a U.S., not British, Supreme Allied Commander (still to be named). Apparent was that the course FDR laid out was to be followed in an alliance in which the United States, henceforward, would take up as "senior partner" the leadership role offered by Churchill in 1942.

As Churchill received Roosevelt's message on European strategy and command of Allied forces, both men knew that until signed by them, negotiation of the secret U.S.-UK atomic agreement would not be complete. Whether or not Churchill had gotten a full and candid oral report from Anderson, filling the gap in his August 10 memorandum, FDR certainly knew from Hopkins that Vannevar Bush and Anderson had succeeded in settling only the process details of implementing information sharing. The two scientists had refined but deferred to the president and prime minister settlement of the four points of substance, then and for the future. There it was, at least implicitly, as their military chiefs were gathering in Quebec for Quadrant and perhaps reprising the conclusion of the Trident Conference: the prospect of a quid pro quo, a cooperative atomic relationship for reaffirmation of Overlord.

On this, each leader now was beyond accepting the other's oral assurance. Since spring, equivocation and double messages from both sides had eviscerated the credibility of any further oral agreement. To settle the issues of strategy for Europe and atomic cooperation, both leaders needed a written commitment. Roosevelt needed Churchill to go first on Overlord.

In their conversation under the tree at Val-Kill on that hot afternoon, Roosevelt and Churchill discussed the details and who would be members of the overseeing Combined Policy Committee, but they did not initial the draft "Tube Alloys Memorandum."[23] When their talk ended, the prime minister did not yet have the signed atomic agreement that he considered to be so critical to his country's postwar future. Roosevelt was not about to initial the atomic agreement until he had received word from his chiefs in Quebec where Allied strategy again was the subject of debate.

Churchill appealed to Roosevelt to return with him to Quebec on the grounds that their joint presence was needed from the outset of Quadrant, a train trip that obviously would afford an extended opportunity for Churchill to discuss the strategy issue with Roosevelt *before* they arrived at the conference. FDR declined, telling Churchill that he had to go back to Washington first and be there on August 16.

Later that afternoon, back at the mansion, Churchill pressed the matter by sending Roosevelt a handwritten note on No. 10 Downing Street stationery. Near the date on the note, August 13, Churchill jotted, "(Blenheim Day)!" invoking the anniversary of actions by his ancestor, the Duke of Marlborough, in 1704, which saved the city of Vienna and the alliance in which Marlborough was fighting for England against a Franco-German enemy. In the note, Churchill again appealed to FDR that they both travel from Hyde Park to Quebec to arrive no later than Sunday or Monday,

August 15–16: "Doubt if much progress will be made [at Quadrant] till we are on the spot."[24] Traveling with Churchill, essentially alone, would have required FDR to drop his plan to go first to Washington before going to Quebec separately. However, the president did not alter his plan, and no written reply has been found to explain why Roosevelt was going to Washington first.[25]

In Friday night's oppressive, still heat, Churchill could not sleep. The prime minister left his bedroom and, by the light of a near-full moon, crossed beneath the bedrooms of the sleeping Roosevelts to the south lawn of Springwood. He sat on a wooden bench just where the land slopes away to afford view of the Hudson valley, perhaps with the smoke of a cigar to fend off mosquitos.[26] Churchill contemplated the day's encounter with Roosevelt.

This Blenheim Day had closed not just with a foretelling of disappointment at the Quebec Conference for Churchill's preferred outcome on strategy for liberating Europe. The day had given stark evidence that the declining trajectory of the British Empire was at its intersection with the ascendency of North America, particularly the United States. Throughout the night, this was palpable in the whistling of New York Central Railroad trains running along both banks of the great river below him with troops and war cargo from across the continent destined for the ports of New York and New Jersey. Whether or not the mental depression that Churchill called his "black dog" had raised its head, his mind surely must have churned.

Churchill's description to Mackenzie King of Roosevelt as a "fine fellow" of strong views who "comes around" had that afternoon bumped against FDR's taking up the leadership of the alliance and the president's now very firm commitment to the U.S. Joint Chiefs of Staff's preferred strategy of cross-Channel attack in 1944. This would commit the Allies to direct engagement of the main body of the Wehrmacht in the West and an overland thrust into the heart of Germany. To be ruled out were expanded operations in the Mediterranean with assault on northwestern Europe reserved as an opportunistic contingency against, hopefully, a foe weakened by internal collapse. The unfolding deployment of a U.S. ground force in Europe that would grow to ninety divisions made a compelling case for appointing an American supreme Allied commander. The British army already had peaked at eighteen divisions and would struggle to maintain the strength and quality of those.[27]

Mackenzie King had been right, three nights earlier, about the reliance of the British armed forces on soldiers, sailors, and airmen of the Dominions. Hosting the conference but not to be present at Quadrant's negotiating table, Canada was far from alone among the Dominions in wanting a stronger say in wartime decisions and the peace to follow. Looking upon the Hudson, flowing down from the north, Churchill hardly could consider Canada's desire for influence without calling to mind his own unresolved, troubled sense of the British Chiefs of Staff's uneven performance. Ambiguous decision making had led to heavy Canadian casualties in the disastrous Dieppe Raid one year earlier almost to the day.[28]

Although strategy for the European theater would be foremost among several military decisions to be reached in Quebec, the consequences of U.S. ascendency as a world power already were far broader. In economic discussions separate from Quadrant, the United States was challenging the Empire Preference that gave British products a tariff-based competitive advantage in international trade.[29] In yet another negotiation, the United States was pushing for open rights of access and overflight for postwar international air travel sure to boom on the foundation of the global network of airways and bases then being built to meet the requirements of war.[30]

As Churchill knew, Canada had its own opinion of the restrictive U.S. position on sharing atomic research as being reasonable in the circumstances of the division of work and investment. Intentionally or not, Canada had allowed the United States to corner the short-term Canadian output of nuclear materials that would be essential if Britain was to have a viable atomic bomb program of its own.[31]

Churchill also knew that the U.S. commitment to the essential four political-military points of his proposal for a secret agreement on atomic weapons research and policy on the postwar role of atomic weapons was only a signature away. Not a treaty but, still, an agreement that as precedent would ease the way toward the Anglo-American treaty of alliance that Churchill wanted for the future. There could be a new framework of a U.S.-UK condominium for control of this powerful new force only if Roosevelt agreed. Roosevelt's need for Churchill's assent to bring to closure the open issue of strategy in Europe gave the prime minister leverage.

As he contemplated these issues, Churchill also was aware that the war provided a most fluid context. He concurred with the sense that the Nazis were beaten. The Allies' contentious debate now was focused on defining the path to the final victory that would be theirs within a year or two at the most. Churchill with particular acuteness shared the Allies' sense, accurate or not, that the Reich was brittle and could implode politically on its own, or be made to do so, much sooner. Whatever the outcome of Quadrant, time still could alter the context for the issues in contention in Quebec. The Allies' reentry into northwestern Europe still might come through an Operation Rankin in response to a German political collapse, rather than by Overlord's direct violent assault.

From all the contentions of that day, Churchill still could find reasons for reaffirmed confidence in his ally. Roosevelt had not snuck off to meet separately with Stalin. Called malleable by some, including Churchill, this day Roosevelt had been resolute on strategy for victory in Europe, but with the realism to hold open a deal in exchange on a matter Churchill held to be vital to Britain, atomic weapons research. Having apparently found some balance, Churchill rose from his overlook of the Hudson at dawn and returned to Roosevelt's mansion "refreshed and relaxed, after the sun had risen."[32]

Late that Saturday morning, August 14, the Roosevelts and the Churchills returned again to Val-Kill for a second picnic and swim. Roosevelt drove Churchill and Mary in his car, and Churchill joined in the swimming. Daisy Suckley's account of the day was effusive. Her impression was that "Churchill *adores* the P., loves him, as a man, looks up to him, defers to him, leans on him. He is older than the P., but the P. is the bigger person, and Churchill recognizes it." Suckley added, "I saw in Churchill, too, an amount of real greatness I did not suspect before."[33]

That evening at dinner, before he departed to return to Quebec City, Churchill talked of his hope to perpetuate the "fraternal relationship of the United States and Great Britain" beyond the war "arguing that the only hope for the United Nations lay in 'the leadership given by the intimacy of the U.S. and Britain in working out misunderstandings with the Russians—and the Chinese too.'" So impassioned was Churchill that he alarmed Eleanor Roosevelt. Fearing a misunderstanding that would weaken the United Nations concept, Mrs. Roosevelt spoke out to challenge Churchill's vision. Already impressed by her imminent trip to the South Pacific, Churchill responded by voicing his respect for her "steel."[34]

Whether or not Daisy Suckley's conclusions from the second picnic were perceptive, drawn as they were from infrequent and limited observation of Churchill and Roosevelt together, the sequence of that day at Hyde Park is revealing. From a sleepless night of brooding, Churchill had emerged with a "refreshed" attitude and gone on to happy intimacy at the picnic that prompted Suckley's observations that so contrast with Churchill's patronizing views of Roosevelt, expressed by him within British circles.[35] At the dinner that followed, Churchill then promoted with feeling an expansive view of Anglo-American postwar relations. The sequence suggests that Churchill had begun to adapt to changed circumstances for the British Empire and a shared global power structure for 1943 and the future. The change would not be easy for Churchill to accept, nor would it happen without overcoming his spirited resistance, but change had begun.

* * *

The dinner over, Churchill boarded his train for the overnight trip back to Quebec City without the president. Waiting for Churchill was a note from his private secretary: "The Lord President

[Sir John Anderson] asked me to report to him the result of your conversation with the President about Tube Alloys. What may I say, please?"[36]

As his train rolled north in the darkness, Churchill considered the issues that he and FDR had and had not covered in their talks. By Churchill's count they had addressed only half out of a dozen points. By the morning of August 15, he had produced a typed letter that began, "My dear Mr. President," above which he wrote, "For you alone," and gave his further thoughts and actions to be taken in follow-up. Among these, he and Roosevelt should make a renewed final offer to meet "U.J." in Fairbanks or at a further point suggested by FDR "as soon as this Military Conference is over." Churchill was "having a fair copy made of the Tube Alloy Memorandum ready for our respective initials." He would "now take up with my Staffs the most important question of the Commands as we outlined them. I am sure the plan you have in mind is the best."[37] On arriving in Quebec, Churchill gave direction that his letter to FDR should be shown to the Chiefs of Staff Committee.[38] The paragraph about Tube Alloy probably was a puzzle to the Committee, except to Churchill's chief military assistant, Sir Hastings Ismay. However, they had in their hands a good hint that the Supreme Allied Commander was going to be an American.

16

Overlord Reaffirmed in Quebec

Good heavens, they've started shooting now!

—Allied officer, Quadrant Conference, August 19, 1943

W hile Churchill made his foray to Hyde Park to meet with Roosevelt, the British Chiefs of Staff Committee and their staff established themselves in the venue for this fourth major Anglo-American wartime conference, the military talks. They would be meeting at the massive Chateau Frontenac located downriver from the Plains of Abraham, where a British army under Gen. James Wolfe had won a pivotal battle that wrested control of North America from the French in 1759, and a short distance from the French-built, early eighteenth-century Citadel, where Churchill and Roosevelt would stay. The hotel soars majestically from the heights above Quebec's old town. Both the Citadel and Chateau Frontenac enjoy commanding views of the Saint Lawrence River. Closer to hand, the British could look down from the high ground onto the roofs of the old town. Through the town in a blizzard and bitter cold on the last day of 1775, a ragged army of American rebels had fought but failed to take these heights. Metaphorically, local history was on the British delegation's side with plenty of eighteenth-century cannon as evidence.

Until the American delegation to Quadrant arrived, however, the cos Committee could only continue to refine positions already prepared during their Atlantic crossing on the *Queen Mary*. On the morning of August 11, they met in Chateau Frontenac to receive an appraisal of the attitude and likely positions of the U.S. Joint Chiefs of Staff from a British officer representing them in Washington. They got important feedback on their own actions since Trident when they were told that "as to the hardening of attitude, this has been distinct since the 'stand still' orders issued by the British in the Mediterranean."[1]

While the British chiefs were meeting in Quebec that Wednesday, U.S. Army Chief of Staff George Marshall in Washington was taking action to follow up on the president's directive given at the White House meeting the day before. His confirmation to FDR of a preponderance of U.S. divisions in the UK for D-Day gave the president affirmation for the case for insisting on an American as supreme Allied commander.[2] To Marshall, his memorandum was a critical step to reassure Roosevelt before the president's meeting with Churchill at Hyde Park.

Through the Army General Staff's Operations Division, Marshall sent a message to General Eisenhower at Allied Headquarters in Algiers that summarized the opinion of the JCS and the Joint Planning Staff that forces then committed to the Mediterranean would be adequate to attain desired ends. Marshall believed this to be consistent with Eisenhower's view, but he personally requested Eisenhower's response and anything additional he wanted to add.[3]

The next day, as Marshall awaited Eisenhower's reply and the fourth train bearing the U.S. delegation departed Washington for Quebec City,[4] an upbeat opinion of bombing effectiveness was on its way to the British in Quebec. From outside London the head of Bomber Command, Air Marshal Arthur Harris, wrote to RAF Chief of Staff Sir Charles Portal in Quebec that the bombing of Germany was "on verge of a final show-down." Operation Pointblank, the night and day effort by Harris's bombers and the U.S. Eighth Air Force would "Knock Germany stiff."[5]

Early in the morning on August 13, Eisenhower's three-and-a-half-page reply to Marshall's message of two days before was received in War Department Message Center. In the message, sent "For Marshall Eyes Only," Eisenhower agreed with the Army chief of staff, but with qualifications. Eisenhower pointed out the danger in making exacting calculations of forces and logistics far into the future. Noting indications of German reinforcement of Italy, Eisenhower wrote that "capabilities for the future are limited by replacements of men and material more than by actual divisional strength and [limited] particularly by shipping and landing craft."[6] Eisenhower implicitly confirmed Marshall's assessment that if invaded by the Allies, Italy would become, in Marshall's phrase, a "suction pump" consuming Allied resources. Eisenhower wrote:

> Once we are committed to operations on the Continent, the question of whether or not the force available to us will be adequate depends entirely on the nature of the German reaction. I doubt whether it will be practicable to limit our occupation to a line just north of Rome and I do not believe we can contemplate an Allied Army in Central Italy and a German force in Northern Italy with a No Man's Land between them. We shall have to gain contact with a view to either destroying the German forces, driving them out of Italy, or if they are strongly reinforced, preventing them from ejecting us.[7]

The jcs pushed to its limit Roosevelt's request that the U.S. chiefs be in Quebec with the British no later than August 14. On the thirteenth, Eisenhower's views as the Allied commander in the Mediterranean in hand, the Joint Chiefs and their aides flew from Washington to Quebec City to be ready for meetings of the full Combined Chiefs of Staff on August 14.[8]

The British Chiefs of Staff Committee had received ccs 303 and, as the U.S. chiefs were en route, met in Chateau Frontenac late in the afternoon of August 13 to discuss the jsc-endorsed strategy draft. They found that the draft approximated the British position better than expected.[9] However, predictably, their assessment fit the framework of their own strategy of flexibility to manipulate relative Allied-Axis strength. That set up a conflict with the U.S. advocacy of "overriding priority" for Overlord.

Affirming the success of Overlord as "being of utmost importance," the British chiefs considered that success to depend less on the total quantitative Allied force assembled for D-Day than on "the relative strength of opposing Allied and German forces." This supported their position that Allied forces in Italy could contribute to creating successful conditions for Overlord by drawing German forces away from France. The British chiefs found the JCS unclear on how far into northern Italy they were prepared to advance.[10]

The British chiefs found that CCS 303 did not highlight the value of northern Italy as a site for air bases from which to attack targets in southern Germany. They also deemed strategically unsound and inflexible its tie to the Trident decisions and endorsement of withdrawing some forces from the Mediterranean when, by retaining them there, in the British chiefs' opinion, "valuable results could be achieved." In their minds were at least two of the three combat-experienced British divisions allotted for transfer to Overlord. They did acknowledge the availability of shipping to make an exchange of divisions, but only to withdraw the British divisions to the UK after replacement divisions had arrived in Italy. If landing craft were short for Overlord, the JCS should draw them from the Pacific.[11]

The Combined Chiefs of Staff started the Quadrant Conference on August 14 at 10:50 a.m., by convening at the Chateau Frontenac for their 106th meeting. They quickly agreed to meet daily in the afternoon at 2:30 p.m. with morning CCS meetings as necessary but, generally, leaving mornings free for the British and American chiefs to conduct their own internal preparatory consultations. The CCS agreed on an overall agenda of topics to be considered "in the sequence in which they are listed," one that conformed to the JCS's preferred agenda. With respect to the European theater, first would be the "Strategic Concept for the Defeat of the Axis in Europe" (CCS 303), the most fundamental of the topics in dispute. Second would be COSSAC's Overlord Outline Plan. This would be followed by the Combined Bomber Offensive (Operation Pointblank), Mediterranean operations, and planning for Operation Rankin. The British Chiefs of Staff then gave their detailed summation of the overall current situation in the European theater, ground, air, and naval by Brooke, Portal, and Pound in turn.[12] The 107th CCS meeting that followed on Saturday was devoted to the Pacific theater.[13]

On Sunday, August 15, the conflict over the issue of two competing strategy visions for the European theater again was joined.

In the morning, the British Chiefs of Staff Committee met to prepare for the afternoon ccs meeting. Before them was jcs-authored ccs 303, now annotated with comments by their own Joint Planning Staff. The British chiefs probably also had been shown Churchill's August 15 "My Dear Mr. President" letter to Roosevelt. They decided to table their strategy position, as developed on the *Queen Mary*, to make clearer to the Americans their intent to carry out Overlord and also their view of the interrelationship between Overlord and operations in the Mediterranean.[14]

Shortly before lunch, Winston Churchill summoned Gen. Sir Alan Brooke to the Citadel. Having just completed a meeting with FDR and Hopkins, Churchill informed Brooke that the position of Supreme Allied Commander would go to an American. The position was not to be Brooke's, despite Churchill's previous promise to him. Brooke may have been told by Churchill that the command would go to Marshall, although in fact that was not set. Missing the appointment as Supreme Allied Commander after having been led to believe the assignment would be his was painful to Brooke.[15] The pain was far from lessened by Brooke's low opinion of Marshall as a strategist.

On the afternoon of August 15 at Chateau Frontenac, the Combined Chiefs of Staff reconvened and took up the jcs paper on strategy for defeat of the Axis in Europe (ccs 303). General Brooke led off, stating that after reading ccs 303, the British chiefs found "great similarity of outlook between" themselves and the jcs. The divergences, Brooke professed, were not fundamental, and they were "in entire agreement that OVERLORD should constitute the major offensive for 1944 and that Italian operations should be planned with this conception as a background." Then, citing the three conditions for a successful Overlord outlined in the COSSAC plan, Brooke built the case for going slow on the cross-Channel attack and taking further action in Italy. He stated that the jcs-proposed stipulation that in the event of a shortage of resources, "OVERLORD will have overriding priority" was "too binding."[16]

General Brooke made his points in a fashion that nibbled away at the total of seven combat-experienced divisions for transfer to the UK as agreed at Trident. His rationale, as he had argued in Washington in May, basically was to retain in the Mediterranean resources earmarked for Overlord for additional military action in Italy so as to create a relative advantage for the Allies in France. Admiral King stated his understanding from this that "the British COS had serious doubts as to the possibility of accomplishing OVERLORD."[17]

General Marshall was more direct. According to the minutes, he stated that unless a decision was taken to remove the seven divisions from the Mediterranean, and unless overriding priority was given to Overlord, he believed that Overlord would become only a subsidiary operation. Marshall raised the JCS-agreed contingency that if Overlord did not get overriding priority, then U.S. forces in the UK might be reduced to a "reinforced army corps necessary for an opportunist cross-Channel operation." Taking up the paper that Maj. Gen. Ray Barker had written for the JCS, Marshall read its main points to the Combined Chiefs. He pressed upon the CCS the combined COSSAC staff conclusion that Overlord would not become impractical if COSSAC's three conditions were not met, only that "more extensive use would have to be made of available means to reduce the enemy's ability to concentrate his forces." Marshall concluded with his long-held criticism of relying on bombing, attrition, and blockade to induce Germany to collapse. He said that "an 'opportunist' strategy would be cheaper in lives but was speculative," and he cited again the possibility of a U.S. shift of priority to the Pacific. Only three CCS meetings into Quadrant, back on the table was the strategy difference, clouded by the specter of abandoning the principle of "Germany first."[18]

Despite this, the Combined Chiefs of Staff with little discussion took two important actions at this meeting that advanced substantive preparation for Overlord. They approved the "Overlord Outline Plan" and endorsed the British Chiefs of Staff authorization for COSSAC, under Lieutenant General Morgan, to begin detailed planning and full preparations for the operation.[19]

The CCS meeting over, the Joint Chiefs of Staff withdrew to their conference room to assess the reopened confrontation. The

JCS chairman, Admiral Leahy, proposed that their purpose be to discuss General Brooke's proposal that a decision on transferring seven divisions from Mediterranean to the UK for Overlord be postponed. The American chiefs were in firm agreement on the importance of getting a decision on strategy with priority for Overlord. To that end, the seven divisions had become a bellwether issue. Admiral King and General Marshall shared the view in hindsight that the British had agreed at Trident in May to moving the seven divisions only to "secure US acquiescence."[20] Suspicions of the British chiefs were expressed openly with much discussion of "decisive" versus "speculative" strategies.

Also growing, however, was a sense that the British staff were not fully aligned with their chiefs. Brig. Gen. Albert Wedemeyer expressed his opinion that lower-level British officers were in agreement with American planners on Overlord. Brigadier General Kuter stated his belief that comments in the parallel meeting of Combined Staff Planners had shown that British planners were in full agreement with CCS 303, the JCS position.

Major General Handy stressed that reaching definite decision at Quadrant was more important than its content. General Marshall agreed. As he had before the JCS left Washington, General Marshall said of the American chiefs' advocacy for Overlord, "We must go into this argument in the spirit of winning." If the Mediterranean strategy was adopted at the end of the fight, the decision should be firm. The JCS directed the staff to prepare a statement to be made to the CCS that "it was the view of the United States Chiefs of Staff that the TRIDENT decision regarding the OVERLORD build-up should be reaffirmed."[21]

During the evening, informal conversations gave a glimmer of hope for agreement. In the American chiefs' morning meeting on August 16 to prepare for the next CCS session, Marshall recounted his conversations with Churchill and Field Marshall Dill the night before. Churchill, fresh from his meeting in Hyde Park with FDR, had told Marshall that he had changed his mind regarding Overlord and that the Allies should use every opportunity to further that operation. Marshall had taken that opportunity to tell Churchill that the ccs had had a difficult meeting with frank differences that afternoon. He told Churchill that he "could not agree to the logic of supporting the main effort [Overlord] by withdrawing strength therefrom in order to bolster up the force in Italy." Ending their discussion, Churchill had replied to Marshall, "Give us time." To Dill, separately, Marshall had said, "It was necessary to consider OVERLORD from the point of view of major strategy and not become involved with details of minor strategy." He said he had warned Dill that the JCS would not stand for "further circumlocution."[22]

Brigadier General Wedemeyer then suggested a further overnight evolvement of the British position. He said that over breakfast, Dill had informed him that the British chiefs were prepared to accept CCS 303 if the JCS's stipulation for overriding priority for Overlord was qualified with language to the effect that the CCS could readjust the allocations in response to new developments. Admiral King said such a qualifier would leave an option to avoid mounting Overlord on the date specified. Wedemeyer and Marshall said they each had told Dill the JCS would not accept a qualifier.[23]

Acutely aware that Churchill, already in Quebec, was getting regular updates from his chiefs, the JCS decided to even the playing field by sending Major General Handy to Washington by air in order to present the situation in detail to President Roosevelt. Handy would take with him CCS 303, the JCS's own update to it, and the minutes of this JCS meeting and the CCS meeting that stimulated them. Although not referred to in this long meeting, the JCS had beefed up their minutes with two annexes. One was General Barker's summary of COSSAC's encouraging projection of the over-the-beach buildup of divisions for Overlord following D-Day.[24] The other was a very pessimistic forecast for a ground campaign in Italy from Eisenhower's chief of staff, Brig. Gen. Bedell Smith. This included Smith's observation that, "'Early exploitation to the Alps' is a delightful thought but is not to be counted upon with any certainty."[25]

At 1:00 p.m., General Handy took off for Washington from Quebec in Lieutenant General Somervell's plane on his special mission. His purpose was to board the president's train and brief FDR, as the president traveled to Quebec, on the situation at Quadrant and the JCS position.[26] He carried plenty of ammunition.

The British Chiefs of Staff Committee also met that Monday morning, August 16, to discuss the American draft modification of CCS 303.[27] They considered the revision to be "quite unacceptable. The paper took no account of the fact that Overlord and Priceless [operations in the Mediterranean] were really parts of one large operation designed to bring about the defeat of the Axis in Europe in Brooke's arguably more expansive view. The British Chiefs agreed that absolute rigidity of the type suggested by the U.S. Chiefs of Staff could not be agreed to." The British chiefs decided to table their own amended version of CCS 303 and "hoped that the amendment would be so slight, and our efforts to meet the U.S. so evident, that the proposal might be accepted by the Americans as the combined resolution for operations in the European Theatre."[28]

The afternoon CCS meeting at Chateau Frontenac, Monday, August 16, found the lines of difference clearly drawn between the British and American chiefs. First topic on the agenda was "Strategic Concept for the Defeat of the Axis in Europe," CCS 303. On the table was the British Chiefs of Staff amended version, crafted to encourage acceptance by the U.S. chiefs while preserving the opportunistic strategy. The chiefs cleared the room of staff and note takers to wrestle again with European strategy in closed session. General Brooke opened the meeting by telling the Americans that "the root of the matter was that we were not trusting each other." He then went over the Mediterranean strategy again and argued for its close relationship to the cross-Channel strategy. He believed that he made some headway with Marshall.[29] The minutes, however, show that the only point of CCS agreement was "to give further consideration to this subject at their next meeting."[30] The report on this meeting to Churchill on behalf of the British chiefs was that after the long, closed session in the afternoon, including a "frank discussion which took place [that] may have cleared the air," the Chiefs of Staff Committee was hopeful that the JCS would "come around."[31]

On General Wedemeyer's copy of CCS 303/2, the British-proposed European strategy revision, his extensive handwritten marginal notes provide a sense of the meeting's confrontation and the conceptual distance from which the Americans would have to "come around." On the British-proposed deletion of U.S. language that in the distribution of resources "OVERLORD will have an overriding priority," the reaction was "Not acceptable." On the British substitution that "operations in the Mediterranean Theater will be carried out with the Forces allotted at TRIDENT except insofar as these may be varied by decision of the Combined Chiefs of Staff"? "Definitely no!" On a more general statement of objectives in northern Italy? "Acceptable, yes." But on replacement of the American constraint to do this "utilizing available Mediterranean forces" with camel's nose language about creating "conditions required for OVERLORD" "Not acceptable. No." And again, on offensive operations against southern France, striking out the same American constraint to do this only with available Mediterranean forces, "Not acceptable. No."[32]

The evening of August 16 at 8:20 p.m., FDR departed Washington by train for Quebec City after spending the day at the White House.[33] Through assistance from Harry Hopkins, Major General Handy was on the train. The following day, over lunch aboard the *Ferdinand Magellan*, the general briefed him on the status of U.S.-UK discussions at Quadrant. The only hitch, which proved minor, came at the outset. On entering FDR's private car, understandably a bit nervous, Handy stepped on the president's Scottie, Fala.[34]

In the war in Western Europe, on August 17 the Allies completed their conquest of Sicily after thirty-eight days of fighting.[35] The American Eighth Air Force, flying out of England, conducted its first raid on ball bearing factories in the Schweinfurt-Regensburg area. Casualties among the American heavy bombers were brutal. Of 376 B-17s taking part, 31 percent were lost to all causes.[36]

As the mauled bomber force was recovering at its bases in East Anglia, the Combined Chiefs of Staff were convened again at Chateau Frontenac. This August 17 meeting, their 110th, was another closed session. This time, the chiefs came to agreement on European strategy. The Americans, indeed, had come around. To General Brooke's "great relief they accepted the proposals for the European theatre so that all our arguing has borne fruit and we have obtained quite fair results."[37] The American chiefs accepted the British-proposed changes "as a brief and concise statement of [the ccs's] agreed strategy concept for operations in the European Theater in 1943–44."[38] The Combined Chiefs directed the Secretariat to put this in a clean copy for presentation to FDR and Churchill.[39]

By the evening of August 17, FDR's train had arrived at Wolfe's Cove Station, Quebec City, and he had transferred to the Citadel where his Map Room already was established.[40] The rounds of dinners and high-level consultations that would continue to the conclusion of Quadrant commenced. These included frequent conversations between Roosevelt and Churchill meeting alone. Of their substance, little is on record.

Wednesday morning, August 18, Churchill's military secretary, Lt. Gen. Sir Hastings Ismay, informed the prime minister of the ccs agreement on strategy for operations in Europe. Ismay's note told Churchill, "I think that you would wish to know at once that we have got precisely what we set out to get."[41]

What had changed for the Americans, who had been so emphatic in their initial reaction less than a day earlier to the British-proposed revision of the language on Overlord? Apparently, a measure of trust had been reestablished. In their morning meeting at Chateau Frontenac, August 18, the British chiefs revoked the general standstill order to British forces in the Mediterranean that they had issued on July 24, well in advance of Quadrant.[42] Barring an unforeseen contingency, on which all the chiefs—American and British—would decide, the way was clear for the seven divisions to redeploy in support of Overlord. Similarly, other resources would be allocated with priority for Overlord. The August 18 action by the Chiefs of Staff Committee tangibly addressed a specific source of the American chiefs' distrust of the British, recognized as such by General Brooke.[43] Therefore, lifting the standstill order likely facilitated the August 17 ccs agreement on strategy.

On the U.S. side, Wednesday morning, Roosevelt met at the Citadel with Marshall, Leahy, Wedemeyer, Hopkins, his naval aide, Rear Adm. Wilson Brown, and press secretary Steve Early.[44] When the Combined Chiefs met at Chateau Frontenac in the afternoon, after a joint luncheon with the two leaders, there was no discussion of European strategy.[45] That had been settled, at least for now.

The chiefs turned to writing their report to Roosevelt and Churchill and to Pacific strategy. The skirmishing had not ended. Getting to closure on the report to the two leaders generated such acrimony between the chiefs that Brooke with Marshall's agreement once again sent the worried staff out of the room so as to continue in closed session. The Combined Chiefs did reach agreement, immediately after which Vice Admiral Mountbatten reminded Brooke that he wanted to demonstrate one of his projects, "Habbakuk." Permission granted, the demonstration inadvertently captured the tenor of all that had gone before at Quadrant.

Habbakuk was the code name for an investigation into the feasibility of building truly enormous aircraft carriers made of frozen wood pulp slurry.[46] At Mountbatten's signal, attendants rolled in carts with a block of water ice on one and on the other a block of "Pykrete" frozen wood slurry. Mountbatten whipped out a revolver, causing the Combined Chiefs to scramble to get behind him. His first shot shattered the block of water ice, showering the Chiefs with chips, proving the expected, Mountbatten said. His second shot bounced off the "Pykrete" and ricocheted between members of the Allies' top military leadership, fortunately claiming as a casualty only the Chateau Frontenac's elegant wood paneling. On hearing gunshots, a member of the long-suffering Anglo-American staff in the next room exclaimed, "Good heavens, they've started shooting now!"[47]

The Combined Chiefs of Staff went to Citadel at 5:30 p.m., August 19, for a plenary session with FDR and Churchill in which the chiefs reported the draft results of their conferences to date and their schedule for future meetings.[48] For all the attention to the strategy for Europe, near-equal time had been devoted to the Pacific theater. Briefing this global strategy to the president and prime minister interactively took time. FDR and Churchill each had comments on the decisions reached and measures that they wished to have studied and reported further. After two and a quarter hours, the meeting adjourned with the agreement that FDR and Churchill would be notified when the chiefs were ready with their final report.[49]

Roosevelt's Joint Chiefs of Staff could report to him written reaffirmation of the British commitment to Overlord as the primary Allied strategy against the Axis in Europe with a date certain for its cross-channel assault, May 1, 1944. Acting on that, the Combined Chiefs had approved COSSAC's "Overlord Outline Plan" and authorized its full development. The way now was clear for Roosevelt to sign the secret "Articles of Agreement" between the United States and the United Kingdom on atomic interchange and collaboration.

The night of August 19 at 9:30 p.m., Roosevelt, the Churchill family, and Harry Hopkins came together for a late dinner at the Citadel. Afterward, FDR and Churchill again had a private conversation for several hours before the president retired.[50] At this meeting, the atomic agreement was typed in two copies on Citadel stationery and signed by Roosevelt and Churchill.[51] Churchill's principal private secretary, John M. Martin, gave one copy to Roosevelt's naval aide, Wilson Brown, for retention.[52]

The next day, FDR and Churchill took time off to fish and picnic at Lac de l'Epaule. Of course, this too "enabled the President and Prime Minister to discuss many details during the drive to and from the fishing ground."[53]

While their leaders relaxed, the Combined Chiefs met again. Having approved the text of their final report and decided on air and naval commanders for Overlord, they shared their evolving observations on Russia. General Marshall remarked on an apparent change in Russian attitudes. To him, the minutes recorded, "It appeared that Russia was turning an increasingly hostile eye on the capitalist world, of whom they were becoming increasingly contemptuous. Their recent 'Second Front' announcement, no longer borne of despair, was indicative of their attitude." He asked for the British chiefs' views, particularly in the context of whether in dire circumstance the Germans might "facilitate our entry into the country to repel the Russians." General Brooke responded that he had in the past considered the possibility of Russian opportunism in Russian demands for part of Poland, part of the Baltic States, and concessions in the Balkans. However, he also foresaw a Russian need for a period of peace in Europe to facilitate Russian recovery from the war's terrible devastation.[54]

On Saturday, August 21, FDR and Churchill sent their telegram to Stalin to inform him of the outcome of the Quadrant Conference, excluding mention of their secret agreement on atomic collaboration.[55] The Combined Chiefs approved minor decisions.[56] Enthused by post-raid reports on Operation Gommorah, Chief of the Air Staff Sir Charles Portal messaged Bomber Command's Arthur Harris this day in anticipation of the RAF's next big strike. "Attacks on Berlin anything like Hamburg scale must have enormous effect on Germany as a whole." The Hamburg raids did throw a scare into the Nazi political leadership and stimulated expanded urban area evacuations. However, Bomber Command's August 23–24 raid on Berlin basically missed the city and incurred heavy losses.[57]

The formal reading to FDR and Churchill of the Combined Chiefs' final report, August 23, at the Citadel brought a reprise of the British caveats. Commenting on Overlord, Churchill stated that "he wished it definitely understood that British acceptance of the planning for Operation OVERLORD included the proviso that the operation could only be carried out in the event that certain conditions regarding German strength were met." These were the three conditions in the COSSAC "Overlord Outline Plan." After adding that he thought the United Nations needed "a second string to their bow" in the form of a prepared plan for Jupiter, an invasion of southern Norway, Churchill returned to Overlord. He said, again, that he "did not in any way wish to imply that he was not wholeheartedly in favor of OVERLORD, but, at the same time, he wished to emphasize that its launching was dependent upon certain conditions which would give it a reasonable chance of success."[58]

Churchill gave his agreement that transfer of the seven combat-experienced divisions from the Mediterranean back to the UK for Overlord was firm at that time but subject to review by the ccs. General Brooke added that return of the seven was planned at present "unless the situation forced the Combined Chiefs of Staff to reconsider on the basis of the enemy situation at the time." Then, restating the rationale that he brought to the conference, Brooke said, "It might be necessary to keep one or two of these trained divisions in the Mediterranean in order to create a more favorable situation for the success of OVERLORD or to avoid a setback in Italy." Churchill said this might be done by an exchange of divisions without prejudice to the move of the seven divisions.[59]

Churchill said that the Overlord plan briefed to him by COS-SAC's Brigadier McLean "seemed sound, but must be strengthened." Marshall agreed and observed that the initial assault actually would have four and a half divisions rather than three as discussed in May at Trident. Responding to Churchill's query as to whether the plan included an attack inside the Cotentin peninsula, Marshall said it did not, but this would be possible to add if more landing craft could be made available.[60] The exchange between Churchill and Marshall presaged Neptune as it would evolve, larger still, for D-Day. Churchill then expressed his interest in assigning the naval command of Overlord to Adm. Sir Bertram Ramsay, who had commanded the invasion fleet for Sicily. Eventually Ramsay got the assignment.

The Quadrant Conference came to an end August 24, with the 116th meeting of the Combined Chiefs of Staff. The ccs concluded their talks with some discussion of the pending amphibious assault, Avalanche, on Salerno outside Naples and Atlantic convoy arrangements.[61] Acting on agreements during Quadrant, convoy movements were about to surge, and the atomic scientists were scrambling.

Roosevelt arrived in Ottawa on August 25, just after leaving the Quadrant Conference in Quebec City. FDR told Prime Minister Mackenzie King, during their drive together, that "he had, he thought, got agreement by effecting a compromise which would mean an attack from Britain to the north of France. That he believed he could get a million men across during the remainder of the summer and on in the autumn." Mackenzie King "pointed out that there were very few divisions in Britain and it was absolutely imperative not only that they should have the numbers but be sure of being able to get on and make real headway after landing." Mackenzie King observed that "the President did not speak of it as a full-scale attack but as one which he thought would meet the purpose."[62]

17

Bolero Unleashed

The most critical thing in World War I and World War II wasn't tanks or airplanes—it was ships.

—Gen. Thomas T. Handy, U.S. Army

Until the Quadrant Conference, two open issues had enabled
the lingering, fractious U.S.-UK indecision over fixing and
adhering to a primary strategy for winning the war in Europe.
One was the absence of a plan for a cross-Channel invasion that
both British and American military chiefs could accept as feasible. The other issue was the absence in the summer of 1943 of a
concentration of Allied forces adequate to win victory in Europe
either from the Mediterranean or across the English Channel. If
cross-Channel attack was to be the strategy, then two additional
major issues loomed among many that had to be addressed: designation of a supreme Allied commander and assembly of the
amphibious force essential to mount and sustain the invasion.

The COSSAC "Overlord Outline Plan," approved by the Combined Chiefs of Staff at the Quadrant Conference, addressed the
first issue. Marshall and the Joint Chiefs of Staff intended to resolve
the second issue by creating the necessary concentration of forces.
They meant to seal the Anglo-American commitment to the cross-
Channel invasion in 1944 by establishing as soon as possible in
Britain the full measure of Allied strength, especially U.S. forces,
required for the invasion. The conditions raised by Churchill and
Brooke yet again at the conclusion of Quadrant heightened the
American chiefs' incentive to act immediately.

Prompt deployment to the UK of an invasion force in full
also would create a tangible buttress against further challenge
by Winston Churchill to Quadrant's reaffirmation of the cross-

Channel invasion, on the date settled by the ccs. The U.S. forces forward deployed for the invasion would fulfill Franklin Roosevelt's precondition for appointing an American as the supreme Allied commander.

General Marshall had assured President Roosevelt on August 11 that the United States could deploy in the United Kingdom nineteen ground force divisions plus the required additional air and sea power, fully equipped and combat ready, in time for the invasion. Fulfilling Marshall's assurance would require prodigious effort. This demanded moving many hundreds of thousands of troops, their equipment, and supplies from the continental United States to the UK. Particularly important was implementing the transfer of the seven U.S. and British divisions from the Mediterranean to Britain for Overlord. Four of these were U.S. divisions whose number would bring the total to well over one million U.S. troops. Movement of the seven divisions had been decided at the Trident Conference in May and reaffirmed at Quadrant in August, but remained to be done.

Major General Handy's decision-framing August 8 memorandum recorded that of the 452,000 U.S. troops confronting the European Axis from the United Kingdom and the Mediterranean at the end of July 1943, only half of these, 238,742, were in Great Britain and Northern Ireland.[1] To reach the May 1, 1944, target for the 1.4 million U.S. troop basis for Overlord and Pointblank, the Allies faced making up the existing shortfall and increasing the pace to deploy 1 million more troops to the UK. This transfer with allowance for time to equip and train the arriving forces for the invasion had to be accomplished in just eight months. The massive movement had to be made through U-boat contested waters and jammed receiving ports, still not free from the threat of nighttime aerial bombing. The deployment had to stay on a schedule tightly crafted around operational needs and logistical constraints. As D-Day neared, planners knew, the buildup would be further challenged. The same receiving ports would have to shift their finite cargo handling capabilities from unloading arriving convoys to loading ships in preparation for the invasion.

Force deployment often was described in terms of divisions and air wings in most discussions at high level. The more-nuanced reality of the 1.2 million troop buildup required a balanced force delivered to the United Kingdom in a sequence and priority designed to support preparation and execution of Operation Overlord. Reorganized on March 9, 1942, for the global conflict, the U.S. Army comprised three basic types of forces, Services of Supply (later renamed the Army Service Force), Army Air Forces, and Army Ground Forces. Argued back and forth, numbers and proportions for the Army's troop basis for the projected May 1, 1944, cross-Channel invasion settled into a still-larger figure of 1.4 million troops of which 44 percent would be ground force, 29 percent air force, and 26 percent service force.

Logic for the buildup, simplified here, assigned Service of Supply units first priority in sequence for overseas transport to the United Kingdom. Their essential mission was to prepare for and support the reception of the vast combat force to follow. Two examples were port battalions to supplement British workers for unloading convoys and moving arriving troops and supplies to cantonment areas and engineering construction units to build bases to receive the arriving forces.[2] Next in sequence were additions to the U.S. Army Air Forces in Britain that already were working with the Royal Air Force in Operation Pointblank to weaken and reduce German capability to resist Overlord. By mid-1943, the Army Air Forces in Britain were struggling with their own shortfall in crews, aircraft, and supplies as well as taking greater combat losses than anticipated. Ground combat forces, the largest U.S. element of the Allied force that would liberate Western Europe from the Axis, followed as third in sequence.

As U.S. forces arrived in ever growing numbers, so their daily requirements for consumable supplies grew proportionately even as materiel and munitions for their coming combat in Europe were transported and stockpiled in the United Kingdom. Ninety-five percent of the buildup would move from the United States to the United Kingdom by sea.

* * *

Beyond emphasis on transatlantic shipping, also to be accomplished was the phased expansion and concentration in the British Isles of the naval amphibious force for Neptune. This would be the opening operation of Overlord, when landing ships and landing craft of very different operational capabilities would surge across the Channel on D-Day.

To develop its Overlord Outline Plan, cossac had been told after the Trident Conference to plan on allocation of 4,504 amphibious ships and craft for Neptune.[3] When the ground force was expanded significantly in the January 1944 modification of cossac's plan, the number of landing ships and craft required also had to grow proportionately. Effectively, this added to the plan another entire naval assault force. Combining U.S. Navy, Royal Navy, and other Allied vessels, Neptune would be a sea force of a magnitude never before or since seen by the world. Major vessel types at the core of the amphibious force were the attack transports, attack cargo ships, landing ships dock, and especially the landing ships tank (LST).

Ponderous and rough-riding, a flat-bottomed LST could carry 1,900 tons of tanks and other vehicles hundreds of miles and land them directly onto a beach over the ramp through its bow doors. This capability was also an asset in embarkation. To load cargo LSTS could nose up to simple, purpose-built concrete aprons ("hards") where roads ended at water's edge in England. That expanded the Allies' capacity to mount and sustain the seaborne invasion beyond the limits of Britain's fully engaged ports. Lamented by their crews as "Large Slow Targets," LSTS were coveted for amphibious operations worldwide and never became available in numbers sufficient to satisfy demands.

Essential complements to the assault landing ships, which were built to cross oceans, were thousands of smaller, inshore steel or plywood landing craft. Many of these themselves required transportation across the Atlantic as deck cargo or as kits for assembly in Britain. A good number, such as the British-designed Landing Craft Tank (LCT), small, flat-bottomed, and vitally needed for their special role in Neptune, were to be drawn out of forces in the Mediterranean. The LCTs could redeploy under their own power from there 1,600 nautical miles to the UK only under favorable maritime weather conditions.

Ramming onto mine and obstacle-strewn beaches to deliver heavy load after load was punishing for the smaller craft. In August 1943, General Eisenhower reported from North Africa a lower than planned availability of amphibious craft for transfer to England as a result of operational and maintenance casualties in the Sicily invasion.[4] Overlord planners were compelled to revise upward their projection of amphibious capacity needed from other sources for the cross-Channel invasion. The margin would have to be made up from vessels needed for operations elsewhere in the world or through still more new construction.

The Combined Chiefs of Staff, on July 20, 1943, already had issued an accelerated schedule. They wanted half of the landing craft flotillas and all of the specialized beach commandos, communication sections, and bombardment groups to join their forces in the United Kingdom by January 1, 1944. They wanted all of the landing ships and craft to join by March 16, 1944. This directive called for the arrival in Britain of 810 amphibious ships and landing craft (exclusive of craft carried aboard attack transports and attack cargo ships) in ten increments by February 16, 1944.[5]

Many of these ships and craft remained to be built in yards in Britain, Canada, and the United States, some hundreds of miles from the ocean in Indiana, Ohio, and Ontario. Steel in the United States to build amphibious ships and craft, like the crews to sail them, had to be obtained at penalty to competing but also critical war priorities. The vagaries of war could, and did, compel the reordering of military materiel priorities much faster than generation of the implements of war could be adapted in response. Output could be driven by the long lead time production of some components. Shifting skilled civilian labor always presented challenging consequences.

The impact of uncertainty about strategy now became evident in hard trade-offs. In 1942, the U.S. Navy had conceded priority for steel to amphibious ships over destroyers and destroyer escorts.[6] At the time, these two combatant types were needed badly for convoy escorts in the Atlantic and also to make up heavy losses in the South Pacific from then-uneven night battle with the Imperial Japanese Navy. The U.S. Navy made this hard choice in favor of amphibious lift for a cross-Channel invasion, however reluctantly, only to see first Roundup and then Sledgehammer deferred and delayed in Allied strategy discussions. Consequently with no repeat of the Navy's support, Roosevelt's January 1943 list of essential war production programs did not include landing craft.[7] When, later in 1943, the U.S. Joint Chiefs of Staff again took up the question of increasing production of amphibious ships and craft to support a 1944 cross-Channel attack, officers charged with expanding and maintaining the U.S. Navy's fleet pushed back.

The vice chief of naval operations, Vice Adm. Frederick Horne, was urged not to change shipbuilding schedules then in force. He was cautioned that "in order to get the present[ly planned] LSTS on time, we have to cut across every single combatant ship program and give them over-riding priority in every navy yard and in every major civilian shipbuilding company."[8] Still, the Navy was able to propose the feasibility of a 50 percent monthly increase in the production of landing ships and craft from LSTS down to the little but vital thirty-six-foot landing craft vehicle personnel (LCVP).

The proposal, radioed from the Pentagon to the U.S. delegation at the Quadrant Conference on August 16, illustrated the "robbing Peter to pay Paul" choices typical at the complex collision of critical priorities with scarcity. The increased production of landing ships and craft depended on allocation of an additional 300,000 tons of steel in 1944 and increased production of diesel engines from 6,000 to 8,000 per month. To increase diesel engine production, the necessary transfer of scarce skilled labor and critical components would impose on the Army reduced production of heavy trucks, trucks essential to sustainment of the armies advancing into France once landed. If the additional steel was not produced, steel would have to be reallocated. Should that be necessary, increased production of LSTS, vital to landing and sustaining the Army over French beaches, would impose reduced production by four per month of Liberty ships, which were vital to transporting the Army's equipment and supplies across the Atlantic for the invasion of Europe. Increased priority for production of Navy landing craft medium (LCM), vital to getting tanks and other armored fighting vehicles ashore in the earliest stages of opposed landings in Normandy, would slow or cancel production of craft needed by the Army in the Southwest Pacific.[9] The needed steel was obtained.

As the U.S. Navy struggled with its two-ocean war priorities, so did the Royal Navy in its areas of responsibility. Concurrently in Britain, steel and facilities had to be reallocated in the race to build components for Mulberry, Neptune's artificial harbors seen to be essential to the success of Overlord. The British Admiralty had to give up a share of production of aircraft carriers and anti-submarine frigates to construct portable piers and pontoons for Mulberry. There would follow an urgent scramble on both sides of the Atlantic to find enough tugboats to tow the artificial harbor components across the Channel to Normandy.[10]

Fundamental joint decisions on strategy turned on the availability of amphibious capacity. Frequently these decisions rose to the highest levels in the alliance. At one point, an exasperated Churchill was reported to complain, "The destinies of two great empires . . . seem to be tied up in some God-damned things called LST's."[11]

* * *

Despite the immensity of the task to create and globally allocate the Allies' combined arms force, by the summer of 1943, a new confidence that it could be done was reflected in General Marshall's August 11 affirmative answer to FDR and in the Quadrant Final Report as to getting divisions to the United Kingdom before D-Day.[12] There were reasons for qualified optimism, about besting the German U-boats. As the need to move a million troops and vast quantities of equipment and supplies from North America to the British Isles became urgent, Allied operations in the Battle of the Atlantic had made a profound shift to the offensive. The U-boat wolves were being hunted not just in the vicinity of convoys and in chokepoints like the Bay of Biscay but as individual threats anywhere in the broad ocean.

At sea in late April and early May 1943, the dramatic running battle of convoys ONS-5 and SC-128 had given hope that a turning point favoring the Allies had been reached. Clear indication of that came from the enemy when a May 24 message was intercepted from Grossadmiral Karl Doenitz to all his U-boat commanders telling them, "The situation in the North Atlantic now forces a temporary shifting of operations to areas less endangered by aircraft."[13] Broader ranging Allied ASW aircraft were not Doenitz's only problem. The Allies changed substantially their code for convoy radio messages, dubbed "Frankfurt" by the Germans, on June 10, 1943. That step shut the Germans out of this source of intelligence on convoy movements. B-Dienst never broke into Frankfurt again, and the unit's access to other Allied naval codes also slipped away.[14]

The Combined Chiefs of Staff and their planners, U.S. and British, cited the marked reduction in U-boat attacks in May, June, and July 1943 as a turning point. In hindsight they were correct. However, their perspective in the moment had to be cautious. In a genuinely global conflict, available merchant ship tonnage everywhere mattered to the margin for victory in specific operations. The Allies worried that the lull in U-boat attacks was not permanent and that the Germans could surge as many as 150 more U-boats into the Atlantic. They pondered possible changes in German weapons and tactics, such as concentrating on hunting still-independently sailing cargo vessels throughout the Atlantic. Expanding operations still more than they already were in the Middle and South Atlantic could stretch Allied ASW assets too thin and enable a U-boat surge force to send sinking of merchant tonnage back up into the grim numbers of 1942.[15]

The U-boats had not been driven from the Atlantic so much

as they now were being neutralized by effective Allied forces in numbers constantly at sea and on watch. The U.S. Navy intelligence assessment at the time of the Quadrant Conference was that Hitler had 429 U-boats operational. Of these, 166 (including 23 in the far north) were operating in the Atlantic, according to Adm. Ernest King.[16] To keep the North Atlantic battle won for safe transfer of the forces from North America that would make Overlord possible, the Allies had to remain constant in their collective purpose. By mid-1943, their organization and resources for doing so were awesome.

The convoy surface escort groups, which once had regularly faced the U-boats virtually alone, now were the convoys' last line in a concentric defense—as they should be. The first line was the integrated Allied intelligence force assigned to the battle. Extensive, penetrating, and highly proficient, Allied intelligence empowered anti-U-boat command and control organizations on both sides of the Atlantic

In Washington, two weeks after forty-four-ship Convoy ONS-5's epic running battle with the twenty-eight U-boats in Gruppe Fink, the U.S. Navy's Tenth Fleet was activated on May 20, 1943, to consolidate all convoy routing and antisubmarine operations in U.S. strategic areas.[17] Intelligence was Tenth Fleet's primary weapon. Located well inland from saltwater, the Tenth Fleet possessed no ships or aircraft of its own. Inside a requisitioned private school on Nebraska Avenue on the heights of Northwest Washington DC, Tenth Fleet staff worked around the clock defensively and offensively. They controlled the Convoy and Routing Section, also in Washington, which set and adjusted the course of convoys as needed to evade, by the best possible margin of distance, identified and suspected locations of U-boats at sea. Offensively, the Tenth Fleet applied detection reports to vector Allied ASW ships and aircraft to locate, attack, and sink U-boats.

This capable organization and its equivalent in the UK worked closely together around the clock to make the most effective use of the now numerous Allied ASW forces. They synthesized time-urgent, integrated signals intelligence, based on position-fixing spot reports from the Allies' network of high-frequency band radio direction-finding (HF/DF) stations around the Atlantic Basin; communications intelligence from decryptions of Enigma messages between German U-boat headquarters and the submarines; and U-boat detections by patrol aircraft and surface escort ships (particularly those with onboard tactical HF/DF).

The Allies had progressed from having too few escorts for adequate close-in defense of the convoys to deploying effective numbers of more capable ships and aircraft. For the U.S. Navy alone, by November 1943, fifty-one new destroyer escorts had been assigned to the Atlantic Fleet.[18] Increased forces and new capabilities supported taking the battle to the U-boats wherever they could be found.

Now available were British and American small escort aircraft carriers (hull classification symbol CVE), each one operating with its flotilla of three or four ASW ships as a hunter-killer group. On a loose tether to screen specific convoys, each CVE would take HF/DF location spot reports from ashore and refine them with their own tactical HF/DF to vector their planes and ASW ships to high probability search areas. Soon more U-boats were being caught on the surface, attacked, and sunk. The Royal Navy had three CVES operating in the Atlantic, and the U.S. Navy had five ready for operations. CVE sailors made self-deprecating comparison of their little ships to "first class carriers," but the results delivered by the CVES were unquestionably first class.[19]

The Allies achieved and then dramatically beat the ratio of exchange of one U-boat sunk for every two merchant ships sunk that they believed Doenitz could not afford. Overall for the first ten months of 1943, absorbing the grim tonnage losses of February through May, one U-boat was sunk for every two and a half merchant vessels sunk. But from June through October, each U-boat sunk represented only half a merchant vessel lost. In September, seventeen merchant vessels were sunk for eleven U-boats sunk. In October, fifteen merchant vessels and thirty-two U-boats were sunk.[20] The ratio of exchange had been inverted by the Allies, catastrophically for Doenitz.

Through late spring and all of July 1943, continued improvement in performance against the U-boat threat by Allied intelligence and antisubmarine forces sustained the chiefs' and planners' confidence about sending massive numbers of troops across the North Atlantic by sea. The battle between codemakers and codebreakers, so important to convoy protection and success in other operations, had tilted further in the favor of the Allies, although the cryptanalysts may not have realized that entirely at the time. Allied ASW operations and tactics became more flexible as they matured. Improved operations, tactics, and new weapons, like the "Fido" air-dropped ASW homing torpedo, increasingly kept U-boats from making contact with convoys even as more submarines were sunk.

* * *

However, current success against the U-boats and relative past success in convoying of troops had to be balanced against the larger and daunting logistical challenge. Despite declining losses to U-boats and surging shipbuilding, there still was a shortage of merchant shipping of all types in 1943. Availability of bottoms for moving cargo and troops to fulfill Bolero always had to be addressed in context with competing requirements and availability—or unavailability—of shipping capacity with specificity on a global basis, literally.

The British Chiefs of Staff, on August 18, 1943, reluctantly approved diversion from South Africa of the Holland America liner *Nieuw Amsterdam* to transport U.S. troops from North America across the Atlantic to the United Kingdom. In doing so, they accepted the need to find another way to move British troops from South Africa to India. They further recommended that Churchill himself cable the prime minister of New Zealand to break the news that the S.S. *Nieuw Amsterdam*'s reassignment would delay by seven months the transfer of New Zealand troops back to closer-to-home combat operations in the South Pacific.[21]

As fast as new cargo ships could be commissioned, their increased capacity was sucked into the maw of burgeoning global requirements of all types. Military cargo vied for space with civil cargo needed to maintain bare subsistence levels of food and fuel for the British people.

Despite severely constraining import consumption and achieving major increases in domestic production of food, by the beginning of 1943 British reserve stocks had declined to levels approaching what the war cabinet considered an irreducible minimum. In response, Britain appealed to the United States in March 1943 to increase transatlantic shipments of critical civilian cargo to keep pace with subsistence consumption.[22] This was done to sustain a people approaching a state of "living hand to mouth."[23]

Sure to compound the issue of food for the British population would be the allocation of open land to accommodate more than one million American troops arriving in the United Kingdom for the invasion. By D-Day, 261,000 acres had been reallocated for American facilities such as bases, airfields, depots, maneuver grounds, and hospitals. Much of this land was taken by necessity from the production of food.[24] A portion of the food produced on the British Isles' remaining agricultural land was allocated to supplement the rations arriving by sea to feed the influx of troops. The earlier British appeal in March 1943 to increase space in transatlantic convoys for critical civilian cargo proved to be well justified.

With Allied victories from the end of 1942 onward came new demands for shipping capacity to assist peoples emerging malnourished from Axis occupation in North Africa and the Mediterranean. Now just beyond the planning horizon were the sustainment needs of soon-to-be-liberated northwestern Europe.

The complex challenge of responding to widely distributed and varying needs, urgencies, and conditions spawned inevitable shipping inefficiencies. At dock level, the panoply of military cargo with its wide range of weights, volumes, and shapes presented a complex physical challenge to loading ships efficiently. Always there was tension between the goal of loading ships to squeeze the most efficiency from scarce cargo space and the goal of timely dispatch of specific military cargo to meet far-flung priority operational needs. Through most of 1942, this conundrum stimulated in the United States civil-military wrangling over loading schemes, who decided them, and who controlled which ships in what circumstances. With the civilian U.S. War Shipping Administration on one side and the Army and Navy on the other, the dispute went to President Roosevelt, who issued an executive order. Still the issue lingered for months before settling into a workable process.[25]

Beyond the scarcity of ships, getting the right ship types to the right ports for loading was influenced not just by distances to be sailed under threat of attack but also by turnaround times in the ports at which they called. The consequences of port delays impeded the number of sailings and availability of shipping needed for new voyages elsewhere. In the European theater in 1943–44, part of the problem was the limited capacity and low efficiency of many North African and Mediterranean ports, reduced still further by war damage.[26] However, even at the much more efficient receiving ports of the United Kingdom, which were subject to attack from the air with bombs and mines, the capacity for unloading ships and for railways to move cargoes inland capped the number of ships that could be received.

The through-put of British ports and the capacity of the British Isles to absorb arriving divisions and air units affected the rate of buildup more than shipping capacity and influenced the size and scheduling of convoys.[27] The finite capacity of Britain's ports had to accommodate imports to sustain the British population at the level of bare subsistence. Allowing for that, the ports could handle at most an average of 150 shiploads per month dedicated to the U.S. military buildup and its sustainment. At an estimated cargo capacity of 10,000 tons for an Atlantic Ocean freighter of the 1940s, such as a Liberty ship, this capped the American inflow at 1.5 million tons per month.[28] In summer months, the ports' performance unloading cargo reached its peak because the longer hours of daylight extended dock work hours and limited the threat of aerial attack from the now-depleted Luftwaffe bomber force.[29] However, with the cross-Channel invasion on, planners could see ahead a spring 1944 deadline on the availability of British ports for receiving troops and materiel arriving from North America.

The through-put at embarkation ports in the United States and Canada, east and west, depended on the efficient, timely arrival for loading of cargo and troops from across the full breadth of North America. Almost all arrived by rail. Movement of a single U.S. division with its equipment to an embarkation port could require up to two hundred trains. Movements of that scale became a daily routine many times over. Unprecedented and not equaled in size since then, that massive rail operation would be threatened with sudden disruption in the United States. Stoppage of movement to embarkation ports would loom just when movement of troops and materiel needed to be at peak efficiency, on the clock against the time when British ports would have to shift their focus to loading for D-Day.

Systemic constraints and disagreement on their solution confronted generation in the United States of troops and equipment ready to ship when needed at embarkation ports. The disparity between the transit time for relatively fast troop ships and for slow-moving cargo ships, combined with the finite handling capacity at British ports and inland depot space, stimulated a long-running argument within the U.S. Army about logistical schema. The Army Service Force in Britain wanted equipment pre-shipped in bulk to build up pre-deployed stocks available for issue to troops as they arrived in Britain.[30] The War Department General Staff resisted ASF's desire, preferring to ship equipment in unit sets with the troops. In an initial compromise with ASF, the General Staff agreed to require units to ship their equipment thirty days in advance of embarking their troops for Britain. Because of the slow transit rate of cargo convoys, the practical effect was that a unit's equipment arrived in Britain just in time for issue to its troops, if nothing went wrong. Looking ahead to moving through British ports at fixed capacity all of the equipment and supplies to support the surge of troops expected in the months immediately prior to D-Day, this compromise was not a satisfactory solution. Negotiation continued within the Army.

However, the vagaries of global war could produce bizarre turns. In the midst of a global premium on all shipping capacity, an abundance of space for shipment of Army equipment and supplies to Britain became available with the sharp curtailment of troop movements from the United States to Britain following the autumn 1942 shift of operations to North Africa. Typically each month, 730,000 tons of shipping space was allocated to the Army for Bolero. However, well into 1943, the Army had difficulty generating sufficient equipment and materiel to use all of its allocated space. In each such month, the Army would have to release back to the civilian War Shipping Administration tens of thousands of tons, sometimes as much as 100,000 tons, of shipping capacity.[31] This did nothing to bolster the chagrined military's case in its arguments with WSA.

Decisions about U.S. shipments of troops and equipment to Britain in anticipation of a cross-Channel attack were made in the shadow of prolonged uncertainty about Allied strategy. As late as July 1943, the emergence of the debate between U.S. planners and leaders in Washington as to whether cross-Channel attack indeed should take priority over operations in the Mediterranean rippled through to cause uncertainty among the logisticians as to whether a cross-Channel attack would happen at all.

* * *

At the Quadrant Conference on August 16, Anglo-American planners agreed to updated monthly troop lift targets through June 1944 that would deliver the invasion force for Overlord called for by COSSAC's "Overlord Outline Plan."[32] Included, in addition to action on transferring the seven divisions from the Mediterranean to Britain, was immediate resumption on a massive scale of U.S. troop convoys to the UK. The troop-carrying capacity of the liners that became legends in the popular memory of World War II would be eclipsed.

Since U.S. entry into the war, sixteen ocean liners, the racehorses of the prewar "Blue Ribbon" Atlantic run, such as *Queen Elizabeth, Queen Mary, Mauretania, Aquitania, Île-de-France,* and *Empress of Scotland,* had supplemented nine escorted AT convoys (discontinued in September 1942) in transporting most U.S.

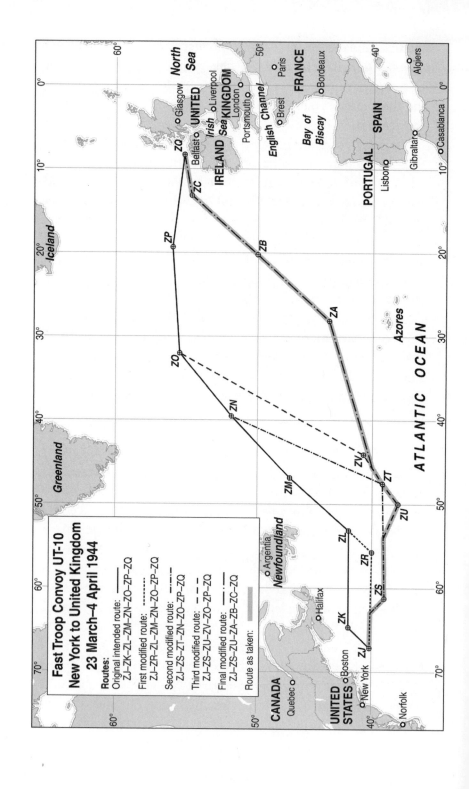

Fast Troop Convoy UT-10
New York to United Kingdom
23 March–4 April 1944

Routes:

Original intended route:
ZJ–ZK–ZL–ZM–ZN–ZO–ZP–ZQ

First modified route:
ZJ–ZR–ZL–ZM–ZN–ZO–ZP–ZQ

Second modified route:
ZJ–ZS–ZT–ZN–ZO–ZP–ZQ

Third modified route:
ZJ–ZS–ZU–ZV–ZO–ZP–ZQ

Final modified route:
ZJ–ZS–ZU–ZA–ZB–ZC–ZQ

Route as taken:

troops to Great Britain.[33] Faster than even surfaced U-boats, the liners most often sailed independently and unescorted between North American ports and Britain. Stripped of their peacetime appointments and converted to carry 15,000 troops each, more than double their peacetime passenger capacity, Cunard's RMS *Queen Mary* and RMS *Queen Elizabeth* were referred to by Allied convoy routers and remembered by their wartime passengers, justifiably, as "monsters."[34] However, the *Queens* and all the other liners combined, "semi-monsters" to the convoy routers, lacked the capacity to transport in time the huge surge of troops to fulfill Marshall's commitment to Roosevelt. By D-Day, 36 percent of troops moved to Great Britain would be transported in the liners, and 5 percent would arrive in Britain by air. The remaining 59 percent would be transported in a new series of twelve heavily escorted fast troop convoys.[35]

Designated UT eastward and TU on their westward return, the twelve fast troop convoys from the United States to Britain started modestly. Three days before the Quadrant Conference concluded, the first of the troop convoys, UT-1, sailed at 7 a.m., August 21, from Norfolk, Virginia, for Liverpool, 3,500 nautical miles across the North Atlantic, with 28,100 troops. UT-1 included five troop-carrying vessels packed to overloading. U.S. Army Transport *Argentina* alone carried 6,497 troops, half again that ship's normal capacity. Others among the convoy's five overloaded transports were USAT *Santa Paula* and USAT *Cristobal*.[36] Faced with a scarcity of troop transports, the War Department adopted a policy of "overloading or double-bunking during the summer months," taking into account open deck space in the UT convoys.[37]

Convoy UT-1 was "fast" relative to other convoys. The slowest vessel allowed to join a UT convoy had to be capable of making 15 nautical miles (knots) per hour. Taking into account sea conditions, the UT convoys averaged a 13.5 knot speed of advance.[38] This compared with 8 knots or less for a typical slow convoy, 19–28 knots for the independently sailing ocean liners, and 17 knots for a surfaced U-boat (8 knots submerged).[39]

UT-1 was carefully protected by a flotilla of antisubmarine escorts that exceeded the number of transports. The convoy left Norfolk in the care of six Royal Navy escorts, three of which broke down on the first day with one rejoining the convoy on the fourth day of sailing. At Argentia, Newfoundland, one Royal Navy and two U.S. Navy escorts were added to increase the five-ship convoy's ASW screen to seven escorts for crossing the North Atlantic. Antisubmarine air patrols supplemented UT-1's escorts, Liberators flying out of Iceland, and up again from British bases when UT-1 was within sight of the Irish coast on September 3.[40]

UT-1 advanced on a course charted to evade the U-boat threat. Consistent with doctrine for all convoys, "the safe and timely arrival of the convoy at its destination [was] the primary object," with sinking U-boats only a secondary goal.[41] Thus Convoy UT-1 reached Liverpool at 9 a.m. on September 4 without encountering any U-boats or losing a single soldier to enemy action.

The eleven UT convoys that followed between September 1943 and April 1944 were much larger than UT-1. Between twenty to thirty-five military transports and merchant ships packed with troops and high priority cargo were in each of these convoys. The number of troops per convoy ranged from 47,600 to 102,000.[42] These convoys also were better protected. Each convoy had an escort task force of ten to eighteen destroyers and destroyer escorts to address the U-boat threat. As a hedge against breakout and attack by a German surface raider, the escort for most UT/TU convoys included one from among the U.S. Navy's many old battleships, either *Arkansas*, *Texas*, or *Nevada*. If not a battleship, then a pair of cruisers was provided. Allied aircraft or blimps overhead, their effectiveness against U-boats well proven by 1943, were a source of reassurance to the convoys, and their absence was a source of anxiety and complaint. The absence of aircraft within view often resulted from one of two reasons: their hunting of U-boats elsewhere, but still in support of the convoy, or bad flying weather.

The antisubmarine ships allocated to the UT convoys were the most capable and up to date that the U.S. Navy had by 1943 and parenthetically another manifestation of the now fully engaged industrial potential of the United States. Of the sixty-one U.S.

destroyers and destroyer escorts that shepherded the twelve UT convoys, three-quarters were new construction that had been in commission less than one year. Designed and built on the Allied navies' hard-learned lessons from four years of battling the U-boats and equipped with better ASW detection systems and weapons capabilities, the first of the new destroyer escorts had become operational in August. They were assigned as a division to the UT convoys.[43] Benefiting from a dedicated oiler in each convoy for mid-ocean refueling, these escorts stayed with the UT convoys all the way from their U.S. ports of departure to the British Isles, avoiding the hand-off between shorter ranged escorts experienced by most slow convoys.

Were the old battleships necessary protection or an excess of prudence? Contemporaneous with the UT/TU convoys, the German Kriegsmarine maintained the battleships *Tirpitz* and *Scharnhorst*, cruiser *Lützow*, and fourteen destroyers as a "fleet in being" in Norway.[44] In July 1943 the new U.S. battleships *Alabama* and *South Dakota* and their escorting destroyers had sortied from Scotland into the Norwegian Sea in an unrewarded attempt to provoke the German ships to engage in a fight.[45] In September most of the German ships did come out from the Norwegian fjords in a grossly disproportionate raid on Allied facilities on the island of Spitzbergen. Between October and December, the *Tirpitz* was badly disabled at its berth in a series of attacks. *Scharnhorst* came out to attack a Murmansk-bound convoy and was sunk in a sea battle with the Royal Navy.

Except for the first of the series, the UT convoys sailed from New York City, past Fort Wadsworth, through a channel swept for mines daily, and past Ambrose Light on the beginning of their journey of 3,200 nautical miles. Usually a section of ships and escorts from Boston joined the convoy off the East Coast. The UT convoys averaged eleven days' sailing time from New York to ports in the British Isles.[46] Uncomfortable days for the troops but more endurable than the three-week crossings experienced by troops in the divisions sent in 1942.

En route, the UT convoys faced the same problems as all the

other Atlantic convoys including collisions at sea, mechanical failures, unreliable communication systems, uncooperative ship masters, fog, and rough weather that could challenge station-keeping and interfere with at-sea refueling of escort vessels. There were merchant ships purported by their owners and masters to be up to the 15-knot standard of the UT convoys that in fact strained to keep up and in doing so made smoke. A surfaced U-boat's most reliable, passive means to find prey were the eyes of its lookouts. A submarine's conning tower view to the horizon was limited even in the best weather by the curve of the earth. However, one ship making smoke to drift above the horizon line could betray the presence of a convoy at a great distance. Of one such ship that he did not want in the westbound return convoy, the commodore of convoy UT-6 reported to his superiors in Washington and London, "Except in foul weather, they are [a] constant menace and source of grave concern."[47]

Potentially, U-boats also could detect convoys at considerable distance hydro-acoustically. The thrashing in the sea of a convoy's many propellers sent a strong hydro-acoustic signature traveling outward. Although many variables bore on probability with uncertainty for both the hunter and the hunted, detection of that signature underwater was possible up to 50 nautical miles away.[48] That meant the prudent margin of distance desired for diverting a convoy's course to evade suspected U-boats was not just beyond line-of-sight but also beyond potential hydro-acoustic detection.

In autumn 1943, as momentum of the UT convoys was building, the Allies suspected that some U-boats carried on-board signals intelligence experts to listen to the convoy escorts' tactical HF/DF reporting and coordination radio frequency.[49] If so, these U-boats' ability to passively detect and track convoys, as well as to avoid probing antisubmarine vessels, would have benefited.

Shortly into the 1943 surge of troops across the Atlantic, the U-boats' means of attacking convoys they located showed new menace. Two days after convoy UT-2 delivered more than 50,000 troops to British ports, the Germans introduced their Zaunkönig ("wren") acoustic torpedo in U-boat attacks on westbound convoys ONS-18 and ON-202, September 19–24. Set to home in on the higher pitched signature of the propellers of warships, the acoustic torpedoes sank three escorts and damaged another. After piercing the convoys' protective screens, U-boats penetrated the convoy to sink six of the merchant ships with conventional torpedoes.[50] Lost to the U-boats' attacks were 357 lives, 36,422 tons of merchant shipping, and the warships.[51]

Loss of the three escort vessels to the new weapon coincided with forthcoming new requirements to commit destroyers and corvettes to other naval operations. So slim was the margin of surface assets available for convoy protection, still, that this loss and diversion combined to ripple throughout ASW operations in the Atlantic. At the end of September, the Royal Navy found that even by withdrawing all escort groups from the Bay of Biscay and reducing the strength of each to six vessels, they still had only four escort groups available for the North Atlantic. In April they had had six groups.[52]

In the intense swirl of measures and countermeasures in the Battle of the Atlantic, the advantage the Germans found in their acoustic torpedo did not last. When convoy UT-3 sailed from New York two weeks later on October 8, Allied escorts were trailing pairs of parallel-rod FXR "Foxer" noise-making deception devices. The Foxer, although vulnerable to heavy weather, could distract the German acoustic torpedo's sensor, but at a penalty to the escort's passive sonar detection of the U-boat. Although not perfect, the Foxer enabled escorts to sidestep acoustic torpedoes and press their attack on the U-boats.[53]

The putting into port of the UT convoys had to be scheduled to avoid coincidence with another convoy's arrival that would overwhelm already congested ports. Arrival in the Clyde Estuary in Scotland especially had to avoid conflict with that of the UT convoy's highest capacity complement, the monster and semi-monster liners, which for a time in 1943 had scheduling restrictions of their own.

As a passenger crossing the North Atlantic with Churchill in *Queen Mary* for the Trident Conference in May 1943, Admiral of the Fleet Sir Dudley Pound made a worrying assessment of the risks and consequences from potential torpedoing of one of the *Queens*. Standing on the deck of *Queen Mary*, Admiral Pound knew the hard fact that speed alone did not make independently sailing liners safe from attack. Two months earlier, off the west coast of Africa, the liner RMS *Empress of Canada* had been sunk by the Italian submarine *Leonardo da Vinci* with the loss of 392 lives.[54] Should the passengers of a *Queen* have to take to the life-boats, the loss of lives would be grim, as "only 3,000 [troops] out of 15,000 on an eastward passage could be accommodated in the boats." Laying up of a torpedo-damaged *Queen* for repairs would impose a far greater impact on available troop lift than adopting a more conservative sailing schedule.[55]

On May 23, acting on Pound's recommendation, the Com-bined Chiefs of Staff had imposed an absolute requirement for added safety. Both of the high troop capacity *Queens* were put on a twenty-eight-day transatlantic sailing cycle. Thus their passage through the submarine-infested waters west of the Bay of Biscay in both directions was restricted to the dark of the moon.[56] In addi-tion to the limits of port through-put, this lunar calendar schedul-ing of the monsters' call on that capacity determined many other convoy sailing dates. Eventually the magnitude and urgency of deploying invasion forces across the Atlantic compelled the waiv-ing of the lunar sailing schedule restrictions.

This then-firm operational restriction on the monsters dictated to Winston Churchill the August 5 date for his westward depar-ture in *Queen Mary* from Faslane, Scotland, and arrival at Hali-fax on August 9 for the Quadrant Conference that he would not join until August 14. Churchill, of course, had a plan to profit from his early arrival by meeting privately with FDR, a plan in the event to little avail.

Beyond the predictable waxing and waning of the moon, unfore-seeable weather and threats of enemy action inevitably compli-cated the careful timing of convoy sailings and arrivals. Thus the escort commander of UT-4 complained that his troop-laden con-voy had to sail at less than its 15-knot capability and remain at risk on the high seas an extra full day so as to meet a requirement not to arrive in Liverpool before November 1, 1943.[57]

The course of eastbound convoy UT-10 was altered four times to avoid suspected or detected U-boats as well as to skirt a major storm. The threat could be close at hand. UT-10's convoy commodore, Rear Adm. Henry D. Cooke, reported that on March 28, 1944, "when U-boats were not far distant, a German voice was heard speaking a few words on the "talk between ships" (TBS) frequency. The escort commander asked if others had heard it, and several ships including USS *Thurston* [the commodore's flagship, a troop transport] replied in the affirmative."[58] TBS was a very high frequency (VHF) voice radio system. VHF range generally is limited to line-of-sight, close indeed for a transmission from one U-boat to another, each riding low at the sea's surface.

The careful planning and protection for the convoys paid off. From the first to the last of the twelve UT convoys, no soldier was lost to enemy action. Slowly at convoy speed, but inexorably, the concentration of forces in Britain for Overlord was building.

18

Sealing the Quebec Decisions

The time has now arrived when further indecision, evasion, and undermining of agreements cannot be borne. In plain American words, the talking stage is over and the time has arrived to "fish or cut bait."

—Gen. George C. Marshall to President Roosevelt, November 8, 1943

Just as the reaffirmation of Overlord at the Quebec Conference set in motion the transatlantic surge in the deployment of military forces, signing of the secret Anglo-American atomic agreement stimulated a scramble among British and American atomic program leaders. What transpired reflected the contrasting leadership styles of Churchill and Roosevelt. Churchill generally shared his thinking and decisions freely with his leaders, even to the point of causing exasperation, as his military chiefs could and did attest. True to his practice, the prime minister also had kept the Tube Alloys leadership current about each stage of his negotiations with FDR. Not so Roosevelt, who once said with a smile, "I never let my right hand know what my left hand does."[1]

On August 19, British Tube Alloy scientists Rudolf Peierls, Mark Oliphant, and Francis Simon arrived in the United States in anticipation of agreement to resume Anglo-American interchange on Tube Alloys/s-1. The fourth member of this British team, Dr. James Chadwick, was to arrive on the next day. Given their arrival in the United States some hours before Churchill and FDR signed the agreement, the trip must have been authorized, planned, and initiated in anticipation of the successful conclusion of the agreement. On August 20 in Washington, with approval from Col. John J. Llewellin, who had been nominated to be a British member of the Combined Policy Committee, Wallace Akers, the permanent British Tube Alloys representative in Washington, talked with Vannevar Bush to "find out what course of action was possible to get collaboration restored as quickly as possible."[2]

Bush was flummoxed. He was FDR's science adviser and a key civilian leader of the U.S. atomic program who had negotiated the draft with Sir John Anderson. Yet he had not been told that the agreement had been signed on August 19. He had no knowledge of its final content or instructions from FDR. So he did not know what to do with the British scientists.[3] Bush told Akers that, until he knew the agreement had been signed and the new Combined Policy Committee had agreed on the action to be taken, nothing could be done with the British scientists. When signature was confirmed, Bush allowed, collaboration could begin within the bounds the Americans had offered back in January and then expanded as the Combined Policy Committee agreed to a broader scope.[4]

Akers, who also may not have known for certain that the deal was in place, went along. The following day, Colonel Llewellin at the British embassy received confirmation from London that the agreement had been signed in Quebec and that the American members of the Combined Policy Committee would be Stimson, Bush, and Conant.[5]

The Americans attempted to catch up with events. The commander of the Manhattan Project, Brig. Gen. Leslie Groves, had his deputy, Col. Kenneth D. Nichols, carry to Quebec a report on the situation with the British in Washington, via a War Department courier plane, "in order that further information would be immediately available." Accounts of what happened then conflict. Groves claimed that General Marshall accepted the report but told Nichols that it was too late because the sharing agreement already had been signed.[6] Bush stated in a memorandum to James Conant that Marshall received the report on Sunday, August 22, and told Nichols he would not have time to read it but would deal with it soon.[7]

At the start of the new week on August 23, Colonel Llewellin initiated attempts to contact and follow up with Henry Stimson, and he persisted through September 2 without success. Stimson was "out of Washington and inaccessible."[8] Llewellin turned to

Bush to attempt to get something started. He found that, almost two weeks since the signing, Bush still was in the dark with "no indication whether the President and the prime minister conferred, and . . . no instructions from the President."[9] After putting Conant in charge with instructions to start interchange with the British as soon as authority and guidance for doing so was in hand, Bush left town for a week.[10]

Finally on September 8, twenty days after FDR and Churchill had signed, Stimson received a copy of the secret agreement and shared its contents with Conant.[11] The U.S. side now made haste. On that day, at an informal U.S.-UK meeting with Stimson presiding and Conant participating, it was agreed to set up the Combined Policy Committee to govern Canada-UK-U.S. interchange on atomic research.[12]

The Americans' Military Policy Committee, established in 1942 to advise FDR on atomic matters, met the next day and took several decisions on action to integrate British scientists into components of the S-1 development program. However, "need to know" remained in effect. The British were to be excluded from development of the graphite pile process and electromagnetic process of isotope separation.[13]

On September 10, in Clinton, Tennessee, close to the Manhattan Project's massive and very secret Oak Ridge atomic facility, the S-1 Executive Committee met and agreed that interchange would be carried out according to General Groves's orders. At last, on September 13, a meeting of British, Canadian, and American scientists in Groves's office marked the reinitiation of atomic information interchange when general progress on theoretical aspects of the fast neutron reaction was discussed.[14] Collaborative Anglo-American work to develop an atomic bomb was under way again.

* * *

Britain's prime minister was burdened by the devastation of his generation in World War I, bearing with personal angst responsibility for the disastrously failed amphibious assault at Gallipoli in 1916. He was troubled also by the bloody failure of the Dieppe Raid in August 1942 and the military's failure to answer adequately his questions about the decision process for that operation.[15] Churchill remained unreconciled to the Quadrant decisions, despite having assented to them. He continued to state reservations about going ahead with Overlord and argued for pursuing instead his strategy based on more attacks from the Mediterranean.

Now he was to bear tangible witness to the post-Quadrant buildup for the cross-Channel invasion that he still opposed. Churchill, as prime minister, not only received continually updated knowledge of the influx of troops for Overlord. In his dual capacity as his own minister of defense, whatever his apprehension, he also was compelled to participate by authorizing the British contribution in various forms to the building of bases and other facilities for the arriving troops.

On September 11, 1943, Churchill, who had traveled with his wife, Clementine, from the Quebec Conference to Washington, participated in a White House meeting of the Combined Chiefs of Staff. Roosevelt was away at Hyde Park. Harry Hopkins left his bed at the Naval Hospital in the Washington suburb of Bethesda, Maryland, to attend the meeting for Roosevelt and keep an eye on Churchill.[16]

The purpose of the meeting was to review Allied strategy in light of the armistice signed with Italy three days earlier. Churchill still advocated directing as many forces as possible to exploit the opportunity he saw in Italy, including continued engagement there by the British Fifty-First Highland Division, one of the seven divisions already designated to return by convoy from the Mediterranean to Britain for Overlord.[17] The U.S. Joint Chiefs of Staff replied to each of Churchill's proposals with their assessment that Allied forces then dedicated to Italian operations were sufficient to the task, consistent with their finding radioed to Eisenhower in Algiers on August 11.[18]

After his return to London, Churchill cabled Roosevelt on October 20 to urge that the two of them meet in advance of their conference with Soviet premier Joseph Stalin, eventually agreed to take place in Tehran and to be called Eureka. Churchill wrote to FDR:

In view of the changes that have taken place since QUADRANT we have had prolonged discussions here about our existing plans for the campaign of 1944. On these the British Chiefs of Staff and the War Cabinet are deeply concerned. We ask for a full conference of the Combined Chiefs of Staff in North Africa in the first or second week of November, that is between the end of the foreign secretaries' conference at Moscow and EUREKA. We ask this irrespective of whether EUREKA takes place or not. It would be best however if this took place on our way to EUREKA.[19]

By October 20, the day of Churchill's cable, convoys UT-2, UT-2A, and UT-3 had arrived in Great Britain with more U.S. troops in addition to the tens of thousands of Allied troops brought aboard the "monsters" and "semi-monsters."[20] The rate of arrival of troops and their equipment for Overlord on a steepening, upward curve made ever more tangible the concentration of forces to implement the cross-Channel attack strategy. The total of new troops arriving in Great Britain by sea in August was 41,681, in September 81,116, and in October 105,557.[21]

The single U.S. Army division left in the United Kingdom after the redeployment for the 1942 North Africa landings, the Twenty-Ninth Infantry Division, had been joined by five more divisions. They were the Second Infantry, Twenty-Eighth Infantry, Fifth Infantry (redeployed from Iceland), Third Armored, and 101st Airborne.[22]

In one week from the date of his cable to FDR, as Churchill certainly knew, most of the ships of just-arrived convoy UT-3 would depart Britain for North Africa, Italy, and Egypt, redesignated as convoy KMF-25A (United Kingdom to the Mediterranean-25A). They would return to Britain as convoy MFK-25A in November with 25,000 U.S. and 13,000 Commonwealth troops, elements from among the seven divisions committed to Overlord, including major units from the U.S. First and Ninth Infantry and Second Armored Divisions.[23] Also to return soon to Britain from the Mediterranean were the U.S. Eighty-Second Airborne Division and British First Airborne Division. All told, the number of troops arriving in Great Britain in the month of November 1943 would rise to 173,860.[24]

The U.S. Joint Chiefs of Staff concluded that Churchill's October 20 cable was a bid to revisit the decision on the primacy of Overlord as the Allied strategy for 1944. Such a discussion could risk renewed indecision and, from that, disruption of the building concentration of tangible military power in Great Britain. The JCS readied itself for another strategy fight. Roosevelt cabled back on October 22 to put off Churchill's requested bilateral meeting until after the conference with Stalin, stating that:

> Regarding another full conference of the Combined Chiefs of Staff early in November, it appears to me that there are several matters which should first be resolved before we meet.
>
> . . . Certain outline plans from Eisenhower and commanders in the Pacific covering operations approved at QUADRANT are to be submitted November 1, and these should receive some consideration before we arrive at the moment of a combined meeting.
>
> . . . At the moment it seems to me that consideration of our relations with Russia is of paramount importance and that a meeting after our special conference with U.J. ["Uncle Joe" Stalin] would be in order rather than one in early November.[25]

With KMF-25A then four days from departing to bring troops back from the Mediterranean for Overlord, Churchill replied to Roosevelt on October 23, urging again the early Anglo-American conference. The prime minister wrote:

> The Russians ought not to be vexed if the Americans and British closely concert the very great operations they have in hand for 1944 on fronts where no Russian Troops will be present. Nor do I think we ought to meet Stalin, if ever the meeting can be arranged, without being agreed about Anglo-American operations as such. . . . I feel very much in the dark at present, and unable to think or act in the forward manner which is needed. For these reasons I desire an early conference.[26]

The following day, Churchill went around Roosevelt with a

personal and private cable to the U.S. Army chief of staff, Gen. George Marshall, sent through British channels and to be conveyed through the British chiefs' Washington liaison, Field Marshal Sir John Dill. Pressing the case he had put to FDR, Churchill wrote: "I hope the President will show you my long telegram to him about our much needed meeting in Africa. Naturally I feel in my marrow the withdrawal of our 50th and 51st Divisions, our best, from the very edge of the battle for Rome in the interests of distant Overlord. We are carrying out our contract, but I pray God it does not cost us dear." Continuing, the prime minister then referred to the vacant position of Supreme Allied Commander, an appointment Marshall dearly wanted but was too principled to seek actively from FDR. Who that commander should be was in the wind, publicly through the press as well as privately, in Washington and London and between Churchill and FDR. Churchill wrote to Marshall, "I do hope to hear of your appointment soon. You know I will back you through thick and thin."[27]

Resolute in his commitment to the Overlord strategy, General Marshall would not be moved by Churchill. Confident in his knowledge of the growing concentration of forces in the UK for Overlord and that FDR now was his partner in its advocacy, Marshall worked with General Handy, through six drafts, on a memorandum that he sent through Admiral Leahy to the president on November 8. The memorandum counseled firmness on the Quadrant strategy agreement. Marshall wrote to FDR, "The battles of manpower that you and I have fought have not been for the purpose of creating a huge military force which is to sit idle, awaiting either the achievement of military victory by our Russian allies, or the success of a gamble on political and psychological disintegration within the German citadel of Europe."[28]

Roosevelt, through messages drafted by Marshall and other members of the JCS, continued to defer action on Churchill's request for a full conference of the Combined Chiefs of Staff in advance of Eureka.[29] FDR introduced a new and diluting factor, third party participation, which he had rejected for Quadrant. On October 25, Roosevelt moved closer to an Anglo-American bilateral meeting, but later on the calendar and with constraints, when he cabled Churchill, "What would you think of you and me meeting, with small staffs, in North Africa or even at the Pyramids, and toward the close of our talks get the Generalissimo [Chiang Kai-shek] to join us for two or three days? At the same time, we could ask U.J. to send [Soviet Foreign Minister] Molotov to the meeting with you and me. Our people propose November 20."[30]

Whether FDR's intention or not, this would narrow the opportunity in advance of meeting with Stalin for the discussion of strategy by senior U.S and British military leaders that Washington feared would revisit the decision on Overlord. The following day, Churchill replied by cable. Bent on a meeting with FDR before they convened with Stalin, Churchill accepted the proposal to invite Chiang Kai-shek. He did so even though this would divert time away from Anglo-American discussion of European strategy for 1944 toward expanded discussion of Asia and the Pacific. Churchill also told FDR, "I hope we need not wait until the twentieth."[31]

Churchill and Roosevelt's back and forth on holding a conference of the CCS before meeting Stalin paralleled the three-way discussion with the Soviets to bring about the Big Three meeting, if that could be done. Two of the Big Three were citing constraints on their geographic movements.

Stalin professed that, as head of the Stavka, the supreme command of Soviet military forces, he was very reluctant to leave the Soviet Union, but willing to venture as far as Tehran. Perhaps just as likely was that the Soviet dictator feared for his position should he be too far away from the safety of the Kremlin for too long.[32]

The communication means of the day were a consideration for Roosevelt. Mindful of the U.S. Constitution's requirement that the president act within ten days on legislation passed by Congress, Roosevelt was reluctant to go farther afield than Basra, Iraq. Where, when, and even whether the meeting of the three leaders could be held lingered as open questions.

Suggesting a contingency in the event of failure to accomplish the meeting of the Big Three, Roosevelt cabled Churchill on October 26 to propose that they invite the Soviets to station a military observer with the Anglo-American Combined Chiefs of Staff. On practical and political grounds, Churchill promptly rejected FDR's proposal as being counter to the close and private Anglo-American consultation that he foresaw as vital to the year ahead. He did so confident of ample support from both the American and British chiefs. Citing the immense Allied operations ahead in Italy and Overlord, Churchill wove into his case with feeling the possibility of major Anglo-American disagreement—on priorities and plans the Americans preferred to consider settled already at Quadrant. These Churchill foresaw as a reason for excluding the Soviets as a third party. He replied to Roosevelt, "I now feel that the year 1944 is loaded with danger. Great differences may develop between us and we may take the wrong turn. Or, again, we may make compromises and fall between two stools." Concluding his cable, Churchill wrote, "I must add that I am more anxious about the campaign of 1944 than about any other with which I have been involved."[33]

* * *

The Germans bloodied a convoy while Churchill and Roosevelt were trading proposals for a meeting of their chiefs of staff, but they attacked too soon. Eastbound convoy KMF-25A, code-named Peacock, was attacked from the air in the Mediterranean on November 7, twelve hours after dropping off the U.S. Army transports USAT *Dorothea Dix* and USAT *Anne Arundel* at Algiers to load U.S. First Infantry Division troops bound for the United Kingdom and Overlord. At dusk off Cap Bougeroun, Algeria, twenty-five Luftwaffe bombers, flying from southern France, attacked the eastbound convoy in four waves, alternately launching glider bombs at the escorts and torpedoes at the ships.

Against the shooting down of six bombers, the U.S.-flagged freighter S.S. *Santa Elena*, Dutch freighter S.S. *Marnix van St. Aldegonde*, and the U.S. destroyer *Beatty* (DD 640) were sunk.[34] However, by attacking when they did, the Germans missed their opportunity. Had they struck during the convoy's critical *westbound* return, they might have inflicted serious loss of life among troops from some of the seven divisions returning to Britain from the Mediterranean for Overlord. Sailing westbound and troop-laden from Sicily and Italy as Convoy MFK-25A, the surviving ships were rejoined by the *Dorothea Dix* and *Anne Arundel* from Algiers and ultimately delivered 38,000 battle-experienced combat troops to the United Kingdom without further losses.

* * *

In the dark at 3:36 a.m. on November 12, where the Potomac River flows into Chesapeake Bay, the sleek new 58,000-ton battleship, USS *Iowa* (BB-61), took aboard FDR and his White House advisers, who had traveled secretly down the river from Washington in the presidential yacht, *Potomac*.[35] Already aboard the battleship were the Joint Chiefs of Staff. No representative of the U.S. State Department was present.[36] Secretary of State Cordell Hull was in Moscow, having just concluded participation in the Conference of Foreign Ministers that was an important preliminary to the Big Three meeting to follow.

After taking fuel at Norfolk, Virginia, *Iowa* put to sea under radio silence. While relays of escorting destroyers kept up and two escort carriers steamed in the vicinity, *Iowa* made a high-speed run at 30 knots across the Atlantic to Oran.[37] The battleship was taking FDR and the JCS on the first leg of their trip to meet Churchill in Cairo, a preliminary to the meeting of the Big Three in Tehran.

Their days aboard *Iowa* were an invaluable, well-timed opportunity for the JCS to converse at length with Roosevelt and receive the commander in chief's intimate guidance on current and future issues. In two formal meetings, totaling more than four and a half hours, their discussions and decisions ranged widely, not just over the current war but with an eye as to the security and role of the United States in the postwar world.

The new thinking about national security, which had taken root among the U.S. foreign policy community and the military at the beginning of 1943, had developed through the Navy, Army, and Army Air Force into assessments and recommendations now ripe for decision. An October 7 query from FDR about the need for bases in northwestern Africa had been used by the Joint Strategic Survey Committee to produce instead a response that was global in scope. From a foundation of assumptions and plans, the JSSC recommended no fewer than seventy-two base sites, thirty-three of which were in the Atlantic and Western Hemisphere and thirty-nine in Asia and the Pacific.[38] The JCS approved the paper as JCS 570 and recommended it to FDR at their second formal meeting aboard *Iowa* on November 19.

The discussion between the president and his military chiefs was long and deep, certainly carrying over informally during the days at sea. FDR generally favored the paper on U.S. postwar basing needs, but wanted to talk with Churchill about many related matters before he acted.[39] Roosevelt's subsequent approval of the report on November 23 did two things: the postwar foundational basis for U.S. national security was confirmed to be global, not just hemispheric, and the wartime practice by the U.S. military services of assessing and planning for national security issues jointly became an agreed principle for the future.[40]

For the immediate future, the Cairo Conference and the Big Three meeting to follow, the president and his chiefs discussed at length the European command question and the relative numbers of U.S. and British forces. To them, these were linked issues. Marshall and Roosevelt were as one on that. To FDR, the number of U.S. forces, Army and Navy, in Europe was at the heart of his case for insisting on an American as Supreme Allied Commander. That number already was large and growing fast. The question of the structure of command rested on whether to have a single supreme commander, the American preference, or to establish also a separate Middle Eastern Command where Churchill had one million troops. Who would be the commander, or commanders, was the question needing an answer ever more urgently.[41]

In Marshall's presence, Roosevelt told the Joint Chiefs, as the minutes recorded, "that it was his idea that General Marshall should be the commander in chief against Germany and command all the British, French, Italian, and U.S. troops involved in this effort." The chiefs and FDR discussed how far into Italy the

Allied armies should advance before their commander, General Eisenhower, was reassigned. What Eisenhower's new assignment would be was not recorded as having been discussed. By November 1943, however, the Joint Chiefs surely had learned that "his idea" often could be far from a firm decision by Roosevelt.[42]

At the time, Roosevelt and Churchill were under pressure at home to publicly name a Supreme Allied Commander. Both appreciated that this had to be done with care as to timing, Allied unity, domestic politics, and, far from least, avoiding telegraphing too much of Allied intentions to the enemy.

* * *

USS *Iowa* steamed on to the east. The Joint Chiefs and FDR continued to deliberate with confidence that the reaffirmed commitment to Overlord at Quadrant and the surge of American troops across the Atlantic had gained for them the strategy debate's high ground. They were united in their commitment to ending the war in Europe through the cross-Channel attack-based strategy. They were persuaded that Hitler's Reich could be brought to its end only by force of combined arms from east and west. One reason for this was that they now were without illusion as to the chance that Germany could instead be bombed into submission.

The Army Air Force chief of staff, Gen. Hap Arnold, had commissioned and given security clearance to a group of eminent American historians to study the prospects of success for the now-intense Combined Bomber Offensive. One task was to examine whether the interwar theory of compelling an enemy nation's political-economic collapse through bombing alone was working or could work. Aboard *Iowa*, Arnold briefed FDR on his historians' draft conclusion that "the complete and highly organized control of the Nazi party gives no encouragement to the hope that any political upheaval can be anticipated in Germany in the near future."[43]

Among the Americans' British counterparts, however, the theory of forcing Germany's collapse through bombing, when weighed together with Russian attacks from the east, still had supporters.

Although the evidence cited from inside Germany was anecdotal, a joint Air Ministry Intelligence–Political Warfare Executive assessment of Allied air attacks and German morale concluded, defensively, "It is not reasonable to infer that no such break in morale can occur, and we do not exclude the possibility that in conjunction with further large-scale military reverses and with the advent of winter, air operations may exercise a decisive influence on conditions inside Germany."[44]

The November 7 Air Ministry bombing progress report that enfolded this intelligence assessment, quite possibly alluding to the approaching cross-Channel invasion as a forcing function, stated: "All evidence indicates that the Combined Bomber Offensive is achieving a profound effect upon Germany's war economy, and upon the morale of her people. In the continuation of the offensive toward a decision, time is a vital factor. The offensive should be pressed on, in accordance with the existing directive, with all vigour, and its intensity increased."[45]

* * *

Since the Quadrant Conference, both the British and U.S. chiefs had begun to see that to succeed, cossac's plan for Overlord needed to be strengthened and expanded. The plan's three proviso conditions were close to mind, and German forces for opposing an invasion from the air were trending in the wrong direction. Although Allied bombing was drawing Luftwaffe fighters into the air to be shot down and fighter manufacturing repeatedly was bombed, the Allies assessed Luftwaffe fighter strength to have increased by more than five hundred aircraft since August.[46] All expected that a scramble for additional resources to make Overlord a success in the spring of 1944 would be a key topic at Cairo and Tehran. The British still were seeing alternative opportunities in the Mediterranean and hope in bombing.

Before the U.S. Joint Chiefs' departure aboard *Iowa*, the British chiefs had forwarded their position for the coming conferences through an emissary to Washington. On the morning of

November 9, just returned British Army brigadier Harold Redman met behind the locked door of his office with U.S. Navy Capt. Forrest Royal and Army Col. A. J. McFarland with an oral message for the JCS from the British Chiefs of Staff. Redman told them that taking Rome and going a reasonable further distance to "make Italy safe from a fierce attack by the Germans," according to Redman, was the British chiefs' sin qua non of the coming conference. Concluding his report to the JCS on the conversation, Captain Royal typed in all capitals and underlined the essence of Redman's message: "If Italy flops, OVERLORD is off anyway, therefore in order to make OVERLORD sure, Italy must be made safe. The British have not 'written off' OVERLORD, have no desire or intention of writing it off, and have no desire to postpone OVERLORD. However, they feel that a successful OVERLORD is to a very large extent dependent on the safety of Italy."[47]

Seeing in this a forewarning, the U.S. Joint Chiefs prepared, once again, the contingency they had threatened since 1942, with or without their commander in chief's support. If, at Cairo, the Sextant Conference decisions did not "guarantee" Overlord, they would recommend reducing U.S. forces in the UK to a level appropriate to Rankin Case "C," relying on the bomber offensive and the Red Army, and shifting U.S. attention and resources to the Pacific.[48]

* * *

Steaming blacked out through the Straits of Gibraltar at 30 knots, but suddenly brilliantly illuminated by Spanish searchlights, and then shadowed by German planes, *Iowa* delivered FDR to Oran. From there, the president and the U.S. delegation flew to Cairo in three C-54s.[49] In Cairo, Roosevelt, Churchill, and Chiang Kai-shek met for the Sextant Conference, in advance of Roosevelt and Churchill's meeting with Stalin, by then arranged for Tehran.

In Cairo, although he did meet with Chiang Kai-shek, FDR declined to formally meet privately with Churchill.[50] However, in another of their many encounters for which there is no formal record of their substantive conversation, FDR did drive with Churchill to visit, appropriately, the Sphinx.

Churchill's requested Cairo meeting of the Combined Chiefs of Staff took place, but was abbreviated by the press of time and an expanded political-military agenda. By no description was this meeting the full CCS conference that Churchill had wanted.

On November 24, at 11:00 a.m. in the president's villa, Churchill, FDR, and their senior military leaders gathered. Roosevelt, immediately establishing his view of the meeting as conditional, was recorded in the minutes as stating that "at this meeting he hoped there would be a preliminary survey of operations in the European theater, including the Mediterranean. Final decisions would depend on the way things went at the conference shortly to be held with Premier Stalin."[51]

According to the CCS minutes of the meeting, Churchill responded by saying "he was in accord with the president's views," and he summarized a year of Allied successes in the war.[52] Churchill then implied a rejoinder to the U.S. Joint Chiefs' September 11 assurance to him of the sufficiency of forces in the Mediterranean by citing stiff German resistance. Doing so, he risked inferring that the Mediterranean was not after all the "soft underbelly" he had claimed in 1942.

Churchill stated that over the intervening two months, the Italian campaign had slowed because in his words, "We did not have a sufficient margin of superiority to give us the power to force the enemy back." Churchill acknowledged poor weather on the Italian peninsula and the possible influence on progress in the ground war of the logistical concentration on buildup of long-range bomber forces in Italy for the Combined Bomber Offensive. However, he ventured, "The departure from the Mediterranean of certain units and landing craft had had, it seemed, a rather depressing effect on the soldiers remaining to fight the battle."[53]

As the CCS met in Cairo on November 24, the buildup for Overlord, agreed in May at Trident and reaffirmed in August at Quadrant, progressed. The CCS minutes record Churchill recounting that he "had agreed, but with a heavy heart, to the return of seven divisions from the Mediterranean Theater." In Italy, the British Fiftieth and Fifty-First Divisions, which were first-class troops, had turned over their equipment in preparation to embark for the UK.[54]

At the end of the meeting, Roosevelt and Churchill "invited the staffs to study the problems as to the scope and dates of the operations to be carried out in the European and Mediterranean Theaters in 1944, with a view to arriving at an agreed view, if possible, before the coming meeting with Stalin."[55] That was to be in Tehran, then four days hence. For the moment, no substantial changes were made to the magnitude or schedule of the Overlord buildup.

* * *

From Cairo and Moscow, FDR, Churchill, and their military and diplomatic lieutenants journeyed to Tehran to meet at last with Soviet premier Joseph Stalin, arriving in the city on Saturday, November 27. Upon landing in Tehran, Churchill endured a long and anxious ride into the city with security that he thought very doubtful.[56] Roosevelt's c-54 landed in Tehran in the afternoon after a twisting flight through mountain passes to avoid flying FDR above 6,000 feet. A presidential motorcade was dispatched over crowd-lined main roads from the airport into the city—with a dummy in the backseat. The motorcade on its way, Secret Service team chief Michael Reilly bundled the president into an unmarked car with a single jeep as its escort for a covert dash—to FDR's delight—through Tehran's ancient back streets to the U.S. embassy. Very shortly, though, security concerns convinced the president to transfer to the Soviet diplomatic compound for the Eureka Conference.[57]

A report of German parachutists, some of whom the Soviet NKVD claimed to have captured, had put the Allies on security alert.[58] As the British and Soviet embassies were adjacent to each other, the three national leaders were located there within a security perimeter. The Americans prudently assumed that their rooms in the Soviet embassy were bugged with microphones. They were correct. Ambassador Averill Harriman remained skeptical of the parachutist alert and the resulting Soviet solicitude for Roosevelt's safety.[59]

In Tehran, as in Cairo, Churchill would try for what would be the last time to deflect Allied effort in the West from a cross-Channel invasion to a Mediterranean strategy. But the die had been cast. In the few months since the Anglo-American decisions in Quebec, a powerful concentration of Allied land, sea, and air forces for Overlord had grown in the United Kingdom. In Tehran, Churchill encountered Roosevelt and Stalin unshakably aligned for Overlord without delay or further diversion.

Roosevelt declined requests from Churchill for private meetings and did all he could to build rapport with Stalin. This included joining with Stalin in teasing at the prime minister's expense. Although FDR told Churchill of his intent in advance and advised him not to take it seriously, the jibes still stung.[60]

The critical exchange on Overlord came in the conference's second plenary session on the afternoon of November 29. Stalin stated clearly the Russians' desire for Overlord to take place sometime during the month of May. Operations in the Mediterranean, he said, had value but were only diversions. An exchange ensued between Churchill and Stalin about how many divisions were where and what opportunities existed in the Mediterranean. That prompted Stalin to ask Churchill what the marshal said in advance was an indiscreet question: "Do the British really believe in Overlord, or are they only saying so to reassure the Russians?"[61] A tense Churchill, with reference to the just-concluded Foreign Ministers Conference, replied that "if the conditions set forth at Moscow were present, it was the duty of the British Government to hurl every scrap of strength across the Channel."[62]

Discussion around the table continued until Stalin circled back to ask who would be appointed to command Overlord. That caused FDR to lean over to Admiral Leahy and whisper, "That old Bolshevik is trying to force me to give him the name of our Supreme Commander. I just can't tell him because I have not yet made up my mind."[63] In the absence of a definitive answer from his allies, Stalin declared, "Then nothing will come out of these operations." Later, as to the conditions of reduced German opposition required for approval to execute Overlord, Stalin asked the same question that had been put to COSSAC's representative in Washington three months earlier: "What if there are thirteen divisions, not twelve?" Through most of this Roosevelt remained silent. Stalin was doing his work for him.[64]

Late that night, Harry Hopkins walked to the British embassy next door. Meeting alone with Churchill, Hopkins convinced the prime minister that he must yield to the Americans and Russians, who were united in their determination to implement Overlord in May.[65] Churchill did yield.

At the third plenary meeting of the Eureka Conference, November 30, with Churchill and FDR's agreement, the Combined Chiefs of Staff informed Stalin that "Anglo-American forces would launch Overlord during the month of May, in conjunction with a supporting operation against the South of France, on the largest scale that would be permitted by the landing craft available at the time."[66]

* * *

There remained the question of who would be Overlord's Supreme Allied Commander. The decision was up to the United States. Stalin, no doubt, saw the situation through the battle-proven Red Army maxim that "not to decide is to decide." With the date now set, the naming of a commander was the remaining proof Stalin sought of Anglo-American commitment to Overlord. For Britain and the United States, designation of a commander for the invasion was the last essential element to be set in place in order to proceed. Roosevelt had gained time with Stalin by promising that a commander would be named within a few days after FDR and Churchill returned to Cairo. Now back in Cairo, time was up and Roosevelt had a dilemma.

Since the close of the Quadrant Conference in early September, the expectation had grown in all quarters that George Marshall would be chosen, to the point of FDR saying as much to the Joint Chiefs aboard the *Iowa*. Katherine Marshall quietly made a start on moving their possessions out of the Army chief of staff quarters at Fort Myer, Virginia. Marshall desired the command as a professional capstone, but wanting to preserve complete freedom of action for his commander in chief, he would not ask for it.[67]

There were problems. FDR had suffered political and editorial attacks in September alleging, wrongly, that he wanted to demote Marshall and get him out of Washington.[68] Roosevelt and the jcs had believed that if the British accepted a single Allied commander over all forces in the west fighting Germany, the posting would be a promotion for Marshall.[69] Recent creation for the British of a separate Middle Eastern Command, however, had eliminated that. Sending Marshall to London to command Overlord and bringing his junior, Gen. Dwight D. Eisenhower, back to Washington to be Army chief of staff, over Marshall was seen as counterintuitive to the military culture. FDR highly valued having Marshall's wise counsel and skill in Washington to deal with all U.S. military matters and services, the British chiefs, Churchill, and Congress. Marshall's biographer, Forrest Pogue, believed that Roosevelt reasoned that with Stalin's "determined advocacy" to counterbalance Churchill, he could "put Eisenhower in London, keep Marshall in Washington, and still have the cross-Channel strategy safe."[70]

Not evident in the record as having been openly discussed at the time is the obvious contrast between the two U.S. generals. Moving beyond early stumbles, by the close of 1943, Eisenhower had grown in his command and demonstrated his ability to lead a huge ground-air-naval, multinational coalition force and win victories. Marshall, for all his superb qualities, had no major combat command experience.

Summoning Marshall to his Cairo villa on December 6, Roosevelt eventually got to his decision. Eisenhower would be the Supreme Allied Commander for Overlord. Explaining his reasoning, FDR closed the meeting with Marshall by saying, "I feel I could not sleep at night with you out of the country."[71]

Immediately, setting aside his disappointment, Marshall took a pencil and wrote in longhand on lined notepaper for Roosevelt the message for transmission to Stalin: "From the President for Marshal Stalin. The immediate appointment of General Eisenhower to the command of Overlord has been decided upon."[72]

* * *

By November 30, when in Tehran, Churchill acquiesced to an unconditional CCS endorsement of Overlord for May 1944, the U.S. component of Allied forces in the British Isles had more than doubled from 278,742 in August, at the start of the UT convoys, to 637,521 troops. Seven of the twelve fast troop convoys and many sailings of the "monsters" were still to cross the Atlantic.[73] The American force projection was on track to have in the United Kingdom in time for a May 1, 1944, D-Day the nineteen divisions promised to FDR; twelve infantry, five armored, and two airborne. Four more divisions, two infantry and two armored, were in the pipeline to arrive in May 1944.[74] This would be one more division than the COSSAC-projected rate of buildup from the United States of three per month. By the end of May 1944, with D-Day a week away, the buildup in the United Kingdom of United States forces would exceed its goal by 100,000, reaching 1,526,965 U.S. troops.[75]

In the final weeks of 1943, troops and cargo were flowing smoothly from North America in a maximum effort to use to its fullest, through the winter and into spring, British port capacity before those same ports had to turn to loading ships for D-Day. Overlord had an objective, a plan, and its commander, and it would have the implementing forces.

Then disaster loomed. The threat sprang not from action on the seas by a resurgent enemy but from the U.S. home front. Relative to the privation and loss of life and property suffered by the populations of other combatant countries, the cause of the crisis had an air of unreasonableness. But the magnitude of its consequences for the Allies made the threat compelling.

The phenomenal wartime output of the U.S. economy could be achieved and sustained only through nationwide acceptance of grueling schedules. Under wartime production's unremitting demands, the pressure of socioeconomic strain was building on all parts of society. The agreement from the outset of U.S. entry into the war that U.S. labor unions would not strike for the duration had begun to unravel earlier in 1943. The success of labor actions by the United Mine Workers, led by John L. Lewis, encouraged others, including steel workers, to initiate wildcat strikes in vital industries.

In October, the thirteen non-operating unions of the U.S. railroads, who unlike other critical war workers did not receive extra pay for hours of overtime, took a cue from the miners and steelworkers by threatening to strike on December 30 if they did not receive an hourly raise of 20 cents.[76] The five railroad worker operating unions, whose members did receive overtime pay, supported their labor brethren.

Government leaders were not unsympathetic to the merits of the railroad unions' case. However, they also had to protect wartime wage caps nationwide, which already were under pressure from wildcat strikes.

Before leaving for the war planning conferences in Cairo and Tehran, Roosevelt had moved U.S. railroad labor negotiations with management into the White House where they continued in his absence, but without result. Upon returning on December 19 from his exhausting trip, FDR found the railroad labor dispute still unresolved. The president initiated a five-hour meeting with the "railroad group" in the Oval Office where he offered himself as arbitrator to the group of railroad management and union officials.[77] Through multiple sessions, an agreement acceptable to all the parties continued to elude the negotiators. Roosevelt began to consider his fallback: taking over all U.S. railroads, as the government had done in World War I, to force upon the unions the prospect of striking against the government.

The consequences of a railroad strike in the United States looked to be grave indeed. Out of deep concern, the civilian leaders of the federal government's military departments, agencies, and boards jointly sent FDR a letter stating, "The war has now progressed to a point where maximum production at the highest possible speed is a vital necessity. A railroad strike would be catastrophic to economic activity and production and supply for the war globally. The lives of millions of men in the Armed Services depend upon the uninterrupted supply of material, ammunition and equipment."[78] For all theaters of the global war, but particularly for Europe with D-Day approaching, they spoke the stark truth.

For Overlord, the accelerated movement of U.S. Army units to Britain was drawing down rapidly the unit equipment sets and stocks of supplies already prepositioned there. Maximum movement of materiel across the North Atlantic had to continue at highest efficiency through the winter if troops set to arrive in the United Kingdom in the spring, on the eve of invasion, were to be equipped and made ready for combat. Supporting the Allied goal of moving 55,600 troops to Britain in December 1943, the transports of Convoy UT-6 were alongside piers in New York and Boston ready to sail December 28–29.[79] Convoy UT-7 was scheduled to sail from New York and Boston on January 15, with the Fourth and Fifth Armored Divisions, to contribute to the goal of 71,800 troops shipped to the UK in January 1944.[80]

In addition to hundreds of thousands of tons of materiel, four more UT troop convoys were to sail before the invasion in 1944, as were the huge liners and many more convoys bearing equipment, munitions, and supplies. All of the troops and cargo the ships would carry first had to arrive at East Coast docks by rail on closely coordinated schedules from throughout the United States.

Secretary of War Stimson saw in the threatened railroad strike "a crisis of major order." General Marshall foresaw in a strike a six-month delay of Allied operations in the war during which the Germans would continue to strengthen their Atlantic defenses.[81]

If anything, Marshall's prediction was optimistic. The vast transatlantic logistical effort, suddenly under threat of disruption by a railroad strike, was crafted to support an invasion in May 1944. The Allies broadly agreed that weather conditions in the Channel would close the opportunity for a 1944 invasion by September, not to open again before May 1945. The Germans' Atlantic Wall certainly would become more formidable by then, and the calculus for a successful invasion (already about to be changed by Generals Eisenhower and Montgomery) would become substantially more demanding. With delay, the operational security risk of exposure to the Germans of the Allies' specific intentions and plans for Normandy would increase.

Any delay in achieving an end to the war in Europe through victory on the ground simply would extend the slaughter of aerial bombing while the horrific machinery of the Final Solution ground on. Having picked up this logistical predicament and sensing hope to postpone for Nazis their Judgment Day, Joseph Goebbels's propaganda machine broadcasts to Allied troops and wavering Axis allies were archly criticizing American ability to deliver on promises.[82]

Since summer, some western military and political leaders had noted that Soviet priorities were shifting away from calls for a second front and toward advancing the Soviet Union's position in Europe upon Germany's defeat.[83] Were the armies of the western Allies to be delayed, who could guess where on the Continent they would meet with Soviet armies? What might that portend for the geopolitics of postwar Europe? With years of contentious delay behind them, strategy set, and timing promised to Stalin, the western Allies simply had to proceed with Overlord on schedule in 1944. A railroad strike in the United States could not be allowed to disrupt that or anything else.

On December 23, Roosevelt met with the railroad group twice more at the White House and also told Stimson and Marshall that if necessary he intended to take over the railroads before a strike could be called. The Justice Department set to work on the complex documents for a federal takeover of the railroads using a similar World War I action as its model.[84] Roosevelt serenely departed Washington by train that evening to enjoy a family Christmas at Hyde Park.[85]

The documents for federalizing the railroads were completed and ready for FDR on his return to Washington on December 27. With the executive order in the president's desk drawer awaiting signature, a last attempt was made in a meeting at the White House to settle the issues, only to collapse in failure to get full agreement among the unions. That evening, the government took over the railroads on Roosevelt's order.[86] They were run by the chief of the Army Service Force, Lt. Gen. Brehon Somervell, with the cooperation of the railroads.[87]

Normally imperturbable, and now relieved, General Marshall told James Byrnes on December 31 that he had been "sleepless with worry" and had debated with himself "whether it was his duty to go on the radio, give his opinion, and then resign."[88]

Twenty-three days after the takeover, at midnight on January 18, 1944, operation of the railroads was restored to their private owners, the unions having accepted a settlement on January 14.[89] Although other wildcat strikes would continue among the steelworkers, the essential, time-urgent flow of troops and materiel had been maintained without interruption.

* * *

Through the UT convoys' evolving composition, the force to conduct Operation Neptune, the crucial amphibious phase of Overlord, could be seen to increase not just in numbers but also in capability. As D-Day grew closer, ship listings for these convoys included more and more attack transports and attack cargo ships with the landing craft they carried. These ships, designed for amphibious assault, stayed in the United Kingdom to take aboard the troops and weapons for Neptune.[90] Concentrating in anchorages throughout the British Isles, the amphibious capability to move Allied armies across the Channel to French beaches emerged. In the final weeks before the invasion, eastward transatlantic shipments declined as British ports cycled up combat loading of vessels.

The UT convoy-escorting old battleships *Arkansas*, *Texas*, and *Nevada* also stayed to join the naval buildup in Northern Ireland. Many of the escorting destroyers stayed, picking up special radios and spotting teams for close-in gunfire support. In that mission, the troops on the beaches, troops they had shepherded across the North Atlantic, would find the destroyers once again crucial.

COSSAC's coordination of planning and preparation for D-Day expanded and intensified. With all of its elements coming together, Overlord advanced through the new year's winter and spring to

D-Day. COSSAC was absorbed into the new, larger organization for which it had been intended from inception to be the prototype. The Supreme Headquarters Allied Expeditionary Force became operational under General Eisenhower. By March 1944, SHAEF's new shoulder flash could be seen increasingly in London and around Britain, a harbinger. Under the arc of a rainbow formed from the colors of all of the Allies' flags and against the black night of Nazi tyranny thrust upward the flaming sword of liberation.

Epilogue

It is on the beaches that the fate of the invasion will be decided... during the first twenty-four hours.

—Field Marshal Erwin Rommel, December 1943

I was on Omaha Beach on D-Day and I tell you we hung on there by our eyelashes for hours.

—Gen. Thomas Handy

The *Texas* Task Group joined with soldier-filled assault ships and craft, from Portland on England's south coast, to become part of Force O. Royal Navy cruiser HMS *Glasgow* took the lead as Force O cleared Point Z, the "Piccadilly Circus" assembly area, in darkness. At General Quarters, steering against a strong westerly crosscurrent, the assault craft pitching miserably in the chop, at 2244 on June 5, 1944, Force O silently proceeded down Swept Channel Three through the minefield leading to Omaha Beach.[1] The gunfire support ships of the *Texas* Task Group would remain at Battle Stations for the next forty-two hours. The troops they supported would fight the battle of their lives.

* * *

The plan for Operation Neptune that was executed on D-Day was not as envisioned in the COSSAC "Overlord Outline Plan," which had sufficed to win conditional approval from Roosevelt, Churchill, and the Combined Chiefs at Quebec. The COSSAC plan and the forces for it had been expanded, just as defenses of the beaches and fields on which the Allies would land were being made much more formidable by the Germans.

Consensus had emerged among the Allies by the end of 1943 to

The COSSAC 1943 Overlord Plan and D-Day as Carried Out (Neptune). Map by
Philip Schwartzberg, Meridian Mapping.

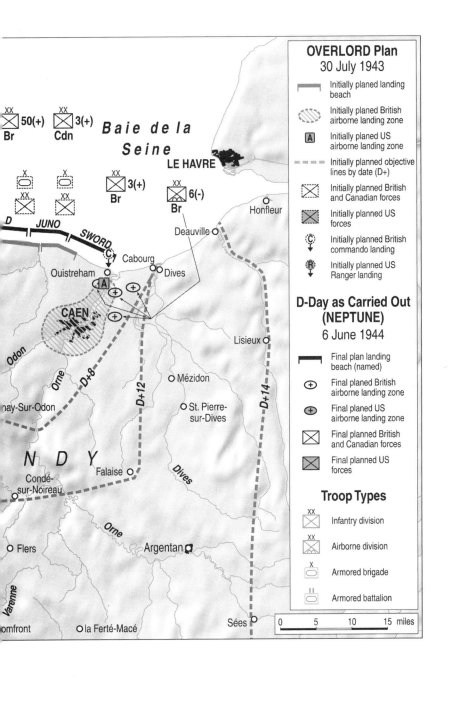

OVERLORD Plan
30 July 1943

Initially planed landing beach
Initially planed British airborne landing zone
Initially planed US airborne landing zone
Initially planned objective lines by date (D+)
Initially planned British and Canadian forces
Initially planned US forces
Initially planned British commando landing
Initially planned US Ranger landing

D-Day as Carried Out (NEPTUNE)
6 June 1944

Final plan landing beach (named)
Final planed British airborne landing zone
Final planed US airborne landing zone
Final planned British and Canadian forces
Final planned US forces

Troop Types

Infantry division
Airborne division
Armored brigade
Armored battalion

50(+) Br 3(+) Cdn

Baie de la Seine

LE HAVRE

3(+) Br   6(-) Br

Honfleur

Deauville

JUNO   SWORD

Ouistreham   Cabourg   Dives

CAEN

Odon   Orne   D+8   D+12   D+14

Mézidon

St. Pierre-sur-Dives

Lisieux

nay-Sur-Odon

N D Y   Falaise

Dives

Condé-sur-Noireau

Orne

Flers   Argentan

Varenne

omfront   la Ferté-Macé   Sées

| 0 | 5 | 10 | 15 | miles |

recognize that cossac's three-division plan for the initial assault into Normandy would be insufficient to achieve success. Quickly, upon taking his post as Supreme Allied Commander, Dwight D. Eisenhower assigned his land force commander for Overlord, British Gen. Bernard Montgomery, to lead a new assessment of what would be required. Montgomery sharply criticized cossac's plan, which had been constrained to the forces the ccs had allotted in May 1943. His recommended increases actually were in line with what General Morgan and his staff would have preferred almost from the outset.[2] By January 24, Eisenhower had the combined recommendations of his land, air, and naval commanders. From his new Supreme Headquarters Allied Expeditionary Force in London, Eisenhower submitted the recommendation to the Combined Chiefs of Staff.[3]

By D-Day, the cossac plan had been expanded from three to six divisions assaulting from the sea onto five landing beaches (increased from three) on a frontage broadened to sixty miles.[4] Three airborne divisions, one British and two American, would jump into Normandy behind the landing beaches. The expanded assault force required in support many more fighter squadrons, hundreds more troop carrier aircraft, and the addition of one more complete naval assault group.[5] To permit assembling this larger force and all its support in the United Kingdom, the date for the invasion was shifted from May 1 to as early as possible in June.

Eisenhower's January request for expansion met not with hesitation but with shared commitment and determination. For Overlord, the Combined Chiefs found the requested additions "reasonable" and fulfilled them. To also sustain the now-delayed supporting landing into southern France (Anvil), they were prepared to get the resources needed "by hook or by crook."[6]

The sober-eyed reassessment of the cossac plan by Eisenhower and his deputies was rooted in the lessons of recent combat and evident fact: the experience they had gained, individually and as a team, in what had been required in North Africa, Sicily, and Italy to fight the Germans and win. They also knew that their enemy was going to test that hard-won knowledge further.

Through signals intelligence, and tactical reconnaissance, they could see for a fact that the defenses they would confront in Normandy were strengthening rapidly for the worse.

Anticipating an Allied invasion in 1944, Hitler foresaw an enormous threat as well as a valuable opportunity. A successful Allied landing in France would be a dagger pointed at the heart of the Reich. If the Allies could be thrown back into the sea, however, they would not be able to try again for at least a year. Should the invasion be defeated, German forces could be transferred from west to east in an attempt to stop the advancing Russians and possibly end the war with German borders unpenetrated.[7]

In December 1943, at Hitler's order, Field Marshal Erwin Rommel had made a tour of inspection of the Atlantic Wall. Surveying with his knowledge of the ferocity of the battlefield attack of which the Allies were capable, particularly with their air power, Rommel saw weaknesses so pervasive as to suggest to him that the Wall was "an enormous bluff."[8] He found much of the Wehrmacht force stationed there to be comprised of poorly equipped and unfit units passed over for or in recovery from fighting on the eastern front. Rommel took particular note of the thin defenses in Normandy.

By D-Day, over the five months since his inspection, Rommel had been beefing up at a furious pace the anti-invasion defenses in depth with fortifications and millions of mines.[9] Although his work was not complete, he had increased and reinvigorated the troops. By May, the Germans' mobile reserve for counterattacking included first line panzer divisions that were positioned relatively forward in Normandy, but not consistently so. Particularly worrisome to Eisenhower were increases in German strength in the Cotentin Peninsula into which the two U.S. paratroop divisions would make a night jump.[10]

However, the Germans were in a strategy disagreement over how to use their mobile armored reserves, the Panzers, in response to an invasion. Field Marshal Gerd von Rundstedt, the commander of the western front, with support from panzer expert Gen. Heinz Guderian, wanted to allow the Allies to move inland before he sought decisive battle in the interior of France beyond the range of the Allies' naval guns. Rommel believed that the strength of Allied tactical air power would never permit the panzers the freedom of maneuver essential to von Rundstedt's strategy.[11] He wanted the armored units well forward for rapid counterattack before the Allies could get off the beaches.[12] Rommel's preference would put the panzers right under the Allies' naval guns. The conflict between von Rundstedt and Rommel, which showed in the positioning of the mobile reserves on the eve of D-Day, was never resolved fully.

COSSAC's "Overlord Outline Plan" had been conditional in part on there being no more than twelve first line German division equivalents in France on D-Day. In their January reassessment of the plan, the Allies had dropped that condition, which would not be met. In late May, British intelligence advised that the German division equivalents in France could be up to sixteen in number, and many would be units of higher quality.[13]

As the Germans were divided on how to deploy their reserves, the massive enterprise of Overlord was the Allies' maximum possible effort and not easily readjusted. On D-Day, both sides would be rolling iron dice.

* * *

Texas had a particular initial fire mission for D-Day morning, one vital to the success of Neptune, Pointe du Hoc. The promontory of Pointe du Hoc lies between Omaha and Utah Beaches. The Germans had established a 155mm gun battery there, protected by thick reinforced concrete fortifications. If not taken out, these guns could sweep the armada and landing beaches with fire at the most critical moment.

At H-Hour, 0630, all along the sixty-mile frontage of the Allies' assault, naval gunfire erupted from battleships, cruisers, and destroyers. Shells from the ten-gun, 14-inch main battery of *Texas* pounded into the German emplacements atop Pointe du Hoc as U.S. Army Rangers scaled its cliff from the sea below despite Germans shooting downward and grenading from above. Fighting at close quarters and scrambling over and around shattered concrete and massive shell craters, still visible today, the rangers who made it to the top found the gun emplacements . . . empty! Later on D-Day, the rangers found the guns hidden a mile inland and spiked them.

Timed to the Channel's tides, the assault troops hit the five beaches in serial from west to east: first the Americans at Utah followed by Omaha, then the British at Gold, Canadians at Juno, and British at Sword. The difference in timing, though slight, afforded the beaches to the east a somewhat longer period of naval preparatory fire. To the east, the British and Canadian assault troops made good progress in establishing themselves ashore. At Utah, tidal crosscurrents put the first wave landing force ashore a mile away from where it intended to land. Unanticipated, this had the good effect of avoiding heavier than expected German defenses, but threatened to disperse the troops to follow. Brig. Gen. Theodore Roosevelt Jr. ashore in the first wave responded under fire to make a decision critical to redirecting the incoming waves of troops: "We'll start the war from right here!"[14]

On Omaha Beach, the American Twenty-Ninth and First Infantry Divisions were in serious trouble. Hundreds of Allied bombers had been assigned to salvo the beach and defenses on the escarpment above it. However, fearful of hitting the inbound landing craft filled with troops, the bombers had dropped their loads moments too late in their flight, causing their bombs to land too far inland. That left the German defenses at Omaha relatively unscathed and created none of the craters among the beach hummocks that the troops hoped to use as cover in their advance. Looking down from the escarpment, the German defenders directed withering fire into the growing mass of troops, soon pinned on the beach, and into the landing craft offshore.[15] The landing stalled with the troops taking heavy casualties only yards beyond the water's edge. The next tide soon would inundate the heavily mined beach, littered with dead and wounded. By 0830, the navy beach masters had stopped further waves of troops and equipment from coming ashore. This set many loaded landing craft to milling around, among Rommel's mines and half-submerged obstacles, while taking shellfire from the Germans. On Omaha Beach, realization of Churchill's worst fears for Overlord appeared imminent.

Navy Lt. George Elsey of the White House Map Room was at Normandy for D-Day, having obtained FDR's approval for this temporary duty to gather information for naval historian Samuel Eliot Morison.[16] Elsey went with the Force O intelligence officer, Cdr. Curtis Munson, in a small boat from the command ship USS *Ancon* to investigate the disturbing reports coming from Omaha Beach. On their harrowing trip, Elsey found that "everywhere was the same: wrecked, swamped, broached, burning boats; tanks, guns, and trucks in a flotsam of fuel cans, cartridge cases, life belts, soldiers' packs—and bodies of men killed by enemy fire or drowned in the onrushing tide." Over the din of gunfire, explosions, and revving boat engines, Munson shouted to Elsey, "It's in the balance now. You can't tell which way it's going."[17]

Overlord advocate Maj. Gen. Thomas Handy and his convert to the strategy, Rear Adm. Savvy Cooke, had flown from Washington to be present for D-Day. They could have observed from relative safety aboard the *Ancon*, miles out in the Channel. Instead, they had gone ashore at Omaha Beach with the troops in the early hours when the issue was in serious doubt. With their firsthand information, Handy and Cooke returned to the *Ancon* to report to V Corps commander Lt. Gen. Leonard Gerow. Withdrawing from Omaha Beach was being seriously considered. Asked his opinion by Gerow, Handy replied, "Gee, the only thing I see that can be done is push the doughs in far enough to get that beach out from under small arms and mortar fire because as Savvy Cooke describes it, 'this is carnage.'"[18]

The Americans would stay and push inland. Handy and Cooke left *Ancon* to go back to observe the fighting along the American beachheads.[19]

On Omaha, the Army could not get its artillery ashore on schedule. To compensate for that, Navy destroyers, some of which had escorted UT convoys, moved inshore, so close that some nearly grounded. Anchoring so as to be more stable gun platforms, despite drifting mines, the destroyers fired thousands of rounds from their five-inch guns to support the infantry and the handful of tanks that had made it ashore. At times, the destroyers' 40 millimeter antiaircraft guns joined the close in battle, firing nearly point blank. Radio communication with the beach largely had been disrupted by casualties among the shore fire control parties. The destroyers effected a silent coordination with the troops by observing through binoculars and directing their own gunfire to where the troops were firing.[20] So it was that in initially small groups the troops advanced up from the beach. Navy Combat Demolitions Units, while taking 41 percent casualties, began to make real progress in clearing obstacles and opening up beach exits to move inland.[21]

D-Day dawned for the people of Normandy bringing the thrill of liberation in equal measure with violence, uncertainty, and fear. Shepherded by his mother, five-year-old Jacques Delente sheltered with his extended family inside a dormant lime kiln. All day long in the dark, they could hear the noise of the battle being fought outside. Too young to be afraid, Jacques peered upward through the kiln's chimney excited to see Allied planes racing across his patch of sky. When the family returned home, they found on their dining room table a German soldier who had died from his wounds and been left by his comrades in retreat.

The day after D-Day, when Lieutenant Elsey went back to Omaha Beach, the scene was being transformed. The escarpment taken, fighting had moved inland. Engineers were clearing obstacles and building roads up to the heights. Troops, tanks, and guns transported from England in LSTS were streaming over the beach and toward the slowly expanding American frontlines. Standing on the beach, Rear Adm. John Hall, a veteran of the Mediterranean landings, said this to Elsey of "Easy Red," a critical section of Omaha Beach where the day before nothing had been easy: "This is the most strongly defended beach I've ever seen. In another month, we might not have made it."[22]

As Americans, up from the western beaches, linked up with the paratroopers and fought field by field through the thick hedgerows in the *bocage*, the Germans were attempting to mount an armored counterattack in the Anglo-Canadian sector to the east. If the Allies were allowed time to establish their armies ashore, Rommel was certain all would be lost.

Between Caen and Bayeux stretches a broad, open plain that slopes down to the beaches where the British and Canadians came ashore. This good tank country had been a concern for the Allies from early in COSSAC's planning. From Juno Beach, on D-Day, according to plan, the tank and mobile artillery-heavy Canadian Third Division had pushed inland to take up a defense of the beachhead on this plain. The Germans needed to capture a "start line" for what Rommel hoped would be a three-division armored attack by the First Panzer Corps to drive the Allies into the sea. But their attempts to capture ground for the start line were frustrated. Repeated, fanatical attacks, June 7–10, by the Twelfth SS Hitler Youth Division broke against the Canadians' skilled and steadfast defense.[23]

While the panzers were trying and failing to gain position for their counterattack, more Allied strengths took decisive effect against the Germans. On D-Day, the Allies owned the skies over Normandy. The growth in the German fighter force in 1943 had been overcome and reversed. The Luftwaffe had been so depleted in defending Germany against the Combined Bomber Offensive that it lacked the planes and pilots to make anything but a token response to Neptune. Allied fighter-bombers roamed the region beyond the beachhead striking any German unit.

Liberation of Europe from the west was in the balance for the Allies in this critical battle. Given that, the Allies' concern about compromising Ultra, their access into German encrypted communications, did not prevent application of this priceless intelligence now, tactically. Movement to the front of German units was hindered and German command and control was particularly hard hit by fighters directed on the basis of sanitized Ultra-based reports to strafe, rocket, and bomb field command posts.[24]

Time to mount a counterattack toward the beachhead was running out when the vast Allied deception program that had supported D-Day for months now induced the maldeployment of

German reinforcements at the critical time. Deceived by the Allies' Fortitude South operation into accepting the existence of an imaginary First U.S. Army Group, still in England, alarm spread in the German command. Normandy was a feint, German High Command and Berlin believed. The real blow was about to land elsewhere. Orders were cancelled for panzer units of the German Fifteenth Army in Belgium and northern France to move south toward Normandy. They were ordered instead to stay to defend against the main Allied landing to come in the Pas de Calais, a fictional threat generated and sustained by Allied deception.[25] Denied position and reinforcement, the greatest potential threat to the Allied beachhead dissipated.

The Germans put up fierce resistance all around the beachhead's perimeter for over a month, but they could not stop the buildup of forces for an Allied breakout to liberate northwestern Europe. Despite a major Channel storm June 19–22 that destroyed one of Neptune's two artificial harbors, the crucial, over-the-beach logistical battle to reinforce and sustain Overlord recovered and continued to great effect, even after French ports were liberated and put back into operation. In July with Operation Cobra, the Allies broke out to begin their eastward dash across France. The critical first phase of Overlord had been won.

Before D-Day ended, elements of twelve divisions were established on the landing grounds and beaches of Normandy, not to be pushed off. Their numbers swelled daily until, after 336 more days of hard fighting, the Allied armies from the west and the Red Army from the east ended the war in Europe. When Germany surrendered unconditionally on May 8, 1945, Operation Overlord concluded in victory.

* * *

Overlord's preparation and implementation was paced by the progress of the atomic bomb project in the United States. Work to develop an atomic bomb at secret locations in the United States had expanded and accelerated dramatically, and since the resumption of Anglo-American atomic cooperation in September 1943,

British scientists were integral to it. The Manhattan Project was developing two bomb designs in parallel. The simplest and most certain but wasteful of fissile material was the gun-type. In this design, a uranium-235 bullet was fired into a uranium target to achieve nuclear fission. The scientists had so much confidence in the gun-type bomb that they froze its design in February 1945 and skipped conducting an explosive test before releasing this bomb (when ready) for combat. The second implosion-type bomb design used an extremely precise conventional explosion to implode a spherical, hollow core of plutonium (U-239), a new element created from uranium. In March 1945 the design for the implosion-type bomb was frozen, but that proved to be no assurance of smooth sailing.[26] Design and production of the implosion-type bomb presented challenges never before addressed that would throw the project into crisis several times.

By November 1943, direct British participation in the Manhattan Project had grown to around two dozen scientists, a dozen of whom were living at the secret Los Alamos Laboratory in New Mexico.[27] Among the British scientists at Los Alamos were the Austrian émigré Otto Frisch and the young German theoretical physicist Klaus Fuchs. Again and again, Frisch's innovative work would prove critical to success in designing the implosion-type bomb.[28] Having slipped through British security screening, Fuchs, on the other hand, had begun covertly passing atomic secrets to the Soviets in London and continued to do so from Los Alamos.[29]

Manhattan Project costs indicate its quickening growth. From $16 million for all of 1942, expenditures increased to $344 million in 1943. That figure was topped in just the first half of 1944 with expenditures in each month to follow projected to approach $100 million.[30] Adjusted for inflation, the cost in 2018 U.S. dollars would be $100 billion through mid-1944 and growing at $1.3 billion per month.

The atomic bomb team still had ahead of it serious obstacles in physics, engineering, and production. However, their progress thus far had a palpable effect of optimism mixed with foreboding. This extended to the worldview of the project's mixed scientific-military-political appointee leadership. Reporting back to Sir John Anderson in London on work of the Anglo-American Combined Policy Committee, unknowingly apace with imminent D-Day, Ronald Campbell wrote on May 31, 1944, that

> we note a natural but increasing sense of American self-confidence and buoyancy as to their ability to carry through this project. On the part of some Americans this is accompanied by a growing sense of responsibility and anxiety about their ability to play their just role in international affairs; on the part of others there is certainly evidence of a thought that this weapon can be kept a tight monopoly and can thus give the maximum protection to America.[31]

On the other side of the Atlantic, too, the dissonance between the promise and danger of atomic energy spurred actions to call attention to the postwar future. In April 1944, Sir John Anderson had appealed to Churchill to approach FDR about eventual postwar control of atomic energy.[32] Supported by Lord Cherwell, Anderson encouraged and facilitated the renowned and like-minded Danish physicist Niels Bohr to meet with Churchill. Bohr held the view that the best opportunity for postwar international control of the atom was to take the Russians into the Allies' confidence at a surface level before the bomb became a demonstrated reality. In this, Bohr was ahead of Anderson who, after Hiroshima and Nagasaki, would come to support inclusion of the Russians in control measures. Bohr certainly was ahead of Churchill and FDR.

Bohr's meeting with Churchill, a week before D-Day, went badly. Bohr already had met at the White House in March 1944 with Roosevelt. In that meeting, as had many before him, the scientist had mistaken ambiguity for encouragement.[33] Bohr's meetings were failures, producing in both leaders only suspicion.

To the postwar military importance of the bomb, Lord Cherwell asked Churchill from London on September 18, 1944, to "try to discover from the President in broad outline what the Americans have in mind about [joint] work on T.A. after the war ends."[34] That day, meeting with Roosevelt at Hyde Park, following the Second Quebec Conference (Octagon), Churchill and FDR agreed to a one-page *aide-memoire* on Tube Alloys that they initialed in the early hours of September 19. They rejected a proposal that the world should be notified about the bomb "with a view to an international agreement regarding its control and use," and specifically directed that Dr. Bohr be prevented from "leakage of information, particularly to the Russians." Roosevelt and Churchill then agreed that "full collaboration between the United States and the British Government in developing Tube Alloys for military and commercial purposes should continue after the defeat of Japan unless and until terminated by joint agreement."[35]

The president never told his advisers on atomic matters, including his secretary of war, of the *aide-memoire's* contents.[36] Vannevar Bush suspected there was an agreement to an exclusive Anglo-American partnership. This both Bush and Conant opposed, fearing that it would stimulate an atomic arms race with the Russians.[37] Stimson had been open to an international control regime that included the Russians if the right conditions could be secured verifiably. But growing friction, suspicion of postwar intentions, and loss of confidence in Russia's word caused Stimson to change his position.[38]

On April 12, 1945, Roosevelt died in Warm Springs, Georgia. Having led the country out of the existential crisis of the Great Depression, he did not live to see victory in the war, in which his leadership had been so essential. He also had not told the vice president who succeeded him about the atomic bomb.

The new president, Harry Truman, was told informally about the atomic bomb by both James Byrnes and Henry Stimson within twenty-four hours of taking office. Not until April 25 did Truman receive a detailed briefing on the Manhattan Project from Secretary of War Stimson and General Groves. Foreign affairs, particularly increasingly adversarial relations with the Soviet Union, were discussed at length in the context of the bomb's political-military implications.[39]

In a conference room at the Pentagon two days later, on April 27, the Target Committee, composed of Army Air Force officers and a small Anglo-American group of Manhattan Project scientists, met for the first time. They were gathered to identify four cities in Japan as candidate targets for an atomic bomb. Theirs was not an easy task. The night firebombing of Japanese cities by Twentieth Air Force B-29s had been under way since March. Not many "pristine" targets remained in Japan.[40] The target selection criteria stipulated by General Groves, to whom the committee would report, assigned secondary importance to military effectiveness. Not an airman but an Army engineer, Groves's primary criterion fit exactly the interwar air power theory of bombing to break a people's morale, a theory not proven in six years of European war. For the committee, Groves recounted in his book, "I had set as the governing factors that the targets chosen should be places the bombing of which would most adversely affect the will of the Japanese people to continue the war. Beyond that, they should be military in nature."[41]

The Target Committee recommended Kyoto and Hiroshima as their first and second choices. Over the weeks that followed, Stimson, who deeply appreciated Asian culture, had become ever more appalled by the human toll of the conventional firebombing raids. In a May 30 meeting with Groves, Stimson learned that the general would deliver the target recommendation to General Marshall the following day. The civilian secretary intervened in this military decision by immediately removing from the list Kyoto, Japan's ancient former capital and storied center of culture.[42]

Into the summer, the scientists at Los Alamos struggled to overcome challenges to prepare the implosion-type bomb for a test while a gun-type device, "Little Boy," was readied for shipment to war. On July 16 at 5:30 a.m. in the desert outside Alamogordo, New Mexico, the first atomic bomb was detonated at Trinity Site with a yield of 18.6 kilotons in a flash brighter than the sun. Four hours later, the cruiser *Indianapolis* departed San Francisco carrying the gun-design bomb, Little Boy, on its long Pacific voyage to be delivered to the B-29 that would drop it on Hiroshima on August 6, 1945.[43] Three days later on August 9, an implosion-type atomic bomb would be dropped on Nagasaki. On August 15, making a radio address to his people, who were hearing his voice for the first time, the emperor announced that Japan would surrender to the Allies. Certainly an important element, the nature and relative weight of the two atomic bombs' influence on Japan's decision to end the war when it did continues to be debated. So bombing casualties suffered by the Japanese remain estimates with the pervasiveness of destruction precluding certainty. In combination, the conventional fire bombing and the two atomic bombs took at least 330,000 lives but possibly as many as 900,000.

At the time of the Trinity test, the victorious Big Three were meeting at Potsdam, Germany, a suburb of Berlin for the Terminal Conference. When President Truman received word of the scientists' success a few hours after the bomb test, he decided to tell Stalin, but asked Churchill's advice on when and how. Apparently unaware of Soviet espionage, Churchill advised framing Truman's communication as a test of which the two of them had just learned. The intent was to avoid being asked in response why the Russians were not told sooner about their allies' Manhattan Project.[44] Truman did so without revealing any details of the bomb test. Not apparent in the Soviet premier's reaction was that Stalin already knew about the atomic project and was confident that he soon would know the details of the Trinity test.

The six-year cataclysm of war in Europe had concluded with the Nazis regime crushed and freedom restored to half of the European continent. The approval for Overlord, so critical to this victory, had in its advocacy intertwined with agreement to cooperate in developing the atomic bomb. With the European war barely ended, an ominous new era of global nuclear anxiety was dawning.

ACKNOWLEDGMENTS

Two incidents over the span of twenty minutes in 1958 led to this book. One shaped my professional life. In hindsight, the other always was along on that journey, tugging at me.

The Cold War made for a tense summer in 1958. The Soviet Union went from first to first in space, while the United States struggled to get into orbit. Both superpowers tested ever larger nuclear weapons in the atmosphere. Tracking their fallout clouds was a staple of the news. Already interested in world affairs, I was a teenager at the start of a five-day canoe trip into the Canadian bush, my first. We pulled off the highway to read the plaque on a stone monument commemorating the 1943 fishing trip in the same area by Franklin D. Roosevelt, less than three weeks before a crucial wartime conference with Winston Churchill in Quebec. Minutes later, at a dock that Roosevelt had used, we met by chance one of FDR's Ojibwe fishing guides. With him was his son, about nine years old, who spoke no English. The boy's black and white dog jumped around us, barking and looking to play. Asked through his father the dog's name, the boy replied, "Sputnik."

Through the day's paddle, I thought about Roosevelt having fished the same waters and about my world's geopolitics penetrating to even this remote place to touch a young boy. By nightfall I had decided that by some means, I wanted a career in international security.

I had that career in a backroom, supporting role through which I witnessed the intensity of effort to gain negotiated decisions for international security, particularly in arms control. In quieter moments, that first encounter with summit history, FDR's, would come back to me as questions. How, at a critical moment, could a president leave Washington, the city then at the center of wartime decision making, to go fishing 760 miles away? Why did he do that? Approaching retirement, I started seeking answers. My queries about a president's ten-day fishing trip led in surprising, multiplying directions that only could be understood in the context of a full year, 1943. *Advocating Overlord* is the result. I owe my deep thanks to many people for helping to make the book possible.

Advocating Overlord attempts to build on the foundation of superb scholarship on Anglo-American wartime relations, D-Day, and development of the atomic bomb created by many fine historians. Robert Sherwood, Forrest Pogue, Margaret Gowing, Samuel Eliot Morison, and others, such as the authors of the U.S. Army's official history (the "green books") made good use of their opportunity to talk with the then still living principals and their staff. Since declassification of many World War II records in all countries, a new generation of historians has continued to refine and expand our knowledge of these events. I am in awe of and grateful for the work of Stephen Ambrose, Rick Atkinson, Graham Farmelo, Doris Kearns Goodwin, John Keegan, Maury Klein, Marc Milner, Ed Offley, Lynne Olson, Richard Overy, Thomas Parrish, Mark Perry, Richard Rhodes, Andrew Roberts, David Roll, Kevin Ruane, Mark Stoler, Nicholas Stargardt, Craig Symonds, and Geoffrey Ward. Their achievements in scholarship informed my own research enormously.

I am especially grateful to Dr. Brian Loring Villa for his encouragement early on and his insightful article, "The Atomic Bomb and the Normandy Invasion," published in 1978 soon after much of the source material on the diplomatic history of the Manhattan Project was declassified. His article remains a reliable window into the circumstances of the intersection of Overlord and atomic diplomacy.

My telling of this story has been facilitated by historians Marc Milner, Richard Overy, and Kevin Ruane. Each graciously answered my questions and offered leads that illuminated important details. So it was, for example, that I found myself in contact with Maj. Mathias Joost, Canadian Forces. The historical weather data that he provided, combined with air transport information from Archangelo DiFante at the U.S. Air Force Historical Research Agency, explain the COSSAC team's suspenseful delay en route to Washington with the OVERLORD plan. Thank you for introducing me to the lively community of people dedicated to understanding this history.

Wherever possible, I relied on primary sources. Each archive and library has its own personality. What they share are wonderful people. The archivists and librarians I encountered were passionate about preserving the record of the past and willing guides to its secrets. I'm especially grateful to Virginia Lewick and Matthew Hanson at the FDR Library and Rene Stein at the National Cryptologic Museum. Rob Martin, a historian at the Canadian Security and Intelligence Service, found sources for my exploration of an intriguing, still-to-be-settled wrinkle. Corporate archivists like Nick Richbell and Lise Noel dug into records for me from seventy-plus years ago. Clemson University's James Cross helped to answer my questions about James Byrnes. Georgetown University's collection of Harry Hopkins's papers illuminated that important figure as a man. The helpful staff at the National Archives and Records Administration in College Park, Maryland, the Library of Congress, the British National Archives at Kew, and the Imperial War Museum made accessible the bulk of the primary sources for the book. That the U.S. military services value their history and its lessons shows in the quality of the historical research centers of each. I've been honored to benefit from that as a civilian researching alongside the services' future leaders. Thank you all.

While the internet continues to expand its enormous facilitation of historical research, it is still possible to hold in your hands a piece of paper that takes you into the moment. I shall always remember holding a minute addressed to the "Prime Minister," bearing Churchill's nearly illegible red initials, and noticing a little brown spot in the margin. It was a scorch from a cigar ember. Every archive visit was a trip to "Wonder Land." As to my longest such trip, I thank Mariasole Piatti, Carlo Pagni, and family for providing a wonderful base and for encouraging me as I explored the archival treasures in Kew. Thanks also to Mike and Linda Swinnerton for a weekend respite in Yorkshire that became a trip back seven decades into wartime Britain.

To bring clarity in organizing my research and thoughts into a manuscript, Shannon O'Neill helped a new writer to find his footing and get serious. David Roll and Christian McBurney were generous with their time and thoughtful, experience-based criticism of my early drafts. Both gave good advice on writing for publication. Thanks are due my writing buddy, Dr. Teodora Salow, for her advice on style and enthusiasm for my project, even as she worked on her own intriguing historical novel, and to Norman Last, a patient and eagle-eyed reader of the manuscript. Philip Schwartzberg of Meridian Mapping created the book's three maps.

An author could not have a better Sherpa than Roger Williams, a lover of history and my steady, effective agent. Roger brought the manuscript to University of Nebraska Press, Potomac Books. There, Tom Swanson, Ann Baker, Natalie O'Neal, Roger Buchholz, Elaine Otto, and the capable production and marketing staff guided *Advocating Overlord* through publication. Thank you.

Writing a book about the diplomacy of D-Day and the atomic bomb is to be humbled by the intertwined complexity of these consequential events. Where this telling has missed or gotten the story wrong, the fault is mine alone.

From the beginning, my daughter, Lauren, has sustained me with her enthusiasm, confidence in Dad's book project, and curiosity about history. Words are inadequate to convey my gratitude to my wife, Mary, for the love, patience, understanding, and encouragement with which she has blessed me. As I poked into the corners of history on this journey whose course may have seemed obvious only to me, Mary and Lauren have been there for me always with love. Thank you.

NOTES

Prologue

1. USS *Texas,* "War Diary," June 1944, RG 38, box 15, NARA, 1–2.

2. USS *Texas,* "War Diary," June 1944, 3. On the concept of not putting all your eggs in one basket, vessels for an amphibious assault are combat loaded to distribute troops, weapons, and resources as evenly as practical. In this way the loss of one vessel may diminish the force, but the complete loss of a particular critical resource might be avoided.

3. Atkinson, *Guns at Last Light,* 37.

4. D-Day casualty figures remain estimates. These numbers for the Allies only on D-Day are from Col. C. P. Stacey, *The Victory Campaign,* 651–52.

5. Beaverbrook, "Memorandum: Present and Future, June 1943," in Sherwood, *Roosevelt and Hopkins,* 735–37.

1. The Casablanca Conference

1. Pogue, *Marshall: Organizer of Victory,* 17.

2. Chief of the Imperial General Staff for a period in 1940–41, Dill often clashed with Churchill. Dill died in Washington in November 1944. He is buried in Arlington National Cemetery across the Potomac from Washington, which marks the high regard in which Dill was held by U.S. military leaders, Congress, and the president.

3. Roll, *Hopkins Touch,* 245–46.

4. Roll, *Hopkins Touch,* 244.

5. Leahy, *I Was There,* 143.

6. Lavery, *Churchill Goes to War,* 160–61.

7. Brooke, *War Diaries,* xlv.

8. Villa, *Unauthorized Action,* 258–59.

9. Lavery, *Churchill Goes to War,* 161.

10. Roberts, *Masters and Commanders,* 316.

11. Lavery, *Churchill Goes to War,* 158–59.

12. Lavery, *Churchill Goes to War,* 156–57.

13. Atkinson, *An Army at Dawn,* 277.

14. Roberts, *Masters and Commanders,* 319.

15. Pogue, *Marshall, Organizer of Victory,* 176–78, and Larrabee, *Commander in Chief,* 329–30.

16. A text of Madame Chiang's February 18, 1943, address to Congress

may be found at the University of Southern California. United States–China Institute, www.china.usc.edu.

17. Parrish, *Roosevelt and Marshall*, 292.

18. Set forth in Admiral Stark's "Plan Dog" memorandum, November 1940. See Stoler, *Allies and Adversaries*, 29–32.

19. Cline, *Washington Command Post*, 157.

20. Despite the confusion with President Roosevelt's constitutional rank and preeminent authority as commander in chief of the U.S. armed forces, King insisted on this title for his naval rank. In World War II, U.S. Navy command diagrams, correspondence, and messages. King was referred to as "COMINCH." Today there is only the chief of naval operations, CNO.

21. Roll, *Hopkins Touch*, 190–91.

22. Roll, *Hopkins Touch*, 211–13.

23. Stoler, *Allies and Adversaries*, 42–43, 114–16.

24. Roberts, *Masters and Commanders*, 138.

25. Roberts, *Masters and Commanders*, 110–13.

26. Keegan, *Second World War*, 312–31.

27. Roll, *Hopkins Touch*, 191, 193, 195.

28. Stephen Peter Hopkins, an eighteen-year-old Marine, died of the wound he received in the invasion of Kwajalein Atoll in the Pacific in February 1944. Army 2nd Lt. Allen Tupper Brown, General Marshall's stepson, was killed in Italy on May 29, 1944.

29. Roosevelt to Churchill re: coordinating atomic research, October 11, 1941, PREM 3/139/8A, NA.

30. Ruane, *Churchill and the Bomb*, 50.

31. Wallace Akers, "General Policy," January 2, 1943, CAB 126/163, NA, 1.

32. S-1 was a section of the Office of Scientific Research and Development that, until establishment of the Manhattan Engineering District under military command on September 17, 1942, had overseen atomic bomb research in the United States. S-1 remained the shorthand designation by which FDR, Bush, Stimson, Hopkins, and others at the highest levels of the U.S. government continued to refer to the atomic bomb project, just as the terms *Tube Alloys* and its abbreviation TA were used by their British counterparts.

33. Sir John Anderson to Churchill, Tube Alloys, January 11, 1943, PREM 3/139/8A, NA, 1–3.

34. Churchill to the paymaster general, May 27, 1944, PREM 3/139/11A, NA, 1.

35. Atomic Energy Commission, excerpt from report to the president by the Military Policy Committee, December 15, 1942, Annexes to the Diplomatic History of the Manhattan Project, RG 374, microfilm roll 12, annex 6, NARA, 267–68.

36. Malcolm MacDonald, telegram no. 48, January 8, 1943, CAB 126/163, NA, 268.

37. Farmelo, *Churchill's Bomb*, 218.

38. Wallace Akers's many communications, preserved at the National Archives in Kew, give testament to qualities and contribution of this capable man.

39. Anderson to prime minister, Telescope no. 151, January 20, 1943, PREM 3/139/8A, NA.

40. Awareness of the project to develop an atomic bomb came to the British Chiefs of Staff much later than it did to the U.S. Joint Chiefs of Staff. General Marshall was on the Military Policy Committee from 1942, and Admiral Leahy, as FDR's chief of staff, was aware. Churchill's letter to FDR, dated August 15, 1943, which he directed be shown to the British chiefs gathered in Quebec, assumes an awareness of Tube Alloys. Dr. Kevin Ruane, author of *Churchill and the Bomb in War and Cold War* (2016), believes the British chiefs were not fully informed until the July 1945 Potsdam Conference, although he states that we cannot know from surviving records what they knew or when informally. Lt. Gen. Sir Hastings Ismay, Churchill's military chief of staff, knew of Tube Alloys and was concerned in 1944 about the extent of atomic knowledge among the JCS compared with ignorance of it among the British COS. Author's email correspondence from Dr. Kevin Ruane, November 10, 2016

41. Roberts, *Masters and Commanders*, 318.

42. Brooke, *War Diaries*, 358.

43. Roll, *Hopkins Touch*, 247.

44. Brooke, *War Diaries*, 359.

45. Brooke, *War Diaries*, 358.

46. Joint Chiefs of Staff, minutes of conference held at Anfa Camp, January 15, 1943, at 1000, RG 218, entry 98, box 1, NARA, 54–55.

47. Morison, *Battle of the Atlantic*, 410.

48. Morison, *Battle of the Atlantic*, 197–98.

49. Morison, *Battle of the Atlantic*, 199.

50. Butcher, *My Three Years with Eisenhower*, 201, 237; Roberts, *Masters and Commanders*, 359.

51. Combined Chiefs of Staff, CCS 57th meeting: minutes of meeting held at Anfa Camp on Friday, January 15, 1943, at 1430, RG 218, entry 98, box 1, NARA, 202–4.

52. Roberts, *Masters and Commanders*, 327.

53. Roberts, *Masters and Commanders*, 320–21.

54. Combined Chiefs of Staff, CCS 57th meeting: minutes, 205–6.

55. Combined Chiefs of Staff, CCS 57th meeting: minutes, 202–6.

56. Wallace Akers, PLYSU 1147w for Perrin DSIR, January 14, 1943, CAB 126/163, NA.

57. Brooke, *War Diaries*, 360.

58. Pogue, *Marshall: Organizer of Victory*, 21–22.

59. Joint Chiefs of Staff, Minutes of conference held at Anfa Camp, 59–60.

60. Brooke, *War Diaries*, 361.

61. Combined Chiefs of Staff, CCS 60th meeting: minutes of meeting held at Anfa Camp on Monday, January 15, 1943, at 1030, RG 218, entry 98, box 1, NARA, 237.

62. Combined Chiefs of Staff, CCS 60th meeting: minutes, 238–39.

63. Brooke, *War Diaries,* 362.

64. Overy, *Bombers and the Bombed,* 107.

65. Brooke, *War Diaries,* 361.

66. Combined Chiefs of Staff, ccs 155/1: Conduct of the War in 1943, January 19, 1943, RG 107, entry 104, box 2, NARA, 18–19.

67. Combined Chiefs of Staff, ccs 155/1: Conduct of the War in 1943, 19.

68. Combined Chiefs of Staff, ccs 166/1/D: The Bomber Offensive from the United Kingdom, January 21, 1943, RG 218, entry 190, box 1, NARA, 1.

69. Overy, *Bombers and the Bombed,* 107–11.

70. Combined Chiefs of Staff, ccs 67th meeting: minutes of meeting held at Anfa Camp on Friday, January 22, 1943, at 1430, RG 218, entry 98, box 1, NARA, 302.

71. Combined Chiefs of Staff, ccs 169: Proposed Organization of Command, Control, Planning and Training for Operations for a Reentry to the Continent across the Channel Beginning in 1943, January 22, 1943, RG 218, entry 190, box 1, NARA, 1.

72. Combined Chiefs of Staff, ccs 169: Proposed Organization of Command, 1.

73. [Brig. Gen. Albert C. Wedemeyer, USA], Analysis of the ANFA and TRIDENT Conferences, May 1943, RG 165, Chief of Staff file, NARA, 1.

74. Ruane, *Churchill and the Bomb,* 51.

75. Thomas L. Rowan to William Gorell Barnes, Tube Alloys re: Churchill communication with Hopkins on Anglo-American cooperation, January 18, 1943, PREM 3/139/8A, NA.

76. Michael W. Perrin to Barnes re: sharing information with Americans, January 19, 1943, and Perrin to Wallace Akers, Cypher telegram SUPLY 1026, January 19, 1943, CAB 126/163, NA.

77. William Gorell Barnes, note for the record, January 22, 1943, CAB 126/163, NA.

78. Anderson to prime minister, Telescope no. 151, January 20, 1943, PREM 3/139/8A, NA.

79. Churchill to Anderson, Stratagem no. 196, January 23, 1943, PREM 3/139/8A, NA.

80. On January 27, from London, Anderson cabled Malcolm MacDonald in Ottawa a note of encouragement that he had "grounds for hoping that the President will go into the matter and may issue instructions to the effect that collaboration between us on this subject should be re-established on a basis of full reciprocity." Nevertheless, in the same cable Anderson directed that "Akers should return to London on January 30 as planned to report personally on the position in Canada and the United States." See Sir John Anderson, telegram no. 258, January 27, 1943, CAB 126/163, NA.

81. Neither Churchill nor FDR liked or entirely trusted the haughty de Gaulle. A good divisional commander who had escaped dramatically from Germany and Vichy in 1942, Giraud proved to be a weak administrator. However, after the assassination of Admiral Darlan, the senior-most French officer in North Africa at the time of TORCH and a reprehensible collaborationist,

Giraud was the only option on site for the Allies. De Gaulle had rejected being summoned to Casablanca until Anthony Eden threatened withdrawal of Allied support. Harry Hopkins stage managed the surprised generals' encounter before reporters, FDR, and Churchill.

82. *FRUS: The Conferences at Washington, 1941–1942, and Casablanca, 1943*, 506, 635.

83. Beitzell, *Uneasy Alliance*, 82.

84. *FRUS: The Conferences at Washington, 1941–1942, and Casablanca, 1943*, 535.

85. Lavery, *Churchill Goes to War*, 171–74.

2. Campaigns of Attrition

1. Air Ministry, Combined Bomber Offensive Progress Report, February 4, 1943–November 1, 1943, November 1943, AIR 8/116/7, NA.

2. Overy, "Weak Link? The Perception of the German Working Class by RAF Bomber Command, 1940–1945," 12–13.

3. Overy, *Bombers and the Bombed*, 25–26.

4. Kennett, *History of Strategic Bombing*, 120, quoted in Rhodes, *Making of the Atomic Bomb*, 342.

5. Overy, *Bombers and the Bombed*, 85.

6. Overy, *Bombers and the Bombed*, 102.

7. Air Chief Marshal Sir Charles Portal, RAF, to Prime Minister re: RAF bombing operations, April 23, 1942, AIR 8/13982, NA.

8. Lord Cherwell, "H2S," January 7, 1944, PREM 3/101, NA.

9. Overy, *Bombers and the Bombed*, 92.

10. Overy, *Bombers and the Bombed*, 92.

11. John E. Singleton, "The Bombing of Germany," May 20, 1942, PREM 3/11/4, NA, 2.

12. Overy, *Bombers and the Bombed*, 158.

13. Combined Chiefs of Staff, CCS 166/1/D: The Bomber Offensive from the United Kingdom, January 21, 1943, RG 218, entry 190, box 1, NARA, 1.

14. Ministry of Economic Warfare, "Joint Report by Ministry of Economic Warfare and Air Intelligence on Effects of Bomber Offensive," November 4, 1943, AIR 8/116/7, NA, 1.

15. Overy, *Bombers and the Bombed*, 256–58, 277.

16. Stargardt, *German War*, 245–48, 364–65.

17. Stargardt, *German War*, 6–7. Attempting to draw reasonable conclusions out of the chaos that swept Europe, estimates of this genocide vary. It is generally accepted that six million Jews and five million other victims were murdered.

18. Quoted in Stargardt, *German War*, 378.

19. Stargardt, *German War*, 418.

20. Overy, *Bombers and the Bombed*, 27, 167; D'Olier, *United States Strategic Bombing Survey*, 5, 6.

21. D'Olier, *United States Strategic Bombing Survey*, 8.

22. Quoted in Keeney, *Pointblank Directive*, 48.

23. Committee of Historians for the Commanding General of the Army Air

Forces, "Germany's War Potential: An Appraisal," December 27, 1943, Henry H. Arnold Papers, Special Reports reel 193; Manuscript Division, LOC, 2.

24. Combined Chiefs of Staff, CCS 155/1: Conduct of the War in 1943, January 19, 1943, RG 107, entry 104, box 2, NA, 1.

25. Morison, *Atlantic Battle Won*, 363.

26. Bell, *Churchill & Sea Power*, 270.

27. Morison, *Battle of the Atlantic*, 311.

28. Offley, *Turning the Tide*, 104.

29. Bell, *Churchill & Sea Power*, 272, 263.

30. Combined Chiefs of Staff, CCS 57th meeting: minutes of meeting held at Anfa Camp on Friday, January 15, 1943, at 1430, RG 218, entry 98, box 1197, NARA.

31. Quoted in Bell, *Churchill & Sea Power*, 262.

32. Winston Churchill quoted in Goette, "Britain and the Delay in Closing the Mid-Atlantic 'Air Gap' during the Battle of the Atlantic," 32

33. Goette, "Britain and the Delay."

34. Bell, *Churchill & Sea Power*, 274.

35. Adm. Sir Dudley Pound, RN, "Security of Sea Communications in the Atlantic and Its Repercussions on Our Strategy (Re-draft by First Sea Lord)," January 12, 1943, AIR 8/1397, NA, 1–2, 35–36.

36. Morison, *Battle of the Atlantic*, 316, 410; Goette, "Britain and the Delay," 37.

37. Morison, *Battle of the Atlantic*, 322.

38. Kahn, *Hitler's Spies*, 221–22.

39. Offley, *Turning the Tide*, 104.

40. Offley, *Turning the Tide*, 412.

41. Anti-U-Boat Warfare Committee, Security of North Atlantic Convoys (AU (43) 68), March 8, 1943, AIR 8/1398, NA, 1–2.

42. Anti-U-Boat Warfare Committee, Security of North Atlantic Convoys (AU (43) 68), 1.

43. Royal Air Force Delegation, Washington, MARCUS 800: Personal for C.A.S. from Foster, March 29, 1943, AIR 8/1399, NA, 1–2.

44. Combined Chiefs of Staff, CCS 189: Very Long Range Aircraft for Anti-Submarine Duty; memorandum from the Joint U.S. Chiefs of Staff, March 16, 1943, AIR 8/1398, NA, 1.

45. Combined Chiefs of Staff, CCS 189: Very Long Range Aircraft, 1.

46. Capt. A. M. R. Allen, USN, "History of Development of Convoy and Routing Section of Tenth Fleet—FX-371, U.S. Navy," November 8, 1943, RG 38, NA, 1.

47. Milner, "The Royal Canadian Navy and 1943: A Year Best Forgotten?" 128.

48. Morison, *Battle of the Atlantic*, 36–37.

49. Morison, *Battle of the Atlantic*, 412.

50. A story well told in Offley, *Turning the Tide*.

3. COSSAC's Ninety Days to Plan

1. Historical Sub-Section, Office of Secretary, General Staff, History of COSSAC (Chief of Staff to Supreme Allied Commander) 1943–1944, file 8–3.6.CA, ACMH, www.history.army.mil/documents/cossac/Cossac.htm, 3.

2. Churchill, personal minute, Serial no. D.69/3, note to General Ismay, April 5, 1943, PREM 3/333/16, NA.

3. Maj. Gen. E. F. Humphreys, BA, Brig. Gen. F. E. Morgan, Staff College Reports–1928, December 20, 1928, PREM 3/333/16, NA.

4. Dr. Maclyn Burg, interview with Gen. Ray W. Barker, July 15, 1972, Oral History Collection, Eisenhower Library, 52.

5. Weighley, *Eisenhower's Lieutenants*, 37.

6. Burg, Barker interview, 56.

7. Burg, Barker interview, 59–60.

8. Morgan, *Overture to Overlord*, 44–45, 23.

9. Burg, Barker interview, 55.

10. Historical Sub-Section, History of COSSAC, 2.

11. Historical Sub-Section, History of COSSAC, 2.

12. Burg, Barker interview, 64.

13. Burg, Barker interview, 2.

14. For the directive and side-by-side comparison of British and U.S. recommended text, see Brig. Gen. Albert Wedemeyer, USA, memorandum for the Secretariat, Joint Chiefs of Staff, April 17, 1943, RG 165, Chief of Staff file, NARA.

15. Historical Sub-Section, History of COSSAC, 4.

16. Stacey, *The Victory Campaign*, 29.

17. Stacey, *The Victory Campaign*, 16.

18. Weighley, *Eisenhower's Lieutenants*, 34–35.

19. Symonds, *Neptune*, 90–92.

20. Weighley, *Eisenhower's Lieutenants*, 35.

21. Morgan, *Overture to Overlord*, 131–32.

22. Harrison, *Cross-Channel Attack*, 64

23. Lt. Gen. Frederick Morgan, RA, COSSAC (43) 6: Battle Experience: Memorandum from COSSAC to Principal Staff Officers, May 19, 1943, RG 331, file 122, NARA.

24. Historical Sub-Section, History of COSSAC, 6.

25. Historical Sub-Section, History of COSSAC, 6.

26. Morgan, *Overture to Overlord*, 128–29.

27. Morgan, *Overture to Overlord*, 135–36.

28. Lt. Gen. Frederick Morgan, RA, "COSSAC (43) 11: Operation 'RUDGE,'" May 25, 1943, RG 331, file 122, NARA, 1, 2.

29. Stoler, *Allies and Adversaries*, 77.

4. The Trident Conference

1. Roberts, *Masters and Commanders*, 358.

2. Roberts, *Masters and Commanders*, 366.

3. [Brig. Gen. Albert C. Wedemeyer, USA], Preparations for the Next United States–British Staff Conference, [July] 1943, RG 218, box 314, NARA, 1.

4. Lippmann, *U.S. Foreign Policy*, 135.

5. JCS 183/1: Air Routes across the Pacific and Air Facilities for International Police Force, quoted in Stoler, *Allies and Adversaries*, 138.

6. Stoler, *Allies and Adversaries*, 131.

7. Cline, *Washington Command Post*, 192.

8. Stoler, *Allies and Adversaries*, 132.

9. Jackson and Bramall, *The Chiefs*, 256.

10. Atkinson, *An Army at Dawn*, 328.

11. Handy and Lincoln, *Commander and System of Command for War against Germany*, September 29, 1943, 2.

12. Keegan, *The Second World War*, 236–37.

13. [Brig. Gen. Albert C. Wedemeyer, USA], Analysis of the ANFA and TRIDENT Conferences, May [25], 1943, RG 165, Chief of Staff file, NARA, I, 3

14. Roberts, *Masters and Commanders*, 358.

15. Combined Chiefs of Staff, TRIDENT minutes 1st meeting, 1–3, and Brooke, *War Diaries*, 402.

16. Combined Chiefs of Staff, TRIDENT minutes 1st meeting, 4, 5.

17. Office of the Combined Chiefs, TRIDENT Conference May 1943: Papers and Minutes of Meetings, Map Room Papers, series 1, box 27, FDRL, 326–27.

18. Office of the Combined Chiefs, TRIDENT Conference May 1943, 326–28.

19. Office of the Combined Chiefs, TRIDENT Conference May 1943, 328.

20. Office of the Combined Chiefs, TRIDENT Conference May 1943, 328–29.

21. Office of the Combined Chiefs, TRIDENT Conference May 1943, 329.

22. FRUS: *The Conferences at Washington and Quebec 1943*, 84.

23. Brooke, *War Diaries*, 405.

24. Brooke, *War Diaries*, 406

25. Combined Chiefs of Staff, CCS 237/1: Resolutions by the Combined Chiefs of Staff (European Operations), May 20, 1943, RG 319, box 10, NARA.

26. Roberts, *Masters and Commanders*, 369.

27. Brooke, *War Diaries*, 407.

28. Roberts, *Masters and Commanders*, 369–70.

29. Brooke, *War Diaries*, 407.

30. Combined Chiefs of Staff, CCS 242/6: Combined Chiefs of Staff Final Report to the President and Prime Minister, May 25, 1943, RG 319, box 11, NARA.

31. Brooke, *War Diaries*, 410.

32. Thomas L. Rowan, Tube Alloys, note to Gorell Barnes re: Churchill communication with Hopkins on Anglo-American cooperation, January 18, 1943, PREM 3/139/8A, NA.

33. Lord Cherwell, Tube Alloys, April 7, 1943, PREM 3/139/8A, NA, I.

34. Churchill to Anderson, Serial no. 270/3, April 5, 1943, PREM 3/139/8A. NA.

35. Gowing, *Britain and Atomic Energy*, 164–65.

36. Anderson, Tube Alloys, note to the prime minister re: history and present position of British research, April 29, 1943, 1–2. Anderson, who certainly was aware of Lord Cherwell's April 7 note that stimulated Churchill's April 15 request, was well armed with recent data when the request came to him. For details of the scientists' estimate at this time, see Akers and Perrin, *T.A. Project—Latest Position*, April 5, 1943, CAB 126/147, NA.

37. Anderson to Churchill, May 15, 1943, PREM 3/139/8A, NA.

38. Wallace A. Akers, Tube Alloy Project: Note on talk with Dean C. J. Mackenzie, May 14, 1943, CAB 126/163, NA, 1.

39. Hewlett and Anderson, *New World, 1939–1946*, 1:271.

40. Churchill to Harry Hopkins, April 1, 1943, PREM 3/139/8A, NA.

41. Eden, *Memoirs*, 657.

42. Eden, *Memoirs*, 658.

43. The text of Halifax's letter can be found in Eden, *Memoirs*, 657–58.

44. Eden, *Memoirs*, 658.

45. White House Usher's Diary, May 24, 1943, FDRL, and Stenographer's Diary, May 24, 1943, FDRL.

46. Vannevar Bush, Memorandum of conference with Harry Hopkins and Lord Cherwell at the White House, May 25, 1943, AEC, Annexes to the Diplomatic History of the Manhattan Project, RG 374, microfilm roll 12, annex 9, NARA. See also *FRUS: Conferences at Washington and Quebec 1943*, 188–89.

47. See, for example, Roberts, *Masters and Commanders*, 371–72.

48. Roll, *Hopkins Touch*, 272, and Pogue, *Marshall: Organizer of Victory*, 212.

49. Quoted from Churchill, *Hinge of Fate*, 801.

50. Brooke, *War Diaries*, 411.

51. Farmelo, *Churchill's Bomb*, 228–29.

52. Bush, Memorandum of conference with Hopkins and Cherwell, May 25, 1943, 1.

53. Bush, Memorandum of conference with Hopkins and Cherwell, 2.

54. Hewlett and Anderson, *New World, 1939–1946*, 1:273.

55. Bush, Memorandum of conference with Hopkins and Cherwell, 3.

56. See Churchill to Hopkins, message 374, 10 June 1943, quoted in assessment of the May 25 FDR-Churchill meeting in *FRUS: Conferences at Washington and Quebec 1943*, 221. For Lord Cherwell's May 30 letter to Hopkins, see ibid., 188.

57. Moran, *Churchill at War*, 116.

58. Bush, personal notes during meeting with Churchill, July 15, 1943, James B. Conant's Personal Files, Records of the Office of Scientific Research and Development, RG 227, m1392, file 10, NARA, 3; and Villa, "The Atomic Bomb and the Normandy Invasion," 483.

59. Churchill, Pencil no. 405: Prime Minister to Lord President, May 26, 1943, PREM 3/139/8A, NA.

60. For Lord Cherwell's May 30 letter to Hopkins, see *FRUS: Conferences at Washington and Quebec 1943*, 188. For Churchill's June 10 cable to Hopkins, see ibid., 630.

61. Moran, *Churchill at War 1940–45*, 117; Lavery, *Churchill Goes to War*, 201; Brooke, *War Diaries*, 412.

62. Roberts, *Masters and Commanders*, 372–73.

63. Brooke, *War Diaries*, 411.

64. Gen. George C. Marshall, USA, draft Churchill-Roosevelt note to Stalin, May 26, 1943, PREM 3/333/5, NA.

65. Parrish, *Roosevelt and Marshall*, 352–53.

66. Parrish, *Roosevelt and Marshall*, 353.

67. Moran, *Churchill at War*, 123.

68. Moran, *Churchill at War*, 122.

69. Pogue, *Marshall: Organizer of Victory*, 218, 220.

70. Stoler, *Allies and Adversaries*, 124.

5. Mission to Moscow

1. Harriman and Abel, *Special Envoy*, 151–64.

2. Harriman and Abel, *Special Envoy*, 152.

3. *FRUS: Conferences at Cairo and Tehran 1943*, 5–6.

4. Joseph Edward Davies, diary, Davies Papers, chronological files, box 1:13, Manuscript Division, LOC, 3.

5. Davies diary, 3.

6. *FRUS: Conferences at Cairo and Tehran 1943*, 3–4.

7. Davies diary, 8.

8. Davies diary, 9.

9. Roll, *Hopkins Touch*, 275.

10. Davies diary, 13.

11. *FRUS: Conferences at Cairo and Tehran 1943*, 5–7.

12. Davies diary, May 5, 1943, 3.

13. Davies, "Advising President Date of Meeting Set for July 15, Paraphrase of Cable Sent on May 21, 1943," chronological files, box 1:13, Manuscript Division, LOC. Had the need arisen, using *jonquils* in a sentence written in Moscow would have been easy for an ambassador half a world away from his home and family in Washington in May. Synonymous with *daffodil* in the American South and Washington's other, more resilient floral glory, fanfares of yellow and white jonquil trumpets brighten the city every spring.

14. Roll, *Hopkins Touch*, 275–76.

15. Tregaron, now owned by the Washington International School, appeared in the 1962 Otto Preminger film based on the Allen Drury novel *Advise and Consent*. Through a zoning board decision that set precedent in the District of Columbia in 1983, Tregaron's twenty-acre wooded grounds were saved from developers by its neighbors.

16. Davies diary, 1–2.

17. Davies diary, 3.

18. Davies diary, 3

19. Based on Averill Harriman's letter to FDR, July 5, 1943, Harriman file, Harry Hopkins Collection, box 157, FDRL.

20. Harriman to FDR, July 5, 1943, 2–3. Given the importance of the subject and his knowledge of Churchill's prompt reply, it is unlikely that Harriman would have waited in silence until July 5 to convey his own time-urgent assessment to FDR in the form of his surviving letter. More probable is that Harriman made an initial report to FDR or Hopkins by cable or orally by ostensibly secure radiotelephone of the gist of the previous night's discussion with Churchill and the June 25 meeting with Churchill and Eden (pos-

sibly in a second communication). There are no surviving cables to this effect from Harriman to FDR. The radiotelephone was available to Harriman. The only such system between London and Washington at the time was the A3 voice-encoded telephone. Security of the A3 had been cracked and system's traffic was monitored and read constantly by the Germans throughout this period. On the compromised A3 voice-encoded telephone and its replacement, see chapter 7.

21. Cable 328: Churchill to Roosevelt, June 25, 1943, FRUS: Conferences at Cairo and Tehran 1943, 10–11.

22. Roosevelt to Churchill, no. 297, June 29, 1943, PREM 3/471, NA, I.

23. Davies diary, 8.

24. Roosevelt to Churchill, no. 297, June 29, 1943, I.

25. Roosevelt to Churchill, no. 297, June 29, 1943, 2.

26. Roosevelt to Churchill, no. 297, June 29, 1943, 2.

27. Cable 334: Churchill to Roosevelt, June 28, 1943, FRUS: Conferences at Cairo and Tehran 1943, 11–12.

28. Cable 336: Churchill to Roosevelt, June 29, 1943, 12–13.

6. COSSAC's Plan Emerges

1. Lt. Gen. Sir Frederick Morgan, RA, COSSAC (43) 20: Notes on visit to war cabinet offices, June 2, 1943, RG 331, file 122, NARA, I.

2. Morgan, COSSAC (43) 28: Operation "OVERLORD" 1944, June 7, 1943, RG 331, file 122, NARA.

3. Morgan, COSSAC (43) 28: Operation "OVERLORD" 1944, 3.

4. Morgan, COSSAC (43) 28: Operation "OVERLORD" 1944, I.

5. The key variable was minutes of flying time available over the combat area.

6. Combined Operations Headquarters, CO (R) 25: "RATTLE" record of a conference held at HMS Warren from 28th June to 2nd July to study the Combined Operations problems of "Overlord," July 1943, ADM 1/13147, NA, 93.

7. Morgan, COSSAC (43) 28: Operation "OVERLORD" 1944, I.

8. Morgan, COSSAC (43) 28: Operation "OVERLORD" 1944, 2.

9. Morgan, Overture to Overlord, 130–31.

10. Morgan, COSSAC: (43) 28: Operation "OVERLORD" 1944, 4–5.

11. COSSAC, meeting to discuss revision of agenda for course at LARGS, June 28–July 2, 1943, June 19, 1943, RG 331, file 210, NARA, I–2.

12. COSSAC, "Conference at LARGS," RG 331, file 210, NARA.

13. Ziegler, Mountbatten, 214.

14. COSSAC, minutes of staff conference held on Friday, July 2, 1943, RG 331, file 122, NARA, I–2; Brown, Bodyguard of Lies, 318.

15. Morgan, Overture to Overlord, 137.

16. Morgan's paper is reproduced in full in Combined Operations Headquarters, CO (R) 25: "RATTLE" record of a conference, 92–98.

17. Stacey, The Victory Campaign, 9–10; Adm. Lord Louis Mountbatten, COS (43) 367 (O) Conference "RATTLE" memorandum by the chief of Combined Operations, July 7, 1943, RG 331, box 130, NARA,I–2.

18. COSSAC: minutes of staff conference held on Friday, July 2, 1943, RG 331, file 122, NARA, 2.

19. Stacey, *The Victory Campaign*, 11.

20. Morgan, *Overture to Overlord*, 138, and Stacey, *Six Years of War*, 108.

21. The First Canadian Army would not reunite in northwest Europe to fight as one until the spring of 1945. Stacey, *Six Years of War*, 109.

22. See "Annex: Points Arising from RATTLE Conference," in Vice Adm. Lord Louis Mountbatten, COS (43) 367 (O) Conference 'RATTLE' memorandum by the chief of Combined Operations, July 7, 1943, RG 331, box 130, NARA, 3–5.

23. Elspeth Shuter Papers, document 13454, IWM, 4.

24. Shakespeare, *Henry V*, act 4, scene 3.

25. Chiefs of Staff Committee, COS (43) 416 (O) Operation "OVERLORD" report and appreciation with appendices, July 30, 1943, RG 165, entry NM-84, 390/30/18/1, box 13, NARA.

26. Chiefs of Staff Committee, COS (43) 416 (O) Operation "OVERLORD" report, iv.

27. Chiefs of Staff Committee, COS (43) 416 (O) Operation "OVERLORD" report, iv.

28. Chiefs of Staff Committee, COS (43) 416 (O) Operation "OVERLORD" report, iv.

29. Chiefs of Staff Committee, COS (43) 416 (O) Operation "OVERLORD" report, iv.

30. Chiefs of Staff Committee, COS (43) 416 (O) Operation "OVERLORD" report, viii.

31. Chiefs of Staff Committee, COS (43) 416 (O) Operation "OVERLORD" report, viii.

32. Chiefs of Staff Committee, COS (43) 416 (O) Operation "OVERLORD" report, viii.

33. Chiefs of Staff Committee, COS (43) 416 (O) Operation "OVERLORD" report, ii.

34. Chiefs of Staff Committee, COS (43) 416 (O) Operation "OVERLORD" report, ii–iii.

7. The Green Hornet

1. Chit from Churchill and response by John M. Martin, September 4, attached to E. E. Bridges, note to the prime minister re: radiotelephone communication security, September 3, 1942, PREM 4/91/3, NA.

2. Kahn, *Hitler's Spies*, 173, and David Kahn, "German Interception of A3 Radio-telephone Calls: Interview of Kurt E. Vetterlein," September 1, 1967, file DK 64–62, CCH, 8.

3. The best American system of the time, SIGABA, added a further stepping of all of that machine's rotors, which themselves spun. This raised the number of possible setting combinations yet again exponentially. SIGABA remained secure until the advent of supercomputers.

4. Weadon, *Sigsaly Story*, 1.

5. Kahn, *Hitler's Spies*, 172.

6. Kahn, *Hitler's Spies*, 172.

7. Kahn, *Hitler's Spies*, 173, and Kahn, "German Interception of A3 Radio-telephone Calls," 1.

8. Kahn, *Hitler's Spies*, 172–73.

9. Kahn, "German Interception of A3 Radio-telephone Calls," 9–10.

10. Kahn, "German Interception of A3 Radio-telephone Calls," 5.

11. The German recordings and raw transcriptions of the calls between Churchill and Roosevelt over the A3 system would be a treasure for historians today, but they have not been found in either captured documents at the National Archives and Records Administration or among records at the Bundesarchives in Germany. They are said to have been destroyed in the bombing of Berlin.

12. B.B., "Cabinet Ministers and the Transatlantic Telephone Service," March 10, 1942, PREM 4/91/3, NA.

13. Chit from Churchill and response by John M. Martin, September 4, attached to E. E. Bridges, note to the prime minister re: radiotelephone communication security, September 3, 1942, PREM 4/91/3, NA.

14. Kahn, "German Interception of A-3 Radio-telephone Calls," 9.

15. E. E. Bridges, Security of the Radio Telephone, March 19, 1942, PREM 4/91/3, NA, 1–2.

16. Weadon, *Sigsaly Story*, 1.

17. Boone and Peterson, SIGSALY–*The Start of the Digital Revolution*, https://www.nsa.gov/about/cryptologic-heritage/historical-figures -publications/publications/wwii/sigsaly-start-digital.shtml.

18. Boone and Peterson, SIGSALY.

19. Boone and Peterson, SIGSALY, appendix A.

20. Boone and Peterson, SIGSALY.

21. Boone and Peterson, SIGSALY.

22. Gen. Sir Hastings L. Ismay, BA, Note to the Prime Minister, February 15, 1943, PREM 4/91/3, NA, 1–2.

23. Boone and Peterson, SIGSALY.

24. Kahn, "German Interception of A3 Radio-telephone Calls," 10.

25. Holmes, *Churchill's Bunker*, 123.

26. For a partial transcript of this apparently unique historical document, see Kahn, *Codebreakers*, 556–57.

8. Hammer and Tongs

1. This building was transferred to the State Department after the War Department moved into the Pentagon. Between 1961 and 1997, the former office of the secretary of war served as the office of the director of the U.S. Arms Control and Disarmament Agency.

2. Henry L. Stimson and W. H. S. Wright, "The Secretary of War's Trip to Iceland, the United Kingdom, and North Africa, July 8–31, 1943," August 1943, Henry L. Stimson Papers, LOC, 1.

3. W. H. S. Wright, "Personal and Secret Memorandum for the Eyes of Mr. Bundy Only," in Stimson and Wright, "Secretary of War's Trip," 2–3.

4. F. S. Low, "Dispatch from Admiral King to Admiral Stark," June 17, 1943, Headquarters United States Fleet, RG 277, entry 170, box 77, NARA, 1.

5. Vannevar Bush, "Sequence of Events Concerning Interchange with the British on the Subject of S-1," August 4, 1943, in *FRUS: Conferences at Washington and Quebec 1943*, 642.

6. Keegan, *The Second World War*, 347–48.

7. Stimson and Wright, "Secretary of War's Trip," 10.

8. The term *Round Hammer* was a combination of the previously considered cross-Channel attack plans, Roundup and Sledgehammer, with a certain logic as to its construction and, briefly, transitory status as a plan. Round Hammer, which became Overlord, was conceived to fall between its two predecessors in size.

9. Stimson, "Observations of Secretary: Trip Overseas, July 8 to July 31/43," August 12, 1943, Henry L. Stimson Papers, LOC, 5.

10. Stimson, "Brief Report on Certain Features of Overseas Trip, August 4, 1943," Stimson Papers, LOC, 7–9; Stimson and Bundy, *On Active Service in Peace and War*, 429–30; E. Morison, *Turmoil and Tradition*, 591.

11. Stimson, "Observations," 5.

12. Stimson, "Observations," 5, 9–10.

13. Stimson, "Observations," 6.

14. Bush, *Pieces of the Action*, 282.

15. Gowing, *Britain and Atomic Energy*, 68n.

16. For the British account of receipt of these communications, see Sir John Anderson, "Tube Alloys," memorandum to the prime minister, January 11, 1943, PREM 3/139/8A, NA, and Sir John Anderson, note to the prime minister re: Conant memorandum, July 23, 1943, PREM 3/139/8A, NA.

17. Bush, personal notes on meeting with Winston Churchill, July 15, 1943, Records of the Office of Scientific Research and Development, Conant's Personal Files, RG 227, m1392, file 10, NARA, 1, 3.

18. Hewlett and Anderson, *New World, 1939–1946*, 1:74–75.

19. Bush, personal notes, 2–3.

20. Bush, personal notes, 1.

21. Bush, *Pieces of the Action*, 282.

22. Overy, *Bombers and the Bombed*, 142, 260.

23. Bell, *Churchill & Sea Power*, 289, referencing Howard, *Grand Strategy IV*, 503.

24. Stimson, "Observations," 6, 39.

25. COSSAC, (43) 28: Operation "Overlord 1944," June 7, 1943, RG 331, file 122, NARA.

26. COSSAC, (43) 28: Operation "Overlord 1944," 6.

27. Roosevelt to Stalin, July 15, 1943, *FRUS: Conferences at Cairo and Tehran 1943*, 16.

28. Roosevelt to Churchill, no. 318, July 16, 1943, *FRUS: Conferences at Washington and Quebec 1943*, 393.

29. Leighton and Coakley, *Global Logistics and Strategy, 1940–1943*, 176.

30. Roosevelt to Churchill, message #297, FRUS: *Conferences at Washington and Quebec 1943*, 391–92.

31. Telephone records 1943, Harry L. Hopkins Collection, box 224, FDRL.

32. E. F. McDonald Jr. to Thomas H. Beck, Crowell-Collier Publishing Co., April 25, 1942, Birch Island file, FDRL.

33. Stimson and Wright, "Secretary of War's Trip," 15.

34. Lavery, *Churchill Goes to War*, 22.

35. Stimson, "Observations," 8, and Stimson and Wright, "Secretary of War's Trip," 15–16.

36. Stimson, "Observations," 8.

37. Stimson, "Observations," 8.

38. Stimson, "Observations," 9–10.

39. Hewlett and Anderson, *New World, 1939–1946*, 1:274–75.

40. Roosevelt to Vannevar Bush, July 20, 1943, Atomic Energy Commission, Annexes to the Diplomatic History of the Manhattan Project, RG 374, microfilm roll 12, NARA, Annex 8.

41. E. A. Shurcliff, Interoffice Memorandum: S-1 Cables, Office of Scientific Research and Development, September 8, 1942, Annexes to the Diplomatic History of the Manhattan Project, RG 227, M1392, file 99, NARA.

42. Carroll L. Wilson, East-905, message to Bush, July 27, 1943, RG 227, entry 176, box 225, folder "Cables Received April 2, 1943–Aug. 31, 1943," NARA. "Essone" is phonetic for "S-1."

43. Carroll L. Wilson to Roosevelt acknowledging transmission of FDR's July 20, 1943, note to Bush, July 28, 1943, PSF Vannevar Bush file, FDRL.

44. James B. Conant, East-913, message to Bush, July 29, 1943, RG 227, entry 176, box 225, file "Cables Received April 2, 1943–Aug. 31, 1943," NARA.

45. Hewlett and Anderson, *New World, 1939–1946*, 1:275

46. Bush, *Pieces of the Action*, 283.

47. Bush, "Sequence of Events Concerning Interchange with the British on the Subject of S-1," 642.

48. Bush, *Pieces of the Action*, 283.

49. See Villa, "The Atomic Bomb and the Normandy Invasion," 485–87.

50. Harvey Bundy, memorandum of meeting at 10 Downing Street on July 22, 1943, Annexes to the Diplomatic History of the Manhattan Project, RG 374, microfilm roll 12, NARA, annex 11, 1.

51. Gowing, *Britain and Atomic Energy*, 167–68.

52. Bundy, memorandum of meeting, 1–2.

53. Bundy, memorandum of meeting, 2.

54. Gowing, *Britain and Atomic Energy*, 168.

55. Bundy, memorandum of meeting, 3.

56. Bundy, memorandum of meeting, 4.

57. Stimson, "Observations," 7–8, 49.

58. Villa, "The Atomic Bomb and the Normandy Invasion," 489.

59. Stimson and Bundy, *On Active Service in Peace and War*, 4.

60. Stimson, "Brief Report," 7–9, and Stimson, "Observations," 12–13.

61. Bush, "Memo to Dr. J. B. Conant," July 22, 1943, Records of the Office of Scientific Research and Development, Conant's Personal Files, RG 227, m1392, file 10, NARA, 2.

62. Roosevelt, Cable 326: Personal and Secret to the Former Naval Person from the President, July 26, 1943, FRUS: Conferences at Washington and Quebec 1943, 636.

63. Bush, Pieces of the Action, 284. The message from Washington informing Bush of new instructions from the president, but with their intent corrupted, did not reach Bush in London until days after the July 22 meeting with Churchill, possibly as late as the following Monday. See Bush, "Sequence of Events Concerning Interchange with the British on the Subject of s-1," 644.

64. Bush, "To Bundy–with the Secretary of War," July 28, 1943, Records of the Office of Scientific Research and Development, James B. Conant's Personal Files, RG 227, m1392, file 10, NARA.

65. Freedom Algiers [Stimson to Bush], "Edited Literal Text," July 28, 1943, Records of the Office of Scientific Research and Development, Conant's Personal Files, RG 227, M1392, file 10, NARA.

66. Churchill, "Cable 372: Former Naval Person to President Most Secret," July 20, 1943, FRUS: Conferences at Washington and Quebec 1943, 394.

67. Churchill, "Cable 374: Former Naval Person to President Personal Most Secret," July 21, 1943, FRUS: Conferences at Washington and Quebec 1943, 394.

68. Stimson, "Brief Report," 9.

69. Stimson, "Brief Report," 9.

70. E. F. McDonald Jr. to Supervising Agent Michael Reilly, July 23, 1943, Birch Island file, FDRL.

71. Hopkins appointment book 1943, entries for July 22, 1943, FDRL.

72. Morison, Breaking the Bismarks Barrier, 128–29.

73. Stimson and Wright, "Secretary of War's Trip."

74. Roosevelt to Churchill, cable 325, FRUS: Conferences at Washington and Quebec 1943, 399–400.

75. Davies diary, 13.

76. Roosevelt, Personal and Secret to the Former Naval Person from the President 297, June 28, 1943, FRUS: Conferences at Cairo and Tehran 1943, 11–12.

77. As a deception to divert attention from his travel to meet Churchill in Argentia Bay, Newfoundland, in August 1941, FDR left New Bedford, Massachusetts, for a very public "fishing trip" aboard the yacht Potomac in Buzzards Bay and cruised slowly through the Cape Cod Canal (easily accessible to press and public) to Cape Cod Bay. The Navy crew of Potomac were dressed in civilian clothes. One crew member with a floppy hat, cigarette holder, and wire rim glasses waved casually to all in sight. FDR, meanwhile, was steaming north in the cruiser Augusta to meet Churchill. See Davis, FDR: The War President, 249–50.

78. Combined Chiefs of Staff, (TRIDENT): Minutes 1st Meeting, The White House, 2:30 p.m., 12 May 1943, RG 107, entry 104, box 276, NARA, 5.

79. Churchill, Former Naval Person to President Roosevelt Personal and Most Secret Nr 383, July 26, 1943, Map Room file, series 1, Messages, box 4, FDRL.

80. COS, Quadrant: Following from Chiefs of Staff COS (W) 734, 26 July 1943, 1857Z, RG 0165, entry 422, box 54, NARA.

81. Michael Reilly, telegram, Reilly to Boos, July 20, 1943, and telegram, Reilly to McDonald, July 22, 1943, Birch Island file, FDRL.

82. Roosevelt, Cable 326: Personal and Secret to the Former Naval Person from the President, 636.

83. Henry L. Stimson, "Summary of General Eisenhower's Views as to Post Husky," July 27, 1943, Henry L. Stimson Papers, LOC.

84. Stimson, "Summary of General Eisenhower's Views as to Post Husky," 4.

85. Stimson, "Summary of General Eisenhower's Views as to Post Husky," 5.

86. Schott, Stimson daybook.

9. Revolt in London and Washington

1. Lt. Gen. Frederick Morgan, BA, COSSAC (43) 14th report: fourteenth report by the chief of staff to the Supreme Commander (Designate), July 19, 1943, RG 331, file 122, NARA, 1–2.

2. Col. Leslie C. Hollis, BA, Chiefs of Staff Committee (43) 162nd meeting (O), minutes, July 22, 1943, RG 331, file 122, NARA, 160–61.

3. Hollis, Chiefs of Staff Committee (43) 168th Meeting (O), July 22, 1943, 2.

4. Morgan, *Overture to Overlord*, 161.

5. Coakley and Leighton, *Global Logistics and Strategy, 1943–1945*, 177.

6. Agarossi, *A Nation Collapses*, 50.

7. Notes for General Marshall for use in conference with the president, July 24, 1943, RG 165, entry 422, box 54, NARA, 1.

8. Notes for General Marshall, 2.

9. Notes for General Marshall, 2–3.

10. Coakley and Leighton, *Global Logistics and Strategy, 1943–1945*, 178.

11. Maj. Gen. Thomas M. Handy, USA, "Conduct of the War in Europe," August 8, 1943, RG 165, NARA, 1–2, 5.

12. Matloff, *Strategic Planning for Coalition Warfare, 1943–1945*, 166–67, and Coakley and Leighton, *Global Logistics and Strategy, 1943–1945*, 178–79.

13. Brig. Gen. John E. Hull, USA, memorandum for General Handy, July 17, 1943, RG 165, entry 4621, box 362, NARA, 3. See also Coakley and Leighton, *Global Logistics and Strategy, 1943–1945*, 164–66, 178, and Matloff, *Strategic Planning for Coalition Warfare*, 166–67.

14. Matloff, *Strategic Planning for Coalition Warfare*, 166–67, and Coakley and Leighton, *Global Logistics and Strategy, 1943–1945*, 166–67, 178–79.

15. Coakley and Leighton, *Global Logistics and Strategy, 1943–1945*, 178–79.

16. Matloff, *Strategic Planning for Coalition Warfare, 1943–1945*, 167.

17. Combined Chiefs of Staff, "Memorandum by the British Chiefs of Staff, CCS 288," July 26, 1943, FRUS: *Conferences at Washington and Quebec 1943*, 400–401.

18. Joint Chiefs of Staff, proposed agenda for Quadrant (CCS 288/1), *Stra-*

tegic Studies and Outline Plans, Book 1, Map Room file, box 27, FDRL, 1, and *FRUS: Conferences at Washington and Quebec 1943,* 402–5.

19. *FRUS: Conferences at Washington and Quebec 1943,* 404–5.

20. Joint Planning Staff, JP (43) 36th Meeting: Minutes of the Meeting of the Joint Planning Staff, May 3, 1943, CAB 84/6, NA, 1.

21. Historical Sub-Section, Office of Secretary, General Staff, History of COSSAC (Chief of Staff to Supreme Allied Commander) 1943–1944, file 8–3.6.CA, ACMH, www.history.army.mil/documents/cossac/Cossac.htm, 22.

22. Col. Leslie C. Hollis, BA, Chiefs of Staff Committee (43) 162nd meeting (O), minutes, July 22, 1943, RG 331, file 122, NARA, 2.

23. Lt. Gen. Sir Frederick Morgan, BA, COSSAC (43) 33: Operation "Rankin," July 27, 1943, RG 331, file 122, NARA, 1.

24. At best, Morgan had a perspective of the enemy constrained by the limits of Allied intelligence and particularly the Allies' incomprehension, unrecognized in 1943, of the resiliency of the Nazis' total dictatorship.

25. Morgan, COSSAC (43) 33: Operation "Rankin," 1.

26. Morgan, COSSAC (43) 33: Operation "Rankin," 2–3.

27. For a detailed, contemporary account of Rankin's three cases and their development, see Historical Sub-Section, Office of Secretary, General Staff, History of COSSAC (Chief of Staff to Supreme Allied Commander), 1943–1944, file 8–3.6.CA, ACMH, www.history.army.mil/documents/cossac/Cossac.htm, 22–26.

28. Historical Sub-Section, Office of Secretary, General Staff, History of COSSAC, 21.

29. For an insightful survey of immediate postwar conditions and events and their impact in Europe and Asia in the year of liberation, see Buruma, *Year Zero: A History of 1945.*

30. Morgan, *Overture to Overlord,* 160.

31. Morgan, *Overture to Overlord,* 160.

32. Dr. Maclyn Burg, interview with Gen. Ray W. Barker, July 15, 1972, Oral History Collection, Eisenhower Library, 84.

33. Burg, Barker interview, 84.

34. Morgan, *Overture to Overlord,* 161–62.

35. E-mail correspondence by the author with Archangelo Difante, Air Force Historical Research Agency, November 21, 2016.

36. E-mail correspondence by the author with Michael Swinnerton, North Yorkshire Moors Railway, October 7, 2013.

37. Morgan, *Overture to Overlord,* 162.

38. E-mail correspondence by the author with Maj. Mathias Joost, Canadian Forces, Directorate of History and Heritage, Canadian Armed Forces, June 23, 2016.

39. Roosevelt to Churchill, cable 326, July 26, 1943, *FRUS: Conferences at Washington and Quebec 1943,* 636.

40. Churchill to Roosevelt, cable 388, July 30, 1943, *FRUS: Conferences at Washington and Quebec 1943,* 637.

41. *FRUS: Conferences at Washington and Quebec 1943,* 637–38, and Atomic

Energy Commission, Annexes to the Diplomatic History of the Manhattan Project, RG 374, microfilm roll 12, NARA.

42. Atomic Energy Commission, annex 10.

10. The Fishing Trip

1. U.S. Secret Service, "Members of the Party," n.d., Birch Island file, FDRL.

2. Hassett, *Off the Record with FDR*, 195.

3. Rigdon, *White House Sailor*, 27.

4. Tully, *FDR, My Boss*, 210.

5. Leahy, *I Was There* manuscript, Adm. William Leahy Papers, LOC; U.S. Secret Service, "Operating Stops, Friday, July 30, 1943," Birch Island file, FDRL, 2.

6. Virginia Tanner, "GPA Dan Moorman Recalls Journeys with President Roosevelt," *Baltimore & Ohio Magazine*, 61–62.

7. Secret Service, "Operating Stops."

8. E. F. McDonald Jr. to Thomas H. Beck, Crowell-Collier Publishing Co., April 25, 1942, Birch Island file, FDRL.

9. Tully, *FDR, My Boss*, 210.

10. Roosevelt to Churchill, cable 326, July 26, 1943, *FRUS: Conferences at Washington and Quebec 1943*, 636.

11. Ward, *Closest Companion*, 227.

12. See "Prime Minister and President Roosevelt to Premier Stalin 19 Aug. 43," quoted in Churchill, *Closing the Ring*, 279.

13. The Secret Service inquired about the length and nature of airfield runways in the vicinity of Georgian Bay, a prudent step for the safety of a traveling president in any situation. However, they apparently limited their inquiry to the U.S. Army Air Force. Had they asked the Canadian Legation, knowledge of the query likely would have reached the British, potentially adding further ambiguity to the "fishing trip." See Guy Hammond, "Message for Riley [*sic*]: Relative Airfields," n.d., Birch Island file, FDRL.

14. Hammond, "Message for Riley."

15. The Soviet intelligence source now is believed to have been Laurence Duggan, a U.S. State Department employee. See Roll, *Hopkins Touch*, 275–76.

16. Ministry of Foreign Affairs of the USSR, *Correspondence between Stalin, Roosevelt, Truman, Churchill, and Atlee*, 70–71, and Eubank, *Summit at Teheran*, 96.

17. Eubank, *Summit at Teheran*, 97.

18. Withers, *The President Travels by Train*, 131.

19. Tanner, "GPA Dan Moorman Recalls Journeys with President Roosevelt," 62.

20. Withers, *The President Travels by Train*, 132.

21. Tanner, "GPA Dan Moorman Recalls Journeys with President Roosevelt," 62.

22. Withers, *The President Travels by Train*, 131–32.

23. Byrnes, *All In One Lifetime*, 194.

24. Hassett, *Off the Record with FDR*, 195.

25. Formally known as the Servicemen's Readjustment Act after its expansion and passage by Congress, the GI Bill enabled eight million veterans to

attend college with federal grants and four million to purchase homes with low-interest federal loans. See Golway, *Together We Cannot Fail,* 231–32.

26. Hassett, *Off the Record with FDR,* 195–96.

27. R. S. Bratton and A. V. S. Pickhardt, Army-Navy daily intelligence reports, July 26 and 29, 1943, Map Room file, box 68, MR 203 (6) Sec. 8, FDRL.

28. White House Usher's Diary, 1943, FDRL.

29. Wood and Jankowski, *Karski,* 196–202. The Polish resistance infiltrated Lieutenant Karski in disguise into the Warsaw Ghetto and into a death camp for the purpose of observing conditions firsthand. During his reconnaissance, he witnessed a mass execution. The resistance then smuggled Karski out of Europe, via Germany, France, and Spain, to report to the western Allies on this as well as Soviet subversion directed against the behind-the-lines forces and leadership of Poland's legitimate government. Some accounts have asserted that Karski described to FDR the atrocities he witnessed in specific detail. However, Karski denied that he did that, stating that he described to the president what was happening conceptually (199).

30. Wood and Jankowski, *Karski,* 202.

31. White House Usher's Diary, July 30, 1943.

32. Secret Service, itinerary, July 30, 1943, Birch Island file, FDRL.

33. See hand notation on Canadian Pacific, Schedule O.D. #1, July 30, 1943, FDRL, 1, and "Roosevelt Trip to Manitoulin Company Triumph," *Canadian Pacific Bulletin,* Canadian Pacific Railway Company Fonds, CRHA, 2, and Secret Service, "Operating Stops."

34. Ward, *Closest Companion,* 228.

35. See Silcox, *The Group of Seven,* 213–14 and paintings at 264, 265, 62.

36. Lt. John Manley, USNR, letter to Lt. Ernest Loeb, September 9, 1943, photostatic copy exhibited at Turner's Store, Little Current, Ontario, 1.

37. Goodwin, *No Ordinary Time,* 451, 480–81.

38. Manley to Loeb, September 9, 1943.

39. Michael F. Reilly, report to Frank J. Wilson, chief, U.S. Secret Service, August 3, 1943, Birch Island file, FDRL, 2.

40. Mitchell, "The President Goes Fishing," 7.

41. R. S. Bratton and A. V. S. Pickhardt, Army-Navy daily intelligence report, August 2, 1943, Map Room file, box 68, MR 203 (6) Sec. 8, FDRL, 1.

42. The correct Romanian spelling courtesy of Dr. Teodora Salow, a native speaker.

43. An Allied on-site, post-strike assessment concluded that the "low level raid of 1st August 1943, caused more damage to refineries attacked that day than all later raids put together." See British Bombing Research Mission, RAC 216/902, cipher message assessing Allied bombing of Romania oil refineries, November 8, 1944, AIR 20/3/180, NA. Statement by Gen. Henry H. Arnold, USAAF, to the Combined Chiefs of Staff. See Combined Chiefs of Staff, (Quadrant) CCS 109th Meeting: Minutes of Meeting held in Room 2208, Chateau Frontenac Hotel on Monday, August 16, 1943, at 1430, RG 165, entry 334, section 5, box 182, NARA, 3,

44. Bratton and Pickhardt, Army-Navy daily intelligence report, August 2, 1943, 1.

45. Doyle, *PT-109*, 115–18.

46. Rigdon, *White House Sailor*, 27–28.

47. Rigdon, *White House Sailor*, 27.

48. See Lt. Col. Chester Hammond, USA, memorandum for General Marshall, forwarding FDR's response to White #25, August 3, 1943; Hammond, memorandum for General Marshall, forwarding FDR's request for JCS recommendation on Rome, August 4, 1943; Hammond, memorandum for General Marshall, forwarding FDR's approval of insistence on use of Azores facilities, August 5, 1943; and Hammond, memorandum for General Marshall, forwarding FDR's approval of JCS report on Rome, August 6, 1943, all in RG 165, box 54, NARA.

49. Rigdon, *White House Sailor*, 34.

11. From One Attorney to Another

1. John W. Schott, appointment clerk, Stimson daybook no. 5168, August 2, 1943, RG 107, NARA.

2. Henry L. Stimson, "Observations of Secretary: Trip Overseas," July 8 to July 31/43, August 12, 1943, Henry L. Stimson Papers, LOC, 63.

3. Schott, Stimson daybook.

4. Stimson, "Observations," 64.

5. Stimson's intent is evident at the start of his subsequent memorandum on the same issue written to Roosevelt five days later on August 10, 1943. See *frus: Conferences at Washington and Quebec 1943*, 496. Stimson had used the tactic of making his argument as though he were an attorney before a judge on February 9, 1942, in a critical White House meeting about the dire situation in the Philippines. Then Stimson literally rose to his feet in the Oval Office and argued his case to the president "standing as if before the court." He carried his point. See Hamilton, *The Mantle of Command*, 180–81, quoting from Stimson's diary.

6. Stimson, brief report on certain features of overseas trip, August 4, 1943, Henry L. Stimson Papers, LOC, 1.

7. Stimson, brief report, 2.

8. Stimson, brief report, 3.

9. E. Morison, *Turmoil and Tradition*, 234–35.

10. Morison, *Turmoil and Tradition*, 3.

11. Stimson, brief report, 3–4.

12. Casey, *Cautious Crusade*, 89–90, and Parrish, *Roosevelt and Marshall*, 297.

13. Persico, *Roosevelt's Centurions*, 221.

14. Stimson, brief report, 8.

15. Stimson, brief report, 9.

16. Stimson, brief report, 11.

17. Stimson, "Observations," 65.

18. Stimson, "Observations," 65.

19. Parrish, *Roosevelt and Marshall*, 87–88.

20. Parrish, *Roosevelt and Marshall*, 87–88, and Pogue, *Marshall: Education of a General*, 324–35.

21. Sherwood, *Roosevelt and Hopkins*, 223–24.

22. Churchill to Roosevelt, December 7, 1940, Map Room Papers, box 1, Churchill–FDR, October 1939–December 1940, vol. 1, Franklin On-line, FDRL, http://www.fdrlibrary.marist.edu/archives/collections/franklin/, 160–179, 15.

23. Sherwood, *Roosevelt and Hopkins*, 224–25.

24. Accounts, all based on Sherwood, vary. See Parrish, *Roosevelt and Marshall*, 162, and Roll, *Hopkins Touch*, 74–75.

25. Sherwood, *Roosevelt and Hopkins*, 225.

26. Churchill, "Speech by Prime Minister Churchill at the Mansion House Regarding Involvement in a U.S.-Japanese War by the British," November 10, 1941, BLI, 1.

27. Pogue, *Marshall: Education of a General*, 324.

28. Marshall to Gen. Asa Singleton, USA, November 22, 1939, quoted in Pogue, *Marshall: Education of a General*, 325.

29. Stimson to Roosevelt, cover letter for secretary of war's July 1943 trip report, August 4, 1943, President's Safe File, Stimson folder, FDRL.

30. *FRUS: Conferences at Washington, 1941–1942, and Casablanca, 1943*, 444.

12. The Happy Time at Birch Island

1. From an early draft of Byrnes, *All in One Lifetime*, courtesy of James Cross, manuscript archivist, Clemson University Library. Provided via email to the author August 16, 2012.

2. Adm. William D. Leahy, USN, journal, August 9, 1943, Leahy Papers, LOC. Harry Hopkins arrived at Birch Island on a Navy PBY Catalina amphibious plane on August 4 from Bangor, Maine. Byrnes may have been on Hopkins's plane. Certain from Byrnes memoir is that he left Washington aboard FDR's train on July 31. Also certain from archived records at Clemson University is that Byrnes was back in Washington on August 2 to chair an Office of War Mobilization meeting on a surge of protest from governors and congressmen about an uncoordinated news release on changes to gasoline rationing. Byrnes certainly had returned to Birch Island by the time Hopkins was there. Byrnes's signature appears below Hopkins's on a commemorative navigation chart that Lt. John Manley circulated among the fishing party. A clue as to whether and how Byrnes suddenly returned to Washington may be a cryptic, post–fishing trip Secret Service telegram to Ford Motor Company security chief Harry Bennett, thanking him for the use of Henry Ford's amphibious plane and pilot: "The only way to get the tiger in the air was to have Hal fly him." See Michael F. Reilly to Harry Bennett, telegram, Ford Motor Company, August 31, 1943, Birch Island file, FDRL. *Tiger* appears nowhere in the lists of Secret Service code names for the fishing trip.

3. Lt. John Manley, USNR, letter to Lt. Ernest Loeb, September 9, 1943, photostatic copy exhibited at Turner's Store, Little Current, Ontario.

4. Rigdon, *White House Sailor*, 32–33, and Manley to Loeb.

5. "E. D. Wilkins Had Brief Exchange with Roosevelt," *Sudbury (ON) Daily Star*, August 9, 1943, Birch Island file, FDRL.

6. Rigdon, *White House Sailor*, 35.

7. Grace Tully, "Thank you letter to Mr. H. A. Heineman," August 13, 1943, Birch Island file, FDRL.

8. Agarossi, *A Nation Collapses*, 73.

9. Amb. John G. Winant, "Most secret to the President from Winant," Message White 47, August 5, 1943, Map Room file, FDRL, 2–3.

10. Churchill, "Former Naval Person to President Roosevelt nr 405," Message White 43, August 4, 1943, Map Room file, FDRL, 1.

11. Churchill, "Former Naval Person to President Roosevelt nr 405," 2.

12. Winant, "Most secret to the President from Winant," August 5, 1943, 1–3

13. "Roosevelt and Cabinet Fish in North," *Sudbury (ON) Daily Star*, August 9, 1943, Birch Island file, FDRL.

14. Manley to Loeb, September 9, 1943, 2.

15. Persico, *Roosevelt's Centurions*, 162–63.

16. Roosevelt, "To the Secretary of War," August 8, 1943, President's Safe File, Stimson file, FDRL.

17. U.S. Secret Service, Schedule A, Saturday, August 7, 1943, Birch Island file, FDRL.

18. Guy H. Spaman to Secret Service chief Wilson re: apprehension of Pete Krug, August 5, 1943, Birch Island file, FDRL.

19. U.S. Secret Service, President's return trip from Birch Island, Ontario, Canada, August 7, 1943, Birch Island file, FDRL.

20. *FRUS: Conferences at Cairo and Tehran 1943*, 18.

21. Roosevelt to Stimson, August 8, 1943. Note the use of the plural *memoranda* between two men who were careful in their use of language. Unless Roosevelt meant to include Stimson's cover letter to him, the record does not explain this.

13. Plain Speaking on the Potomac

1. Hamilton, *Commander in Chief*, 319.

2. Chiefs of Staff Committee, COS (43) 471 (O) Part B 'Quadrant' Record of Chiefs of Staff meetings held on board RMS *Queen Mary* and in Quebec August 1943, September 11, 1943, CAB 99/23, NA, 4–5, and COSSAC (43) 23rd meeting, minutes of COSSAC staff conference held on Saturday, August 28, 1943, August 30, 1943, RG 331, file 122, NARA, 1–2.

3. COSSAC (43) 32 (Final) Digest of Operation "Overlord," in Chiefs of Staff Committee, COS (43) 416 (O) Operation "Overlord" report and appreciation with appendices, July 30, 1943, RG 165, entry NM-84, 390/30/18/1, box 13, NARA, viii.

4. Chiefs of Staff Committee, COS (43) 471 (O) Part B 'Quadrant' Record of Chiefs of Staff meetings held on board RMS *Queen Mary* and in Quebec August 1943, September 11, 1943, CAB 99/23, NA, 5.

5. Churchill, *Closing the Ring*, 67.

6. COSSAC (43) 23rd meeting: minutes of COSSAC staff conference held on Saturday, August 28, 1943, August 30, 1943, RG 331, file 122, NARA, 3.

7. Gen. Sir Hastings Ismay account quoted in Lavery, *Churchill Goes to War*, 463.

8. Roosevelt, Cable 326: To the Former Naval Person from the President, July 26, 1943, *FRUS: Conferences at Washington, 1941–1942, and Casablanca, 1943*, 636.

9. Churchill to Sir John Anderson re: negotiation of Articles of Agreement, August 1, 1943, PREM 3/139/8A, NA.

10. See Farmelo, *Churchill's Bomb*, 218, and Gowing, *Britain and Atomic Energy*, 172.

11. *FRUS: Conferences at Washington and Quebec 1943*, 640–41.

12. Sir John Anderson, draft Articles of Agreement, August 4, 1943, Atomic Energy Commission, Annexes to the Diplomatic History of the Manhattan Project, RG 374, microfilm roll 12, NARA, annex 13.

13. Vannevar Bush, memorandum: sequence of events concerning interchange with the British on the subject of s-1, August 4, 1943, Atomic Energy Commission, Annexes to the Diplomatic History of the Manhattan Project, RG 374, microfilm roll 12, NARA, annex 10.

14. Bush, memorandum: sequence of events.

15. Quoted in Ruane, *Churchill and the Bomb*, 61.

16. Derivative from timeline described in Bush to Anderson, August 6, 1943, PREM 3/139/8A, NA.

17. Stimson appointment book, August 5, 1943, RG 107, NARA.

18. Gowing, *Britain and Atomic Energy*, 170.

19. Gowing, *Britain and Atomic Energy*, 170.

20. Harvey Bundy, memorandum of meeting at 10 Downing Street on July 22, 1943, Annexes to the Diplomatic History of the Manhattan Project, RG 374, microfilm roll 12, NARA, annex 11, 4.

21. For an exposition of the reasoning for limiting cooperation with the British recommended to FDR and the end of 1942 and which was the foundation for resistance to cooperation by Vannevar Bush, his deputy James Conant, and Manhattan Project commander Gen. Leslie Groves, see Bush, "Excerpt from Report to the President by the Military Policy Committee, 15 December 1942, with Particular Reference to Recommendations Relating to Future Relations with the British and Canadians," Annexes to the Diplomatic History of the Manhattan Project, RG 374, microfilm roll 12, NARA, annex 6.

22. Bush to Anderson, August 6, 1943, PREM 3/139/8A, NA. Bush's decision to defer negotiation on the draft agreement's four substantive points had consequences unforeseen at the time. Point Three prohibited each government from sharing atomic information with a third party without the prior agreement of both governments. In September 1942, the British government had entered into an agreement with exiled French scientists on an exchange of patent rights and information related to atomic research. By foreclosing discussion of the point, Bush also precluded an opportunity for Anderson to cite this preexisting commitment before Roosevelt and Churchill signed the Atomic Sharing Agreement. In 1944, this became an issue between the British and the Americans. In hindsight, General Groves felt that with knowledge

in advance of signing, an accommodation of the Anglo-French commitment could have been incorporated. See Groves, *Now It Can Be Told*, 224–28.

23. Bush to Anderson, August 6, 1943, PREM 3/139/8A, NA.

24. Groves, *Now It Can Be Told*, 135.

25. Bundy, memorandum for the secretary, August 6, 1943, *FRUS: Conferences in Washington and Quebec*, 648–49.

26. "A reasonable basis for a quid pro quo" is from Bundy, memorandum for the secretary, 648–49.

27. Anderson to Bush re: draft Articles of Agreement, August 6, 1943, PREM 3/139/8A, 1943, NA.

28. Bush to Roosevelt, August 7, 1943, Annexes to the Diplomatic History of the Manhattan Project, RG 374, microfilm roll 12, NARA, annex 17.

29. Bush, memorandum of conference with Mr. Harry Hopkins and Lord Cherwell at the White House, May 25, 1943, Atomic Energy Commission, Annexes to the Diplomatic History of the Manhattan Project, RG 374, microfilm roll 12, NARA, annex 9, I.

30. See James B. Conant, memorandum: exchange of information on S-1 project with the British, July 30, 1943, Annexes to the Diplomatic History of the Manhattan Project, RG 374, Annex 10, roll 12, NARA, annex 10, and Conant, memorandum: exchange of information on S-1 with the British, August 6, 1943, Annexes to the Diplomatic History of the Manhattan Project, RG 227, M 1392, roll 5, frame 33, NARA.

31. Coakley and Leighton, *Global Logistics and Strategy, 1943–1945*, 180.

32. See report by Joint War Planning Committee 5, "Strategic Concept for Defeat of the Axis in Europe," August 1943, cited in Coakley and Leighton, *Global Logistics and Strategy, 1943–1945*, 180.

33. Coakley and Leighton, *Global Logistics and Strategy, 1943–1945*, 179.

34. Quoted in Coakley and Leighton, *Global Logistics and Strategy, 1943–1945*, 101–2.

35. Joint Chiefs of Staff, Quadrant Information Bulletin, no. 1, August 5, 1943, RG 165, box 54, NARA.

36. Lt. Gen. Sir Frederick Morgan, BA, COSSAC /3182/Geo. notes on conversation with Maj-Gen Barker, August 5, 1943, RG 331, box 210, NARA, I.

37. Morgan, COSSAC /3182/Geo. notes, I.

38. For Marshall's questions to Barker, see Joint Chiefs of Staff, 100th meeting: minutes of meeting held in room 240, Combined Chiefs of Staff Building, August 6, 1943, at 1200, RG 165, entry 334, box 184, NARA, 4–5, and Matloff, *Strategic Planning for Coalition Warfare*, 173–74.

39. Joint Chiefs of Staff, 100th meeting, 6.

40. Joint Chiefs of Staff, *Strategic Studies and Outline Plans, Book I*, Map Room files, box 27, FDRL, I.

41. Coakley and Leighton, *Global Logistics and Strategy, 1943–1945*, 181.

42. "Estimate of the Enemy Situation, 1943–1944 European Area," July 30, 1943, I in Joint Chiefs of Staff, *Strategic Studies and Outline Plans, Book I*.

43. Joint Chiefs of Staff, Quadrant Information Bulletin, no. 1, August 5, 1943, RG 165, box 54, NARA.

44. Roberts, *Masters and Commanders,* 392.

45. Harriman and Abel, *Special Envoy,* 221.

46. Maj. Gen. Thomas Handy, USA, "Conduct of the War in Europe," August 8, 1943, RG 165, NARA.

47. Handy, "Conduct of the War in Europe," 10.

48. Handy, "Conduct of the War in Europe," 1–2.

49. Total end-of-month strength for August 1943, in Ruppenthal, *Logistical Support of the Armies,* 1:192.

50. Ruppenthal, *Logistical Support of the Armies,* 1:55–59.

51. Harrison, *Cross-Channel Attack,* 87.

52. Stimson, brief report on certain features of overseas trip, August 4, 1943, Stimson Papers, LOC, 13.

53. Handy, "Conduct of the War in Europe," 3–4.

54. Handy, "Conduct of the War in Europe," 5.

55. Handy, "Conduct of the War in Europe," 5–6.

56. Brooke, *War Diaries,* 438.

14. A Presidential Directive

1. 1. U.S. Secret Service, president's return trip from Birch Island, Ontario, Canada, August 7, 1943, Birch Island file, FDRL.

2. Telephone records 1943, Harry L. Hopkins Collection, box 224, FDRL.

3. Stimson appointment book, RG 107, NARA.

4. Telephone records 1943, Hopkins Collection, box 224, FDRL.

5. Joint Chiefs of Staff, 102nd meeting: Joint Chiefs of Staff supplementary minutes, August 11, 1943, RG 165, box 185, NARA.

6. Joint Chiefs of Staff, CCS 303: Concept for the defeat of the Axis in Europe, August 9, 1943, in Joint Chiefs of Staff, *Strategic Studies and Outline Plans, Book I,* Map Room files, box 27, FDRL; Coakley and Leighton, *Global Logistics and Strategy, 1943–1945,* 181.

7. Cline, *Washington Command Post,* 223, 223n.

8. Coakley and Leighton, *Global Logistics and Strategy, 1943–1945,* 2.

9. Joint Chiefs of Staff, CCS 303: Concept for the Defeat of the Axis in Europe; Coakley and Leighton, *Global Logistics and Strategy 1943–1945,* 3, 9–11.

10. Stimson and Bundy, *On Active Service,* 434–35; Hopkins appointment book 1943, series 3, box 53, folder O, Harry Hopkins Collection, GUL; and Stimson appointment book, RG 107, NARA.

11. Stimson appointment book, RG 107, NARA.

12. White House Usher's Diary, August 9, 1943, FDRL.

13. Matloff, *Strategic Planning for Coalition Warfare, 1943–1945,* 211–12.

14. Gen. George C. Marshall, USA, memorandum for General Handy, August 9, 1943, RG 165, box 59, NARA.

15. Matloff, *Strategic Planning for Coalition Warfare, 1943–1945,* 213, and Joint Chiefs of Staff, 102nd meeting: minutes of meeting held in Room 240, the Combined Chiefs of Staff Building, August 9, 1943, at 1130, RG 165, box 185, NARA, 5–6.

16. Maj. Gen. Thomas Handy, USA, memorandum for the Chief of Staff: movement of additional divisions to the Mediterranean, August 9, 1943, RG 165, NARA.

17. Stimson appointment book, RG 107, NARA.

18. Stimson, "Observations," 80–81.

19. Hopkins appointment book 1943.

20. Vannevar Bush to Roosevelt, August 7, 1943, Atomic Energy Commission, Annexes to the Diplomatic History of the Manhattan Project, RG 374, microfilm roll 12, NARA, Annex 17.

21. Roberts, *Masters and Commanders*, 392.

22. Harriman and Abel, *Special Envoy*, 222

23. White House Usher's Diary, August 9, 1943, FDRL.

24. Stimson, "Observations," 81. Built in 1801 and modified by the succession of public figures who lived there, Woodley survives as the library and administrative office of Maret International School. Kilborne, *Images of America: Woodley and Its Residents*, 121.

25. Stimson and Bundy, *On Active Service in Peace and War*, 435, and Stimson, "Observations," 81.

26. Stimson, "Dear Mr. President," August 10, 1943, 2, found in Stimson, "Observations," 80–90.

27. Stimson and Bundy, *On Active Service in Peace and War*, 435, and Stimson appointment book, August 10, 1943, RG 107, NARA.

28. Maj. Gen. Thomas Handy, USA, memorandum for the Chief of Staff: movement of additional divisions to the Mediterranean, August 9, 1943, RG 165, NARA.

29. Matloff, *Strategic Planning for Coalition Warfare, 1943–1945*, 213.

30. Joint Chiefs of Staff, Quadrant Information Bulletin, no. 1, August 5, 1943, RG 165, box 54, NARA.

31. Joint Chiefs of Staff, 103rd meeting: minutes of meeting held in room 240, Combined Chiefs of Staff Building, August 10, 1943, at 1200, RG 165, box 185, NARA, 1–2.

32. Stimson and Bundy, *On Active Service in Peace and War*, 435.

33. Stimson, "Observations,"83.

34. Stimson, "Observations,"83, 84. In his memoir, published almost thirty years before U.S. declassification of the 1943 Anglo-American secret agreement on atomic research and policy, Stimson made no other mention of the atomic negotiation.

35. Stimson, "Observations," 84.

36. Stimson and Bundy, *On Active Service in Peace and War*, 438, and White House Usher's Diary, August 10, 1943, FDRL.

37. Coakley and Leighton, *Global Logistics and Strategy, 1943–1945*, 185.

38. Larrabee, *Commander in Chief*, 187, and Stimson and Bundy, *On Active Service in Peace and War*, 439.

39. Wedemeyer, *Wedemeyer Reports!* 242.

40. Quoted in Stimson and Bundy, *On Active Service in Peace and War*, 439.

41. Joint Chiefs of Staff, Quadrant Information Bulletin, no. 1, August 5, 1943, RG 165, box 54, NARA.

42. Roberts, *Masters and Commanders*, 392.

43. Gen. George C. Marshall, USA, memorandum for the president: divisions for Overlord on May 1, 1944, August 11, 1943, RG 165, box 54, NARA.

44. Operations Division, wdgs, outgoing message no. 4751, Commanding General Freedom, Algiers, August 11, 1943, RG 165, box 54, NARA.

15. Blenheim on the Hudson

1. William Lyon Mackenzie King, memorandum of conversation Mr. Mackenzie King had with Mr. Winston Churchill, Quebec City, August 10, 1943, LAC, http://www.bac-lac.gc.ca/eng/discover/politics-government /prime-ministers/william-lyon-mackenzie-king/Pages/diaries-william-lyon -mackenzie-king.aspx, 1318–26.

2. Mackenzie King, "Memorandum of Conversation," 1318.

3. Mackenzie King, "Memorandum of Conversation," 1318–19.

4. Mackenzie King, "Memorandum of Conversation," 1319, 1321.

5. Mackenzie King, "Memorandum of Conversation," 1320.

6. Mackenzie King, "Memorandum of Conversation," 1321–22.

7. Bush to Anderson, and Anderson to Bush re: draft articles of agreement, August 6, 1943, PREM 3/139/8A, NA, 1.

8. Anderson, "Tube Alloys," August 10, 1943, PREM 3/139/8A, NA, 1.

9. John M. Martin, "Welfare 51 NOCOP," cypher telegram to Lord Cherwell, August 11, 1943, PREM 3/139/8A, NA.

10. Gowing, *Britain and Atomic Energy*, 192–93, 196–97.

11. Mackenzie King, "Memorandum of Conversation,"1322.

12. Mackenzie King, "Memorandum of Conversation,"1325.

13. Mackenzie King, "Memorandum of Conversation," 1322, 1324.

14. Mackenzie King, "Memorandum of Conversation," 1323–24.

15. Churchill's doctor, Lord Moran, recorded that Mackenzie King shared with him this observation of Churchill. Quoted from Lord Moran's papers in Hamilton, *The Mantle of Command*, 122.

16. Mackenzie King, "Memorandum of Conversation,"1325–26.

17. Mackenzie King, "Memorandum of Conversation," 1326. According to Dr. Marc Milner, Mackenzie King was correct that, by the summer of 1943, the Royal Canadian Navy was providing at least 40 percent if not more of the transatlantic convoy escorts. E-mail correspondence by the author with Dr. Marc Milner, director, Gregg Centre, University of New Brunswick, February 11, 2015.

18. Mackenzie King, "Memorandum of Conversation,"1326.

19. Guy H. Spaman, "Train from A to H.P.," August 11, 1943, Birch Island file, FDRL; *FRUS: Conferences at Washington and Quebec 1943*, 412

20. Ward, *Closest Companion*, 228.

21. This was the only painting that Churchill made during the war. Moran, *Churchill at War*, 100.

22. Ward, *Closest Companion*, 229.

23. Churchill, "My dear Mr. President," August 15, 1943, PREM 3/139/8A, NA.

24. Churchill, note to Roosevelt, August 13, 1943, President's Secretary's File, Diplomatic, box 37, Great Britain–Churchill, Winston 1942–1943, FDRL, 84–85.

25. *FRUS: Conferences at Washington and Quebec 1943*, 412.

26. Goodwin, *No Ordinary Time*, 457.

27. Jackson and Bramall, *The Chiefs*, 256.

28. Villa, *Unauthorized Action*, 252–53.

29. *FRUS: General; the British Commonwealth; the Far East 1942*, 1:533–36.

30. *FRUS: Diplomatic Papers 1944: General Economic and Social Matters*, 533–35.

31. Gowing, *Britain and Atomic Energy*, 16.

32. Churchill, *Closing the Ring*, 82; Goodwin, *No Ordinary Time*, 457.

33. Ward, *Closest Companion*, 230.

34. Goodwin, *No Ordinary Time*, 457; Harriman and Abel, *Special Envoy*, 222.

35. For a later example of Churchill's view, see Eden, *Memoirs*, 491.

36. John M. Martin to Churchill re: outcome of Tube Alloys conversation with Roosevelt, August 14, 1943, PREM 3/139/8A, NA.

37. Churchill, "My dear Mr. President," August 15, 1943, PREM 3/139/8A, NA.

38. Churchill, direction to show his letter to Roosevelt of August 15 to the Chiefs of Staff Committee, August 15, 1943, PREM 3/139/8A, NA.

16. Overlord Reaffirmed in Quebec

1. Chiefs of Staff Committee, COS (Q) 7th meeting: August 11, 1943, in Chiefs of Staff Committee, COS (43) 471 (O) Part B Quadrant Record of Chiefs of Staff meetings held on board ss *Queen Mary* and in Quebec August 1943, September 11, 1943, CAB 99/23, NA, 199.

2. Gen. George C. Marshall, USA, memorandum for the president: divisions for Overlord on May 1, 1944, August 11, 1943, RG 165, box 54, NARA.

3. Marshall, USA, message 4751 to General Eisenhower, Algiers, August 11, 1943, RG 165, box 54, NARA.

4. Joint Chiefs of Staff, Quadrant Information Bulletin, no. 1, August 5, 1943, RG 165, box 54, NARA.

5. Overy, *Bombers and the Bombed*, 148.

6. Gen. Dwight D. Eisenhower, USA, incoming message no. 7205 for Marshall eyes only, August 13, 1943, RG 165, box 54, NARA, 1–2.

7. Eisenhower, incoming message no. 7205, 1.

8. Joint Chiefs of Staff, Quadrant Information Bulletin, no. 1.

9. COS (Q) 10th meeting: minutes, August 13, 1943, in Chiefs of Staff Committee, COS (43) 471 (O) Part B 'Quadrant' Record of Chiefs of Staff Meetings Held on Board ss *Queen Mary* and in Quebec August 1943, September 11, 1943, CAB 99/23, NA, 32.

10. COS (Q) 10th meeting: minutes, August 13, 1943, 33.

11. COS (Q) 10th Meeting: Minutes, August 13, 1943, 33.

12. Combined Chiefs of Staff (Quadrant), CCS 106th meeting: minutes of meeting held in room 2208, Chateau Frontenac Hotel on Saturday, August 14, 1943, at 1030, RG 165, entry 334, section 5, box 182, NARA.

13. C.C.S. 107th meeting: minutes of meeting, August 14, 1943, in Office of

the Combined Chiefs, Quadrant Conference August 1943: papers and minutes of meetings, August 1943, Map Room Papers, series 1, box 27, FDRL, 423–29.

14. COS (Q) 12th meeting: minutes, August 15, in Chiefs of Staff Committee, COS (43) 471 (O) Part B 'Quadrant' record of Chiefs of Staff meetings held on board ss *Queen Mary* and in Quebec August 1943, September 11, 1943, CAB 99/23, NA, 135–36.

15. Brooke, *War Diaries*, 441–42.

16. Combined Chiefs of Staff (Quadrant), CCS 108th meeting: minutes of meeting held in room 2208, Chateau Frontenac Hotel on Sunday, August 15, 1943, at 1300, RG 165, entry 334, box 182, NARA, 2, 3.

17. Combined Chiefs of Staff (Quadrant), CCS 108th meeting: minutes, 4.

18. Combined Chiefs of Staff (Quadrant), CCS 108th meeting: minutes, 15 August 1943, 4–5.

19. Combined Chiefs of Staff (Quadrant), CCS 108th meeting: minutes, 6.

20. Joint Chiefs of Staff, 104th meeting: minutes of meeting held in room 2104, Chateau Frontenac Hotel, August 15, 1943 at 1700, RG 165, box 185, NARA, 2.

21. Joint Chiefs of Staff, 104th meeting: minutes, 5.

22. Joint Chiefs of Staff, 105th meeting: minutes of meeting held in room 2104, Chateau Frontenac Hotel, August 16, 1943 at 1000, RG 165, entry 334, section 5, box 185, NARA, 1–2.

23. Joint Chiefs of Staff, 105th meeting: minutes, 3.

24. Joint Chiefs of Staff, Annex B, 105th meeting: minutes of meeting held in room 2104, Chateau Frontenac Hotel, August 16, 1943, at 1000, RG 165, entry 334, section 5, box 185, NARA, 1943, 11.

25. Joint Chiefs of Staff, Annex A, 105th meeting: minutes, 10.

26. G.O. Jr., memorandum for General Hull, August 16, 1943, RG 165, NARA.

27. Joint Chiefs of Staff, CCS 303/1: "Combined Chiefs of Staff: Strategic Concept for the Defeat of the Axis in Europe: Memorandum Submitted by the U.S. Joint Chiefs of Staff, August 16, 1943," RG 319, box 15, NARA.

28. Combined Chiefs of Staff, CCS 303/2: Strategic Concept for the Defeat of the Axis in Europe, August 16, 1943, copy no. 4, RG 165, NARA; Brigadier Sir Edward Ian Jacobs to Churchill re: state of CCS discussion of European strategy, August 16, 1943, PREM 3/333/15, NA, 1.

29. Brooke, *War Diaries*, 443.

30. Combined Chiefs of Staff (Quadrant), CCS 109th meeting: minutes of meeting held in room 2208, Chateau Frontenac Hotel on Monday, August 16, 1943, at 1430, RG 165, entry 334, section 5, box 182, NARA, 1.

31. Gen. Ian Jacobs to Churchill, re: state of CCS discussion of European strategy, August 16, 1943, PREM 3/333/15, NA, 1.

32. Combined Chiefs of Staff, CCS 303/2: Strategic Concept for the Defeat of the Axis in Europe.

33. Secret Service, Trips of the President, 1939–1945: Quebec Conference, August 1943, FDRL.

34. Pogue, *Marshall: Organizer of Victory*, 245, 634n15.

35. Pogue, *Marshall: Organizer of Victory*, 248.

36. Overy, *Bombers and the Bombed,* 150–51.

37. Brooke, *War Diaries,* 443.

38. Combined Chiefs of Staff, CCS 110th meeting Quadrant Conference, minutes, August 17 at 1430, in Office of the Combined Chiefs, Quadrant Conference August 1943: papers and minutes of meetings, August 1943, Map Room Papers, series I, box 27, FDRL, 446.

39. Combined Chiefs of Staff, CCS 303/3: Strategic Concept for the Defeat of the Axis in Europe, August 17, 1943, RG 165, NARA.

40. Roosevelt Day by Day, August 17, 1943, FDRL, http://www.fdrlibrary.marist.edu/daybyday/.

41. Lt. Gen. Sir Hastings Ismay, note to the prime minister, August 18, 1943, PREM 3/333/15, NA.

42. COS (Q) 33: "The Standstill Order in the Mediterranean," August 18, 1943, in Chiefs of Staff Committee, COS (43) 471 (O) Part B 'Quadrant' record of Chiefs of Staff meetings held on board SS *Queen Mary* and in Quebec August 1943, September 11, 1943, CAB 99/23, NA, 140.

43. Brooke based that on "something the PM had said to Stimson" during the U.S. Secretary of War's visit to London. See Roberts, *Masters and Commanders,* 409.

44. Roosevelt Day by Day, August 17, 1943, FDRL

45. Combined Chiefs of Staff (Quadrant), CCS 111th meeting: minutes of meeting held in room 2208, Chateau Frontenac Hotel on Wednesday, August 18, 1943, at 1500, RG 165, entry 334, box 182, NARA.

46. Roberts, *Masters and Commanders,* 405. Habbakuk is a prophet in the Hebrew Bible and Christian Old Testament. Within God's response to Habbakuk's complaint that the deity was ignoring destruction and violence is this: "Look at the nations and see! Be astonished! Be astounded! For a work is being done in your days that you would not believe if you were told." Rev. Emily Guthrie in email correspondence with author, March 10, 2017.

47. Brooke, *War Diaries,* 445–46.

48. See Combined Chiefs of Staff, CCS 319: Combined Chiefs of Staff progress report to the president and prime minister, August 19, 1943, Map Room files, box 169, FDRL.

49. Chief William Rigdon, USN, log of the president's visit to Canada, August 16–26, 1943, September 1943, George Elsey Papers, item 6, FDRL, 8.

50. Rigdon, log of the president's visit to Canada, August 16–26, 1943, 8.

51. Ruane, *Churchill and the Bomb,* 62–63.

52. John M. Martin to Adm. Wilson Brown, USN, conveying copy of the Roosevelt-Churchill "Articles of Agreement," August 19, 1943, PREM 3/139/8A, NA.

53. Rigdon, log of the president's visit to Canada, August 16–26, 1943, 9.

54. CCS 113th meeting Quadrant Conference minutes, August 20, 1943, in Office of the Combined Chiefs, Quadrant Conference, August 1943: Papers and Minutes of Meetings, August 1943, Map Room Papers, series I; box 27, FDRL, 465–73, 472.

55. Roosevelt and Churchill, "Secret and Personal to Marshal Stalin," August 21, 1943, Yale Law School, http://avalon.law.yale.edu/wwii/q004.asp.

56. Combined Chiefs of Staff, CCS 114th meeting Quadrant Conference minutes, August 21, 1943, in Office of the Combined Chiefs, Quadrant Conference, August 1943: papers and minutes of meetings, August 1943, Map Room Papers, series 1, box 27, FDRL, 475–77.

57. Overy, *Bombers and the Bombed*, 148, 262, 152–53

58. Combined Chiefs of Staff, 2nd meeting of the president and prime minister with the Combined Chiefs of Staff, August 23, 1

59. Combined Chiefs of Staff, 2nd meeting.

60. Combined Chiefs of Staff, 2nd meeting.

61. Combined Chiefs of Staff (Quadrant), CCS 116th meeting: minutes, August 24, 1943.

62. Mackenzie King, "Memorandum of Conversation," 2584.

17. Bolero Unleashed

1. Ruppenthal, *Logistical Support of the Armies*, 1:129, table 3.

2. Gen. Sir Thomas Riddell-Webster, QMG, minute to the secretary of state for war, Sir P. J. Grigg, on the rate of accepting U.S. troops, January 1, 1943, PREM 3/454/3, NA, 1–2, and Sir Findlater Stewart, "Bolero" Movement and "Overlord," August 11, 1943, CAB 21/1503, NA.

3. Harrison, *Cross-Channel Attack*, 65.

4. Gen. Dwight D. Eisenhower, USA, incoming message no. 7205 for Marshall eyes only, August 13, 1943, RG 165, box 54, NARA.

5. British Chiefs of Staff, CCS 286: Formation by U.S. assault forces for Operation 'Overlord' memorandum by the representatives of the British Chiefs of Staff, July 20, 1943, RG 319, file 14, NA.

6. Morison, *The Battle of the Atlantic*, 205, and Leighton and Coakley, *Global Logistics and Strategy, 1940–1943*, 624.

7. Harrison, *Cross-Channel Attack*, 63, and Leighton and Coakley, *Global Logistics and Strategy, 1940–1943*, 683.

8. Memorandum from Rear Adm. W. S. Farber, Fleet Maintenance Division, to Vice Admiral Horne, quoted in Harrison, *Cross-Channel Attack*, 63.

9. Army Service Force, Transportation Corps, outgoing message no. 8Q, RG 165, entry 422, box 29, NARA.

10. Historical Sub-Section, Office of Secretary, General Staff, *History of COSSAC (Chief of Staff to Supreme Allied Commander) 1943–1944*, file 8–3.6. CA, ACMH, www.history.army.mil/documents/cossac/Cossac.htm, 32–33.

11. Harrison, *Cross-Channel Attack*, 64, referencing an April 26, 1944, memorandum from Assistant Secretary of War John J. McCloy to General Marshall quoting Churchill.

12. Gen. George C. Marshall, USA, memorandum for the president: divisions for Overlord on May 1, 1944, August 11, 1943, RG 165, box 54, NARA, 1–2, and Combined Chiefs of Staff, CCS 319/4: Combined Chiefs of Staff Final Report to the President and Prime Minister, August 23, 1943, RG 107, entry 104, box 277, NARA, 251.

13. See Offley, *Turning the Tide*, 281–335, 364.

14. Kahn, *Hitler's Spies*, 221–22.

15. Allied Anti-Submarine Survey Board, "Employment of CVE's in Offensive Action against U-Boats," August 27, 1943, CCS 335, RG 319, box 18, NARA, 1–2.

16. Combined Chiefs of Staff (Quadrant), CCS 111th meeting: minutes of meeting held in room 2208, Chateau Frontenac Hotel on Wednesday, August 18, 1943, at 1500, RG 165, entry 334, box 182, NARA, 4.

17. Offley, *Turning the Tide*, 229, 284, and Headquarters of the Commander in Chief, United States Fleet and Commander Tenth Fleet, "History of Convoy and Routing, 1939–1945," Navy Department, RG 38, NARA, 2.

18. Combined Chiefs of Staff, CCS 338: Report on recent and prospective developments in anti-submarine operations since Quadrant: memorandum from the United States Chiefs of Staff, November 18, 1943, RG 319, box 20, NARA, 1.

19. Lt. Charles Dillon, USNR, Narrative, USS *Bogue*, September 23, 1943, RG 38, entry 11 170/65/20/1–5, box 7, NARA, 2, 8

20. Combined Chiefs of Staff, CCS 338: Report on recent and prospective developments in anti-submarine operations since Quadrant, 1.

21. Chiefs of Staff Committee, COS (43) 130th meeting: minutes of meeting held on Wednesday, August 18, 1943, at 10:30 a.m., CAB 79/27, NA, 1.

22. Leighton and Coakley, *Global Logistics and Strategy, 1940–1943*, 678.

23. Bell, *Churchill & Sea Power*, 276–77.

24. Calculated from Symonds, *Neptune*, 139.

25. For an account of the dispute, see "The Pressure for Economy in Ship Operations" in Leighton and Coakley, *Global Logistics and Strategy, 1940–1943*, 616–23.

26. Leighton and Coakley; *Global Logistics and Strategy, 1940–1943*, 612.

27. Ruppenthal, *Logistical Support of the Armies*, 1:121.

28. Ross and Romanus, *The Quartermaster Corps: Operations in the War against Germany*, 317.

29. Ruppenthal, *Logistical Support of the Armies*, 1:136.

30. Ruppenthal, *Logistical Support of the Armies*, 1:132–34.

31. Ruppenthal, *Logistical Support of the Armies*, 1:137–9.

32. U.S. Delegation, Quebec, Message no. 32-W-17, Action: General Somervell, August 16, 1943, RG 165, box 54, NARA.

33. Morison, *Atlantic Battle Won*, 133, and Headquarters of the Commander-in-Chief, United States Fleet and Commander Tenth Fleet, "History of Convoy and Routing, 1939–1945," Navy Department, RG 38, NARA, 47–48.

34. Author's conversation in 2013 with Madge Darneille, Kensington, Maryland. Mrs. Darneille, as a Royal Navy civilian employee, crossed the Atlantic westward in the *Queen Elizabeth* to reach her wartime assignment at the Admiralty Mission in Washington.

35. Ruppenthal, *Logistical Support of the Armies*, 1:234.

36. Capt. Paul P. Blackburn, USN (Ret.), Comment re Convoy UT-1, September 16, 1943, RG 38, file 370, box 162, NARA, 1.

37. Blackburn, Comment re Convoy UT-1, Second Endorsement, September 16, 1943, 2.

38. Blackburn, Report of Convoy UT-1, September 6, 1943, RG 38, file 370, box 162, NARA, 1.

39. UT Convoy Reports, RG 38, file 370, boxes 162–63, NARA; Headquarters of the Commander-in-Chief, United States Fleet and Commander Tenth Fleet, "History of Convoy and Routing, 1939–1945," Navy Department, RG 38, NARA, 48.

40. Headquarters of the Commander-in-Chief, United States Fleet and Commander Tenth Fleet, "History of Convoy and Routing, 1939–1945," 48.

41. Royal Navy, Atlantic Convoy instructions, quoted in Offley, *Turning the Tide*, 309.

42. Bolero-Sickle Combined Committee, UK troop movements (tentative schedule), July 7, 1943, RG 165, box 203, NARA, 1.

43. Morison, *Atlantic Battle Won*, 115

44. Morison, *Atlantic Battle Won*, 230–31.

45. Morison, *Atlantic Battle Won*, 230.

46. Average time calculated from departures and arrivals reported in twelve UT convoy reports, RG 38, file 370, boxes 162–63, NARA.

47. Commander Task Force 60, CTF 60 Reports to COMNAVEU, naval message, January 7, 1944, RG 38, file 370, box 163, NARA.

48. Author's discussion with Capt. Lee Moss, USN (Ret.), former attack submarine commander, March 24, 2013.

49. British Chiefs of Staff, CCS 399/1 (SEXTANT): Memorandum: progress report on the U-boat war—September–October 1943, November 23, 1943, RG 319, file 20, NARA, 2.

50. Morrison, *Atlantic Battle Won*, 138–46.

51. Offley, *Turning the Tide*, 378.

52. Admiralty, Message 301621A: Appreciation of the present situation in the North Atlantic, September 30, 1943, AIR 8/1399, NA.

53. British Chiefs of Staff, CCS 399/1 (SEXTANT), 5.

54. Jordan, *World's Merchant Fleets, 1939*, 110.

55. British Chiefs of Staff, CCS 246: movement of the *Queens*, 23 May 1943, RG 319, NARA, 1.

56. Combined Chiefs of Staff, (Trident): CCS 94th Minutes of Meeting Held in the Board of Governors Room, Federal Reserve Building on Sunday, 23 May 1943, at 1400, RG 107, entry 104, box 277, NARA, 2, and Combined Chiefs of Staff, (Trident): CCS 93rd meeting: minutes of meeting held in the Board of Governors Room, Federal Reserve Building, on Saturday, May 22, 1943, at 1030, RG 107, entry 104, box 277, NARA, 2.

57. Commander Task Force 69, "Early Arrival of UT Convoys," November 1, 1943, RG 38, file 370, box 163, NARA.

58. Rear Adm. Henry D. Cooke, USN, Convoy Form D: Mercantile Convoy no. UT-10, Annex B, n.d., RG 38, file 370, box 163, NARA.

18. Sealing the Quebec Decisions

1. Goodwin, *No Ordinary Time*, 137.

2. Wallace A. Akers, "Tube Alloy Project: Negotiations with the Ameri-

cans after the Signing of the Quebec Agreement," September 13, 1943, CAB 126/164, NA, 1.

3. Vannevar Bush to Dr. James Conant," August 23, 1943, Records of the Office of Scientific Research and Development, Conant's Personal Files, RG 227, M1392, file 10, NARA.

4. Akers, "Tube Alloy Project," 1.

5. Akers, "Tube Alloy Project," 1.

6. Groves, *Now It Can Be Told,* 135–36.

7. Bush to Conant, August 23, 1943.

8. Akers, "Tube Alloy Project," 1.

9. Bush to Conant, September 2, 1943, Records of the Office of Scientific Research and Development, Conant's Personal Files, RG 227, M1392, file 10, NARA, 2.

10. Akers, "Tube Alloy Project," 1.

11. Akers, "Tube Alloy Project," 1.

12. Harvey Bundy, minutes of informal meeting, September 8, 1943, Records of the Office of Scientific Research and Development, Conant's Personal Files, RG 227, M1392, file 10, NARA.

13. Brig. Gen. Leslie R. Groves, USA, extract minutes of the meeting of the Military Policy Committee, September 9, 1943, Records of the Office of Scientific Research and Development, James B. Conant's Personal Files, RG 227, M1392, file 10, NARA.

14. James B. Conant, memorandum re: progress of the work on interchange with the British on the S-1 project, September 15, 1943, Records of the Office of Scientific Research and Development, Conant's Personal Files, RG 227, M1392, file 33A T-3, NARA.

15. Villa, *Unauthorized Action,* 243.

16. Roll, *Hopkins Touch,* 297.

17. Churchill to Field Marshal Dill, October 24, 1943, RG 165, entry 422, box 29, NARA.

18. Marshall to Eisenhower, message 4751, Algiers, August 11, 1943, RG 165, box 54, NARA.

19. *FRUS: Conferences at Cairo and Tehran 1943,* 34.

20. FX3714, Convoy: UT-2, September 5, 1943, and Convoy: UT-3, October 17, 1943, RG 38, file 370, box 162, NARA.

21. Ruppenthal, *Logistical Support of the Armies,* 1:232, table 5.

22. Col. Harold P. Tasker, USA, "Buildup of U.S. Divisions in the United Kingdom," October 12, 1943, RG165, entry 421, box 362, NARA.

23. Tasker, "Buildup of U.S. Divisions in the United Kingdom"

24. Ruppenthal, *Logistical Support of the Armies,* 1:232.

25. *FRUS: Conferences at Cairo and Tehran 1943,* 37–38.

26. *FRUS: Conferences at Cairo and Tehran 1943,* 38–39.

27. Churchill to Field Marshal Dill," October 24, 1943.

28. Gen. George C. Marshall, USA, memorandum for the president: subject: conduct of the European war, November 8, 1943, RG 165, (NM-84) box 362, NARA, 2–3.

29. Stoler, *Allies and Adversaries*, 176.

30. FRUS: *Conferences at Cairo and Tehran 1943*, 39–40.

31. FRUS: *Conferences at Cairo and Tehran 1943*, 41.

32. Eubank, *Summit at Teheran*, 103.

33. FRUS: *Conferences at Cairo and Tehran 1943*, 7, 47–48.

34. COMNAVNAW (Naval Intelligence Unit), "Enemy Air Attack on Peacock," Office of Chief of Naval Operations, November 22, 1943, RG 38, file 370, box 163, NARA, 1–3.

35. Parrish, *Roosevelt and Marshall*, 374–75.

36. Roll, *Hopkins Touch*, 301.

37. Roll, *Hopkins Touch*, 301.

38. Stoler, *Allies and Adversaries*, 159.

39. For the record of their discussion, see Joint Chiefs of Staff, "Minutes of Meeting: Between the President and the Chiefs of Staff, held on board ship in the Admiral's Cabin, on Friday, 19 November 1943, at 1500," RG 165, entry, NM-84, box 7, NARA, 9–13,

40. Stoler, *Allies and Adversaries*, 160.

41. Joint Chiefs of Staff, minutes of meeting: between the president and the chiefs of staff, held on board ship in the admiral's cabin, on Friday, 19 November 1943, at 1500, RG 165, entry, NM-84, box 7, NARA, 2–4.

42. Joint Chiefs of Staff, minutes of meeting: between the president and the chiefs of staff, held on board ship in the president's cabin, on Monday, 15 November 1943, at 1400, RG 165, entry, NM-84, box 7, NARA, 5, 3.

43. Casey, *Cautious Crusade*, 134, and Committee of Historians for the Commanding General of the Army Air Forces, "Germany's War Potential: An Appraisal," December 27, 1943, Henry H. Arnold Papers, Special Reports reel 193; Manuscript Division, LOC, 2.

44. Air Ministry Intelligence and Political Warfare Executive, "Allied Air Attacks and German Morale–IV," November 7, 1943, in Air Ministry, Combined Bomber Offensive progress report, November 1943, AIR 8/116/7, NA, 8.

45. Air Ministry, Combined Bomber Offensive progress report, ii.

46. Air Ministry, Combined Bomber Offensive progress report, 9, and chart "Distribution of German Air Force Fighters."

47. Capt. Forrest B. Royal, USN, Memorandum for the record, November 9, 1943, RG 218, box 306, CDF HM 1944, NARA, 1–3.

48. "Appendix A: Memorandum from the United States Chiefs of Staff," in OPD Strategy Section, "SS 133/5: United States Courses of Action in the Case Sextant Decisions Do Not Guarantee Overlord," November 12, 1943, RG 165, entry 421, box 363, NARA.

49. Lt. E. D. H. Johnson, USN, "USS *Iowa*: Trip to Oran with President Roosevelt, June 5, 1945," RG 38, entry 11 170/65/20/1–5, box 14, NARA, 3; J.C.S., "Memorandum (Ship) Number 3 Disembarkation and Plane Transportation; November 14, 1943," Map Room Papers, Naval Aide's file A16, box 170; FDRL, 1–2.

50. Stoler, *Allies and Adversaries*, 166–67.

51. *FRUS, Conferences at Cairo and Tehran,* 330.

52. *FRUS: Conferences at Cairo and Tehran,* 330–34.

53. *FRUS: Conferences at Cairo and Tehran,* 331.

54. *FRUS: Conferences at Cairo and Tehran,* 331.

55. *FRUS: Conferences at Cairo and Tehran,* 334.

56. Churchill, *Closing the Ring,* 342–43.

57. Reilly, *Reilly of the White House,* 178–79.

58. Reilly, *Reilly of the White House,* 175–77.

59. Harriman and Abel, *Special Envoy,* 264–65.

60. Moran, *Churchill at War,* 172–73, and Roberts, *Masters and Commanders,* 444–45.

61. Chester Bohlen, "Minutes" in *FRUS, Conferences at Cairo and Tehran 1943,* 539.

62. Referring to the declarations of the just-ended Moscow Foreign Ministers Conference, Chester Bohlen, minutes in *FRUS, Conferences at Cairo and Tehran 1943,* 538–39.

63. Leahy, *I Was There,* 208.

64. Combined Chiefs of Staff, minutes in *FRUS, Conferences at Cairo and Tehran 1943,* 541, 548.

65. Roll, *Hopkins Touch,* 323.

66. Combined Chiefs of Staff, minutes in *FRUS, Conferences at Cairo and Tehran 1943,* 579.

67. Sherwood, *Roosevelt and Hopkins,* 803.

68. Pogue, *Marshall: Organizer of Victory,* 321.

69. Joint Chiefs of Staff, minutes of meeting: between the president and the Chiefs of Staff, held on board ship in the admiral's cabin, on Friday, 19 November 1943, at 1500, RG 165, entry, NM-84, box 7, NARA, 1.

70. Pogue, *Marshall: Organizer of Victory,* 320.

71. Marshall's account in Sherwood, *Roosevelt and Hopkins,* 803.

72. Roosevelt to Marshal Stalin re: Overlord commander, December 6, 1943, RG 165 (NM-84), box 59, NARA.

73. Ruppenthal, *Logistical Support of the Armies,* 1:232, table 5.

74. Col. Harold P. Tasker, USA, "Buildup of U.S. Divisions in the United Kingdom," November 20, 1943, RG165, entry 421, box 362, NARA.

75. Ruppenthal, *Logistical Support of the Armies,* 1:45.

76. Klein, *Call to Arms,* 624.

77. White House Usher's Diary, December 19, 1943, FDRL; Klein, *Call to Arms,* 624.

78. Quoted in Klein, *Call to Arms,* 625.

79. Commander Task Force 60, Convoy UT-6, December 30, 1943, RG 38, file 370, box 163; NARA, 1–2.

80. Capt. Ross A. Dierdorff, USN, Convoy Form D: Mercantile Convoy no. UT-7, n.d., RG 38, file 370, box 163, NARA, 1–2.

81. Klein, *Call to Arms,* 625.

82. Klein, *Call to Arms,* 625.

83. CCS 113th meeting Quadrant Conference minutes, August 20, 1943, in Office of the Combined Chiefs, Quadrant Conference, August 1943: Papers and Minutes of Meetings, August 1943, Map Room Papers, series 1, box 27, FDRL, 472.

84. Klein, *Call to Arms*, 624–25.

85. White House Usher's Diary, December 23, 1943, FDRL.

86. Byrnes, *All In One Lifetime*, 200.

87. Klein, *Call to Arms*, 625–6.

88. Byrnes, *All In One Lifetime*, 201.

89. Klein, *Call to Arms*, 626.

90. See, for example, FX3714, Convoy: UT-8, February 23, 1944, and Convoy: UT-9, February 28, 1944, RG 38, file 370, box 163, NARA.

19. Epilogue

1. USS *Texas*, "War Diary," June 1944, RG 38, box 15, NARA, 2–4.

2. Eisenhower, *Crusade in Europe*, 230.

3. Combined Chiefs of Staff, "CCS 465/1: Recommendations of Supreme Commander AEF on 'Overlord' and 'Anvil,'" January 24, 1944, RG 319, box 25, NARA, Enclosure A.

4. Harrison, *Cross-Channel Attack*, map 3.

5. Combined Chiefs of Staff, CCS 465/1: recommendations of supreme commander AEF on 'Overlord' and 'Anvil,' January 24, 1944, RG 319, box 25, NARA, 3–4.

6. Combined Chiefs of Staff, CCS 465/1: Recommendations, 2.

7. Mitcham, *Rommel's Last Battle*, 3–4.

8. Ambrose, *D-Day*, 61.

9. Mitcham, *Rommel's Last Battle*, 21–24.

10. Milner, *Stopping the Panzers*, 66–67, 89.

11. Ambrose, *D-Day*, 64, 114.

12. Mitcham, *Rommel's Last Battle*, 9.

13. Milner, *Stopping the Panzers*, 89.

14. Ambrose, *D-Day*, 278–79.

15. Today the American Military Cemetery is located on this escarpment where, with the wind whispering through stately pines, there is a poignant view down to Omaha Beach.

16. Lieutenant Elsey's firsthand experiences, on-scene interviews, and two trunks of documents and maps became the foundation for a significant part of Morison's volume covering Overlord. See Morison, *The Invasion of France and Germany, 1944–1945*.

17. Elsey, *An Unplanned Life*, 54–55.

18. Lt. Col. Edward M. Knoff Jr., USA, interview with General Thomas T. Handy, ACMH, 48.

19. Eventually Handy and Cooke returned to Portland aboard a destroyer to report to Eisenhower. See Cdr. J. G. Marshall, USN, USS *Doyle* (DD494) deck log, June 8, 1944, RG 24, file 470, box 952, NARA.

20. For examples, see Cdr. R. O. Beer, USN, USS *Carmick* (DD-493) narra-

tive report, June 5–17, 1944, June 23, 1944, RG 38, file 370, box 897, NARA, 3, and Lt. J. L. Semmes, USN, USS *Frankford* (DD497) action report, shore bombardment June 6, 1944, June 24, 1944, RG 38, file 370, box 989, NARA, 2–4.

21. Lt. Cdr. Joseph H. Gibbons, USN, "Naval Combat Demolitions Units in Force 'O,' Normandy Invasion, June 6, 1944," September 27, 1944, RG 38, entry 11 170/65/20/1–5, box 10, NARA, 2.

22. Elsey, *An Unplanned Life*, 57.

23. Milner, *Stopping the Panzers*, 224, 310.

24. Milner, *Stopping the Panzers*, 309–10.

25. Milner, *Stopping the Panzers*, 311–12.

26. Hewlett and Anderson, *The New World, 1939–1946*, 1:317–18.

27. Hewlett and Anderson, *The New World, 1939–1946*, 1:310; Ruane, *Churchill and the Bomb*, 71.

28. Rhodes, *The Making of the Atomic Bomb*, 610–12.

29. Ruane, *Churchill and the Bomb*, 71. Convicted of espionage, Fuchs served a fourteen-year sentence in Britain, after which he emigrated to East Germany.

30. Hewlett and Anderson, *The New World, 1939–1946*, 1:290

31. Ronald I. Campbell to Sir John Anderson, May 31, 1944, PREM 3/139/11A, NA, 3.

32. Ruane, *Churchill and the Bomb*, 79.

33. Rhodes, *The Making of the Atomic Bomb*, 526–27.

34. Lord Cherwell, Tube Alloys, memorandum to the prime minister, September 18, 1944, PREM 3/139/118A, NA.

35. Roosevelt and Churchill, Aide-memoire: Tube Alloys, September 19, 1944, PREM 3/139/11A, NA.

36. Eight months after the signing, Churchill, on May 21, 1945, authorized the British representative on the Coordinating Committee to give a copy to Henry Stimson, noting when he did so that "on this topic, no agreed record appears to exist." See Churchill, "Chancellor of the Exchequer," May 21, 1945, PREM 3/139/11A, NA.

37. Sherwin, *A World Destroyed*, 115.

38. Stimson and Bundy, *On Active Service in Peace and War*, 363.

39. Rhodes, *The Making of the Atomic Bomb*, 617, 623–26.

40. Rhodes, *The Making of the Atomic Bomb*, 626.

41. Groves, *Now It Can Be Told*, 267.

42. Rhodes, *Making of the Atomic Bomb*, 640–41.

43. Rhodes, *The Making of the Atomic Bomb*, 677–78.

44. Churchill, Summarized note of the prime minister's conversation with President Truman at luncheon, July 18, 1945, PREM 3/139/11A, NA.

BIBLIOGRAPHY

Archives and Manuscript Material

ACMH: U.S. Army Center for Military History, Carlisle, Pennsylvania
Thomas T. Handy Papers

BTCC: Bell Telephone Company of Canada, Toronto, Ontario
W.H. Mitchell, "The President Goes Fishing: Whitefish Region Entertains a World Leader," *Blue Bell* 22, no. 9 (September 1943)

CCH: Center for Cryptologic History, Fort Meade, Maryland
David Kahn Collection

CRHA: Canadian Railway History Archives Exporail, Montreal, Quebec
Canadian Pacific Railway Company Fonds

EL: Eisenhower Library, Abilene, Kansas
Oral History Collection

FDRL: Franklin D. Roosevelt Library, Hyde Park, New York
George Elsey Papers
Averill Harriman Papers
Harry Hopkins Collection
Map Room File
President's Safe File
President's Secretary's File, Diplomatic Papers
William Rigdon Papers
Trips of the President Collection
Grace Tully Collection
White House Usher's Diary

GUL: Georgetown University Library, Washington, DC
Harry L. Hopkins Papers

IWM: Imperial War Museum, London
Elspeth Shuter Papers

LAC: Library and Archives Canada, Ottawa, Ontario
William Lyon Mackenzie King. *A Real Companion and Friend: The Diary of William Lyon Mackenzie King, 1893–1950,* http://www.bac-lac.gc.ca/eng /discover/politics-government/prime-ministers/william-lyon-mackenzie -king/Pages/diaries-william-lyon-mackenzie-king.aspx.

LOC: Library of Congress, Washington, DC

Henry H. Arnold Papers

Joseph Edward Davies Papers

Henry L. Stimson Papers

Lt. John Manley to Lt. Ernest Loeb, September 9, 1943, photostatic copy exhibited at Turner's Store, Little Current, Ontario

NA: National Archives, Kew, United Kingdom

Admiralty Correspondence and Papers, Series I: 1938–1945

Air Ministry Combat Records, Second World War Bomber Command, AIR 20/3/180

Cabinet Office and Predecessors, Registered Files (1916–65), statistics relating to the war effort of the United Kingdom, CAB 21/1201

Ministry of Home Defense: Intelligence Branch Registered Files

Prime Minister's Office, Operational Correspondence and Papers (1940–1945)

Records of the Department of Scientific and Industrial Relations, Anglo-American Relations

Tube Alloys Consultative Council and Combined Policy Committee (Atomic Energy) Minutes and Papers: Anglo-Canadian-U.S. discussions of security standards, CAB 126/148

Tube Alloys Consultative Council and Combined Policy Committee (Atomic Energy) Minutes and Papers: Cooperation and Exchange of Information between the U.S. and the UK, CAB 126/163

Tube Alloys Consultative Council and Combined Policy Committee (Atomic Energy) Minutes and Papers: Correspondence with Dr. Vannevar Bush and Mr. Malcolm MacDonald, High Commissioner in Canada, CAB 126/41

Tube Alloys Consultative Council and Combined Policy Committee (Atomic Energy) Minutes and Papers: Estimated Expenses 1943–44, CAB 124/24

Tube Alloys Consultative Council and Combined Policy Committee (Atomic Energy) Minutes and Papers: Negotiations Culminating in the Quebec Agreement, August 1943, and Later Correspondence Relating to the Agreement, CAB 126/164

Tube Alloys Consultative Council and Combined Policy Committee (Atomic Energy) Minutes and Papers: Summary and Observations on General Policy of the TA Projects in Canada and the United Kingdom, CAB 126/147

Tube Alloys Consultative Council and Combined Policy Committee (Atomic Energy) Minutes and Papers: Technical Committee Minutes and Papers, CAB 126/46

War Cabinet and Cabinet: Chiefs of Staff Committee Memoranda, CAB 79/64

War Cabinet and Cabinet: Chiefs of Staff Committee Minutes, CAB 79/64

War Cabinet and Cabinet: Joint Planning Staff Minutes and Memoranda, CAB 84/6

War Cabinet and Cabinet: Record of "Quadrant" Conference, Plenary Meetings and Meetings of the Combined Chiefs of Staff, CAB 99/23

War Cabinet and Cabinet: Record of "Trident" Conference in Washington and North Africa 1943, CAB 99/22

NARA: National Archives and Records Administration, College Park, Maryland

Log Books of U.S. Navy Ships and Stations, 1941–83

Records of the Allied Operational and Occupation Headquarters, World War II

Records of the Army Staff

Records of the Atomic Energy Commission: Annexes to the Diplomatic History of the Manhattan Project

Records of the Office of the Chief of Naval Operations

Records of the Office of Scientific Research and Development

Records of the Office of the Secretary of War

Records of the U.S. Joint Chiefs of Staff

Records of the War Department General and Special Staffs

Yale Law School, New Haven

Roosevelt, Franklin D. and Winston S. Churchill. "Secret and personal to Marshal Stalin from the United States Government and His Majesty's Government in the United Kingdom," August 21, 1943. http://avalon.law.yale.edu/wwii/q004.asp

Published Works

Agarossi, Elena. *A Nation Collapses: The Italian Surrender of September 1943.* Cambridge: Cambridge University Press, 2000.

Ambrose, Stephen E. *D-Day, June 6, 1944: The Climactic Battle of World War II.* New York: Simon & Schuster, 1994.

Atkinson, Rick. *An Army at Dawn: The War in North Africa.* New York: Henry Holt, 2002.

———. *The Day of Battle: The War in Sicily and Italy, 1943–1944.* New York: Henry Holt, 2007.

———. *The Guns at Last Light: The War in Western Europe, 1944–1945.* New York: Henry Holt, 2013.

Beitzell, Robert. *The Uneasy Alliance: America, Britain, and Russia, 1941–1943.* New York: Alfred A. Knopf, 1972.

Bell, Christopher M. *Churchill & Sea Power.* Oxford: Oxford University Press, 2014.

Brooke, Alan. *War Diaries, 1939–1945: Field Marshal Lord Alanbrooke.* Edited by Alex Danchev and Daniel Todman. Berkeley: University of California Press, 2001.

Brown, Anthony Cave. *Bodyguard of Lies.* New York: Harper and Row, 1975.

Buruma, Ian. *Year Zero: A History of 1945.* New York: Penguin Books, 2014.

Bush, Vannevar. *Pieces of the Action.* New York: William Morrow, 1970.

Butcher, Harry C. *My Three Years with Eisenhower.* New York: Simon and Schuster, 1946.

Butler, Susan, ed. *My Dear Mr. Stalin: The Complete Correspondence between*

Franklin D. Roosevelt and Joseph V. Stalin. New Haven: Yale University Press, 2005.

———. *Roosevelt and Stalin: Portrait of a Partnership.* New York: Alfred A. Knopf, 2015.

Byrnes, James F. *All in One Lifetime.* New York: Harper & Brothers, 1958.

Casey, Steven. *Cautious Crusade: American Public Opinion and the War against Nazi Germany.* Oxford: Oxford University Press, 2001.

Churchill, Winston S. *The Second World War.* Vol. 5, *Closing the Ring.* Boston: Houghton Mifflin, 1951.

———. *Never Give In! The Best of Winston Churchill's Speeches.* Compiled and edited by Winston S. Churchill. London: Pimlico, 2003.

Clarke, Peter. *The Last Thousand Days of the British Empire: Churchill Roosevelt and the Birth of Pax Americana.* New York: Bloomsbury Press, 2008.

Cline, Ray S. *Washington Command Post: The Operations Division.* Washington DC: Office of the Chief of Military History, Department of the Army, 1951.

Coakley, Robert W., and Richard M. Leighton. *Global Logistics and Strategy, 1943–1945.* Washington DC: Office of the Chief of Military History, Department of the Army, 1968.

Conant, James B. *My Several Lives: Memoirs of a Social Inventor.* New York: Harper & Row, 1970.

Crane, Conrad C. *American Airpower Strategy in World War II: Bombs, Cities, Civilians, and Oil.* Lawrence: University Press of Kansas, 2016.

Davis, Kenneth S. *FDR: The War President, 1940–1943.* New York: Random House, 2000.

D'Olier, Franklin. *The United States Strategic Bombing Survey.* September 30, 1945. Reprint, Maxwell Air Force Base, AL: Air University Press, 1987.

Doyle, William. *PT 109: An American Epic of War, Survival, and the Destiny of John F. Kennedy.* New York: William Morrow, 2015.

Dyer, Gwynne. *Canada in the Great Power Game, 1914–2014.* Toronto: Random House Canada, 2014.

Eden, Anthony. *The Reckoning: The Memoirs of Anthony Eden, Earl of Avon.* Boston: Houghton Mifflin, 1965.

Eisenhower, Dwight D. *Crusade in Europe.* Garden City: Doubleday & Company. 1952.

Elsey, George McKee. *An Unplanned Life.* Columbia: University of Missouri Press, 2005.

Eubank, Keith. *Summit at Teheran.* New York: William Morrow, 1985.

Farmelo, Graham. *Churchill's Bomb: How the United States Overtook Britain in the First Nuclear Arms Race.* New York: Basic Books, 2013.

Foreign Relations of the United States: Diplomatic Papers, 1944: General Economic and Social Matters. Washington DC: U.S. Department of State, 1967.

Foreign Relations of the United States: General; the British Commonwealth; the Far East 1942. Vol. 1. Washington DC: U.S. Department of State, 1960.

Foreign Relations of the United States: The Conferences at Cairo and Tehran, 1943. Washington DC: U.S. Department of State, 1961.

Foreign Relations of the United States: The Conferences at Washington, 1941–1942, and Casablanca, 1943. Washington DC: U.S. Department of State, 1968.

Foreign Relations of the United States: The Conferences at Washington and Quebec 1943. Washington DC: U.S. Department of State, 1970.

Gallagher, Tim. "Espanola Prisoner of War Camp, 1940–1943." In *Through the Years: Manitoulin District History and Genealogy*, 4–36. Gore Bay ON: Manitoulin Media, Autumn 1996.

Gilbert, Martin. *Winston S. Churchill.* Vol. 7, *Road to Victory, 1941–1945.* New York: Houghton Mifflin, 1986.

Goette, Richard. "Britain and the Delay in Closing the Mid-Atlantic 'Air Gap' during the Battle of the Atlantic." *Northern Mariner/Le Marin du Nord* 15, no. 4 (October 2005): 19–41

Golway, Terry. *Together We Cannot Fail: FDR and the American Presidency in Years of Crisis.* Naperville IL: Sourcebooks MediaFusion, 2009.

Goodwin, Doris Kearns. *No Ordinary Time: Franklin and Eleanor Roosevelt: The Home Front in World War II.* New York: Simon & Schuster, 1994.

Gowing, Margaret. *Britain and Atomic Energy, 1939–1945.* London: Macmillan, 1965.

Groves, Leslie M., General. *Now It Can Be Told: The Story of the Manhattan Project.* New York: Da Capo Press, 1983.

Hamilton, Nigel. *Commander in Chief.* Boston: Houghton Mifflin Harcourt, 2016.

———. *The Mantle of Command: FDR at War, 1941–1942.* Boston: Houghton Mifflin Harcourt, 2014.

Harriman, W. Averill, and Elie Abel. *Special Envoy to Churchill and Stalin, 1941–1946.* New York: Random House, 1975.

Harrison, Gordon A. *Cross-Channel Attack.* Washington DC: Office of the Chief of Military History, Department of the Army, 1951.

Hassett, William D. *Off the Record with FDR, 1942–1945.* New Brunswick NJ: Rutgers University Press, 1958.

Hewlett, Richard G., and Oscar E. Anderson Jr. *The New World, 1939–1946.* Vol. 1, *A History of the United States Atomic Energy Commission.* University Park: Pennsylvania State University Press, 1962.

Holmes, Richard. *Churchill's Bunker: The Cabinet War Rooms and the Culture of Secrecy in Wartime London.* New Haven: Yale University Press, 2009.

Jackson, Sir William, General, and Field Marshal Lord Bramall. *The Chiefs: The Story of the United Kingdom Chiefs of Staff.* London: Brassey's, 1992.

Jones, Reginald V. *The Wizard War: British Scientific Intelligence, 1939–1945.* New York: Coward, McCann & Geoghegan, 1978.

Jordan, Roger W. *World's Merchant Fleets, 1939: The Particulars and Wartime Fates of 6,000 Ships.* Annapolis MD: Naval Institute Press, 2006.

Kahn, David. *The Codebreakers.* Rev. ed. New York: Scribner, 1996.

———. *Hitler's Spies: German Military Intelligence in World War II.* New York: Macmillan, 1978.

Keegan, John. *The Second World War.* New York: Penguin Books, 1989.

Keeney, L. Douglas. *The Pointblank Directive.* Oxford: Osprey, 2012.

Kennett, Lee B. *A History of Strategic Bombing*. New York: Scribner, 1982.

Kilborne, Al. *Images of America: Woodley and Its Residents*. Charleston, SC: Arcadia, 2008.

Kimball, Warren F. *Forged in War: Roosevelt, Churchill, and the Second World War*. New York: William Morrow, 1997.

Klein, Maury. *A Call to Arms: Mobilizing American for World War II*. New York: Bloomsbury Press, 2013.

Larrabee, Eric. *Commander in Chief: Franklin Delano Roosevelt, His Lieutenants, and Their War*. Annapolis MD: Naval Institute Press, 1987.

Lavery, Brian. *Churchill Goes to War: Winston's Wartime Journeys*. London: Conway, 2008.

Leahy, William D., Fleet Admiral. *I Was There*. New York: McGraw-Hill, 1950.

Leighton, Richard M., and Robert W. Coakley. *Global Logistics and Strategy, 1940–1943*. Washington DC: Office of the Chief of Military History, Department of the Army, 1955.

Lelyveld, Joseph. *His Final Battle: The Last Months of Franklin Roosevelt*. New York: Alfred A Knopf, 2016.

Lippmann, Walter. *U.S. Foreign Policy: Shield of the Republic*. Boston: Little, Brown, 1943.

Matloff, Maurice. *Strategic Planning for Coalition Warfare, 1943–1945*. Washington DC: Office of the Chief of Military History, Department of the Army, 1959.

Meacham, Jon. *Franklin and Winston: An Intimate Portrait of an Epic Friendship*. New York: Random House, 2003.

Milner, Marc. "The Royal Canadian Navy and 1943: A Year Best Forgotten?" In *1943: The Beginning of the End*, ed. Paul D. Dickson, 123–36. Ottawa: Canadian Committee for the History of the Second World War, 1995.

———. *Stopping the Panzers: The Untold Story of D-Day*. Lawrence: University Press of Kansas, 2014.

Ministry of Foreign Affairs of the USSR. *Correspondence between Stalin, Roosevelt, Truman, Churchill, and Atlee during WWII*. 1957. Reprint, Honolulu HI: University Press of the Pacific, 2001.

Mitcham, Samuel W., Jr. *Rommel's Last Battle: The Desert Fox and the Normandy Campaign*. New York: Stein and Day, 1983.

Mitchell, W. H. "The President Goes Fishing: Whitefish Region Entertains a World Leader." *Blue Bell* 22, no. 9 (September 1943): 7, 32.

Montgomery, Bernard. *The Memoirs of Field Marshal Montgomery*. New York: Da Capo Press, 1958.

Moran, Lord. *Churchill at War, 1940–45*. New York: Carroll & Graf, 2002.

Morgan, Sir Frederick. *Overture to Overlord*. New York: Doubleday, 1950.

———. *Peace and War: A Soldier's Life*. London: Hodder and Stoughton, 1961.

Morison, Elting E. *Turmoil and Tradition: A Study of the Life and Times of Henry L. Stimson*. New York: History Book Club, 2003.

Morison, Samuel Eliot. *The Battle of the Atlantic, September 1939–May 1943*. Vol. 1 of *History of United States Naval Operations in World War II*. Annapolis MD: Naval Institute Press, 2010.

————. *The Atlantic Battle Won, May 1943–May 1945.* Vol. 10 of *History of United States Naval Operations in World War II.* Boston: Little, Brown, 1975.

————.*The Invasion of France and Germany, 1944–1945.* Vol. 11 of *History of United States Naval Operations in World War II.* Annapolis, MD: Naval Institute Press, 2011.

Mount, Graeme S. "Myths and Realities: FDR's 1943 Vacation on Lake Huron." *Northern Mariner/Le Marin du Nord* 11, no. 3 (2001): 23–32.

Offley, Ed. *Turning the Tide.* New York: Basic Books, 2011.

Olson, Lynne. *Citizens of London: The Americans Who Stood with Britain in Its Darkest, Finest Hour.* New York: Random House, 2010.

Overy, Richard. *The Bombers and the Bombed: Allied Air War over Europe, 1940–1945.* New York: Viking, 2013.

————. "Weak Link? The Perception of the German Working Class by RAF Bomber Command, 1940–1945." *Labour History Review* 77, no. 1 (April 2012): 11–33.

Parrish, Thomas. *Roosevelt and Marshall: Partners in Politics and War.* New York: William Morrow, 1989.

Perry, Mark. *Partners in Command: George Marshall and Dwight Eisenhower in War and Peace.* New York: Penguin Press, 2007.

Persico, Joseph E. *Roosevelt's Centurions.* New York: Random House, 2013.

Pogue, Forrest C. *George C. Marshall: Education of a General, 1880–1939.* New York: Viking Press, 1963.

————. *George C. Marshall: Organizer of Victory, 1943–1945.* New York: Viking Press, 1973.

————. *United States Army in World War II: European Theater of Operations: The Supreme Command.* Washington DC: Office of the Chief of Military History, Department of the Army, 1954.

Porter, Cecil. *The Gilded Cage: Gravenhurst German Prisoner of War Camp 20, 1940–1946.* Gravenhurst ON: Gravenhurst, 2003.

Reilly, Michael F. *Reilly of the White House.* New York: Simon and Schuster, 1947.

Rhodes, Richard. *The Making of the Atomic Bomb.* New York: Touchstone, 1988.

Rigdon, William M. *White House Sailor.* Garden City NY: Doubleday, 1962.

Roberts, Andrew. *Masters and Commanders: How Four Titans Won the War in the West, 1941–1945.* New York: Harper Perennial, 2009.

Roll, David L. *The Hopkins Touch.* New York: Oxford University Press, 2013.

Ross, William F., and Charles F. Romanus. *The Quartermaster Corps: Operations in the War against Germany.* Washington DC: Office of the Chief of Military History, Department of the Army, 1965.

Ruane, Kevin. *Churchill and the Bomb in War and Cold War.* London: Bloomsbury Academic, 2016.

Ruppenthal, Roland G. *Logistical Support of the Armies.* Vol. 1, *May 1941–September 1944.* Washington DC: Office of the Chief of Military History, Department of the Army, 1953.

Sherwin, Martin J. *A World Destroyed: Hiroshima and Its Legacies.* 3rd ed. Stanford, CA: Stanford University Press, 2003.

Sherwood, Robert E. *Roosevelt and Hopkins: An Intimate History.* New York: Grosset & Dunlap, 1950.

Silcox, David P. *The Group of Seven and Tom Thomson.* Richmond Hill ON: Firefly Books, 2011.

Stacey, C. P. *Six Years of War: The Army in Canada, Britain, and the Pacific.* Vol. 1 of *Official History of the Canadian Army in the Second World War.* Ottawa: Queen's Printer and Controller of Stationery, 1957

———.*The Victory Campaign.* Vol. 3 of *Official History of the Canadian Army in the Second World War.* Ottawa: Queen's Printer and Controller of Stationery, 1960.

Stargardt, Nicholas. *The German War: A Nation under Arms, 1939–1945.* New York: Basic Books, 2015.

Stimson, Henry L., and McGeorge Bundy. *On Active Service in Peace and War.* New York: Harper & Brothers, 1947.

Stoler, Mark A. *Allies and Adversaries: The Joint Chiefs of Staff, the Grand Alliance, and U.S. Strategy in World War II.* Chapel Hill: University of North Carolina Press, 2004.

———. *The Politics of the Second Front: American Military Planning and Diplomacy in Coalition Warfare, 1941–1945.* Westport CT: Greenwood Press, 1977.

Symonds, Craig L. *Neptune: The Allied Invasion of Europe and the D-Day Landings.* Oxford: Oxford University Press, 2014.

Tanner, Virginia. "GPA Dan Moorman Recalls Journeys with President Roosevelt." *Baltimore & Ohio Magazine,* May 1945, 61–62.

Tully, Grace. *FDR, My Boss.* New York: Charles Scribner, 1947.

Villa, Brian Loring. "The Atomic Bomb and the Normandy Invasion." *Perspectives in American History* 11 (1977–78): 461–502.

———. *Unauthorized Action: Mountbatten and the Dieppe Raid.* Don Mills ON: Oxford University Press, 1989.

Ward, Geoffrey C., ed. *Closest Companion: The Untold Story of the Intimate Friendship between Franklin Roosevelt and Margaret Suckley.* New York: Houghton Mifflin, 1995.

Weadon, Patrick D. *Sigsaly Story.* Fort Meade MD: National Security Agency, Central Security Service, 2000.

Wedemeyer, Albert C. *Wedemeyer Reports!* New York: Henry Holt, 1958.

Weighley, Russell F. *Eisenhower's Lieutenants: The Campaign of France and Germany, 1944–1945.* Bloomington: Indiana University Press, 1981.

Williams, Mary H. *United States Army in World War II; Special Studies: Chronology, 1941–1945.* Washington DC: Office of the Chief of Military History, Department of the Army, 1960.

Withers, Bob. *The President Travels by Train: Politics and Pullmans.* Lynchburg, VA: TLC, 1996.

Wood, Lewis. "Roosevelt Back after a Vacation of Week in Canada." *New York Times,* August 10, 1943.

Wood, Thomas E., and Stanislaw M. Jankowski. *Karski: How One Man Tried to Stop the Holocaust.* New York: John Wiley, 1994.

Ziegler, Philip. *Mountbatten.* New York: Alfred A. Knopf, 1985.

INDEX

Page numbers in italics refer to maps

A3 radiotelephone voice encryption system, 114, 115–17, 119–20, 329n20, 331n11
acoustic torpedoes, 270–71
aerial bombings: of Germany, 34, 41–49, 168, 248; of Japan, 313–14; of London, 44; resources for, 51–52; theory of, 42–43, 313. *See also* Combined Bomber Offensive (CBO)
aerial patrolling, 28, 51–52, 54, 142, 268
aide-memoire on Tube Alloys program, 312, 357n36
air bases on Italian mainland, 146
Air Ministry Intelligence—Political Warfare Executive assessment, 286
Airplane Conference of 1938, 180
air travel hostile interception, 142, 146
Akers, Wallace, 25–26, 30, 160–61, 192, 274–75, 320n38
Algiers planning meeting, 91–92
Allied Anti-Submarine Working Group, 122
Allied conferences, 6, *38–39*; Cairo Conference, 283, 284, 287–89. *See also* Casablanca Conference; Eureka Conference; Quadrant Conference; Trident Conference
American Military Cemetery, 356n15
American Telephone and Telegraph Company, 115
amphibious forces for Neptune, 254–57. *See also specific amphibious ships and craft*
amphibious landings history, 63
Anakim, Operation, 31, 33
Anderson, John: and Anglo-American atomic agreement, 160–61, 165, 192–95, 197, 213, 222–24; and atomic bomb information, 11, 23, 36–37, 81–82,

135–36, 322n80, 326n36; and atomic energy, 311
Anfa, Morocco, 14
Anfa Camp, 15
Anfa Hotel, 14
Anglo-American atomic agreement: background of, 6, 125, 130–31, 137–38, 139–40, 160–61; drafting of, 192–98, 207, 222–23, 233–34, 342–43n22; FDR and Churchill meetings on, 228–29; FDR and draft of, 213, 217–18; signing of, 247, 274–75
Anglo-American Combined Policy Committee, 195, 311
the *Anna H.*, 171, 184–85, 188
antisubmarine warfare (ASW): and attrition campaigns, 50, 51–52, 55; and Bolero, 153, 258–61, 267–69, 271; and Casablanca Conference, 28–29; German threat to, 142
Anti-U-Boat Warfare Committee, 52, 53–54
Arcadia Conference, 15
armada size, D-Day, 3
armaments production: German, 48; U.S., 181–82, 255–57, 294–95
Army Service Force (ASF), 253, 264, 297
Arnold, Henry "Hap": about, 11; and aerial bombing, 44, 45–46, 48; and Casablanca Conference, 11, 27; and meetings aboard USS *Iowa*, 285; and Quadrant Conference, 208, 218
artificial ports, 108, 110, 112, 190, *191*, 200, 257, 309
ASF. *See* Army Service Force (ASF)
ASW. *See* antisubmarine warfare (ASW)
AT convoys, 265
Atlanticism, 71
Atlantic Wall, 63, 295, 303

atomic bomb: accelerated development of, 309–11; British development of, 80–82, 135; and Canada, 223–24, 231; information sharing on, 22–27, 80–89, 122, 124–27, 130–40, 320n32, 321n40; restoration of U.S.-UK collaboration, 274–76, 309–10; target site selection for, 312–13; test and use of, 313–14. *See also* Anglo-American atomic agreement

atomic energy: commercial applications of, 85, 87, 125, 136, 137, 192; postwar control of, 311–12

attack cargo ships, 254, 255, 297

attack transports, 254, 255, 297

attrition campaigns, 41–56; aerial bombings, 41–49, 215; Battle of the Atlantic, 49–56

attrition versus direct assault strategies, 31, 68, 72, 208–9, 240

Avalanche, Operation, 130, 146, 249

B-24s, 13, 51–53, 55, 142, 171, 268

Badoglio, Pietro, 149, 186

Barker, Ray: and COSSAC establishment and directives, 58–59, 60, 62, 66–67; and Overlord Outline Plan, 113, 126–27, 158–60, 199–201

Barnes, William Gorell, 36

Battle of Kursk, 123

Battle of the Atlantic, 49–56, 201–2, 226, 257–61, 271, 346n17

battleships, 1–2, 268–69, 297. *See also* the *Lützow*, the *Scharnhorst*, the *Tirpitz*, USS *Alabama*; USS *Arkansas*; USS *Iowa*; USS *Nevada*; USS *South Dakota*; USS *Texas*

Beaverbrook, Max, 7, 98–99, 147

Beck, Thomas, 141

Belfast, Ireland, 1

Bell Telephone Company of Canada, 171

Bell Telephone Laboratories, 117–18

Bennett, Harry, 340n2

Beobachtung-Dienst, 53

Bessell, William W., 151–52

Big Three meeting. *See* Eureka Conference

Big Three relationship, 166–67

bilateral meeting of Roosevelt and Stalin,

93–102; and Churchill, 98–102, 143–44, 328–29n20; and Joseph Davies in Moscow, 94–97; Stalin's request to make trilateral, 189; waiting for, 162, 166–67

Birch Island, Canada, 170, 172. *See also under* fishing trips of Franklin Roosevelt

the Blitz, 44

Bolero, Operation. *See* Operation Bolero

Bomber Command, RAF, 43, 51–52, 248

bombers: antisubmarine warfare and, 28–29, 54–55; B-24s, 13, 51–53, 55, 142, 171, 268. *See also* aerial bombings; bombing strategy

bombing offensives. *See* aerial bombings

bombing strategy, 41, 43–44, 45

Brady, Dorothy, 163

the *Bristol*, flying boat, 90–91

British Post Office, 115

Brooke, Alan: about, 13, 14; and Casablanca Conference, 13, 29, 30, 31, 32–33; and COSSAC, 57, 158; and post-Trident in-flight meeting, 90–91; and Quadrant Conference, 147, 206, 239–40, 243, 245, 246, 248, 249; and Trident Conference, 76–77, 78–79, 86

Brown, Allen Tupper, 320n28

Brown, Wilson, 163, 172, 185, 227, 246, 247

Buckley, O. E., 118

Bundy, Harvey: and atomic bomb, 122, 126, 134–36, 140, 194, 196–97; and cross-Channel option, 216, 218–19

Burma, 27, 31, 33, 206

Bush, Vannevar: about, 24; and Anglo-American atomic agreement, 192–95, 196–98, 207, 213, 342n22; and atomic bomb information, 24–26, 82, 85–88, 132–36, 139–40, 161, 165, 334n63; Britain trip of, 122, 124–26; and postwar atomic partnership, 312; restoring atomic collaboration, 275–76

Byrnes, James, 163, 168, 184, 185, 312, 340n2

Caen, France, 108, 110–12

Cairo Conference, 283, 284, 287–89

campaigns of attrition. *See* attrition campaigns

Campbell, Ronald, 186–87, 311
Canada: and atomic bomb, 81, 82, 223–24, 231, 276; war participation of, 225–26, 231
Caroline Islands, 33
Casablanca Conference, 11–40; American meetings of, 27–28; arriving at and location of, 11–15; atomic bomb and, 26, 30, 35–36; background of, 16–27; and bomber allocation, 52; British meetings of, 32; ccs meetings of, 28–35; conclusions of, 37–40, 49, 73; plenary sessions of, 30; purpose and challenge of, 15–16
casualties: of Allied aerial bombing, 47–48, 244; of Battle of the Atlantic, 49, 271; of D-Day, 3, 307, 319n4; of *Empress of Canada*, 272; in Japan, 314; of Operation Gomorrah, 126; of Operation Jubilee, 63
CCS. *See* Combined Chiefs of Staff (ccs)
Chadwick, James, 274
Chateau Frontenac, 235, 246
Cherbourg, port of, 108, 111, 112
Cherwell, Lord. *See* Lindeman, Frederick
Chiang Kai-shek, 281, 287
Chiang Kai-shek, Madame, 17
Chief of Imperial General Staff (cigs), UK, 32
Chief of Staff to the Supreme Allied Commander (cossac). *See* cossac
Chiefs of Staff (cos), UK: and atomic bomb, 26–27, 321n40; and ccs 303, 237–38; and Churchill, 21, 231; and cossac, 57, 62, 113, 147–48, 159, 190; and Italy invasion, 148–49, 286–87; and merchant shipping, 261; and Quadrant Conference, 238–39, 243; and Quadrant Conference preparations, 152–53, 235–36, 237–38; and Rankin planning, 155; and Trident Conference, 72–73. *See also* Combined Chiefs of Staff (ccs)
China, 17, 27, 31, 75, 77
Churchill, Winston: about, 14, 274; and aerial bombing, 42–43, 44; and Anglo-American atomic agreement, 8–9, 161; and atomic bomb information sharing, 22–23, 35–37, 80–86, 88–89, 124–26, 130–

32, 134–40; and atomic bomb UK development, 6; and Battle of the Atlantic, 52; and bilateral initiative between FDR and Stalin, 93, 95, 98–102, 128, 143–44; and Cairo Conference, 287–89; and Casablanca Conference, 13, 16, 26, 37–40; and cossac, 57–58, 190–91; cross-channel invasion strategy position of, 6, 74, 89; cross-Channel strategy commitment of, 123–24, 129–30, 131, 138–39, 186–88, 277–82, 293; and Eureka Conference, 289–91; and Italy invasion, 92, 124, 126, 186–87, 277; and post-Trident in-flight meeting, 90–91; and postwar atomic energy, 311–12; and Quadrant Conference, 128–29, 141, 162, 227–33, 247, 248–49; quotes of, 1, 41; relationship of cos with, 21; and Stalin, 93, 224–25; and Trident Conference, 74, 79, 80, 88–89; and voice communications, 114, 116–17, 119–20; and William Mackenzie King, 221–22; writing to FDR, 181–82
Ciechanowski, Jan, 168–69
cigs. *See* Chief of Imperial General Staff (cigs), UK
Citadel, 221, 235, 245
civil affairs planning and capabilities, 156–57
Clyde Estuary, 271
Coastal Command, raf, 51, 52, 55
Cobra, Operation, 309
Cockade, Operation, 61, 107, 308–9
Combat Demolition Units, 307
Combined Bomber Offensive (cbo): about, 45–49; Casablanca Conference decisions on, 34, 124; and D-Day, 308; and Germany's collapse theory, 236, 253, 285–86; and Italy, 288; and priorities, 54–55, 153, 201, 209–10, 212, 238; and resources, 205, 252
Combined Chiefs of Staff (ccs): and Battle of the Atlantic, 49, 52, 54, 258; and Cairo Conference, 288; and Casablanca Conference, 15, 18, 28–35; and ccs 303, 208; and Churchill cross-Channel commitment, 277–79; and Combined Bomber Offensive, 46; and cossac, 60–61, 62, 64, 148, 201; and expanded cross-Channel plan, 302; formation of, 15; and Italy invasion,

Combined Chiefs of Staff (continued) 128, 149; and Neptune amphibious forces, 255; and Quadrant Conference, 129, 153, 238–40, 243–46, 247–48, 249; and Trident Conference, 70, 74, 75–77, 78–79, 85

Combined Commanders Committee, UK, 62

Combined Operations Headquarters, UK, 62

Combined Policy Committee, 195, 224, 229, 274–76, 311

complicity, German citizens' sense of, 47

Conant, James: and Anglo-American atomic agreement, 139, 193–94, 196–97, 198; and atomic bomb, 24–26, 82, 125, 132–33, 139, 161, 275–76; memorandum of, 30, 125, 192–93; and postwar atomic partnership, 312

"Conduct of the War in Europe" (Handy), 202–6

constitutional limits of U.S. presidential war powers, 24, 87, 131, 134

Convoy and Routing Section, 259

Convoy Conference, 55

convoys: AT, 265; KMF and MFK, 278, 279, 282–83; ON and ONS, 258, 259, 271; SC, 258; UT and TU, 265–73, 266, 278, 293, 295, 297, 352n46

Cooke, Charles M. "Savvy", Jr., 152, 199, 306, 356n19

Cooke, Henry D., 273

COS. See Chiefs of Staff (COS), UK

COSSAC (Chief of Staff to the Supreme Allied Commander): coordinating D-Day, 297–98; establishment, directives, and purpose of, 57–62, 64–67; expanded plan of, 299–303, 300–301, 304; and Overlord entry point options, 67–68; Overlord Outline Plan of, 109–13, 126–27, 154–60, 190–91, 198–201, 240, 254, 304; and Overlord plan elements, 103–6; and Overlord resources, 68–69; planning challenges of, 62–65; and Rankin planning, 154–57, 336n24; and Rattle Conference, 102, 106–9

Cotentin Peninsula, 62, 108, 111, 249, 303

Cripps, Stafford, 122, 124

cross-beach efficiency, 108

cross-Channel attack strategy: and atomic bomb information sharing, 84–85; and Casablanca Conference, 18, 20, 29, 31, 34–35; and CCS 303, 209–10; and Eureka Conference, 290–91; Henry Stimson memo to FDR on, 173–80, 185, 186, 188, 189, 339n5, 341n21; overview of, 5, 6, 8–9; and post-Trident in-flight meeting, 89–91; and pre-Quadrant Conference, 228–29, 230–31; and Quadrant Conference, 147, 239–42, 245–46, 248–49; and Quadrant Conference preparations, 215–16, 236–38; and Sledgehammer, 19; and Trident Conference, 75–77, 78–79; U.S. revolt against, 152, 154, 158, 165, 198–99. See also COSSAC (Chief of Staff to the Supreme Allied Commander)

CVE. See escort aircraft carriers (CVE)

Davies, Joseph E., 93, 94–98, 101

D-Day, 2, 3, 304–9

Deane, John, 141, 218

deception operations, Allied, 61, 107, 308–9

decryption, 50, 53, 114, 118–19

de Gaulle, Charles, 37, 322–23n81

Delente, Jacques, 307

demobilization, 168

Democratic Party, 16–17, 176–77

deployment of U.S. troops for Overlord, 251–53, 265–73, 266, 278–79, 295, 297

destroyers: as convoy escorts, 256, 260, 268–69, 271, 297; on D-Day, 306–7

Deutsche Reichspost, 115

Devers, Jacob, 58, 67, 109, 127, 131, 147, 158, 199–200

Dieppe Raid, 14, 63, 231, 276–77

diesel engine production, 256

digitizing speech, 117–18

Dill, John, 11–12, 26–27, 32, 189, 241–42, 316n2

divisions by nationality, 103–4

the Dixie Clipper, flying boat, 12

Doenitz, Karl, 53, 258, 260

Doolittle, Jimmy, 145, 178

double-bunking convoys, 267

Dover, England, 130

Duggan, Laurence, 337n15

Eaker, Ira, 124
Early, Steve, 172, 246
Eden, Anthony, 37, 83–84, 100, 123, 187, 323n81
Eisenhower, Dwight D.: about, 18–19; as American Supreme Allied Commander in North Africa, 15, 29, 73, 91–92; invading Italy, 78, 128, 145–46, 178, 220, 255; and Overlord forces, 204, 220, 236–37; quotes of, 70; as Supreme Allied Commander, 285, 292, 298, 302, 303
Elsey, George, 306, 307, 356n16
encryption systems, 50, 53, 114–20, 330n3, 331n11
Enigma, 50, 53, 120
entry point options for cross-Channel attack, 67–68, 104–5, 110, 111–12, 329n5
equipment shipping, 264–65, 295
escort aircraft carriers (CVE), 260
escort fighters, 45, 48
escort vessels: and antisubmarine warfare, 28–29; for D-Day, 3, 297; and trade routes, 50, 51, 52, 54, 55, 346n17; for troop deployment, 1, 256, 259–60, 267–71
Essone. See S-1
ETOUSA. See European Theater of Operations, U.S. Army (ETOUSA)
Eureka Conference: meetings of, 289–91; planning for, 189, 234, 277–78, 279, 281, 283; preliminary meetings for, 283, 284, 287–89
European Theater of Operations, U.S. Army (ETOUSA), 58, 109
European theater war strategy options. See cross-Channel attack strategy; Mediterranean strategy
evasive routing of convoys, 53, 54
expanded Overlord plan, 299–303, 300–301, 304

the Ferdinand Magellan, presidential railroad car, 163, 168, 170, 185, 188, 244
"Fido" homing torpedoes, 261
Fiftieth Division, UK, 288–89
Fifty-First Division, UK, 289
fireside chats, 168

fire support for assault troops, 3, 65, 108, 297, 302, 306–7
First Airborne Division, UK, 278
First Canadian Army, 109, 330n21
First Canadian Infantry Division, 109
First Panzer Corps, 308
fishing trips of Franklin Roosevelt: at Birch Island, 170–72, 184–89, 340n2; of December 1940, 181–82; in Ontario, 129; planning of Birch Island, 141, 143, 145; as a ruse, 144, 344n77; train ride from Birch Island for, 189, 207; train ride to Birch Island for, 162–64, 165–66, 168, 169–70
food supplies and production, 262
Force O, 299
forces for Neptune. See amphibious forces for Neptune
forces for Overlord: deployment of U.S., 251–53, 265–73, 266, 278–79, 295, 297; and Overlord Outline Plan, 103–4, 110, 126–27, 191, 200, 251; and Quadrant Conference, 239–40, 249, 251; and Quadrant Conference preparations, 211, 212, 216, 218, 219–20, 236–38. See also amphibious forces for Neptune
Force Utah, 3
Foxer (FXR), 271
France: Churchill broadcasting to, 1; invasion of southern, 152, 199, 210, 220, 244, 302. See also cross-Channel attack strategy; Free French
"Frankfurt" inercepted convoy radio messages, 53, 258
Free French, 2–3, 37, 73, 322–23n81, 342–43n22
Frisch, Otto, 310
Fuchs, Klaus, 310, 357n29
funding for the war, 180–81
FXR. See Foxer (FXR)

Gallipoli, battle at, 63, 276
George Leygues, French cruiser, 2–3
German parachutists, 289
Germany: aerial bombing of, 41–49, 168, 248; and Battle of the Atlantic, 201–2; citizen sense of complicity, 47; and scenario

Germany *(continued)*
of Allied D-Day loss, 303; strengthening of defenses by, 303–4; theory of forcing collapse of, 33–34, 43–44, 46, 285–86
Germany first strategy, 16, 18, 31, 32, 123, 175, 176, 240
Gerow, Leonard, 306
Ghost Train, 159–60
GI Bill of Rights, 168, 337–38n25
Giraud, Henri, 37, 322–23n81
Goebbels, Josef, 47, 296
Gold Beach, 301, 305
Gomorrah, Operation, 126, 248
Green Hornet, 118–19, 120
Groom, Victor, 190–91
Group of Seven, 170
Groves, Leslie, 24–26, 82–83, 133, 197, 275, 312–13, 342–43n22
Guderian, Heinz, 303–4
gun-type atomic bomb, 310, 313
Gymnast, Operation, 19

Habbakuk, 246, 349n46
Halifax, Lord, 83–84
Hall, John, 307
Handy, Thomas: "Conduct of the War in Europe" memo of, 202–6, 252; and cross-Channel option , 200, 212, 280; and D-Day, 299, 306; and Quadrant Conference, 210, 241, 242–43, 244
Harriman, Averill: and bilateral initiative with Soviet Union, 93, 98–100, 102, 328–29n20; and Casablanca Conference, 13, 27; and Churchill, 202; and Eureka Conference, 289; and Quadrant Conference, 213, 227.
Harris, Arthur, 51, 236, 248
Hassett, William D., 163, 168
headquarters ships, 14, 107
"Heads of Agreement," 161, 193
high-frequency band radio direction-finding (HF/DF) stations, 260, 270
Hiroshima, Japan, 313–14
Hitler, Adolf, 42, 303
HMS *Bulolo*, 14
HMS *Dun Donald*, 106–7
HMS *Glasgow*, 2, 3, 299

the Holocaust, 47, 169, 323n17, 338n29
homing torpedoes, 261
Hopkins, Harry: about, 21, 320n28; and atomic bomb, 35, 80, 82–84, 89, 125, 132, 213–14; and Casablanca Conference, 13, 27, 37, 323n81; and Eureka Conference, 291; and fishing trip, 141, 184–85, 340n2; and Henry Stimson cross-Channel memo, 180, 182–83, 186, 188; and Joseph Davies, 97–98; and Lend-Lease program, 182; and Quadrant Conference, 129, 172, 207, 210, 213–14, 227; and strategy, 7, 18, 19–20
Hopkins, Stephen Peter, 320n28
Horne, Fredrick, 256
Howard, Leslie, 142
Howe, C. D., 224
Hull, Cordell, 97, 169, 211, 283
Hull, John E., 72, 151
Husky, Operation, 74, 76, 109, 122. *See also* Sicily, Italy
hydro-acoustic signatures, 270

Imperial Chemical Industries (ICI), 25, 192
Imperial Japanese Navy, 256
implosion-type atomic bombs, 310, 313
Inönü, Ismet, 40
intelligence: and Battle of the Atlantic, 51, 53, 201, 259–61; and Combined Bomber Offensive, 286; and encryption, 114–15, 116, 117, 120, 258, 308
Ismay, Hastings "Pug": and COSSAC, 57–58, 191; and Quadrant Conference, 245; and Sigsaly, 118–19; and trilateral meeting, 225; and Tube Alloys, 234, 320n40
isolationists, 20–21, 71, 180
Italy: British support for invading, 138, 149, 175, 202, 206, 222, 277; forces transfer from, 202, 220, 249, 283, 288–89; invasion of, 225, 288; and Operation Avalanche, 145–46; Overlord supporting invasion of, 178, 287; post-Mussolini, 119–20, 162, 186–87; and proposal for attacking south of Rome, 128, 131; Quadrant Conference discussion on, 236–38, 239–40, 242, 244, 249, 277; Sardinia, 28, 30, 92, 220; Trident Conference discus-

sion of, 74–75, 78, 85, 86, 88, 92, 98. *See also* Mediterranean strategy; Sicily, Italy

Japan: bombing of, 313–14; decryption and, 114, 117; priority for defeat of, 15, 16, 18, 74, 76, 123; and resources, 31; and U.S. Marine Corps, 63

JCS 570, 284

Joint Chiefs of Staff (JCS), 284, 570: and atomic bomb, 321n40; and Battle of the Atlantic, 54–55; and Casablanca Conference, 11–12; and COSSAC, 61, 147–48; and Franklin Roosevelt, 21; and meetings aboard USS *Iowa*, 283–84, 285; and Overlord Outline Plan, 200–201; and postwar preparations, 71–72; and Quadrant Conference, 145, 152–53, 204, 207–9, 218–19, 240–42; strategy conflict between British, 149, 279; and Trident Conference, 76, 77, 79, 80; and war priorities, 18. *See also* Combined Chiefs of Staff (CCS)

Joint Planning Staff, 152, 198, 199, 220, 239

Joint Strategic Survey Committee (JSSC), 199, 201, 203, 284

Joint War Planning Committee (JWPC), 151–52, 198–99

Jubilee, Operation, 14, 63, 231, 276–77

Juno Beach, 301, 305, 308

Jupiter, Operation, 248

Kahn, David, 116–17

Karski, Jan, 169, 338n29

Kennedy, John F., 171

King, Ernest: about, 12; and Casablanca Conference, 11, 19, 27, 31, 32; and forces for Overlord, 216, 259; and Quadrant Conference, 128, 208, 218, 240, 241, 242; and strategy, 119, 320n20; and Torch, 20; and Trident Conference, 72, 75–76

KMF-25A convoy, 278, 279, 282–83

Kriegsmarine, 53, 269

Krug, Peter, 189

Kuter, Laurence, 198–99, 241

Kyoto, Japan, 313

labor unions, 293–94, 296

land for troop accommodations, 262

landing beaches of Overlord Outline Plan, 110–11

landing craft, 3, 64, 93, 191, 254–57, 305. *See also specific craft*

landing craft medium (LCM), 257

landing craft tank (LCT), 3, 254–55

landing craft vehicle personnel (LCVP), 256

landing ship tank (LST), 3, 254, 256, 257, 307

Lanza d'Ajeta, Blasco, 186–87

LCM. *See* landing craft medium (LCM)

LCT. *See* landing craft tank (LCT)

LCVP. *See* landing craft vehicle personnel (LCVP)

Leahy, William: and atomic bomb, 321n40; and Casablanca Conference, 13; and fishing trip, 163, 172, 184, 185; and Quadrant Conference, 129, 208, 218, 241; and Trident Conference, 75

Lee, John C. H., 127

Lend-Lease Act, 182

the *Leonardo Da Vinci*, 272

Lewis, John L., 294

Liberators, 13, 51–53, 55, 142, 171, 268

Liberty ships, 257, 263

Lindeman, Frederick (Lord Cherwell), 43–44; and atomic bomb, 23, 80, 84, 86–89, 134, 135–36, 198; postwar control of atomic energy, 311.

Lindsay, Richard C., 151–52

Lippmann, Walter, 71–72

Little Boy, 313

Llewellin, John J., 274–76

loading schemes, 262–63

Loeb, Ernest, 184

Long, Dewey, 129, 145, 163

Los Alamos Laboratory, 310, 313

Lovett, Robert, 174

LST. *See* landing ship tank (LST)

Luftwaffe: Battle of the Atlantic and, 142; and the Blitz, 44; and convoy KMF-25A, 282; and D-Day, 308; defending Germany by fighters of, 45, 48–49; and Overlord planning, 61, 111, 286

lunar sailing schedule, 272

the *Lützow*, German pocket battleship, 269

MacArthur, Douglas, 17
MacDonald, Malcolm, 322n80
Mackenzie, C. J., 82
Mackenzie King, William: and Churchill, 221–22, 224–26, 230, 346n15; and FDR, 226, 250; as host of Quadrant Conference, 141, 231
Magic, 114
Manhattan Engineering District, 320n32
Manhattan Project. *See* atomic bomb
Manley, John, 184–85, 188–89, 340n2
Mansergh, M. J., 190
Maret International School, 345n24
Marshall, George C.: about, 9, 12, 21–22, 320n28; approach to dealing with FDR of, 180–82, 188; and Anglo-American atomic agreement, 194, 196–97; and atomic bomb, 24, 275, 321n40; and Casablanca Conference, 11–12, 27–28, 30–31; and communication security, 117; and cross-Channel option, 149–51, 154, 200, 211–12, 219–20, 252, 274, 280; and Henry Stimson, 121, 124, 173–74; and Henry Stimson's cross-Channel memo, 179–80, 189; invading Italy, 92, 128, 130, 131; and post-Trident in-flight meeting, 90–91; and postwar national security, 284; preparing for Quadrant Conference, 207–8, 215–16, 218, 236–37; and Quadrant Conference, 144, 240, 241–42, 246, 247, 249, 257; and railroad dispute, 295, 296–97; and strategy, 9, 12, 19; as Supreme Allied Commander candidate, 280, 284, 291–92; and Trident Conference, 76–77, 78
Marshall Islands, 33
Martin, John M., 114, 247
McCarthy, Frank, 90, 144
McDonald, E. F., 129, 141
McFarland, A. J., 287
McIntire, Ross, 163, 185
McKenzie, Donald, 188
McLean, Kenneth, 190–91, 249
McNarny, Joseph, 199
McNaughton, Andrew, 109
Mediterranean strategy: and Casablanca Conference, 19–20, 26–28, 29–30, 31, 32, 33; Churchill supporting, 90, 92,

126, 130, 144, 186, 277, 290; and COSSAC, 107, 109; Henry Stimson's case against, 175–76, 178–79; and Quadrant Conference, 153, 201, 203, 209, 236–37, 240, 243–44; and Trident Conference, 74, 75–77, 78, 85, 89; U.S. support of, 148, 151–52, 154, 158, 199, 265
Mediterranean theater: deploying U.S. troops to, 211–12, 216; movement of forces for Overlord from, 79, 127, 149, 210, 220, 249, 252, 277, 278; operations in, 204, 220, 288–89, 290
merchant shipping, 49–50, 258, 261–65, 268, 270, 271
MFK-25A convoy, 278, 283
Middle Eastern Command, 284, 292
Mid-Ocean Air Gap, 51, 52, 54, 55
Milch, Erhard, 48
Military Policy Committee: and Anglo-American atomic agreement, 193–94, 195, 276; and atomic bomb, 24, 25, 121, 125, 133, 134, 321n40
Milner, Marc, 346n17
Mission to Moscow, 94–98
Molotov, V. M., 94
the *Montcalm*, French Cruiser, 2–3
Montgomery, Bernard, 295, 302
Moorman, Daniel, 163
morale: as a factor in direct action, 28, 31, 33, 34; theory of bombing to break, 33–34, 42, 43, 44, 46–47, 285–86, 313
Moran, Lord, 88, 92, 346n15
Morgan, Frederick: and COSSAC, 57–60, 64, 65–68; and Overlord Outline Plan, 103, 105–6, 107, 112–13, 126–27, 157–59, 199; and Quadrant Conference, 147; and Rankin planning, 154–55
Morison, Samuel Eliot, 306, 356n16
Morocco, 15, 63
Mountbatten, Louis, 13–14, 62, 67, 106, 108, 109, 246
Mount Royal, private railway car, 227
Mulberry artificial harbors, 108, 110, 112, 190, 191, 200, 257, 309
Munson, Curtis, 306
Mussolini, Benito, 149–50
Mustang, P-51, 48–49

Nagasaki, Japan, 313
national security, postwar, 283–84
Navy, Free-French, 2–3
Navy, Imperial Japanese, 256
Navy, Royal. *See* Royal Navy (RN)
Navy, Royal Canadian, 226, 346n17
Navy, U.S. *See* U.S. Navy (USN)
Navy Patrol Torpedo Boat, 109, 171
need to know principle: and atomic
   bomb, 6, 25–26, 82, 86–87, 132–33, 134,
   135, 276; and COSSAC, 57
Neptune, Operation, 1–3, 103, 108, 254–
   57, 297, 299–302, 300–301, 304–8
New Zealand troops, 226, 261
Nichols, Kenneth D., 275
Night Mail, 159–60
Norfolk House, 59
Normandy as an Overlord entry point
   option, 67–68, 105, 110, 111–12
Normandy residents, 307
North Africa, 15, 19, 20–21, 29, 30, 73,
   205. *See also* Operation Torch

Oberkommando der Wehrmacht, 116, 120
ocean liners for troop deployment, 265–
   67, 271–72. *See also specific ocean liners*
Office of Scientific Research and Develop-
   ment (OSRD), 24, 132–33, 135, 320n32
Oliphant, Mark, 274
Omaha Beach, 3, 299, 300, 304–7, 356n15
ON-202 convoy, 271
ONS-5 convoy, 258, 259
ONS-18 convoy, 271
OPD. *See* U.S. Army Operations Divi-
   sion (OPD)
Operation Anakim, 31, 33
Operation Avalanche, 130, 146, 249
Operation Bolero, 218, 251–73; and
   amphibious craft, 254–57; and Bat-
   tle of Atlantic offensive, 257–61; and
   Churchill, 123, 126; and force assem-
   bly, 251–53; Mediterranean operations
   competition to, 28, 151, 204, 216; and
   Quadrant Conference, 153, 204; and
   shipping, 261–65
Operation Cobra, 309
Operation Cockade, 61, 107, 308–9

Operation Gomorrah, 126, 248
Operation Gymnast, 19
Operation Husky, 74, 76, 109, 122
Operation Jubilee, 14, 63, 231, 276–77
Operation Jupiter, 248
Operation Neptune, 1–3, 103, 108, 254–57,
   297, 299–302, 300–301, 304–8
Operation Overlord: entry point options
   for, 67–68, 104–5, 110, 111–12, 329n5;
   expanded plan of, 299–303, 300–301,
   304; outline plan of, 109–13, 126–27,
   154–60, 190–91, 198–201, 240, 254,
   304; overriding priority of, 237, 239–
   40, 242, 244. *See also* COSSAC (Chief
   of Staff to the Supreme Allied Com-
   mander); cross-Channel attack strategy;
   D-Day; forces for Overlord
Operation Pointblank. *See* Combined
   Bomber Offensive (CBO)
Operation Priceless. *See* Mediterranean
   theater
Operation Rankin, 61–62, 148, 149, 154–
   57, 232, 238, 287
Operation Roundhammer, 69, 123, 131,
   138, 146, 177–78, 332n8. *See also* Opera-
   tion Overlord
Operation Roundup, 19, 20, 69, 75–77
Operation Rudge, 67–68
Operation Sea Lion, 42
Operation Sickle, 153, 201, 216
Operation Skyscraper, 62
Operation Sledgehammer, 19–20, 69, 75,
   76, 256
Operation Tindall, 107
Operation Torch, 20, 21–22, 26, 65, 107,
   177, 205
Oppenheimer, Robert, 24
opportunistic strategy, 72, 155, 199, 203,
   209, 230, 240, 243. *See also* Operation
   Rankin
overloading convoys, 267
Overlord, Operation. *See* Operation Overlord

P-51 Mustang, 48–49
Pacific first strategy, 17, 18, 31
Pacific theater, 17–18, 32, 75, 238, 247
Paget, Bernard, 67

Panzers, 303–4, 308, 309

paratroopers, 110, 303, 307

Pas de Calais: and D-Day deception, 309; as an Overlord entry point option, 67–68, 104–5, 110–11, 329n5

Peacock convoy, 278, 279, 282–83

Pearl Harbor, 117

Peierls, Rudolf, 274

Pershing, John J., 180–81

"Piccadilly Circus," 3, 299

plutonium, 23, 310

Pogue, Forrest, 292

Pointblank, Operation. *See* Combined Bomber Offensive (CBO)

Pointe du Hoc, 304–5

Poland, 96, 169, 248, 338n29

Polish-Soviet border, 96

Portal, Charles, 13, 32, 45–46, 52, 236, 238, 248

port battalions, 253

port efficiencies, 263–64, 293

Potomac River, 191–92

Pound, Dudley, 13, 28, 52, 238, 272

precision bombing, 34, 44–45, 46

Prettyman, Arthur, 163

Priceless, Operation. *See* Mediterranean theater

production, wartime: of Germany, 43, 48; of U.S., 4, 181–82, 256–57, 293–94

Quadrant Conference: agenda for, 152–53, 172, 238; and Anglo-American atomic agreement, 9, 247; background and overview of, 9, 99, 102, 128–29, 141, 143, 144–45, 235; British preparations for, 221–24, 226, 235–36; and CCS 303, 208–10; CCS meetings of, 238–40, 243–46, 247–48, 249; COS meetings of, 243; and cross-Channel option, 147, 149; and FDR and Churchill meetings, 227–29; final report of, 257; JCS meetings of, 240–42; plenary sessions of, 246–47, 248–49; U.S. preparations for, 150–51, 162, 165, 198, 201, 202–4, 213–20, 236–37

Quebec Conference. *See* Quadrant Conference

radar, bombing, 43, 44, 45

radio-telephones, 114–20

RAF. *See* Royal Air Force (RAF)

Ramsay, Bertram, 249

Rankin, Operation, 61–62, 148, 149, 154–57, 232, 238, 287

Rattle Conference, 102, 106–9

RCMP. *See* Royal Canadian Mounted Police (RCMP)

reconnaissance, 120, 156

Redman, Harold, 287

Reilly, Michael, 129, 141, 145, 163, 289

relationships between military chiefs, 5, 6–7

Republican Party, 17

Revolt Against Overlord, 151–52, 154, 158, 165

Rigdon, William, 163, 172

RMS *Empress of Canada*, 272

RMS *Queen Elizabeth*, 267

RMS *Queen Mary*, 144, 166, 190, 206, 213, 265, 267, 271–72

Romania oil refinery raid, 171, 338n43

Rommel, Erwin, 299, 303–4, 308

Rooks, Lowell, 220

Roosevelt, Eleanor, 143, 169, 228, 233

Roosevelt, Franklin D.: about, 12–13, 14, 274; and aerial bombing, 42–43; and Anglo-American atomic agreement, 213, 217–18; and atomic bomb, 9, 22, 82, 84, 88–89, 91, 125; and atomic bomb information sharing, 88–89, 91, 125, 132–33, 135, 140, 145; and Battle of the Atlantic, 54–55; and bilateral initiative with Stalin, 93–94, 96–101, 127–28, 143–44; and Cairo Conference, 287–89; and Casablanca Conference, 12–13, 16, 19–20, 27–28, 30, 37–40; controlling postwar atomic energy, 311–12; and cross-Channel option, 9, 150–51, 202–3, 206, 211–12, 218–19; dealing with, 180–82, 188; death of, 312; and deployment of U.S. forces for Overlord, 252; and elections, 16–17; and Eureka Conference, 289–91; meeting aboard USS *Iowa*, 283–84, 285; and postwar national security, 284; and pre-Quadrant Conference meetings with Churchill, 227–29, 232–33; and Quadrant Conference, 128–

29, 216–19, 244, 245, 246, 247, 248; and railroad dispute, 294–97; traveling by train, 167–68; and Trident Conference , 70, 74–75, 79; and voice communication, 116, 117, 119–20; and William Mackenzie King, 226, 250. *See also* fishing trips of Franklin Roosevelt

Roosevelt, Theodore, Jr., 305

Roundhammer, Operation, 69, 123, 131, 138, 146, 177–78, 332n8. *See also* Operation Overlord

Roundup, Operation, 19, 20, 69, 75–77

routes for convoys, 53, 54, 266

Royal, Forrest, 287

Royal Air Force (RAF): and aerial bombings of Germany, 41–42, 43, 126, 168; and Battle of the Atlantic, 260; and Combined Bomber Offensive, 34, 43, 44–45, 47, 51–52, 55, 168; nationalities in, 226

Royal Canadian Mounted Police (RCMP), 169

Royal Canadian Navy, 226, 346n17

Royal Navy (RN): and Battle of the Atlantic, 52; and D-Day, 2, 3, 299; and Neptune, 254; and Overlord resources, 257, 260, 268, 269, 271

Ruane, Kevin, 321n40

Rudge, Operation, 67–68

sailing time of UT convoys, 269, 352n46

Salerno, Italy, 130, 145, 249

Sardinia, Italy, 28, 30, 92, 220

SC-128 convoy, 258

the *Scharnhorst*, German battleship, 269

scheduling troop deployment convoys, 271–72

Sea Lion, Operation, 42

second front, 37, 91, 93–94, 96, 97, 167, 248

Sextant Conference, 283, 284, 287–89

Shangri-La, 150

Sherwood, Robert, 182

shipping capacities, 262–65

Sicily, Italy: discussions of invasion of, 28, 30, 31, 33, 40, 78, 92, 151; invasion of, 109, 122–23, 138, 171, 205, 225, 244

Sickle, Operation, 153, 201, 216

Sigsaly, 118–19, 120

Simon, Francis, 274

S-1 project, 23, 133, 134–35, 193–94, 196–97, 320n32

Skyscraper, Operation, 62

Sledgehammer, Operation, 19–20, 69, 75, 76, 256

Slessor, John, 32

Smith, Bedell, 242

Somervell, Brehon, 297

Soviet Union: and atomic bomb, 81, 136, 310, 311, 312, 314; and Casablanca Conference, 11, 19, 32, 33; Joseph Davies visiting, 94–98; Quadrant Conference discussion on, 247–48; and Sledgehammer, 19, 69; Trident Conference discussing, 91, 92; and war in Europe, 91, 123, 167, 296. *See also* Eureka Conference; Stalin, Joseph

Spaatz, Carl "Tooey," 44, 145, 146, 178

speed of convoy vessels, 267

Speer, Albert, 48

Spitzbergen, 269

S.S. *Marnix van St. Aldegonde*, 282

S.S. *Nieuw Amsterdam*, 261

S.S. *Santa Elena*, 282

Stalin, Joseph: and atomic bomb, 314; and bilateral initiative with FDR, 93–97, 127, 143–44, 162, 166–67, 189; and Casablanca Conference, 11; and Churchill, 93, 224–25; and cross-Channel invasion, 91, 290–91; and Eureka conference, 281, 290–91; and Quadrant Conference, 248

standstill order in Mediterranean, 149, 150, 245–46

Stargardt, Nicholas, 46–47

steel supply, 81, 255–57

stereotyping, 8

Stimson, Henry Lewis: about, 18, 121, 175–76; and Anglo-American atomic agreement, 161, 173, 194, 196, 217–18, 345n34; and atomic bomb, 24, 124, 133–38, 140, 275–76, 312, 313; Britain trip of, 122–24, 129–31, 138–39; cross-Channel strategy memo by, 173–80, 182–83, 185, 188, 189, 339n5, 341n21; Dwight Eisenhower meetings with, 145–46; flying to North Africa, 142; and Overlord Outline Plan,

Stimson *(continued)*
113, 126–27, 131, 158; controlling postwar atomic energy, 312, 357n36; and Quadrant Conference , 141, 207, 210, 212–13, 214–15, 216–19; and railroad dispute, 295, 296; and Walter Lippman book, 72
Stoler, Mark, 72
"Strategic Concept for the Defeat of the Axis in Europe," 203, 208–10, 237–38, 239, 242–44
strikes, labor, 293–97
Suckley, Margaret "Daisy," 166, 227, 232–33
Sudbury Daily Star, 185
supplies shipping, 264–65, 295. *See also* merchant shipping
Supreme Allied Commander: creation of, 34–35; designation of, 239, 251, 280, 284–85, 290, 291–92; recommendations of George Marshall for, 179, 212–13, 215, 218
Supreme Headquarters Allied Expeditionary Force (SHAEF), 60, 298
Surles, Alexander, 131, 145–46
sustainment needs of liberated peoples, 262
Sword Beach, 301, 305
Symbol Conference. *See* Casablanca Conference

"talk between ships" (TBS), 273
Target Committee, 312–13
Task Group 129.2, 1–3
TBS. *See* "talk between ships" (TBS)
Terminal Conference, 314
terror bombings. *See* aerial bombings
Texas Task Group, 299
Third Division, Canadian, 308
Tindall, Operation, 107
the *Tirpitz,* German battleship, 269
Torch, Operation, 20, 21–22, 26, 65, 107, 177, 205
Tovey, John, 52
Tregaron, 97, 328n15
Trident Conference: and atomic bomb, 81–83, 84–89; background and overview of, 70–74; CCS meetings of, 75–77, 78–79; conclusions of, 79–80, 85–86,

88–89, 92, 98, 167, 203; and Overlord, 103, 104; plenary meeting of, 74–75; and second front, 93–94; studies done at, 77–78
trilateral conference. *See* Eureka Conference
Trinity test, 313, 314
Truman, Harry, 312, 314
Tube Alloys (TA) project, 23; progress report on, 180–81; subject to confirmation, 223. See also atomic bomb
TU convoys, 267
Tully, Grace, 163
Turing, Alan, 117, 119
Turkey, 33, 40, 74
Turner, G. R., 62
Twelfth SS Hitler Youth Division, 308

U-boats: Allied offensive of, 257–61; attacks of, 28, 41; and Battle of Atlantic, 49–56, 226; and priority of ASW, 28, 33, 49; targeting production of, 45; and troop deployment convoys, 270–71, 273
Ultra, 114, 308
unconditional surrender, 37–40, 157
United Mine Workers, 294
U.S. 101st Airborne division, 278
USA. *See* U.S. Army (USA)
USAAF. *See* U.S. Army Air Force (USAAF)
U.S. Army (USA), 17, 253. *See also specific force types*
U.S. Army Air Force (USAAF), 34, 44–45, 51, 181, 253
U.S. Army Ground Forces, 252, 253
U.S. Army Operations Division (OPD), 199, 202, 220
U.S. Army Services of Supply, 253
U.S. Army Transport (USAT), 267, 282–83
U.S. ascendency as a world power, 230, 231
USAT. *See* U.S. Army Transport (USAT)
USAT *Anne Arundel,* 282–83
USAT *Argentina,* 267
USAT *Cristobal,* 267
USAT *Dorothea Dix,* 282–83
USAT *Santa Paula,* 267
U.S. Eighth Air Force, 44, 48, 124, 146, 205, 236, 244

U.S. Eighty-Second Airborne Division, 278

U.S. elections, 16–17, 123, 175, 176–77

U.S. Fifth Armored Division, 295

U.S. Fifth Infantry, 278

U.S. First Infantry, 278, 282, 305–6, 309

U.S. Foreign Policy: Shield of the Republic (Lippmann), 71–72

U.S. Fourth Armored Division, 295

U.S. Marine Corps, 63

USN. See U.S. Navy (USN)

U.S. Navy (USN): and Battle of the Atlantic, 55; Battleship Division Five of, 1–3; and D-Day, 307; and FDR fishing trip, 171; and Neptune, 254; Tenth Fleet of, 259–60; and troop deployment convoys, 268; and war priorities and resources, 16, 17–18, 51, 256–57, 263

U.S. Navy Battleship Division Five, 1–3

U.S. Navy Tenth Fleet, 259–60

U.S. Ninth Infantry, 278

U.S. railroad operations, 264, 294–97

USS Alabama, 269

USS Ancon, 306

USS Arkansas, 1, 268, 297

USS Beatty, 282

USSBS. See U.S. Strategic Bombing Survey (USSBS)

U.S. Second Armored Division, 278

U.S. Second Infantry, 278

USS Indianapolis, 313

USS Iowa, 283–84, 285, 287

USS Nevada, 1, 3, 268, 297

USS Potomac, 283, 334n77

USS South Dakota, 269

USS Texas, 1–2, 3, 268, 297, 299, 304

USS Thurston, 273

U.S. Strategic Bombing Survey (USSBS), 48

USS Tuscaloosa, 181

USS Wilmette, 171, 188

U.S. Third Armored Division, 278

U.S. Twentieth Air Force, 313

U.S. Twenty-Eighth Infantry, 278

U.S. Twenty-Ninth Infantry, 205, 278, 305–6

U.S. War Shipping Administration (WSA), 263, 265

UT-1 convoy, 267–68

UT-2 convoy, 270, 278

UT-3 convoy, 271, 278

UT-4 convoy, 272–73

UT-6 convoy, 270, 295

UT-7 convoy, 295

UT-10 convoy, 266, 273

Utah Beach, 300, 304, 305

UT convoys, 267–73, 278, 293, 295, 297, 352n46. See also specific UT convoys

Val-Kill, 228, 229, 232

very long range bombers (VLR), 28–29, 51–53, 54, 55, 142

Vetterlein, Kurt, 114, 115–17

voice communication, 114–20, 330n3, 331n11

von Rundstedt, Gerd, 303–4

Wallace, Henry, 24, 84, 194

War Cabinet Anti-U-boat Committee, 122

War Department, 199–200, 264, 267

War Department Building, 121, 331n1

war powers of U.S. presidents, 24, 87, 131, 134

Watson, Edwin "Pa," 162, 163, 185

Wedemeyer, Albert C., 11, 198–99, 219, 241, 242, 244, 246

wildcat strikes, 294, 297

Wilkins, E. D., 185

Wilson, Carroll L., 132–33, 140

Winant, John Gilbert, 123, 124, 186–87, 210

Wolfe, James, 235

Woodley, 214, 345n24

World War I, 20–21, 44, 63, 111, 215, 251, 276, 296

WSA. See U.S. War Shipping Administration (WSA)

Yamamoto, Isoroku, 142

Zaunkönig acoustic torpedoes, 270–71